Problems and
Prospects in
European Education

Problems and Prospects in European Education

EDITED BY
Elizabeth Sherman Swing,
Jürgen Schriewer, and
François Orivel

PRAEGER

Westport, Connecticut
London

Library of Congress Cataloging-in-Publication Data

Problems and prospects in European education / edited by Elizabeth Sherman Swing,
  Jürgen Schriewer, and François Orivel.
     p. cm.
   Includes bibliographical references and index.
   ISBN 0–275–95202–9 (alk. paper)
    1. Education—Social aspects—Europe. 2. Education—Economic aspects—Europe. I.
Swing, Elizabeth Sherman. II. Schriewer, Jürgen. III. Orivel, François.
LC191.8.E85P86 2000
370'.94—dc21   99–055882

British Library Cataloguing in Publication Data is available.

Library of Congress Catalog Card Number: 99–055882
ISBN: 0–275–95202–9

First published in 2000

Praeger Publishers, 88 Post Road West, Westport, CT 06881
An imprint of Greenwood Publishing Group, Inc.
www.praeger.com

Printed in the United States of America

The paper used in this book complies with the
Permanent Paper Standard issued by the National
Information Standards Organization (Z39.48–1984).

10 9 8 7 6 5 4 3 2 1

For Raymond Ryba

(1930–1999)

Contents

1

European Educational Systems: The Framework of Tradition, Systemic Expansion, and Challenges for Restructuring

Jürgen Schriewer, François Orivel, and
Elizabeth Sherman Swing

This volume is about education in Europe. It deals, accordingly, with European education's common heritage and the distinct national traditions it preserves; with overall processes of growth and the institutional forms within which growth has taken place; with the interpretations of European educational systems put forward in the shape of educational theories or reform-oriented programs, policies, and ideologies; as well as with the social actors, forces, and movements that have fueled reform. The book's chapters also address, then, the challenges European education has to face as a consequence of change occurring at multiple levels: at the levels of cultural values, socio-political reconstruction, intercultural migration, supranational integration, and, not least, ongoing global interconnection. It goes without saying that a volume dealing with a socio-cultural reality of this complexity can do so only in a selective way. This holds true all the more because it is co-authored by experts coming from different national and theoretical backgrounds. In what follows, therefore, some of the conceptual links that join up the book's ten substantive chapters will be clarified. In particular, this introduction is meant to highlight, both historically and conceptually, a number of salient features related to the constitution of modern education in the form of public *educational systems* displaying structural characteristics, which typically include:

- a general administrative framework, or "meta-organization," normally established, funded, and controlled by the state;
- a coherently defined "ladder," or "macro-organization," of institutionalized schooling including successive levels, different tracks, and corresponding end-of-school examinations;

- the "micro-organization" of teaching and learning processes in the classroom according to distinct age groups and uniform time units;
- the regulation of these teaching and learning processes by public authorities and through more or less detailed requirements in the form of syllabi, directives, and examination plans;
- the use of certificates, diplomas, and credentials to link school careers with occupational careers;
- the professionalization of the teacher role; and finally,
- the institutionalization of system-related reflection, legitimization, and analysis in the form of educational research and educational theory as a particular field of academic study.

EDUCATIONAL SYSTEM FORMATION AND INCLUSION

Educational systems are, in spite of their worldwide dissemination and implementation since the second half of the 20th century (Thomas, Meyer, Ramirez, and Boli 1987; Meyer and Ramirez 1999; Schriewer 1999), definitely a modern type of educational organization. Comparative social history of education has shown that the processes of the formation and eventual consolidation of "the modern educational system," although starting toward the end of the 18th century, came to completion only toward the turn from the 19th to the 20th century (Müller, Ringer, and Simon 1987). Corresponding research has also cleared up that educational system formation, or "systematization," was carried through in close correspondence with the far-reaching transformation processes leading to specifically modern patterns of social organization.

Prominent 19th-century authors such as Matthew Arnold in Britain (1861–1868), Edmond Dreyfus-Brisac in France (1882–1897), or Lorenz von Stein in Germany were well aware of the radical newness of these processes. In particular, the latter provided, in his monumental *Treatise on Public Administration* (*Verwaltungslehre*), a comparative study of the emergence, in connection with modern nation-state building, of European educational systems and, at the same time, a historical document that mirrored, in terms of participatory observation, early-19th-century processes of constitutional struggle and societal reorganization. In a large-scale historical overview, Stein reviewed, thus, the sequence of organizational forms in which education had successively taken place since ancient times. He then went on to enthusiastically welcome the eventual formation of educational systems as the "incorporation [of previously uncoordinated patterns of schooling] into an all-encompassing unity of the educational process," an occurrence that presupposed, he argued, the concomitant incorporation of varying patterns of school tutelage into "a public legal organism":

Just as more than a thousand years had been necessary in order to transform early forms of schooling into educational establishments organized under the tutelage of public authorities, so more than another thousand years were needed in order to shape the totality of these establishments, which had successively come into being, and which originally were lacking any kind of coherence, into a unified system of public instruction and to create, thus, what we call an organic component of national legislation and administration. (Stein 1884, 123 ff.)

Stein sought to give additional weight to this idea by establishing the correspondences between his sequence of increasingly institutionalized forms of schooling and a sequence, likewise developed from a macrohistorical perspective, of successive regimes of societal organization. In this sense, he outlined the succession of first, a social regime based on clan and lineage (*Geschlechterordnung*), next, an estate-based corporate social regime (*ständische Ordnung*), and finally, the essentially modern form of civil society based on constitutional law (*staatsbürgerliche Ordnung*), in order to point out that only under the conditions of the latter regime was it possible for educational system formation to come to fruition.

It is, thus, three aspects that according to Stein, make up the specific "systems" character of educational systems: (1) the unity of meaning pervading, as "all-encompassing unity of the educational process," all teaching and learning activities; (2) the unity of an administrative and organizational whole resultant from the incorporation of educational institutions into a "public legal organism"; and (3) the—as Stein emphasized—"intimate connection" of educational system building with intrinsically modern principles of state organization and societal order. In largely similar, though more elaborate, forms, these aspects are taken up again in conceptual models developed by recent social theory. Particular reference is made here to the theory of social differentiation developed by Niklas Luhmann in terms of systems theory closely associated with communication theory and the theory of evolution. Luhmann distinguished three schemes of the primary differentiation of society—that is, segmentation characteristic of archaic societies; stratification characteristic of nearly all premodern civilizations; and functional differentiation essentially realized in modern European and North American societies—but in much of his work, dwelled particularly upon the latter scheme. Under the heading of "functional differentiation," he developed both a theory of the evolutionary processes leading to European modernity and an analysis of the patterns, risks, and potentialities typical of contemporary society (Luhmann 1982; also Luhmann 1995 [1984]).

While explaining, then, with reference to these frameworks, the formation and operation of functionally specific subsystems of society—such as the political system, the legal and the economic system, or the system of scientific research—Luhmann also provided the conceptual tools for analyzing the emergence, from the late 18th century onward, and the subsequent "systematization," up to the early 20th century, of particular subsystems for education. Not least in consideration of this wider social context it takes into account, the Luhmannian model throws into relief educational systems' inherent modernity. Moreover, the model makes it possible to specify further the nature of these systems in terms of networks of highly specialized communication, the meaning of which refers to a special function to be fulfilled at the level of society itself. Finally, going well beyond the systems' aspects already spelled out a century ago by Lorenz von Stein, the Luhmannian model emphasizes a further criterion—and a decisive one—intrinsic to the constitution of functionally specific social subsystems. This criterion is inclusion.

Inclusion refers to one of the central aspects of modern, that is, functionally differentiated, societies, namely the access of a population as a whole to all of the functional subsystems constituted at the level of society. By this is not meant, to be sure, that everybody can or will become a politician, a physician, a merchant, or a teacher. Although such "service roles" had been in existence for long periods of time and had more or less been closely associated with well-defined layers, classes, or estates within a hierarchically ordered society, *inclusion* means the universalization, not of these roles, but of their counterparts, namely the roles of the electorate, of patients, of consumers, or of pupils respectively. What characterizes, in other words, the transition from a premodern, stratified social order to modern society is the differentiation not of "service roles," but of functionally specific "service-receiving roles" and the attendant universalization of the latter. *Inclusion* means, accordingly, that each person has access to every subsystem of society independently of the role he performs in other social subsystems.

The educational correlate to the inclusion process at the level of society at large was, in current terminology, the "universalization of primary education." This process started in the Protestant countries of Central and Northern Europe as early as the 17th century, was largely achieved in most of Western Europe by the end of the 19th century, but came about, in some countries of Southern Europe, only in the first half of the 20th century. At the level of national legislation, important steps tending toward universalizing primary education often went hand in hand with measures undertaken with a view to assuring greater inclusion in the political and legal systems as well. As illustrated by the historical experience, not only of England and Italy but in varying forms of France and Prussia and to some extent of Russia, such measures consisted in, for example, the extension of the franchise or in more general steps meant to turn hitherto dependent subjects into national citizens (Frijhoff 1983). At the local level, on the other hand, national school laws were successively implemented as an answer to the radically altered communication requirements that were attendant upon social structures increasingly characterized by new patterns of differentiation and ensuing processes of rationalization, mobilization, and industrialization (Thabault 1971 [1944]; Gellner 1983). In this sense, the process of inclusion in the emerging educational system did correspond to the gearing of that system to its actual function—a function that has exactly been described in terms of laying the foundation of the capability for universal communication across all subsystems of society, hence of "socializing persons as the adequate environment of future social systems" (Luhmann 1982). One may conclude, then, that—although a multitude of different types of schools and educational establishments, supported by a multitude of individual and corporate actors, had been in existence for centuries—it was essentially the achievement of universal mass schooling that marked the decisive transition toward the constitution of institutionalized education as a modern "system."

META-ORGANIZATION

To the extent that since the late 18th century the traditional union of schools and church(es) made way for the differentiation between education and religion, conceived of and organized as distinct spheres of social action and meaning, it was the increasingly rationalized and secularized nation-state that was considered to serve as the natural support and guardian of the education of its citizens. This view had implications in distinct but complementary respects. On the one hand, the eventual achievement and continuous running of an inclusive educational system presupposed organizational resources and required an administrative infrastructure, which no corporate social actor other than the state was deemed able to provide. On the other hand, the state and state-supported agencies were ready to use compulsory mass schooling also for pushing through the realization of more general state-related goals: be this the goal of ensuring a more complete realization of individual citizens' political rights, as Condorcet had stipulated in his famous project for the overall organization of public instruction submitted in 1792 to the National Assembly of revolutionary France; be this the goal of preventing social unrest on the part of the impoverished industrial working classes, which was of prime importance to social reformers and policymakers in 19th-century Victorian England; or be this the goal of fostering, by means of political socialization and/or nationalist indoctrination, processes of accelerated nation building, as was practiced in the Central and Eastern European nation-states that had come into being only toward the end of the 19th and in the first decades of the 20th century.

Thus, in nearly all European countries, the realization of an all-inclusive educational system by way of the universalization of compulsory mass schooling went hand in hand with the increasing intervention of central state agencies and the building of comprehensive administrative frameworks. Education ministries were established with a view to securing the financial resources and to establishing the administrative infrastructure—that is, the meta-organization—necessary not only to guarantee generalized supply, but also successfully to run standardized networks of institutionalized schooling. Again, just as held true for the realization of compulsory mass schooling, this process took more than a century to come to its achievement. It was a long way, indeed, from the late-18th-century program of establishing a state organism patterned on Catholic Church organization, and called, in the case of the pioneering Italian principalities of Parma and Piemont, or in the case of Imperial France, the *university*—meaning the totality of a hierarchically structured pyramid of all institutionalized schooling—to the all-encompassing modern educational systems considered as components of public policy and organized as branches of the respective country's state administration and legislation.

Moreover, the particular shape of a given system of education, as well as its way of operation, largely mirrored, and to some extent continues to mirror, the respective state's pattern of public and constitutional law. Thus, they mirror the outcomes of historical "struggles between the state and particular social interests"—as Stein put it—or, in terms of present-day comparative sociology—the specific solution to the "legitimization conflict" between the centralizing and secularizing nation-state and more traditional corporate actors, such as the church(es), craft guilds, estates, trusts, and so on (Rokkan 1970). Along such lines of reasoning, present-day analyses go on to differentiate between political systems according to whether "they developed articulated party systems before, after, or concurrent with the establishment of centralized national bureaucracies" (Flora and Heidenheimer 1981, 296 ff.). Accordingly, the constitutional character of political systems, as well as their different religious backgrounds, did heavily impinge on the manner and the sequence in which they nationalized social services in general and education in particular:

- The transferral of duties and services from associations to public bureaucracies, and from local to national officials, though everywhere gradual, was a more rapid process in the "early bureaucratic" systems—such as France or Germany—because these could command relatively greater resources to "police" and assimilate the functions of local authorities.

- Regarding educational services, the pace of transfer from church to state was affected by both constitutional and religious characteristics. It was especially rapid in the Lutheran absolutist states—such as Prussia and Sweden—which encouraged the first crusade for mass education that the West has ever seen.

- The "party first" systems—such as Britain and the United States, or, in a sense, the Netherlands—remained more pluralist because religious, local, and entrepreneurial interests remained freer to offer a variety of services in competition with the public services the national and state governments were gradually evolving (Flora and Heidenheimer 1981, 269ff.).

MACRO-ORGANIZATION

As mentioned above, educational systems in Europe were not created in a vacuum. Their system formation processes started, rather, from quite an array of existing institutions stemming from premodern establishments such as medieval cathedral schools and Renaissance universities, church-run colleges and academies for the sons and daughters of the nobility, endowed grammar schools and *Gymnasien* established by enlightened princely rulers, to municipal petty schools and the more recent forms of drawing schools, science schools, higher-grade, technical, and vocational schools. It was, then, a significant feature of the differentiation process that the emergent educational systems, during the initial stage of inclusion, and from such origins, were rather decentralized, uncoordinated, and open in their organization. Their services were called on not so much by the lower, but by the middle and upper classes. The more the continuing process of inclusion advanced, however, the more acute the need for internal specification and rational articulation made itself felt. Specification, on the one hand, implied the removal of mere ambiguities and unregulated competition between institutions that were to become clearly defined alternative tracks or types of schooling. The systems' articulation, on the other hand, raised the issue of connecting hitherto uncoordinated institutional components with a view to constructing a rational "sequence," or "ladder," of successive levels of education.

The structural outcomes of defining educational systems' macro-organization can be conceived of, then, from the perspective of social theory, as ways of coping with divergent expectations and requirements, such as inclusion (by organizing universal access to elementary schooling for all potential pupils) and selection (by channeling them consecutively into different tracks and levels); qualifying for universal communication across all fields of society and inculcating differential "habitus" (Bourdieu 1970) as adapted to particular groups, trades, and areas of activity; and in more general terms, the educational system's very functional orientation toward the encompassing society at large and its output performances related to other functionally specific subsystems, such as the economic system. As a consequence, the issue of defining an educational system's macro-organization has always been closely associated with a nation's public policy in general, and with its social, economic, and science policy in particular. This applied particularly to the construction of sequence between the "lower" or vernacular schools (e.g., the so-called English or German schools) and the "learned" or Latin-based establishments, between—to take up a graphic phrasing coined by Prost (1968)—*"l'école du peuple"* and *"l'école des notables."* Thus, from the late-19th-century "systematization" of the educational systems in France, Britain, and Germany (Müller, Ringer, and Simon 1987); over the definition, during the inter-war period, of examination-based transition procedures from the primary to the secondary level of education; up to the successive introduction of comprehensive schooling in many, but not all, European countries, in the post–World War II era, contrasting models, programs, and policies for educational macro-organization have been in the very core of educational policy debate in Europe. These models and policies have not only led to the construction, in different European nations, of "disparate ladders"—as Heidenheimer (1997) put it—but have also considerably fostered the production both of educational research and theory building and of educational reformative reflection and ideology.

REFLECTION

Educational systems, just as social systems more generally, are intrinsically self-reflexive. They typically develop self-observations and self-descriptions, which in turn, influence the working of the system in question. It is, then, a significant feature of modernity that in the societal subsystems that have built up in the course of the far-reaching transformation processes attendant on "functional differentiation," system-specific self-descriptions intensify to such an extent that they crystallize into explicitly stated reflection theories. Such are, for example, the political and constitutional theories developed, from the 17th century onward, within the emerging political system, or the economic and legal theories elaborated, from the 18th century on, within the economic and legal systems, respectively. Likewise, educational theorizing pursued within the emergent educational system follows this common pattern of self-referential theories *of* a societal subsystem developed *within* that system (Luhmann 1995 [1984]).

On the one hand, this explains the tremendous increase in educational knowledge, educational ideologies, and educational theories produced, from the second half of the 18th century onward, in conjunction with programs advocating the establishment of universal state-supported "national systems of education." On the other hand, this general feature intrinsic to self-referential social systems casts new light on the emergence, in close temporal and ideological connection with the passing of the decisive laws on compulsory schooling in most of the Western European nations, of education as a particular field of academic study. The historically unprecedented scale, the inclusive character, as well as, especially in the Catholic countries of Southern Europe, the secularized organization of universal mass education not only presupposed new patterns of an administrative infrastructure or meta-organization, but required also new forms of both reflection and systematized teacher training. Thus, in Britain, the establishment of the first chairs in education in Scottish universities, and in English universities, of courses in educational theory, immediately followed the 1870 and 1880 legislation on compulsory elementary schooling. Likewise, in France, the first courses and, later, chairs of education were established in the French faculties, from 1883 onward, in close conjunction with the all-encompassing educational reforms pushed through those same years by the dominant political and intellectual elites of the early Third Republic. In Italy, the creation of the first education chair (1872) even preceded the introduction of compulsory schooling, though as part of a political project formally adopted. Following a similar rationale, the creation of the first Spanish chair in education (1905) was conceived as a major initiative meant to fuel a significant rise of universal primary education. Developments in Germany, on the other hand, were a bit more complicated, in that university courses in educational theory had been in existence since the late 18th century—thereby reflecting the early start of the inclusion process in the German *Länder*—whereas particular chairs were erected only in the first decades of the 20th century, in connection with controversial debate about macro-organization, or, more exactly, about the extent to which the German educational system should be organized according to the contrary principles of inclusiveness or selectivity (Drewek, Lüth et al. 1998).

Finally, although educational studies are nowadays firmly established in universities, research institutes, and teacher training colleges throughout Europe, the field continuously has had to cope with problems both of adequate method and of academic reputation (Shen 1999). These are associated, at long last, with the ambiguities of transplanting educational systems' reflection into the institutions of science. Educational studies are, in other words, not just an academic discipline like sociology or biology; the field is constituted, rather, as a "composite area of study" (Hirst 1983). It combines components of knowledge as diverse as the traditional wisdom and normative doctrines embedded in the writings of the grand educators and philosophers of the past; philosophical reasoning and hermeneutic reflection; social-scientific theory building and research largely based on psychology and sociology; and the development of applied knowledge suited to educational planning and practical assistance. The structural reason for this is the fact that functional differentiation of society entails also a disjunction of scientific research and systemic self-reflection. Whereas the former is carried out according to the distinctive commitment to "truth" of the functionally specific subsystem for science, the latter embodies the particular communication processes that are meant, within each of society's subsystems, to interpret its distinctive unity and identity, and to provide orientation for the practitioners working in relevant fields. As a consequence, educational studies allow room for a considerable variety of theoretical constructions of reality, the varying presuppositions of which ensue from their being related to distinct system imperatives and problem perspectives: to either the logic of discovery specific to modern science, or to the need for self-interpretation, practical orientation, and professional knowledge emerging from within a given educational system and resulting in the style of theorizing described as systemic self-reflection. The respective proportions, however, in which these component modes of reasoning give shape to educational studies as an institutionalized field are subject to historical and socio-cultural variation. Such variation, finally, arises from distinct national configurations of the relations between corporate actors (such as the state, the teaching profession, political associations, or the academic community), individual actors (such as eminent philosophers, social scientists, or politicians), relevant institutions (such as the university or the educational system as a whole), and the intellectual traditions prevailing in each of the countries concerned.

STRUCTURAL ELABORATION

Thus, although clearly sharing structural features that are not random but involved in their systemic organization, European educational systems are, at the same time, socio-cultural entities bearing the imprint both of their societal environment and of the historical period most decisive for their "systematization." The expositions that preceded on topics such as inclusion, meta-organization, macro-organization, or reflection have sufficiently pointed up, indeed, that socio-historically specific educational systems, in spite of their being structured according to the logic of self-referential social systems, are not just the predetermined outcome of anonymous societal forces as once predominant versions of functionalism and Marxism used to contend. Educational systems take shape, rather, through multiple communication and interaction processes that bear different meanings and give rise to different outcomes, according to different stages of development and depending on different periods of time. These communication and interaction processes take place, moreover, between—often conflicting—social actors who are, on their part, bound to varying socio-cultural settings. Suffice it to recall here the outstanding role teachers and their associations as well as the increasing number of educational experts and the knowledge, models, and ideologies they produce have played, and continue to play, in different periods of time and under varying circumstances (Popkewitz 1999).

"Realist social theory" seeking to overcome the conventional divide between "systems" and "actors" has been developed with a view exactly to grasping the intricate combination of cultural settings, structural factors, and social interaction (Archer 1979 and 1982). In so doing, it has also provided the conceptual tools suited to analyzing the social construction of educational systems. By focusing on the recurrent sequences of "initial conditioning" (by given institutions and settings); "interaction" (both between context and environment and between corporate and individual actors); and resultant "structural elaboration" (serving, in turn, as conditioning for subsequent interaction), this approach insists upon the "morphogenetic character" of socio-cultural systems in general, and educational systems in particular. Accordingly, it throws into relief not only these systems' "elaboration over time," but also the fact that they follow an irrevocably unique developmental path.

EXPANSION

The concept of structural elaboration has particularly been taken up in debates concerning an appropriate interpretation of the spectacular expansion that European educational systems have experienced during the post–Word War II era (Archer 1982). Depending on varying preconditions of context, structure, and environment, educational expansion did not take place evenly in every European country. It was, rather, initiated by two groups of countries: by Northern European, especially Scandinavian, countries on the one hand, and on the other, by the East Central and Eastern European countries under predominant political and ideological influence of the former Soviet Union. Educational expansion then spread to Western and Southern Europe as well, first to Britain, France, Belgium, and Germany, and in a second wave, to the Mediterranean region, catching up countries such as Italy, Greece, Spain, and Portugal.

First of all, educational expansion meant the extension of the inclusion process, constitutive of educational system building in general, from the lower level of compulsory mass education to the higher levels of—using the International Standard Classification of Education (ISCED) terms—junior secondary education, upper secondary education, and finally, higher education. Again, the extent to which, and the speed at which, different European countries implemented these changes were quite different. The formerly socialist countries of East Central and Eastern Europe, after an early expansion of junior secondary education, followed by only limited growth of higher education in the 1950s, stabilized their educational system by and large at a level of expansion reached in the 1960s. As a consequence, in these countries, the participation rate in higher education is considerably behind that of the rest of Europe. On the other hand, the gap, which used to be important in the 1950s, between (non-socialist) Northern and Southern European countries, has substantially narrowed.

Educational expansion, however, was connected with yet another aspect of this extension of the principle of inclusion to the upper levels of the educational pyramid, namely with the definite inclusion of women. Although compulsory mass schooling had, for decades, become virtually all-inclusive for boys and girls alike, postcompulsory education still was characterized by marked gender inequalities, at least until the 1960s. In this respect, European countries have undoubtedly achieved a great improvement. Nevertheless, the likelihood of access to upper secondary and higher education remains in some instances unequal. In countries that have developed technical and/or vocational education and training at the end of junior secondary or at the level of upper secondary education, fewer girls than boys tend to enroll in these tracks. This is because of the division of sex roles, which still prevails on the job market. Industrial jobs are more likely assigned to men, whereas employees in the service sector are more likely to be women. Accordingly, girls are more likely to be enrolled in general education. As a consequence of this, however, the issue of sex roles in education has already been reversed in some cases. Thus, male teenagers are increasingly at a disadvantage to the extent that schools attach greater importance to values more connected with girls' socialization than with that of boys. In addition, since school systems tend to recruit more women than men as teachers, except in higher education, the predominance of women at the primary and secondary levels may generate new perceptions of sex roles and thus induce a disequilibrium at the expense of men. By contrast, men still dominate in the elite segment of the educational system, particularly when mathematics is used as a tool for access to elite institutions.

Moreover, educational expansion went hand in hand with a far-reaching reconsideration and eventual restructuring of educational macro-organization as it had been defined in the major European nations at the turn of the century. Inevitably, however, in spite of the by and large quite similar push toward expansion, structural elaboration led to fairly different organizational patterns. Thus, one major pattern, which has been driven mostly by social equity objectives, is based on the concept of comprehensive schooling. In this model very little differentiation takes place in types of schools or programs at the junior secondary level. The majority of pupils is thus exposed to a similar school menu. This pattern has triumphed in Eastern Europe as well as, subsequently, in all of the Northern European and the majority of Western European countries. Another model, however, continues the traditional tripartite structure of macro-organization that was characteristic, with some variation, of most of the European educational systems prior to World War II. This pattern is based on an early differentiation of the tracks offered to children; some tracks are more academically oriented, whereas others are more likely to lead to early vocational education. Typical of this model are the educational systems of Germany and Switzerland. A third model is embodied by the French educational system. While in principle adopting the comprehensive school model for junior secondary education, France has implemented it in a flexible way and preserved, thus, a certain degree of internal differentiation, hence of selectivity. In some schools, for instance, pupils may be regrouped according to scholastic achievement criteria and are exposed, accordingly, to slightly different curricula, especially in foreign languages (Heidenheimer 1997; Leschinsky and Mayer 1999).

Finally, and most important, the expansion of European educational systems has been legitimated with respect to different objectives, linked with economic and social policies respectively, and has consequently been fueled by different social actors. To begin with, economic policy objectives dominated, particularly during the postwar reconstruction and modernization period of European societies. Educational expansion was considered to be in close correspondence with the growing needs of modernizing economies for qualified labor. Economic growth led to important new investments and to the rapid development of more productive technologies, both requiring a higher level of general and vocational training within the workforce. At the same time, the number of farmers was declining rapidly, and new jobs in the industrial and service sectors were created. It was also the time during which economists invented the concept of human capital, according to which the nature of education was no longer a consumption good but an investment good, generating, just like physical investment, a profitable economic return for both the individual and the society as a whole.

This new perception of education also fostered the development of new conceptual and methodological frameworks for the analysis of education. A new discipline emerged in the form of the economics of education. Economic analyses have highlighted, inter alia, changing patterns of the evolution of cost and finance. Thus, at the beginning of educational expansion, in the 1950s, European public authorities were spending 2.5% of their consolidated gross domestic product (GDP) on education. Twenty-five years later, this figure was close to 6%. This period has therefore experienced an unprecedented increase in public expenditure on education. It is likely that private expenditure has declined, at least in relative terms, but unfortunately this point has never been properly documented. Given the fact that the growth of the GDPs has been quite rapid, the total amount of public resources allocated to public education has multiplied by a factor of 5 to 6.

After 1975 the increase in public expenditure for education within the GDP stopped. The average for Europe fell to 5.5% in 1992 (from a maximum of

6%). The main feature of European education budgets during the 1975–1992 period is a trend toward a greater convergence between countries. Southern countries, which used to spend less than the average, have continued an increase in public expenditure for education, whereas most Northern countries, which used to spend more than the average, have tended to reduce their effort. This convergence toward an average level does not concern the newly independent successor states of the former Soviet Union, in which the percentage of public education expenditure within the GDP has dramatically gone down to a level between 1 and 4%. Indeed, a striking effect of the split of the former Soviet Union is the deep decline of public resources, not only in the Russian Federation, but even more drastically in the peripheral republics such as the Ukraine, Belarus, or Georgia. In Western Europe, by contrast, a small decline in public resources for education may be explained by the conjunction of three phenomena: first, a tendency toward a diversification of sources of finance for education; second, the beginning of greater concern for better (i.e., more cost-effective) utilization of existing resources; and third, a decline in a majority of countries of the school-age population after the baby boom that followed World War II. There are, however, some exceptions to this trend. In France, for example, a slight increase in expenditure for public education parallels a slight increase in the total number of pupils and is linked with recent policies attempting to enlarge access to upper secondary and higher education.

On the other hand, the economists' view of education as an investment good stimulated, in turn, social demand. Education came to be seen as a powerful tool, not only for economic development, but also for promoting upward social mobility. Social policy objectives such as equality of opportunity and equitable access to the upper secondary and higher levels of the educational system led to an increased enrollment, from the early 1960s onward, of children of low economic status. And just as the postwar economic concerns with education had been translated into the economics of education as a new field of study, so the social equity issues gave rise to a substantial body of research and analysis. Relevant studies have indeed amply demonstrated the high correlation that existed, and continues to exist, between low socio-economic status and unequal access to postcompulsory education. As a consequence, large sectors of the public—parents' as well as teachers' associations, educationalists as well as social scientists, politicians as well as trade unions—held the view that in order to reduce inequities in access to upper secondary and higher education successfully, an important quantitative expansion of the system had to take place in connection with its overall restructuring.

Undoubtedly, then, the overall expansion of educational systems all over Europe has significantly increased the access to non-compulsory education for children belonging to middle-level or low-level economic status. In spite of this expansion, however, inequities still exist in most European countries. In particular, access to the elite segment of the educational pyramid is still largely monopolized by children from higher socio-economic strata. On the other hand, a significant proportion of each generation leaves the educational system with an alarmingly low level of school competencies, particularly in reading. This holds true irrespective of the fact that the proportion of illiterates in a given population depends on one's definition of illiteracy and may vary from 5 to 20%. Up to now, very few remedial programs have successfully addressed this issue. It is less a question of improving the internal quality of education services than a question of unfavorable socio-economic background. Children whose parents are illiterate, or who belong to one-parent families, the immigrant population, or families whose heads are unemployed are more likely to be low achievers than are others. Such patterns of inequity go hand in hand with new patterns of diversification that gain acceptance in spite of the adoption by the majority of European countries of the model of comprehensive schooling. Diversification is because of, for instance, the existence of a private sector in education specifically oriented toward excellence and requiring a heavy investment from parents to finance high fees in elite schools. Typical of this pattern are private schools in Switzerland or the United Kingdom. But one has also to mention, in this connection, the de facto organization in countries such as France, which share a strong tradition of public education, of an elitist sector—or of elitist tracks— within that public system. Diversification of this type corresponds to a recent trend in parental attitudes toward schooling, namely, the spread of a consumerist behavior, a demand for more choice among schools. Such consumerism is an important reason for the continued existence of private schools with religious affiliations, even though religion is no longer the predominant reason for the enrollment of pupils in such schools. Parents of high socio-economic status are more likely to insist on the right to have choice than are others.

Paradoxically, then, educational expansion, although considerably extending the inclusion of the totality of young generations into the higher levels of the education pyramid, has at the same time introduced new patterns of diversification among post–junior secondary schools. Such diversification is associated with unequal employment prospects and income profiles during the lifecycle. Therefore, families have developed strategies to put their children on tracks leading to the most attractive careers. Families are, however, unevenly prepared to develop such strategies.

RECONSTRUCTION

Although all educational systems in Europe have experienced an unprecedented expansion during the last decades, some of them are now more involved in large-scale restructuring. This has become a matter of necessity as a consequence of the breakdown of socialist regimes in East Central and Eastern Europe. Structural elaboration, then, is currently taking shape by way of highly controversial interaction and negotiation processes, both between the context of formerly socialist systems and a radically altered environment of social actors and, within the latter, between actors supporting opposite models of educational meta-organization, macro-organization, and last but not least, micro-organization.

Thus, socialist education reflected a state monopoly aimed at uniformity. Post-socialist education builds on national identity and on political pluralism, a development that appears to presage a new pluralism. In addition, a process of renationalization is under way in each of the former Soviet bloc countries, and with it the creation of a national school system consciously reflecting indigenous cultural, spiritual, and historical traditions. Nevertheless, the transformation of what were once unified school systems has been an ambivalent process. A major issue is how to provide a bridge between general education and the demands of a weak market system. Schools are underfunded. The old educational establishment has suffered loss of status and income. Patterns of dogmatic belief still persist in places that lack a tradition of democracy.

Since 1992 a full spectrum of schools not tolerated under socialism has appeared, or reappeared, in the cities of East Central and Eastern Europe: *Gymnasien*, private and confessional schools—a development widely interpreted as the triumph of freedom and pluralism. Such schools, however, are not without their critics. That some private schools get partial state support may be interpreted as an excuse for the state to reduce its subsidy to public education. Private schools, furthermore, are widely viewed as evidence of a return to class distinctions. At the same time there is a lively interest in alternative and reformed pedagogy in the former socialist states, even attempts to link with the international activity school movement and with reforms called the "new education" in Europe.

Excessive centralization was one of the most restrictive factors of the former system, although there were attempts to change even before the fall of the Soviet bloc. In the 1970s these attempts increased, but even in the 1990s many of the new republics carried over an old administrative structure in which teachers were subjected to a highly authoritarian system. In Russia, moreover, where each administrative unit enjoyed a high level of autonomy, the real need was to balance central state control with regional interests. Another difficulty was how to bring professional quality to school administrations in the midst of political and financial crisis. In some post-socialist countries, administrators continued in their jobs. In the former East Germany, however, many administrators were dismissed and replaced by experienced administrators from the West German *Länder*, who had little understanding of crises faced by the new *Länder*. Others were replaced by novices. These difficulties notwithstanding, greater choice and variety is now possible throughout the former Soviet bloc. With the state monopoly gone, teachers in schools have the right to make their own decisions about curriculum for the first time in many years.

CULTURAL HOMOGENIZATION

The emergence of modern society based on functional differentiation and inclusion, and closely connected to the rise of modern technology, societywide communication and transportation, as well as of a market-based economy, also implied a high degree of cultural homogenization. In fact, the project of modern nation building actually consisted in making congruent political structures of state organization and territorial sovereignty with cultural and linguistic structures defined in ethnic terms (Gellner 1983). The very function assigned, then, to national systems of education was exactly to achieve and guarantee this homogenization both at the level of linguistic mastery of the national language and at the level of rationalized problem-solution habits and mental attitudes appropriate to a new, industrializing social environment. In this sense, the historical mission of the emerging national systems of education in 19th-century Europe exactly mirrored the function, spelled out above in theoretical terms, of the functionally specific subsystem of society for education, namely to qualify people for universal communication across all subsystems of society. Toward the turn of the second millennium, however, late-19th-century patterns of cultural homogenization inevitably are confronted with new challenges. These are challenges coming both from inside European societies—that is, the assertive presence of immigrants, migrant workers, and non-dominant indigenous groups—and from outside—that is, the processes of increasing European integration as symbolized by the European Union and the Council of Europe.

In many European countries—in addition to long-established indigenous ethnic groups such as the Basques and Catalonians in Spain, or the Welsh in the United Kingdom—guest workers, immigrants, and refugees have formed their own ethnic enclaves, some for three generations. Recent easing of naturalization restrictions makes an accurate demographic count difficult, but it is not an exaggeration to point out that in countries such as Belgium and Germany, 8 to 9% of the population may be of foreign citizenship. In some neighborhoods in urban centers such as London and Brussels, they may make up 90 to 100% of a school population (Swing 1992). A special concern at the close of the 20th century is how to provide a fair and equitable education for these "others" that provides for economic success in the larger society while honoring ethnic identity.

Europeans have experimented with several patterns of educational accommodation of such ethnic groups. The most dramatic, *separatism*, is a pattern frequently found among indigenous minorities but not specific to them. An example of separatism is the case of Belgium, a country that was once a nation-state but is now a federation of semi-autonomous cultural communities, each of which controls an education system in its own language (Swing 1997). Another pattern of separatism is possibly under way in Wales, where Welsh is now a required language in all schools. Welsh Nationalists are no less fervent than were Flemish Nationalists in the past, but whether their drive for linguistic recognition will take the same route the Flemings took is far from clear. A third pattern of separatism occurs within ethnic groups—for example, Muslims petitioning for separate schools in England or Turks seeking separate schools in Germany. Such programs are the least likely to attain permanence, unless they are generated from within the separate communities.

Another pattern of accommodation might be labeled *segmented pluralism*, that is, the coexistence of indigenous majorities and immigrants—"others," *Ausländer* in Germany, for example. Ethnic Germans, even those who have not lived in Germany for several generations, are not *Ausländer*, but other newcomers are, particularly Turks, the largest ethnic group in Germany and the most vocal. Although educated in German schools, some in a variety of bicultural and bilingual programs, they remain non-assimilated, a defiantly separate group, whether or not they wish to be one, in a world in which the concept of Turkish-German does not exist. To one degree or another, such segmented pluralism exists throughout Western Europe—but in spite of, not because of, the efforts of supranational agencies such as the Council of Europe and the European Union, which have funded a plethora of bilingual, bicultural, and intercultural programs for immigrants and migrant workers.

Although countries such as France and England have been host to multicultural, pluralist pilot projects of this kind, their dominant mode of accommodation is *assimilationist* rather than pluralist. But unlike the third generation in the United States who frequently adopt a hyphenated identity, a non-national foreigner in many European countries is likely to be viewed as an "outsider," an "other," a stateless person. The overt intent of the National Curriculum in England, for example, is to provide equality of educational opportunity for everyone through a uniform course of studies; but underlying this intent is the assumption that all students, even minority students from India, Pakistan, or Africa, should become acculturated to the same worldview, an assumption that may be compared to Americanization school programs of the first half of the 20th century in the United States (Swing 1980).

On the other hand, with the creation of the Council of Europe and the European Economic Community—today the European Union—European nations have at last begun to achieve a degree of unity. In contrast to the Council of Europe, an organization with essentially educational and cultural goals, which has provided an important forum for debate but has no legislative power, the European Union actually *does* have legislative powers, and increasingly so. According to its founding document, the Treaty of Rome (1957), the European Community's competencies initially were focused almost exclusively on economic and political matters. It is only from 1976 onward that an educational program directed toward the development of a European dimension of education was established. Subsequently, the term *European dimension of education* has come to be used instead of older terms such as *Europeanization*. Even so, despite a commitment by national governments in 1988 to the introduction of a European dimension into the curricula of European schools, pressures to preserve historical and national elements in education continue to dominate many school systems.

On the eve of the 21st century, therefore, Europe is attempting to achieve a new form of cultural homogenization defined, henceforth, at the supranational union level, and related to the conscious promotion of a European identity in the curricula of schools. Much remains to be done, particularly within national education systems of the member states of the European Union and the Council of Europe, where implementation in curricula and teacher preparation still remain limited. Of particular concern is the position of a European dimension in the schools of East Central and Eastern European countries, where priority is given, after a long period of Soviet-dominated "socialist internationalism," to restrengthening national identity. Within this context, it seems likely that both the European Union and the Council of Europe will continue to develop their own activities in the promotion of the European dimension in school programs and teacher training. How successful this will be is a question for the next generation.

Having outlined some of the key concepts and features characteristic both of "the modern educational system" (Müller, Ringer, and Simon 1987) and of European educational systems' current state and ongoing transformation, we shall conclude our introductory considerations by assigning to these concepts and features the individual chapters that make up the book. Selected aspects typically linked with the systems character of modern institutionalized education—such as educational meta-organization, the teachers in their capacity as a key group of social actors constantly involved in structural elaboration processes, and educational system reflection—are dealt with in greater detail in Part I: chapter 2, by Hermann Avenarius and Theo M. E. Liket, "Systems of Public Administration: Patterns of School Legislation and Management"; chapter 3, by António Nóvoa, "The Teaching Profession in Europe: Historical and Sociological Analysis"; and chapter 4, by Jürgen Schriewer, "Educational Studies in Europe." The issue of establishing a "sequence," that is, the integration of different levels and types of schooling into a coherent macro-organization, is taken up in Part II, where chapter 5, by Bernd Zymek, "Equality of Opportunity: Expansion of European School Systems Since the Second World War," makes the transition between "systematization" and post–World War II expansion. Complementary aspects of expansion are expounded in chapter 6, by François Orivel, "The Economics of Education: Incentives, Control of Costs, Allocation of Resources," and in chapter 7, by Marie Duru-Bellat and Agnès van Zanten, "The Impact of Family Socialization Processes and Educational Strategies on the Adaptation and Academic Success of Students." Margaret Sutherland analyzes the late inclusion of girls, particularly in the upper levels of secondary, higher and/or technical education, in chapter 8, "Gender Issues in European Education Today." Finally, Part III is particularly devoted to analyzing problems and challenges of European educational systems after the breakdown of socialism and in an era of global change. Chapter 9, by Jürgen Wichmann and Val D. Rust, "The Heritage of Socialism and *Perestroika*: Transformation Processes in Central and Eastern European Education," provides an analysis of changes in education in those areas. Chapter 10, by Elizabeth Sherman Swing, "Schools, Separatism, and Assimilation: The Education of 'Others' in Europe," examines migration, immigration, and minority education. Chapter 11, by Raymond Ryba, "Developing the European Dimension in Education: The Roles of the European Union and the Council of Europe," looks at the challenges European education systems are facing as a consequence of supranational integration. Although far from a complete description of European education, the book's chapters nevertheless provide the reader detailed insight into what we consider core issues. Both the authors and the editors hope that the book will open up better understanding and invite further reading. The up-to-date reference lists that conclude each chapter provide a wide range of sources for that purpose.

REFERENCES

Archer, Margaret S. 1979. *Social Origins of Educational Systems*. Beverly Hills and London: Sage.

Archer, Margaret S., ed. 1982. *The Sociology of Educational Expansion*. Beverly Hills and London: Sage.

Arnold, Matthew. 1861. *The Popular Education of France with Notices of that of Holland and Switzerland*. London: Longman.

———. 1864. *A French Eton or Middle-Class Education and the State*. London: Macmillan.

———. 1868. *Schools and Universities on the Continent*. London: Macmillan.

Bourdieu, Pièrre, and Jean-Claude Bourdieu. 1970. *La réproduction. Eléments pour une théorie du système d'enseignment*. Paris: Minuit. (English translation: *Reproduction in Education, Society and Culture*. London: Corwin, 1990.)

Drewek, Peter, Christoph Lüth, Richard Aldrich, Harald Scholtz, Jürgen Schriewer, and Heinz-Elmar Tenorth, eds. 1998. *History of Educational Studies. Geschichte der Erziehungswissenschaft. Histoire des Sciences de l'éducation*. Vol. 3 of *Paedagogica Historica*, Supplementary Series. Gent, Belgium: C.S.H.P.

Dreyfus-Brisac, Edmond. 1882–1897. *L'Education nouvelle: études de pédagogie comparée*. 3 vols. Paris: G. Masson.

Flora, Peter, and Arnold J. Heidenheimer, eds. 1981. *The Development of Welfare States in Europe and America*. New Brunswick and London: Transaction Books.

Frijhoff, Willem, ed. 1983. *L'Offre d'École: Eléments pour une étude comparée des politiques éducatives au XIXe siècle/The Supply of Schooling: Contributions to a comparative study of educational policies in the XIXth century*. Paris: Publications de la Sorbonne & Institut National de Recherche Pédagogique.

Gellner, Ernest. 1983. *Nations and Nationalism*. Oxford: Basil Blackwell Ltd.

Heidenheimer, Arnold J. 1997. *Disparate Ladders: Why School and University Policies Differ in Germany, Japan, and Switzerland*. New Brunswick and London: Transaction Books.

Hirst, Paul H. 1983. "Educational Theory." In *Educational Theory and Its Foundation Disciplines*. Edited by Paul H. Hirst. London: Routledge and Kegan Paul, 3–29.

Leschinsky, Achim, and Karl Ulrich Mayer, eds. 1999. *The Comprehensive School Experiment Revisited: Evidence from Western Europe*, 2nd updated and enlarged edition. Vol. 2 of Comparative Studies Series. Frankfurt am Main, Germany: Peter Lang.

Luhmann, Niklas. 1982. *The Differentiation of Society*. Translated by S. Holmes and C. Larmore. New York: Columbia University Press.

———. 1995. *Social Systems*. Stanford, CA: Stanford University Press. (Original

German edition under the title *Soziale Systeme: Grundriss einer allgemeinen Theorie*. Frankfurt am Main: Suhrkamp, 1984.)

Meyer, John W., and Francisco O. Ramirez. 1999. "The World Institutionalization of Education." In *Discourse Formation in Comparative Education*. Edited by J. Schriewer. Vol. 10 of Comparative Studies Series. Frankfurt am Main, Bern, New York: Peter Lang, forthcoming.

Müller, Detlef K., Fritz Ringer, and Brian Simon, eds. 1987. *The Rise of the Modern Educational System: Structural Change and Social Reproduction 1870–1920*. Cambridge: Cambridge University Press; Paris: Editions de la Maison des Sciences de l'Homme.

Popkewitz, Thomas S., ed. 1999. *Educational Knowledge: Changing Relationships Between the State, Civil Society, and the Educational Community*. Albany, NY: SUNY Press, forthcoming.

Prost, Antoine. 1968. *Histoire de l'enseignement en France 1800–1967*. Paris: Armand Colin.

Rokkan, Stein, et al. 1970. *Citizens, Elections, Parties. Approaches to the Comparative Study of the Processes of Development*. Oslo: Universitetsverlaget.

Schriewer, Jürgen. 1999. "World-System and Interrelationship-Networks." In *Educational Knowledge: Changing Relationships Between the State, Civil Society, and the Educational Community*. Edited by Th. S. Popkewitz. Albany, NY: SUNY Press, forthcoming.

Shen, Jianping. 1999. *The School of Education. Its Mission, Faculty, and Reward Structure*. New York, Bern: Peter Lang.

Stein, Lorenz von. 1884. *Die Verwaltungslehre. 7. Teil. Die Innere Verwaltung. Zweites Hauptgebiet: Das Bildungswesen*. Stuttgart: Cotta.

Swing, Elizabeth Sherman. 1980. *Bilingualism and Linguistic Segregation in the Schools of Brussels*. Quebec, Canada: International Center for Research on Bilingualism/Centre international de recherche sur le bilinguisme.

———. 1992. "Bilingual/Multilingual Education: Reaction and Reform in Belgium, Wales, and England." *European Education* 23 (4)(Winter):32–44.

———. 1997. "Education and Separatism in Multicultural Belgium: An American Perspective." In *Studies in Comparative, International, and Peace Education. Liber Amicorum Henk Van daele*. Edited by Karel de Clerck and Frank Simon. Ghent, Belgium: C.S.H.P., 235–252.

Thabault, Roger. 1971. *Education and change in a village community. Mazières-en-Gâtine 1848–1914*. London: Routledge and Kegan Paul. (Original French edition under the title *Mon village. Ses hommes—ses routes—son école*. Paris: Delagrave, 1944.)

Thomas, George W., John W. Meyer, Francisco O. Ramirez, and John Boli. 1987. *Institutional Structure, Constituting State, Society, and the Individual*. Beverly Hills, CA: Sage.

PART I

THE STRUCTURES OF EUROPEAN EDUCATION

2

Systems of Public Administration: Patterns of School Legislation and Management

Hermann Avenarius and Theo M. E. Liket

INTRODUCTION

This chapter deals with the development and the current situation of four representative European educational systems: those in France, Germany, England and Wales, and the Netherlands. These systems exemplify the main characteristics of those in other Western European countries, which are either similar or only slightly different.[1]

One should realize that the educational systems of European countries are strongly influenced by history, by national traditions, and by norms and values often rooted in religion. European history, which is characterized by strong national identities established long ago and reinforced over the centuries by bilateral and worldwide wars, has determined the form of educational systems. During the last decades a growing understanding has emerged that although national diversity in Europe is and has been very important from a historic, economic, and cultural point of view, national ambitions that led to conflicts and to destructive wars have been counterproductive. The slow but irreversible process of integration within the European Union has also led to the exchange of information about educational systems and educational practice.[2]

General Developments

Recent developments also play an important role in the change of attitudes among states and individuals. First, of course, is the collapse of the Soviet system and the liberation of a series of Central and Eastern European countries from Communist domination. The European Union as a whole and all individual Western European states are involved in developing relations with the former communist countries. In education,[3] too, many exchanges take place between participants on both sides of the former Iron Curtain (Van der Meer 1995).

Other events stimulate international contacts in a continent in which there are problems too large for nation-states alone to master. For instance, the confrontation with internationally organized criminals; the growing concern over problems in the environment; the consciousness that local conflicts anywhere in the world influence all national and individual well-being and make cooperative international action necessary; economic interdependence in the widest sense; a communication revolution that makes international labor-market politics essential; the exchange of students all over the world; the explosion of the tourist industry, bringing people in contact with different cultures; the power of global advertisement in all domains of society; international cooperation in the "health industry" and the worldwide actions to protect against diseases—all these factors and many others show that national identity is relative in an era that is moving at an accelerating pace toward more international understanding and collective problem solving (UNESCO 1996).

At the same time there is an increasing demand for more democracy on a local and regional level. People try to preserve their local traditions, their norms and values. Areas such as Flanders, Wallonia, and the German communities in Belgium and the *comunidades autónomas* in Catalonia and the Basque country in Spain fight for the preservation of their identities and for more political autonomy. The trend toward regionalization is underlined by the division of Czechoslovakia into two countries, by the disintegration of Yugoslavia, and the transformation of the Soviet Union into a federation. In all these cases, which are only examples of a general trend, education remains one of the instruments to preserve the local or regional identity.

We therefore observe two tendencies: There is, on the one hand, a growing internationalization, not at the very least stimulated by the European Union through its action programs such as SOCRATES, that is, exchanges of teachers and students (see *Official Journal of the European Communities* 1994). This will result in more and better understanding of the differences and similarities of educational systems. The windows are now open, and this openness will have an influence on the respective national systems. On the other hand, a growing regionalization, which fosters local features and peculiarities in educational philosophy and daily practice, is also taking place.

These developments go hand in hand with a tendency toward more relative autonomy for individual educational institutions in primary, secondary, and higher education, a trend not restricted to Europe (Carl Bertelsmann Prize 1996). This trend can be observed in most countries of the Western Hemisphere: for example, the United States, Canada, Australia, and New Zealand. In international conferences the autonomy of schools and universities, on the one hand, and systems of quality control (a combination of quality assessment and quality improvement), on the other, are dominant themes. The international exchange of information in this area is growing, and these exchanges are also influenced by internationally constituted visiting committees for quality assessment.

The development of more autonomy for the individual school or university has educational, social, financial, and psychological dimensions: There is far *greater tolerance of diversity and variety in educational philosophies.* The increasing importance of schools that have a specific educational design and background, such as the Montessori schools and Dalton schools, illustrates this trend. Parents and professional educators have a growing awareness that top-down educational and didactic models are no longer adequate to solve pedagogical and social problems. Responsible people in education, therefore, look for designs more appropriate to the challenging diversity of professions and of life. Academic freedom is a necessity in universities, but it is also needed on a reasonable scale in primary and secondary education. There is a consensus that professional responsibility should be balanced with governmental responsibility, provided there is a good system of accountability (Mertens 1994). The belief of many practitioners in schools is that the traditional, almost "natural," organization of the teaching process by timetables and other restricting regulations does not stimulate the transfer of knowledge, skills, and attitudes in a way that corresponds to how youngsters nowadays perceive reality and use modern communication media.

There is a growing understanding that in view of the *diversity of the school population in a multicultural society* and other specific features of school reality, uniform and detailed regulations are not suitable instruments for teachers and heads of schools to solve daily problems. One must face the fact that central regulations are not in tune with particular regional problems and the necessary flexibility of school-based problem solving. The growing demand for the participation of larger groups of the population leads to the demand by parents and students for more influence on educational institutions (Liket 1993).

Given scarce *financial resources*, national and local governments have to set priorities in overall budgeting for different issues. Education is only one area of governments' responsibilities. It competes with other tasks such as fighting organized crime, environmental concerns, traffic problems, public health, and the progressive aging of society. This conflict of interests leads to questions about the availability and reasonableness of financial resources for education. In addition, there is a need for more efficient use of money and more efficient management in educational institutions. Systems of lump-sum financing appear to have the advantage of guaranteeing not only a better farsighted planning of governmental and local budgets but also of making schools and universities more conscious of their own responsibility for the spending of public money.

There is more and more consensus that efficiency increases if decisions are made on the lowest level possible. It follows, therefore, that most responsibilities should be transferred to the educational institutions themselves. Experience shows that *motivation of teachers, parents, and students* is higher if programs and methods can be discussed on the school level and if there is a feeling of "ownership" of the school's particular philosophy. Teachers, parents, and students demand that their school have its own profile; they are convinced that educational options are more important than organizational conditions, and that teamwork and functional differentiation support the professional attitudes of staff members.

The Two Main Scenarios in European Educational Systems

National educational systems were established in Europe at the end of the 18th century. There are in principle two different approaches toward organization, content, and division of responsibilities in educational systems. We call them *state-oriented* versus *school-oriented* approaches. Most educational scenarios resemble in substance one of these two "philosophies." The development of one or the other model has been dependent on some fundamental characteristics of the respective countries. These models are

- the concept of the "state" in a political and organizational sense;
- the relation between the individual citizen and the state;
- the relation between the economic development of society and educational reality;
- the need for developing a national identity;
- ideas about guarantees for the quality of education and for equality of opportunities for young people;
- the question of the desirability of pedagogical and didactic uniformity in educational management;
- tolerance toward diversity in society; and
- the acceptance of personal responsibility in education by parents and students.

State-Oriented Systems

Most educational systems in continental Europe have their origin in the Napoleonic period. The first educational laws were enacted between the end of the 18th century and the year 1813, when French domination collapsed. This system presupposes an equality of educational opportunities for every citizen by providing the same course of studies to all students. Regulations, which are influenced by these theoretical assumptions, are strong. Teacher training is uniform so that teachers are in principle exchangeable. The schools work along central and detailed guidelines, and the teacher in the end operates as a person who transmits knowledge, practice, norms, and values as a representative of a uniform national educational policy system.

It comes as no surprise that teachers in this scenario are civil servants. Because of national or state uniformity of aims and guidelines and the uniformity of teacher training, they can easily be transferred from one school to the other. In this model the individual teacher is far more the extended arm of government than a member of a team of teachers with common aims and objectives. Therefore, the pedagogical supervisor of the teacher is not the head of the school but an inspector who, in the name of the state, controls the achievement of the teacher in the respective subjects and has the power to give instructions. As with any ideal type, this model does not correspond totally to the reality of the administration of schools. It explains, however, the underlying educational philosophy according to which regulations and central control guarantee uniformity and efficiency of the system and equality of opportunities.

School-Oriented Systems

This philosophy, mostly practiced in Anglo-Saxon countries, accepts as a principle different ways to reach educational aims and objectives and gives people the opportunity to establish an educational reality rooted in their religious and philosophical convictions. To guarantee quality of education, nationwide evaluation is the crucial factor. This leads to a dialogue between reviewers of educational performance and the staff of schools. Individual teachers are, more than in the state-oriented system, responsible for their own choices as a result of open discussions. The teaching staff has a common pedagogical and didactic concept. Sometimes this may result in a lack of continuity in the maintenance of the educational philosophy so that the profile of the individual school can occasionally change. In any case, the teachers have to conform to this philosophy and profile. Consequently, they cannot be centrally transferred from one school to another.

Such traditional differences between these two systems will last, although the overall tendencies may in the long run cause more overlapping. Two factors account for the expectation that these differences in European educational systems will not change dramatically in the near future. First, the Maastricht Treaty emphasizes that member states shall be responsible for educational policies. The influence of the European Union in the domain of education is limited to international exchange of teachers and students, to the mutual recognition of national certificates and diplomas, to support of the mobility of students who want to attend educational institutions in another member state, and to promotion of the learning of foreign languages. The second reason that these differences in European educational systems will continue for the time being is the fact that systems change slowly. Implementation of reforms in education, as in other sectors of society, is a long-term process that takes years and sometimes decades. Therefore, diversity in education will continue to contribute to the challenging phenomenon of differences among nations, regions, and individual schools in Europe.

Table 2.1
State-Oriented Systems versus School-Oriented Systems

State-Oriented	School-Oriented
Detailed national or state regulations	National or state regulations limited to general issues
Detailed school curriculum	National or state curriculum containing only aims and objectives
Teachers as civil servants	Teachers not civil servants, but employees of the school or the local authority
Head of the school as representative of national or state government	Head of the school relatively independent from national or state government
Members of national educational hierarchy as key decision makers	Members of separate influence groups in the educational system as key decision makers
Central appointment of staff	Appointment of staff by the local authority or the school itself
Central budgeting	Budgeting the responsibility of school and/or local authority

CHARACTERISTIC FEATURES OF THE LEGAL AND ADMINISTRATIVE ORGANIZATION OF FOUR EDUCATIONAL SYSTEMS: FRANCE, GERMANY, ENGLAND AND WALES, THE NETHERLANDS

France

General Overview

The French system is still very near to its original starting point, although it is also influenced by tendencies described in the first part of the chapter and by developments pointing toward decentralization of power (Vasconcellos 1993; Vaniscotte 1996). The principles of the educational system were inspired by the French Revolution in 1789 and reformulated in laws enacted between 1881 and 1889. These principles are still the basis of the current educational system, which guarantees public education at all levels as "a duty of the state" and a right also to private education.

The Legal Framework

The legal basis of the educational system is laid down in the constitution, which guarantees equality of opportunities and a national responsibility for education. Except in private schools, the teachers are civil servants. Approximately 17% of pupils attend these private schools, most of which are based on religion and governed by the Catholic Church or by boards related to the church. Private schools are not spread evenly over the country, but are found mostly in four areas: Brittany and Normandy, the north of the country, the city of Paris, and the city of Lyon.

Private schools can be subject to relatively strict regulations similar to those in state schools (*le contrat simple*). In this case the state pays the salaries of the teaching staff. Or private schools can be autonomous and have their own regulations (*le contrat d'association*). In this case they are subject only to the national inspectorate.

The main principles of the *éducation nationale* are as follows: The state is *responsible* for the existence of a public school system and guarantees private education under its supervision. Private schools are entitled to negotiate a treaty with the state. They must guarantee an education that complies with the programs defined by the state. *Education is compulsory* for all children living in France from the age of 6 until the age of 16. Education in schools and public institutions is *free of charge*. In primary education and in the *collèges* (from ages 11 or 12 to 15 or 16), books and other materials are also free of charge. Public education must be *neutral* in the domains of religion, philosophy, and politics. Religious education is not part of the school program; in primary schools it can be given outside the school timetable. In order to secure *equivalence of certificates*, it is the state that extends diplomas and university degrees.

Diplomas granted by private schools have official status only if the schools are accredited by the state.

Organization and Management

This centrally organized system has identical and very detailed curricula for all schools. The results of the examinations in all *lycées* are published so that schools know how each performs in comparison with all other French *lycées*.[4] This shows that the system is rather competitive. Students can attend certain highly regarded institutions of higher education that have a limited number of places only after a *concours*, a competitive examination. Learning results, therefore, play a very central role in school life. Every year the best students of a class are publicly mentioned and get awards. There is much extrinsic motivation. The uniformity of the organized top-down educational system reflects the conviction that every student throughout the country should have the same opportunity.

Education until the age of 15 or 16 (end of the *collège*) is comprehensive. After that, students attend the *lycée d'enseignement général et technologique* (general and technical school) or the *lycée professionnel* (vocational school). Both lead to different diplomas. Some *lycées* have preparatory classes after the final examination (*baccalauréat*) that prepare and select students for the prestigious *écoles nationales*. The competition in those *classes préparatoires* is very strong.

The administration of the system is as follows: On top of the educational system is the minister of education in Paris. The people responsible for education are civil servants, including the teaching staff of the schools. The country is divided into thirty *académies*, among which, three are in Paris, two are in Lyon, and two are in overseas areas. Those academies are distinct from the civil territorial divisions in France. The departments, as the smallest administrative units, and the regions, each comprise several departments.

The head of the academy is the *recteur*, who is responsible for education within the area of the academy. *Recteurs* are usually rather young, politically appointed civil servants. Usually they have started their professional career in a university to which they may return in case of political changes. The second important administrative position within the academy is that of the *inspecteur d'académie*, who is responsible for the management of personnel and buildings. He takes care of the *carte scolaire* in which, year by year, the placement of teaching staff in schools is organized. Teachers are normally appointed to one school, but they can be transferred to a school elsewhere in the academy or even in the country if necessary. Nevertheless, the status of civil servants is rather safe: although they can be transferred, they may not be dismissed, except in very extreme cases.

Another body that is organized on the national level looks after pedagogical-didactic aspects of the educational system: the general inspectorate (*inspection général*) (Vandevoorde 1993). Members of this institution are the *inspecteurs généraux*, their chief being the *doyen*. The internal organization of the inspectorate is subject-oriented. Therefore, every school has to cope with as many inspectors as there are subjects in the school. To approve the school as a whole, two decades ago the inspectorate added a branch of *inspecteurs généraux de la vie scolaire* (inspectors for school life), who are responsible for aspects not covered by the subject-oriented inspectors.

The inspectorate was formerly responsible also for the periodic assessment of teachers' work and behavior. This task has in the meantime been transferred to regional inspectors (*inspecteurs pédagogiques régionaux*). The function of the inspectorate has changed insofar as nowadays it covers more mixed subject groups, plays a role also in the development of decentralized educational aspects, and performs more evaluative duties. International exchanges and the experience of inspectors in other European countries have strongly influenced this inspectorate. Also, the tendency toward slightly more decentralization is reflected in a change of working styles and attitudes within the national inspectorate ("Critères et indicateurs" 1991).

The head of a school is appointed after a competitive examination, the *concours*. This person is the formal representative of the state in the institution. He is *chef d'établissement*, that is, chief of the institution, and is obliged to take residence in the school building. His function implies responsibility for running the school according to the relevant regulations. These (national) regulations cover three areas: administrative responsibilities, pedagogical responsibilities, and external relations.

Developments

In certain areas, strictly prescribed and limited, there is more decision making available for heads and inspectors of academies and for heads of schools. In these cases the control by the central administration is organized a posteriori. This so-called decentralization is to be extended. The *collèges* and the *lycées*, which until recently were officially national institutions with administrative character, will now be "local public institutions for education." They share their responsibilities with the respective local authority (departments for the *collèges*, regions for the *lycées*) and the state. This change gives local authorities and their councils, which represent different groups—teaching and administrative staff, parents—more freedom in administration and management of education.

It has already been mentioned that education in France is characterized by centralization and is still organized on the basis of the principles of the French Revolution. Nevertheless, international developments in the domains of management and pedagogy have an impact nowadays on the national school system. The organization of national education is, however, part of the system of public administration as a whole. This is organized top-down, emphasizing the principles of uniformity and equal opportunity. It is not expected that the system will substantially change in the near future.

On the other hand, there is increasing public criticism of the system. The differences between schools, moreover, are often far greater than the principles of uniformity and equal opportunity might suggest. In particular, the development of a growing multicultural population and the huge problems in metropolitan suburbs show that the traditional way of governing education by central rules and regulations is no longer suitable for solving problems in an efficient way. One could even fear that traditional governance would evoke additional tensions. The French educational system might have been appropriate for a homogeneous society. Its meritocratic character appears to be specifically attractive to the elite. But for students with more limited potential, it has its shortcomings.

Germany

General Overview

There have been two lasting characteristics of the development of schools in Germany since the eras of enlightenment and absolutism. The state governments maintain control of schools, and in this regard, education in Germany fits the continental model. But this state is not identical with a "central" government. It is the "provincial" state that is responsible for schooling in the Federal Republic of Germany, the respective *Länder*, that is, Hesse or Brandenburg, to mention two of the sixteen *Länder*. Although the state legally does not have a monopoly on schools, the federal and most *Länder* constitutions guarantee the right to private schooling. But in practice, private schools play a marginal role; only about 6% of students attend these institutions, most of which are controlled by Catholic or Protestant denominations.

Two instruments ensure the stability of the educational systems of the sixteen *Länder*. The Federal Constitutional Court (*Bundesverfassungsgericht*) in Karlsruhe may review laws enacted in the *Länder*. The court decides whether such laws are in agreement with the federal constitution (the so-called Basic Law). The judgment of this court is final, unlike the situation in the Netherlands, where Parliament has the last word. Secondly, the Conference of Ministers of Education (*Kultusministerkonferenz*, KMK) coordinates educational policies among the different *Länder*. Legally, the decisions of the KMK are only recommendations to the respective *Länder*, but in practice they play an important role in keeping the sixteen educational systems together.

The Legal Framework

According to article 7, section 1 of the Basic Law, "the entire school system shall be under the supervision of the state."[5] The term *supervision* does not contain all implications of the corresponding German word *Aufsicht. Aufsicht* implies an active role in the guarantee of efficient education, in the obligation to disseminate the necessary resources, in granting equal opportunities to all citizens, and in securing the quality of education.

Schooling is compulsory between the ages of 6 and 18 years and must be undertaken in either a state school or a private school approved by the state school authority. Primary schooling (classes 1 to 6 in Berlin and Brandenburg) has become a kind of comprehensive education since the 1918 revolution and is therefore uniform. After this, depending on the children's ability and their parents' preference, children go on to either the *Hauptschule* (Secondary Modern School, classes 5 to 9 or 10), the *Realschule* (Intermediate School, a technically oriented type of semi-academic school, classes 5 to 10) or the *Gymnasium* (Grammar School, an academic secondary school, classes 5 to 13 or 12). In some *Länder* these different schools have occasionally been combined in one school, the *Gesamtschule* (comprehensive school), of which there are two types: the integrated and the cooperative (additive) comprehensive school. In some *Länder*, particularly in the East, *Hauptschule* and *Realschule* are integrated into one school type. On completing *Hauptschule* or *Realschule*, most students go on to three years of vocational or technical training, a "dual system" comprising apprenticeship or traineeship and part-time *Berufsschule* (vocational or technical school).

State schools are caught between the state and the municipality. The state is responsible for pedagogical matters, that is, the curriculum, school-leaving examinations, educational structures as a whole, and most importantly, for the staffing of teachers and headmasters. The municipality takes care of everything pertaining to material and local management. This includes construction, administration, and organization of the individual schools.

Organization and Management

Within the state school administration there are as a rule three levels: the final authority, which is the minister of education; the intermediate authority at the regional level; and the lower supervisory authorities at the municipality level. Schools are not independent administrative units. As institutions subject to the authority responsible for them, they do not possess legal capacity. The municipality is responsible for their management, but can transfer responsibility for the day-to-day running of the school to the head of the school. The municipality represents the school, both in and out of court. In its own name a school does not negotiate legal transactions such as contracts for textbooks or contracts for accommodation during school excursions, but only on behalf of the municipality, provided that the latter has not reserved this power for itself. The municipality is owner of all school property. The land on which the school stands is registered in the name of the municipality.

According to long-standing administrative tradition, in fulfilling its pedagogic obligations, the school is formally at the lowest level of the state school administration, in principle bound by the instructions of the state supervisory school authority. One could say that the educational systems in the different *Länder* have been centralized in a way similar to the French model. Most important in this context is the fact that as in France, a teacher is usually a civil servant for life. In other words, the teacher has "tenure." The decision about staff appointment rests with the state school authorities in each *Land*. This approach has obvious drawbacks. Neither the school itself nor the municipality can improve the school's reputation by practicing its own staff policy. But there are also advantages. Less attractive schools, such as those in decaying inner cities, in municipalities with large immigrant populations, or in rural areas do not have to fear that they will suffer local discrimination (Avenarius 1995).

As a civil servant, the teacher is in principle subject to directives and obliged to obey regulations, but pedagogic freedom gives him or her a certain scope for independent instruction and education. The principle of pedagogic freedom both complements and modifies the teacher's status as a civil servant. In substance, it is recognized in the school legislation of all *Länder* and is taken for granted in the administration of justice. This does not alter the fact that the rigid status of the teaching staff and its organizational background of relatively strong labor unions may hamper a flexible personnel policy (Bildungskommission 1995).

The number of detailed rules and regulations in the respective *Länder* is still rather high. For almost each and every problem there is a legal solution, and the effort to solve these problems in a legal way has caused a tremendous growth of laws and directives. The administrative courts, too, play an enormous role in this process of *Verrechtlichung*.

In organizing education, the inspectorate (*Schulaufsicht*) has remarkable powers. It is responsible for the appointment of teachers and heads of schools. Also, in most *Länder* it assesses the work of the teachers and in some, the final evaluation of students' examinations at the end of secondary education. A large portion of inspectors' time is spent dealing with conflicts between parents and the school. There is much concern among inspectors that for this reason, the time available for pedagogical tasks is not sufficient.

Traditionally, the school as a whole has little scope for its own initiatives. Class time is usually a strict forty-five minutes. Teachers, according to the type of school they belong to, have to teach a specific number of subject-oriented hours a week. Many activities organized by the head of the school need the permission of the inspector. The influence of the school on appointment of teachers is rather small, at least in legal terms. Books and other learning materials, furthermore, can be chosen only from a list agreed upon by the minister of education.

The advantage of these structures and regulations is clear. At the least they suggest the realization of the principle of equality. Prescribed curricula, materials, and fixed timetables guarantee a formal equality of education. This is the more important because choice of a school is not always free. Pupils living in the respective school districts must attend primary school in their geographic area. There is, however, a growing concern about the inflexibility of this system in relation to developments in society. In particular, the presence of cultural minorities and immigrants poses challenges. Moreover, the fact that individual schools cannot extend their decision-making power to meet problems not foreseen in the state regulations evokes more and more irritation on all levels of educational management (Rosenbusch 1994).

Developments

The overall trends described in the first part of this chapter influence more and more the legal and administrative framework of education in Germany. The first attempt to change the educational structure dates from 1970. Brandenburg, Bremen, Hamburg, Hesse, Lower-Saxony, Northrhine-Westphalia, Rhineland-Palatinate, Saxony-Anhalt, and Schleswig-Holstein have enacted or are preparing new laws to give schools more autonomy and flexibility.[6] Berlin recently started a three-year experimental project to open up the possibility for schools to develop their own pedagogic profiles, to control their own administration and finance, and to get influence on personnel management.[7]

In all these cases there is broad consensus that development toward more diversity and more responsibility at lower levels of the system has to be accompanied by efficient evaluation. This may affect the role of the inspectorate. The tendency, as in other countries, is to give the inspectorate a more specific evaluative role and less direct responsibility for the administrative aspects of the job. In addition, the schools themselves need the support of the inspectorate in their exercise of internal evaluation. For this reason, some *Länder* have started training courses on a broad scale to raise the professionalism of school inspectors.

These new tendencies will without doubt lead to more responsibility by the lower levels of the educational system. On the other hand, there is general concern about the guarantee of educational standards and the fundamental topic of equal opportunities for students (Avenarius 1994). It remains to be seen along which lines both of these fundamental aspects will develop.

England and Wales

General Overview

The insular location of Britain on the European map and the fact that British political interests were for centuries directed to other parts of the world caused development quite different from that in European continental countries. The British Empire was not only the world's dominant nation, in competition with the Netherlands, Portugal, and Spain during the 16th, 17th, and 18th centuries, and with France in the 18th and 19th centuries. It also formed strong cooperation with countries such as the United States, Canada, Australia, and New Zealand after independence of these former colonies. After World War II, Britain became an important but no longer dominant power on the European scene. In that light it has not been easy to master the transition from world power to relatively small European nation. The traditional feeling of independence, however, is unbroken and is partly responsible for the restrictive attitude toward too much influence of supranational ("federal") organizations such as the European Union and its institutions. At the same time, British politicians know very well that the current situation in the world makes it almost impossible for Britain to stay away from the political, military, economic, and cultural reality of a common Europe today.

These considerations are also important when one looks at education. Although differing significantly from the continental systems, the relative independence of parts (England and Wales, Scotland, Northern Ireland) have led to remarkable differences in the educational structure within the United Kingdom itself. Separate legislation exists for England and Wales, for Scotland, and for Northern Ireland respectively. The secretaries of state for Wales, Scotland, and Northern Ireland are ministers in the United Kingdom government and responsible to parliament for the operation of their respective offices. The fact that the educational systems for England and Wales, for Scotland, and for Northern Ireland are subject to different legislation results in variations in organization, administration, and control of the systems, as well as in educational terminology. In the following the focus will be on the education system in England and Wales,[8] the part of the United Kingdom that comprises almost 90% of the overall population (Ministry of Education and Science in England and Wales 1984).

The Legal Framework

There is one fundamental aspect that is peculiar to England: Whereas in all other European states educational rights and obligations have been laid down in a constitution, England has no written constitution. Although the laws that regulate education are sometimes as dense as in other countries, they are not anchored in a constitution. This means that even laws that introduce fundamental educational changes do not need a qualified majority in Parliament. For this reason, educational policy can react flexibly, even radically, to new challenges, perhaps sometimes at the expense of stability and reliability.

Another difference from continental systems is the fact that in England, decision making at the lowest level has always been characteristic of the democratic principle. Every citizen should be able to decide on his or her own in many domains of life without the control of the state. In many fields this has led to very distinct solutions to societal problems. It also explains the variety of educational institutions spread over the country. It is quite normal that parents choose a school for their children relatively freely from among schools with quite distinct identities and profiles. On the other hand, this freedom of choice may result in increasing inequality. Upper-class children usually attend private (mostly boarding) schools in which only 7% of English students get their primary and secondary education.

Organization and Management

Characteristic of the educational system is the fact that the role of the state is rather restricted. There are only a few rules and regulations at central level. Under the Education Act of 1944, a balanced partnership between local and central authorities was established, according to which the Local Education Authorities (LEAs) govern the public school system in their respective regional area.

Although the head teacher in England has far more competencies than col-

leagues in most continental schools, the regulations passed by the local authorities can be very dense and strict so that sometimes the autonomy of schools is
in practice rather small. The fact that central government is far away does not
mean that the school is free from external intervention. The scope of autonomy
strongly depends on the way local authorities organize the management of
schools. Approaches may differ from LEA to LEA, with the consequence that
salaries and regulations for retirement (even the age of retirement) are different.
In addition, party politics within the local authorities may be of great importance.
The debate on comprehensive education, for instance, resulted in significant
differences between local authorities that reflected their politics. The cost of
education is shared between central and local governments. LEAs set a budget
for the whole education service in their area. The school governing body and
the head teacher are informed of the school's total annual budget and are entirely
responsible for its expenditure.

Until recently, Her Majesty's Inspectorate (HMI), under the leadership of the
inspector-general, played an important role. This organization was responsible
for the evaluation of the system and for the evaluation of individual schools.
Groups of inspectors visited all primary and secondary schools to assess their
educational achievement and their organization and management. In this way
the inspectorate published more than 300 reports on individual schools per year.
These reports had an important impact on the policy making of the respective
LEAs. They made it necessary for the local authorities, even though independent, to cope with general standards. Therefore, HMI was one of the instruments
by which central government could influence the quality of education in the
country.[9]

Developments

During the last decades the debate on the shortcomings of the educational
system has been very intense. Politicians and educators complained of a low
educational level. According to their view, the achievement of students in public
education, compared with that in other countries, was below an acceptable standard. Therefore, efforts have been made to share responsibility for education
fairly between government and schools through a system of greater accountability. Connected with this development was the intent to give parents more
choice among a variety of schools in order to make schools more achievement-
oriented and more prepared for competition.

Two attempts are particularly interesting. First, after a long debate in Parliament, a National Curriculum was introduced by the Education Reform Act of
1988. Many people in England, especially among educators, perceived this to
be a development toward far more centralization.[10] Such an assumption is at
least one-sided. The core of the curricular innovation is to produce national
standards in three subjects—English, mathematics, and science—and to test students in these subjects at the ages of 7, 11, 14, and 16 years. These tests are
intended to raise the quality of education. Since they are anonymous, as far as

the individual students are concerned, they give information only through so-called "league tables" about the performance of individual schools compared with national results.

Implementation of the National Curriculum produced many problems, in particular the skepticism and sometimes open obstruction of teachers. Teachers were already involved in other conflicts with local authorities over union politics in the domains of status and salaries. Therefore, for a long period, they refused any "extra work" in addition to their normal teaching load.

Another problem was that private education was excluded from central control. The argument for this exclusion of private schools, the so-called public schools, is that these schools allegedly had higher standards. In addition, the government feared that the House of Lords would never accept a law that would allow the state to intervene in private education.

Another important reform consisted of giving individual schools the right to "opt out" of the local authority, with the result that they no longer remain under the responsibility of the respective LEA but are under direct control of the central government (Heller and Edwards 1992). This corresponded to the introduction of a market economy by what was then the Thatcher government. Almost 10% of schools made use of this opportunity and thus became "grant-maintained schools." Though the number of schools that have opted out is rather low, the government's encouragement of schools to do so undermined the LEAs in their key role as strategic planning agencies. There are now three types of schools in England: schools under the responsibility of the respective Local Education Authority, grant-maintained schools and independent private ("public") schools.

Although these innovations have resulted in a certain redistribution of power in educational decision making by strengthening the influence of the national government on standards and accountability, the new model, despite the perception of some critics, does not deserve the qualification as purely "centralized." The only assumption one can make is that tendencies in continental countries toward more school autonomy and in England toward more accountability may in the end reduce the hitherto fundamental differences between the systems.

One may wonder why at the very moment when more central control of standards has been introduced, the instrument par excellence to achieve this end, Her Majesty's Inspectorate, has been partly abolished. It is still responsible for overall national aspects of evaluation. But the evaluation of the individual school, which is prescribed by law, has to be executed by teams of inspectors who have been specifically trained and registered by a new authority, the Office for Standards in Education (OFSTED). Schools are free to choose the evaluating agency and must pay for the evaluation. So it comes as no surprise that former members of HMI have established private agencies to do the same work as they did before in their public function. One can hardly view this development as symptomatic of a tendency to centralize educational politics and management.

The Netherlands

General Overview

One should keep in mind that the Dutch educational system was established in the period of French oppression and therefore followed the Napoleonic model. The first educational laws bear the date of 1806, the period in which the *Bataafse Republiek* was part of the French Empire. Almost two centuries later, however, the system has changed so that now it resembles the Anglo-Saxon type.

The new tendencies started in the middle of the 19th century. From 1850 onward, public schools were financed by the state. Thereafter, Roman Catholic and Protestant churches each demanded subsidies from the state for their schools. This conflict led to the famous "school battle." In 1917 during World War I, in which the Netherlands was not involved, a crucial, radical change took place: the "pacification" of Roman Catholic, Protestant, and state school systems. Since then, the constitution has guaranteed freedom of education (free appointment of teachers, free pedagogical and didactic choices, free choice of teaching materials), limited only by general global educational aims: national final exams after secondary education and a national inspectorate. All schools (private and public) receive a 100% subsidy from the state. The result is that more than two-thirds of schools are private (Ministry of Education and Science 1994). In this respect, the Netherlands is quite distinct from most other countries within the European Union.

A "second wave" of reforms, leading toward more independence and strongly influenced by national and international developments, started in the 1980s. This decade is marked by still more autonomy of institutions in all parts of the educational system (primary, secondary, and higher education). The "second wave" was initially introduced in higher education (Parliament of the Netherlands 1985–1986).

The Legal Framework

As already mentioned, the Dutch constitution guarantees freedom of education, which means that establishing a school is free (depending on a minimum number of students attending the school). Before the changes during the 1980s, educational quality was more or less secured by state rules and regulations; fewer than in France and Germany, but nevertheless rather strict, so that in spite of this fundamental freedom, schools were not as different from one another as the constitutional freedom would suggest.

The fundamental change, which has taken place since then, offers far greater autonomy to individual schools and universities. Roughly speaking, the characteristics are the following:

- central laws that contain only global aims and regulations;
- lump-sum financing;

- development of its own profile by the individual school;
- free appointment of teaching staff;
- freedom of curriculum and organization;
- responsibility of the school for its program and time schedule;
- obligation of the school for self-evaluation;
- external evaluation of individual schools and the school system as a whole (Liket 1983).

Organization and Management

It is the school (the school board, the leaders among the teachers, the teaching staff, and also in some aspects the parents and students) that is responsible for developing plans for determining the internal aspects of school life. The national laws prescribe the topics that have to be covered in the planning document; that is, aims or objectives of the school (educational philosophy), internal organization, division of work among the teaching staff, curriculum, assessment of student performance, the guidance system, the participation of parents and students, and the organization of self-evaluation. This planning document, decided upon by the school board—which usually consists of interested members of the community, representatives of churches and of industry—is the official charter through which the school informs the public about its educational program. This planning document must be adapted to new developments and experiences every two years. The role of the inspectorate is restricted to making sure it complies with national laws and regulations.

In addition, each second year the school has to produce a self-evaluation document that is sent to the National Inspectorate. This must assess the performance of the school on the basis of both the planning and the evaluation documents. Every five to six years the inspectorate organizes an external evaluation, during which an outside group similar to American visiting committees visits the school.

The crucial element in the relationship between external experts (the inspectorate) and the schools is dialogue in which the differences between planning documents and evaluation reports, on the one side, and the educational reality, on the other, are discussed. The inspectorate has no power to change planning documents and other decisions of the school board. The concept is that experts' open and relevant feedback gives enough motivation for the responsible actors in school to take the recommendations of professional evaluators seriously. The practice until now confirms the soundness of this approach. The feedback leads to adoption of relevant suggestions and to change in the planning documents. This process initiates a continuous circle of high-quality care within the school. Since parents and students are entitled to choose among schools freely, the adoption of external advice also has repercussions on competition among schools.

Although the formal responsibilities of the inspectorate do not differ significantly from its former tasks, working style and organization have changed dramatically (Ministry of Education and Science 1990). Therefore, the Dutch inspectorate (after intense cooperation with the English inspectorate) has lost its original "continental" character. The most important aspects of the new style of the inspectorate are

- a relatively independent organization (outside the ministry) under direct responsibility of the minister of education;
- change from individual work to teamwork;
- professionalization in evaluation methods and techniques;
- expertise based on work in visiting committees;
- problem-oriented reports on general aspects of the national educational system; and
- advice to schools about methods and techniques of internal evaluation.

There is no formal administrative level between the Ministry of Education and the school board in private education (75% of schools). In public schools—where, by the way, teachers are not civil servants but employees—the municipality plays a certain role. It delegates, however, many aspects of management to the individual school. It is the school board that has the final responsibility, and it delegates most of the daily decision making to the head of the school.

Therefore, in the process of increasing autonomy in schools and in view of new methods of internal and external quality control, the local management of schools and the function of heads of schools and head teacher teams has changed. The role of the head teacher is more important than in most other European countries. The head of the school, under the ultimate accountability of the school board, is responsible for pedagogical/didactic issues, for the organization of labor, for personnel and finance (lump-sum financing), and for public relations. A statute enacted by the board delineates the roles, the responsibilities, and the rights of teaching staff, parents, and students. Because of the assumption that innovations take place only if the teaching staff is convinced of their advantages, much effort is given to a cooperative leadership and to the involvement of teachers, parents, and students in the decision-making processes.

The heads of schools already in office are subject to in-service training. For incoming heads, universities have in the meantime organized two-year post-academic courses.[11] A master's degree in educational management for candidates who successfully complete that course does not imply, however, that they will be automatically appointed; the school boards are free to choose. But the certificate serves more and more as a very important recommendation of the applicant's skills and capabilities.

The implementation of this new concept of school autonomy and quality care takes some time, of course. Although changes usually take a number of years, the educational system is on its way toward new arrangements between partners in the system (government, municipalities, school boards, and teaching staff), and a new balance of powers and influences.

Developments

Even in the Netherlands, the rather far-reaching autonomy of schools has its limits. In recent years, additional testing on the national level has been introduced. After the eight-year primary school (4 to 12 years of age), students and their parents may choose among different types of schools, mostly on the recommendation of the head teacher of the primary school. Although the students are therefore already selected in some way, they have to finish what is called the basic study for all. This can take place in two, three, or four years within the different school types and has to be completed by a test in the most important subjects, which is prepared by the National Testing Institute (CITO) in Arnhem. CITO is also responsible for final national examinations at the end of all types of secondary education, tests that primarily cover the cognitive aspects of education and count for only 50% of the evaluation on the exam. The schools in their turn are responsible for the other 50% of the evaluation.

A major problem is the growing number of immigrants. Larger cities such as Amsterdam and Rotterdam try to support special schools by extra money; experiments with the so-called magnet schools give hopeful results. There is also a tendency to integrate different types of educational approaches into the school system (vocational education, youth work, continuous education, and distance learning). The coordination between education and the labor market is a point demanding increasing attention.

CONCLUDING REMARKS: THE EUROPEAN PERSPECTIVE

A remarkable consequence of the growing autonomy of schools and universities in Europe is increasing cooperation between institutions across national borders. This is a general trend leading to new forms of cooperation of educational institutions, not just a development initiated by international and supranational organizations. There is hardly a university or polytechnic in the member states of the European Union that does not belong to one or more networks. These networks—for the time being mostly in higher education—not only set out to exchange professors and students, but also to implement common curricula so that students receive credits that can be used in several universities in the European Union. Similar associations for the exchange of students and teachers exist among secondary schools. These exchanges open up windows toward more international understanding and are an incentive for educational innovation. It is evident that these networks promote the educational profile of the individual schools and the innovational attitude of the teaching staff. In this way the development of European integration supports the emergence of more autonomy in educational institutions.

Inspectorates in the European Union member states are also committed to more cooperation. Initiatives include plans to organize a permanent body of representatives of national inspectorates, where standards for education, working methods, and in-service training can periodically be exchanged. This may also lead to the exchange of experiences and innovations between educational systems. Cooperation and communication are not intended to diminish the variety of the diverse patterns of school legislation and management but can serve as a contribution to better international understanding and may raise the problem-solving capacity of politicians and practitioners in education.

NOTES

1. A possible exception is Switzerland, where the autonomy of the twenty-six cantons in educational domains was extremely high. That is now slightly changing, and Switzerland is therefore going more in the direction of the general developments in Europe described in this chapter.

2. Cf. the various publications of Eurydice, the Information Network on Education in the European Union.

3. Significant is the project METROPOLIS introducing modern educational management in the context of a close relationship between Amsterdam and Moscow.

4. Every year complete reports are published in *Le Monde de l'Education* in a special issue in autumn.

5. The original German text is "Das gesamte Schulwesen steht unter der Aufsicht des Staates."

6. All these developments can be followed in new laws and drafts.

7. "Schule in erweiter Verantwortung." This project (1995 to 1998) received scientific guidance by the German Institute for International Educational Research, Frankfurt-on-Main/Berlin.

8. When we deal with the system of England and Wales, we will indicate this as the "English" system without mentioning Wales continuously.

9. This practice, which led to a change in the mode of operation of HMI in the direction of more teamwork and a growing professionalization in evaluating methods and techniques, was also applied in the assessment of educational systems in other European countries. On this basis HMI also influenced the work of the inspectorates in the Netherlands, Belgium, France, and Sweden. It also initiated an exchange twice a year of ideas and working methods among inspectorates in Europe.

10. It is worth noting that the political philosophy on which the introduction of the National Curriculum had been based was being applied not only to education but to many other areas of the public services such as health, social services, transport, and so on. For a critique of this approach see Wragg (1993).

11. Netherlands School for Educational Managment (University of Amsterdam, Pedagogical Department) issues information brochures periodically.

REFERENCES

Avenarius, Hermann. 1994. "Schulische Selbstverwaltung. Grenzen und Möglichkelten." *Recht der Jugend und des Bildungswesens* 2: 256 ff.

―――. 1995. "Educational Decision-Making in Open Societies: The Case of West and East Germany." In *Pluralism and Education. Current World Trends in Policy,*

Law, and Administration. Edited by Peter M. Roeder, Ingo Richter, and Hans-Peter Füssel. Berkeley: Institute of Governmental Studies Press, University of California; Berlin: Max Planck Institute for Human Development and Education, 193 ff.

Bildungskommission North Rhine Westphalia. 1995. In *Zukunft der Bidung. Schule der Zukunft*. Neuwied et al.: Luchterhand, 151 ff.

Carl Bertelsmann Prize. 1996. "Innovative School Systems in an International Comparison." Gütersloh: Bertelsmann Stiftung.

"Critères et indicateurs pour l'évaluation d'un établissement d'enseignement supérieur." 1991. *Bulletin du Comité National d'Evaluation*. Paris.

Heller, Harold, and Peter Edwards. 1992. In *Policy and Power in Education. The Rise and Fall of the LEA*. London: Routledge.

Liket, Theo M. E. 1993. In *Freihelt und Verantworfung. Das nierderländische Modell des Bildungswesens*, Gütersloh: Verlag Bertelsmann Stiftung, 33 ff. The original version of this book was published in Dutch, *Vrijheid en Rekenschap*, 1992. Amsterdam: Meulenhoff Educatief bv.

Mertens, Ferdinand J. H. 1994. Opening address to the conference "Restructuring Education." Haarlem, the Netherlands. Ministry of Education and Science, Zoetermeer.

Ministry of Education and Science. 1990. "Education Inspectorate. Duties, Methods, and Organization." The Hague, the Netherlands.

———. 1994. "Facts and Figures on Education and Science." Zoetermeer, the Netherlands.

Ministry of Education and Science in England and Wales. 1984. "Inspection and Reporting. Working Programme for Her Majesty's Inspectorate" (internal report). London.

Netherlands School for Educational Management. University of Amsterdam, Pedagogical Department. Information brochures (published periodically, n.d.).

Official Journal of the European Communities. 1994. (C 37) 66: 3 ff.

Parliament of the Netherlands. 1985–1986. *Higher Education. Autonomy and Quality*. The Hague, the Netherlands.

Rosenbusch, Heinz. 1994. *Lehrer und Schulräte—Ein strukturell gestörtes Verhältnis*. Bad Heilbrunn: Klinkhardt Verlag.

UNESCO. 1996. *International Commission on Education for the Twenty-First Century: Learning: the Treasure Within*. Report to UNESCO, Paris.

Van der Meer, A. W. 1995. "Education in a Russian Metropolis." In *Reflections on Education in Russia*. Edited by Ferdinand J. H. Mertens. Leuven: Acco, 197–207.

Vandevoorde, Pierre. 1993. "De inspection à èvaluation?" *Education et Administration. Revue de l'Association Française des Administrateurs de l'Éducation* (4): 15 ff.

Vaniscotte, Francine. 1996. *Les écoles de l'Europe. Systèmes éducatifs et dimension européenne*. Paris: Institut National de Recherche Pédagogique.

Vasconcellos, Maria. 1993. *Le système éducatif*. Paris: Edition La Découverte.

Wragg, E. C. 1993. *Education. A Distant Vision, an Alternative White Paper*. London: Institute for Public Policy Research.

3

The Teaching Profession in Europe: Historical and Sociological Analysis

António Nóvoa

INTRODUCTION

The number of surveys, studies, and analyses of teachers that have appeared in European countries has doubled in the past thirty years. Academic research, documents from professional organizations, and politically oriented texts all attempt to understand questions of increasing importance at the end of this century. The intention of this chapter[1] is not to add an additional text to a literature already so abundant. Instead, it attempts an overview of reflections in recent years on the history and challenges facing the teaching profession. The structure of this study reflects three concerns: teachers as a group without emphasis on sociological differences dividing "primary" and "secondary" school teachers; teachers in the public sector, those who have carried out principal changes in the profession; and the role of the European Union, a unit of analysis that reflects a generic approach rather than the specifics of each country.

These generalizations establish the contours of this document, which is based on a number of national surveys but attempts to define a comprehensive reading of European reality. This is undoubtedly a strange undertaking because of the differences that mark European space, notably between Catholic and Protestant countries, between the north and the south, between the center and the periphery, or between continental Europe and the United Kingdom, to mention a few. However, I will make an effort to ensure that this synthesis does not obscure the specifics of each context.

The discussion is based on a central concept—that of *professionalization*, a concept that will be examined not on the basis of (static) criteria for verifying attributes, but on the basis of (dynamic) processes by which a professional group evolves. From this vantage point, it will be possible to understand major changes in the history of teaching (first section) and to note current conflicts around the teaching profession (second section). The concept of professionalization thus acquires historical significance that is put into place pragmatically with the goal of making it possible to understand teachers' efforts to improve their professional status (Nóvoa 1987). This emphasis does not detract from an analysis of professionalization as a discourse leading to new practices for control and social regulation of teachers.

It goes without saying that the concepts of *profession* and *professionalization*, terms strongly influenced by Anglo-American connotations, do not have the same meaning in different parts of the world. Today, however, these terms no longer carry just Anglo-American connotations. "The word *profession*, sometimes with its English pronunciation, as an expert legitimated by science, is injected into national discourses about education" (Simola and Popkewitz 1996, 6). This fact does not lead to a definition that remains constant from one country to the next, but instead to recognition of "a certain international currency in discourses about professions, while, at the same time, making those discourses problematic as they are historically realized in educational fields" (Simola and Popkewitz 1996, 6). It is this trans-national acceptance of the concept of *professionalization* that will be mobilized in a pragmatic manner in the text, both to illuminate processes for enhancing the status of teachers (the development of specialized knowledge, claims for a greater professional autonomy, definition of ethical and deontological rules, improvement in salaries, etc.), and to understand the reorganization of the technologies of control and regulation of the teaching profession. This analysis thus acquires a historical dimension, directly tied to the manner in which questions of power/knowledge are played out, not only within the professional group, but also in its relations with the state and with society. These reflections place the professions at the very heart of social conflicts and goals, and attract attention to the role played by the state in professionalizing teachers.

In this context, the question *Are teachers professionals?* becomes totally useless, as it is more reflective of an ideological position than a scientific inquiry (Perrenoud 1996). On the other hand, it is useful to identify the major lines of power that characterize the work of a group attempting to professionalize its activities. The diachronic analysis of large collective movements makes it possible to see the strong points (and the contradictions) of the process. This text pays particular attention to the struggles and actions of teachers seeking certain social and economic privileges (Goodson and Hargreaves 1996). Thus, it views professionalization both as a historical project undertaken by teachers and as a process that has been opposed by arguments over costs, by state-run bureaucracies and governmental powers, and by social interests.

Model for Analyzing the Process of Teacher Professionalization

Relations between the state and teachers are central to the process of professionalization. Magali Larson (1988) is correct in noting that professions constitute a material connection between the state and the deployment of specialized knowledge in civil society. In the case of teaching, however, these relations are even closer, to such an extent that it is possible to charter the history of teachers through analysis of their interactions with the state. Independent of the status granted to teachers in different countries (civil servant, contractual worker, etc.), this perspective remains essential for understanding past and present ways that teaching is organized as a profession.

In most European countries toward the end of the 18th century, along with profound changes in the way social and economic life was organized, the state created conditions propitious for the emergence of a professional group dedicated to teaching as its primary activity. Without referring to actions accomplished through state intervention, it is impossible to understand this first moment in the process of professionalization—the occupation of a social domain by a group of individuals who dedicated the majority (or all of) their work hours to teaching.

At the same time, questions about the selection and recruitment of teachers, especially about authorization to undertake these activities, become more and more important. What had remained, up to this point, in the control of religious authorities, local communities, or private initiatives became a function of the state, which now had to put appropriate mechanisms of regulation into place. A fundamental step in the process of turning teachers into professionals is the creation by public or state authorities of legal support: a license or a diploma. This is an essential moment, especially in bureaucratic professions; it created a legal framework for gaining access, fixing conditions of entry, and instituting specific and precise procedures for recruitment such as tests and examinations.

Study of interactions between the state and teachers constitutes, therefore, one of the central elements in analysis of the process of professionalization. Its two essential dimensions are

1. The development by the teaching profession of a body of knowledge and techniques. These can be explored through an examination of teacher training institutions. This body of knowledge and techniques should be capable of reproduction and transmission to others, because it cannot be seen without taking conditions of its production and diffusion into account. It is fundamental to understand the development of teacher training institutions in the production of professional knowledge. This professional knowledge cannot be attained solely through practical apprenticeship; it requires a long training period (several years), and should contain theoretical (academic and intellectual) procedures.

2. The definition of a set of norms and values unique to teachers. This activity is accomplished to a large degree within training institutions but also finds its reference point in professional organizations. Performing a profession inevitably involves norms and ethical behaviors orienting the practices and relationships of practitioners to other social actors. For this reason, it is more productive to relate norms and values to the development of professional associations of teachers, who participate in the definition of rules for the profession, who defend the socioeconomic interests of their members, and who safeguard ethical and deontological norms. In the case of teachers, the problem of professional autonomy takes on a heavy burden to the extent that it is central to the construction of this profession's relationship with the state and with local communities.

It is fundamental that analysis of different dimensions and stages in the process of professionalization are closely linked to an understanding of the evolution of the social image and the professional status of teachers. This frame of reference sees professional history as a collective enterprise in social mobility, casting light on conflicts that cut across the teaching corps, as well as on different visions of the teaching profession inhabiting the social and political field.

These concepts are represented in Figure 3.1, which gives the model adopted throughout this chapter. The hope is that the criteria just described will not limit the sociological history of teaching but will instead provide a base from which to construct a reasonable approach to the history and current challenges facing teachers.

Figure 3.1
Model for Analyzing the Process of Teacher Professionalization

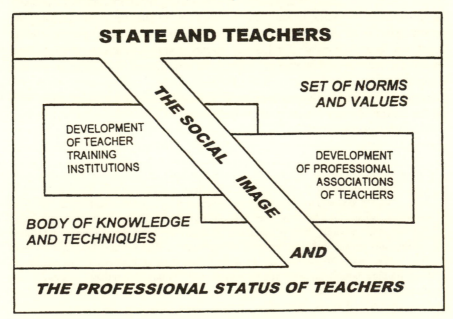

THE HISTORICAL PROCESS OF THE PROFESSIONALIZATION OF TEACHERS (18th–20th CENTURY)

The State and Teachers

The end of the 18th century in Europe was a key period in the history of education, and thus of the teaching profession. Despite the specifics and socio-economic context of each country, people everywhere were asking what constitutes a good teacher: Should the teacher be religious or secular? Should the teacher be part of a teaching force or not? How should the teacher be chosen and named? How paid? What authority should control teachers? (Julia 1981). This collection of questions was fundamental to the secularization movement that led to state control of education. The new *teaching states* instituted rigorous control over education, that is to say, over the process of reproduction (or production) of the way people view the world (Bourdieu 1993). The success of this process depended to a large degree on the recruitment of a new corps of teachers, chosen and supervised by the state (Archer 1979).

Chartier and Julia (1989) have established a cartography of educational reforms in 18th-century Europe. Theories that centered on the nature and process of state formation show that creation of national educational systems corresponds to several needs: to train personnel for state functions, to spread dominant national cultures, and to create political and cultural unity within the new nation-states (Green 1990; Soysal and Strang 1989). From one area to another, reform efforts were of course marked by the particularities of national histories and circumstances; but they were also guided by a common transnational project that was to lead to the formation of the modern state. Ernest Gellner (1983) argues that centralization of the state was a consequence of centralizing education. He believes that an educational system was a necessary condition for the economic development of modernity. The reconstruction in the 18th century of the principle of citizenship must be seen in the context of this reform movement and the affirmation of nation-states in Europe.

The teaching activity, which developed in a subsidiary and non-specialized manner—first in Protestant and later in Catholic countries, thanks to the action of religious congregations—acquired new contours. The improvement of teaching tools and methodologies, the introduction of more sophisticated teaching methods, and the broadening of curricula and educational programs all made it difficult to practice teaching on a purely accessory or marginal level. Teaching became a "collection of practices," the domain of specialists able to devote sufficient time and energy to it. In general terms, despite the specifics of each country, state intervention was to provoke national homogeneity as well as a unification and hierarchization of the different groups dedicated to teaching. In the beginning it was the state framework, not a corporate conception of the profession, that made teachers into a professional group.

One of the first concerns of 18th century educational reformers was to establish uniform procedures for the selection and nomination of teachers. In fact, the teaching profession was one of the first professions to adopt methods of selection "based on the formalized recognition of individual merit, demonstrated by diplomas and specific tests" (Viñao Frago 1994, 119). Nevertheless, the emergence of new professional models did not come without resistance, a fact that helps explain, according to Dominique Julia (1994), the quasi-secular separation that distinguished declared intentions from their realization in practice. It was necessary to remove teachers from the influence of local populations and authorities and to envision them as a state-sponsored group, or at least as a group operating under the aegis of state protection. The teachers themselves were to adhere to this project, to the extent that it gave them a measure of autonomy and independence, vis-à-vis the priests, the local authorities, and the local populations; nevertheless, they had the protection of the state with all the rights and responsibilities that implied. This was a project supported simultaneously by teachers and states, the former attempting to transform themselves into an autonomous and hierarchized administrative group, the latter attempting to guarantee its control over the educational institution (Hamilton 1989).

Since the end of the 18th century, teaching licenses or permits have in general been obligatory in Europe. These documents have been granted by state authority (or some other agency given authority by the state) after an individual passed an examination or competition open to anyone who has a certain number of necessary attributes such as literary prowess, age, or good moral character. This procedure represents an important step in professionalization because it creates conditions for the elaboration of a canon of technical competencies based on educational criteria that could serve as a base for recruitment and, as a corollary, as a blueprint for a teaching career. The license or permit functions as a "guarantee" by the state to teachers that they can use to improve their professional status.

To say that in most countries teachers are state employees is insufficient if one does not add that they are *a particular type of state employee* (Robert 1995). It is, furthermore, important to understand that "the blanket use of the term *state functionaries* hides too many historical, local and particular possibilities and, importantly, ignores teachers' attempts at working class alliances on education and their varied interpretation of their role as perceived by the State, and their resistances to it" (Lawn and Ozga 1981, 49). The teaching profession is closely tied to goals and expectations and is strongly linked to a political intent. Teachers, as carriers of a message, are aligned with national ideals: they must be understood from the dual perspective of integration and independence. At the end of the ancien régime, the status of state functionary was convenient for teachers, as it assured them independence with respect to local influences (Cornu 1992). However, teachers attempted to combine the privileges of functionaries (for example, tenure) with those of independent employees. To a certain extent, it can be said that the ideal model of teaching is situated somewhere between that of the civil servant and the independent professional—that is one reason why the model of the liberal professions remains, whether explicitly or implicitly, a point of reference for members of the teaching profession even if it has never served as a base for their organization. In their collective history, teachers have never given up asking for regulations that are less administrative (in the bureaucratic sense) and more professional (in the liberal sense) (Terral 1997).

Development of Teacher-Training Institutions

The creation of teacher-training institutions, a primordial step in the process of professionalization, is the fruit of action on the part both of teachers and of states. The former saw it as a way of enhancing their status; the latter saw it as a powerful instrument of control. Institutionalizing the procedures of training through the creation of normal schools has permitted, on the one hand, the development of teaching as a profession aimed at social improvement for its members, and on the other hand, the establishment of stricter state control. The project of creating teacher-training institutions is fairly old, but in the majority of European countries it was not realized until the 19th century. The action taken by teachers explains to a large degree the success of normal schools since that time. Up to that point, teachers, like other professionals, would include two demands in each of their struggles: increased request for access to normal schools, plus a longer curriculum with higher academic standards. They thus demonstrated their adherence to the idea that social stratification should be based on academic criteria and on the superiority of the educated. Normal schools represent a profound change, a sociological revolution among people teaching in primary schools. The impoverished and poorly educated teachers of the beginning of the 19th century were to give way to professionals, trained and prepared to exercise the activity of teaching (Gardner 1995; Nique 1991).

Teacher-training institutions were initially oriented toward primary-school teachers. An increasing preoccupation with secondary-school teachers dates from the second half of the 19th century (Wideen and Grimmett 1995). Obviously, these two levels of teaching have different strategies and problems; primary-school teachers are expected to show more concern for the student, whereas secondary-school teachers construct their identity through an academic discipline (Judge, Lemosse, Paine, and Sedlak 1994). In both cases, however, the importance of this moment in the professionalization of teachers is obvious. A long-term analysis of the evolution of teacher training, furthermore, reveals a growing similarity between these two institutional tracks. In a historical analysis of initial training over the last century recently published by the European Union, the following conclusion emerges: "To sum up, three broad approaches to teacher training for primary education characterize the development of teacher training during the course of this century: post-primary education in a specialized vocational school, training in post-secondary level institutions, and finally training in higher education, generally at university. These models are found almost everywhere in Europe, but have been established at different times during the century" (European Commission 1996, 91). Concerning secondary education, the same document suggests "that initial training for secondary teachers based only on knowledge of the subject matter is inadequate to guarantee a high level of success in democratic school systems which are open to pupils from all social backgrounds" (European Commission 1996, 92).

Body of Knowledge and Techniques

Teacher-training institutions are points of reference for the production of a body of knowledge and techniques exclusive to the teaching profession. At first, the normal schools (for primary teachers) and later the universities (for secondary teachers) put into place curricula that attempted to determine the knowledge and techniques necessary for "professional" teachers. It is for this reason that a history of professionalization cannot ignore the relationship between teachers and knowledge, especially pedagogical knowledge. However, it is not sufficient to consider the genealogy and the diffusion of a specialized knowledge. It is also necessary to take the social meaning of this knowledge into account, and its penetration into individual and collective consciousness as the bridge to different sites of power (academic, professional, and political) that inhabit the field of education.

The ambiguities of the professional status and the social condition of teachers are well illustrated by their relationship to this knowledge. The *intermediate* position of teachers is particularly shown by their dependence on the epistemologies produced by other groups in other social spaces. In the 19th century, two axes of reflection developed: on the one hand, the axis of *pedagogy*, closer to the normal schools and the practices of teacher training; on the other hand, the axis of the *science of education*, a theoretical dimension often in the space of the university. There is disconnection between the science of education as an academic discipline, and pedagogy as practical knowledge for teachers (Schriewer and Keiner 1992). This bias produces cleavage between theory and practice (between theoreticians and practitioners) that highlights the importance of analyzing the professionalization of teachers on the basis of knowledge and powers in place in a given period.

The professionalization of teachers is in fact tied to the possibility of a pedagogical knowledge that is not strictly instrumental and that can produce a corpus of reference both theoretical and practical. In reality, it is not surprising that the high-points of the production of scientific reflection in education are also the high points of the professional affirmations of teachers. Nevertheless, these periods also contain elements of a devaluation of the teaching profession. They provoke simultaneously the delegitimation of teachers as producers of knowledge and the investment of new groups of experts affirmed as "scientific authorities" in the field of education. It is important to understand this paradox. With every advance in the educational sciences, there is an improvement in the image of teachers, but at the same time a decrease in their competencies, es-

pecially in the status accorded their knowledge—that is, any knowledge produced by experience and reflection on practice.

For normal schools there was an important change toward the end of the 19th
century in a majority of European countries. The coursework stretched out to
two or three years, and took on a clear dimension of professional training that
justified the expert status conferred on teachers. One finds, for the first time, a
conception of teacher training in which pedagogical knowledge becomes independent of methods, thus bringing about new power relationships between those
who produce theory and those who produce practice. This division was accentuated at the beginning of the 20th century when the psychology-sociology-
pedagogy triangle, as the base of the *sciences of education* kaleidoscope, was
constructed. The new scientific élan was viewed as central to a logic of innovation. Therefore, it had to furnish instruments useful to administration and
social regulation. This involved a change in teacher training from the normative
and philosophical approach of the late 19th century to a reformist tendency
based on scientific knowledge.

This explosion of the educational sciences brought teachers closer to a general
body of knowledge, but also brought risk that they would pay less attention to
specific aspects of the field. We can see periodically, especially within the normal schools, a methodological emphasis that reveals the need to build links
between theory and practice—a reflection of the presence of hierarchies among
the holders of knowledge (the scientists), the guardians of methodology (the
normal-school teachers and the school inspectors), and the men and women of
action (the teachers). During the first decades of the 20th century, therefore, we
are confronted with contradictory processes that mark an incontrovertible
launching point for the teaching profession, but at the moment that showed the
limit of its autonomous development. Despite differences among countries, the
obligation of completing a relatively long and theoretically based specialized
training constitutes a significant step in the professionalization of teachers
throughout Europe.

The Development of Professional Teacher Organizations

The first teacher associations were organized at the beginning of the 19th
century as friendly associations or mutual aid societies. Sometimes formed for
collective defense and protection, sometimes for promoting culture and teaching,
these associations first appeared among secondary-school teachers and were later
enlarged to include primary-school teachers. At first the modalities of organization were fragile, although they already reflected the corporate interests of the
profession (Bernard, Bouet, Dommanget, and Serret 1966). These organizations
formed slowly and according to different rhythms throughout the whole first
half of the 19th century (Robert 1995).

Toward the middle of the 19th century, however, a series of sociological
changes, especially the progressive consolidation of training institutions and the

beginning of compulsory schooling, created conditions favorable to the development of the teachers movement. This movement took on a collective task: to convert teachers into a unified group and to elaborate a common ideology. This corporate actor was born as the result of a long collective enterprise that gives witness to the way teachers had become conscious of their own interests as a professional group.

In the image of the different rationales in their training, an important cleavage separated primary- and secondary-school teachers. The former adopted a more combative role, gradually approaching the perspective of labor unions as they developed within workers' and civil service movements. The latter organized in different ways, trying to achieve a more corporate identity, although the demands of their movement also reflected collective claims. One could see in this difference the classic opposition between professionalism linked to defense of general interests and public service, and unionism linked to class interests. However, this opposition does not stand up to a careful and critical examination. Such a distinction is based more on ideological differences than on the functions actually performed by the different professional organizations: it is not possible to "contrast *professionalism with unionism* like two systems of values exclusive of one another" (Maurice 1972, 222).

Nevertheless, the choice of the associative model as appropriate to describe the teachers movement is controversial, as shown by the ambiguity of teachers' socio-professional status. Teacher associations have adopted diversified forms of organization, taking either professional groups or labor unions as models (Lawn 1985). This choice has been legitimated by distinct discourses, which are loaded with political meaning and which change considerably, depending on socio-political contexts and historical situations. On the other hand, the practice of professional teacher associations is almost always characterized by somewhat hybrid behavior organized around two dimensions: the defense of their members' corporate interests and the defense of teaching in terms of public service and social utility.

At the beginning of the 20th century, after several decades of struggle and collective efforts, the union model began to dominate. This, however, has not hindered the maintenance, until today, of other associative models: friendly associations, pedagogical associations, including teachers from a specific discipline, groups of specialists, pedagogical movements, or even the beginnings of professional orders (Robert 1995). A study published in 1925 by the *Internationale des Travailleurs de l'Enseignement*, however, shows clearly that despite political difficulties and the immense diversity of organizational forms, the union perspective had acquired a solid base in the majority of European countries (Boubou 1925). Ida Berger would even write that "this strong syndicalization is a trait obvious to the highest degree in the physiognomy of teachers" (1979, 152). Speaking of the Swedish situation, Christina Florin would insist on the fact that "the increasing influence of this organization [Association of the Elementary Teachers of Sweden] contributed to making teachers more professional" (1991, 22).

Set of Norms and Values

The prestige and power that teachers enjoyed at the beginning of the 20th century is indistinguishable from the actions carried out by their associations: they added to the extrinsic unity of the teaching corps imposed by the state through their status as functionaries, an intrinsic unity built on the basis of professional solidarity and the defense of common interests. In this framework, the state opposed in different ways the autonomous organization of teachers. The establishment of an esprit de corps and a common strategy was not accomplished without conflict, given the different ethical, ideological, and political dispositions in the movement.

This rapport of powers, both *ad intra* and *ad extra*, progressively built an apparatus that shaped the contours of teachers' professional identities. This process undoubtedly had individual referents, but it played itself out primarily in a collective dimension. Professional associations occupied a primordial role in the elaboration of collective reservoirs of beliefs, norms, rules, meanings, and values that defined the profession of teacher. Under their influence, an expansion of the press and a multiplication of conferences and congresses took place in the transitional decades at the end of the 19th and beginning of the 20th century. These became regular laboratories of common ideals, with schools and instruction representing the "progress" in which teachers were invested.

Teachers' norms and values were first defined against the background of a social dimension (the school and its role in progress). They were later played off against a standard of pedagogical responsibility (the child and his or her rights as a student). From this standpoint we can view the ethical debate and its consequences to the regulation of the profession. It is important to understand that if from the point of view of the professions' regulations, teachers submitted to ethics imposed by the state, they succeeded collectively in producing values reflecting their daily activities and professional demands. This is why ethical questions cannot be understood without looking at the work accomplished within the teachers' representative organizations.

Social Image and the Economic Status of Teachers

The second half of the 19th century is a key period for understanding the ambiguity of the position of teachers and the improvement in their socio-economic status. Creation of normal schools (and university-based institutions for teacher training), development of the educational model (the "grammar of schooling"), and belief in the virtues of instruction as a factor in progress transformed the teaching profession into an aspiration for different social classes and a road to social improvement. To become a primary-school teacher was to manage an escape from conditions marked by images of pain: "that of the peasant, exhausted at night from cutting hay, that of the maker of wooden shoes, who sweats heavily turning his drill, and that of the weaver, who is combing dusty hemp" (Ozouf 1967, 63). Normally coming from underprivileged social groups, primary-school teachers felt superior to villagers because of their knowledge; nevertheless, their pitiful remuneration made it impossible for them to adopt a middle class lifestyle (Ozouf and Ozouf 1992). The sociological isolation of teachers was similar to that of priests (it was crucial to maintain relations with everyone without favoring anyone) and reinforced solidarity within the teaching corps. The situation of secondary-school teachers was completely different. Coming from more privileged backgrounds, they were, until the middle of the 20th century, that is to say until the period of explosive growth in schooling, part of the local elite (Chapoulié 1987). Their university training, their salaries, and the fabric of the social, cultural, and political relations that they maintained favored this assumption, which marked an obvious divide between primary- and secondary-school teachers (Neave 1992).

In neither case was professionalization a process built endogenously. The history of teaching cannot be disassociated from the place its members occupied in society and the role they played in the maintenance of the social order. Teachers were not only responding to a social need for education; they created this need. The social operation of schooling would never have been possible without the juncture of several social and economic factors, but it is teachers who were the agents of this enterprise. At the moment when the school became a privileged instrument of social stratification, teachers were invested with enormous power. From then on, they held the keys to social ascension (and stagnation). This placed them at the crossroads of frequently contradictory socio-economic interests: functionaries of the state and agents for reproduction of the dominant social order, they personified hopes for social mobility held by different social strata. Here lies all of the ambiguity and the importance of the teaching profession. As cultural agents, teachers are also inevitably political agents. Furthermore, as Philippe Perrenoud reminds us, public images represent a big enough challenge, as much for professionals as for the organizations that train or employ them: in fact, "no corporation can be indifferent to its public image, to the extent to which its reputation depends on it, so does its prestige, its revenue, and the power of its members" (1996, 69).

The Feminization of the Teaching Profession

The feminization of the teaching corps—a phenomenon that despite specific national circumstances, can be clearly perceived in all European countries since the middle of the 19th century—is an essential component of an analysis of the social image and economic status of teachers. Traditional sociological explanations are insufficient for understanding the complexity of this question, especially the inference that the teaching profession is devalued because it is predominantly feminine, and vice versa (Albisetti 1993). Instead of classical analyses, which view women as an "obstacle" to improvement of the image and status of the profession, it is necessary to go further and to use the more sophisticated conceptual tools that make it possible to understand the *positive* contribution of women to a professional definition of teachers. It is important, however, to point out that women have played a fundamental role in the professionalization of teachers, both in the production of knowledge and values and in the definition of professional attitudes and competencies. The need is to study that "added value" if one wishes to understand the historical dilemmas cutting across the teaching profession.

In this respect, the question of salaries is both significant and contradictory. On the one hand, it is a struggle that brings together successive generations of women who fight, often with the support of professional organizations, for equal pay for men and women. On the other hand, and contrary to what could be expected from traditional explanations, the recognition of this right by public powers has not had very significant consequences for the sociological profile of the teaching profession. Curiously—and here we see another contradiction— equal wages were first obtained in some countries of Southern Europe (at the end of the 19th century) and did not reach the rest of the continent until the middle of the 20th century (Araújo 1993; Owen 1988). Nevertheless, even with differential wages, teaching was one of the few careers open to women, as is demonstrated by the growth in registrations in normal schools in the last decades of the 19th century.

An analysis of iconography concerning teachers produced at the beginning of the 20th century reveals an absence of *public* images of women teachers. Nevertheless, by 1900, women constituted a majority of primary-school teachers: more than 50% in France and Belgium, more than 60% in Sweden and Italy, and more than 70% in England. In spite of this, the dominant images of teachers were *masculine* images, images that seemed a better fit with a professional image. There were some feminine images, but these were often "private" images (the teacher with her students, or in her class). At the same time, ideologies of *motherhood* were disseminated throughout the field of education, notably by a new generation of doctors and hygienists. The more useful image, especially in union struggles and in the search for greater social recognition, remained masculine. The feminine dimension of teaching was recognized, but did not constitute a point of reference identifying the profession.

The continuation of female participation in the profession shows that gender has a fundamental role in the identity of teachers. To avoid classical arguments, it is more interesting to pose another question: Are we confronted with an essential change in the teaching profession? This problem cannot be approached from the standpoint of simple statistical or quantitative reasoning. It needs to be situated within the field of complex and contradictory influences on the teaching profession. At the same time, for reasons simultaneously political, social, and cultural, teachers were to be removed, little by little, from the forefront of the public scene. Since the 1930s a cloak of silence has fallen on teachers, enclosing them inside educational spaces. This retreat was accompanied by rhetoric, adapted to the female universe, that reinvented a concept of mission, or of religious vocation. The profession of teacher adopted a feminine identity, and this brought with it essentially *private* images. Along with this transition, we also see reinforcement of an apparatus for controlling teachers, which especially in the case of women, impacted both professional and private areas. Primary-school teachers became the objects of a close surveillance, which put into place policies that discriminated against women's work.

The feminine image of the profession became definitively fixed toward the middle of the 20th century, a time when women were already a substantial majority of primary-school teachers and a substantial percentage of secondary-school teachers. It is crucial to underscore the differences between primary and secondary teaching; for the latter, the percentage of women remains around 50% in the European Union (European Commission 1996). Within the European Community, the proportion of women in the teaching force has grown very little since the 1960s, although a country by country examination of this evolution indicates how much this tendency hides important national disparities (European Commission 1996).

These facts are significant because they indicate the arrival of a threshold of professionalization: a relatively stable teaching force with consolidation of certain rules in teacher training and in the practice and regulation of professional activity. The consolidation of this social image and the professional status of teachers was not accomplished without struggles or contradictions. Toward the middle of the 20th century, we can identify processes, called by some writers *de-professionalization* (or *proletarization*), that contradict the dynamics of the professional affirmation of teachers. It is undeniable, however, that *mass schooling*, along with consolidation of the status of teachers and the setting of a *professional image*, confirm the end of a historical cycle in the teaching profession.

SOCIOLOGICAL REFLECTIONS ON THE TEACHING PROFESSION

The first cycle in the professionalization of teachers lasted until the 1920s and 1930s: from the start of state-sponsored schooling at the end of the ancien régime, until the consolidation of mass schooling at the beginning of the 20th century. Despite tensions and conflicts, this was a relatively "coherent" period in the life of teachers, a period when they created themselves as "professionals." However, during World War II and in the postwar educational expansion, teachers confronted a number of contradictory processes in which professional affirmation mixed with devaluation and with authoritarian control over the profession, a process some authors call *de-professionalization* or *proletarization* (Lawn and Grace 1987; Ozga 1989; Ozga and Lawn 1981).

It is possible to identify characteristics of this phenomenon: a separation between conceptualization and realization, which brings about surveillance of teachers by experts; a standardization of tasks, which provokes a technical and instrumental definition of teachers; the reduction of remuneration, which causes devaluation of teachers' socio-economic status; the intensification of demands vis-à-vis everyday educational activities, which makes a reflexive approach to teaching more difficult. At the heart of the debate is the question of professional autonomy, the internal or external regulation of the activity of teaching. It is obvious that during the middle decades of the 20th century, teachers did not stop striving to reinforce their social image or professional status. They were obliged, however, to deal with contradictory and opposing tendencies (Lawn 1987).

By the 1970s, teachers, thanks to their representative organizations, had achieved a number of professional objectives (Grace 1991; Goodson and Hargreaves 1996). These achievements concern primarily Northern European countries; the situation in the South was substantially different because of authoritarian regimes that blocked professional development. Nevertheless, "within a remarkably short period of time, the decade of the 1980s, the professional gains made by the teachers over a long historical period were either weakened or eliminated by the action of the central state in education" (Grace 1991, 3). Despite political and social differences, it is undeniable that debate over the professionalization of the teaching profession has had similar contours in the 1980s and 1990s in the majority of European countries, a circumstance that has obvious political explanations.

Thinking About Relations Between the State and Teachers

A sociological analysis of the teaching profession cannot overlook an important quantitative fact: for the last three decades the total number of teachers in the European Union has practically doubled, currently comprising about 4 million members. It is true that this evolution has not been consistent in all of the states, but it represents a change in size, as well as content, in the definition of the teaching profession. The crisis of teaching talked about since the 1960s is not unconnected to this phenomenon, which carries paradoxical implications: on the one hand, there is a devaluation of teachers and their professional status; on the other hand, teachers remain in political discourse and in the social image one of the most crucial groups for building the future. Understanding current challenges facing the profession requires special attention to this gap between the real condition of teachers and the weight given to their actions.

Ivor Goodson and Andy Hargreaves (1996) have clearly demonstrated the complexity of this debate, highlighting its conflicts and contradictions. This reconfiguration of the teaching profession is a process that reflects a profound alteration in the forms of state intervention in each country in the European Union, but that is being supported by similar discourses and educational policies.

At the risk of overestimating the importance of these similarities, it is possible to mention two processes that are closely linked: the *rationalization* and the *privatization* of teaching.

Understanding tendencies pointing to the rationalization of teaching requires a look at the development of educational sciences and the groups of experts (in curriculum, teaching methodologies, and evaluation) who claim power over the organization of teachers' activities. This contributes to confirmation of a technical definition of the profession and to practices of control based on "scientific" rationalities. That the relationship between teachers and knowledge is directly at stake through separation of conception, realization, and standardization of tasks makes a reflective approach to teaching impossible. The rationalization of teaching brackets knowledge and subjectivities—in a word the personal and collective histories of teachers. In this way a professional logic is constructed that turns the subjective and experiential dimensions of teachers' reflections on their own work and informal moments of exchange and cooperation into a tabula rasa.

The rapid growth of specialists after the 1980s has brought about a reconstitution of the field of education, a reconfiguration of the teaching profession, and a new attitude toward political decision making (Charlot and Beillerot 1995). It is important to understand the role of specialized systems of knowledge in the management of professional work and in the organization of peoples' lives (Giddens 1990). Establishing the educational sciences as "rational," "scientific," or "objective" obscures ideological dimensions and different points of view about teaching. The prestige of educational researchers depends on the "naturalization" of their worldview and on an increasing proximity between academic and university spaces. Increasingly, states tend to abandon a normative (or prescriptive) role and to put into place technologies of surveillance, evaluation, and regulation based on concepts produced by experts. Efforts to rationalize teaching by the educational sciences is based on a logic that values the knowledge of experts and disqualifies the knowledge of teachers.

Rationalization and privatization of teaching are two moments in the progress of outside control of teachers. They are part of a political agenda defining teachers by the criteria of technical rationality, thus reinforcing the gap between theory and practice and the ambiguity of teachers' relationship to knowledge. Pedagogical experts produce discourses on autonomy, on capacity for self-reflection, or on the importance of teachers' academic or scientific qualifications. At the same time, educational reforms seek legitimacy through a rhetoric of decentralization giving teachers greater control over their work. To improve the "quality" and the "efficiency" of teaching, however, educational policies look to experts who impose ever more stringent procedures of evaluation and control over content, processes, and results. Teachers, furthermore, are pressured to adopt conformist perspectives and technical orientations that threaten professional autonomy (Pereyra, García Minguez, Gómez, and Beas 1996; Popkewitz 1993).

The concept of the *privatization* of education hearkens back, on the one hand, to the neo-liberal policies that introduced new work regulations for teachers, and on the other hand, to the weight acquired by "laws of the market" in the definition of educational space. Strategies of management and administration tend to replace bureaucratic or administrative mechanisms (Helsby 1995). Maeve Landman and Jenny Ozga stress, correctly, that "the space left for teachers in the new model of market-driven client-led and state-regulated education provision is not comfortable" (1995, 24). The call for decentralization, for example, sanctifies political strategies based on controls lying close to the work of teachers, either through the intervention of local authorities or through a logic of client accountability. The reference to greater autonomy of teachers also implies self-regulation, both individual and collective, which embraces criteria originally conceived outside of the profession. This is why the political rhetoric of teacher professionalization must be analyzed as an element in a redefinition of relationships between the state, civil society, and the scientific world.

These two processes (*rationalization* and *privatization*) denote contradictory tendencies, especially concerning relations between the state and teachers. Rhetorical inflation of the mission of teachers contributes to greater social visibility, reinforcing prestige, but it also contributes to stricter governmental and scientific controls. These controls bring with them depreciation of teachers' competence and work. European societies at the end of the 20th century manifest an ambiguous attitude toward teachers. Teachers are regarded as professionals who lack qualifications and competence but who represent, nevertheless, the greatest hope for social and cultural change. This identity of teachers is produced through a game of power and counterpower between images that carry different projects, and that make it necessary to define a new conception of teaching.

Perspectives and Challenges in Teacher Training

The training of teachers is one of the most decisive domains of change in European education. Throughout its history, teacher training has balanced academic models, centered on specific institutions and "fundamental" knowledge, with practical models, based on schools and on "applied" methodologies. This dichotomy could be overcome by adopting professional models of partnerships between institutions of higher learning and the schools (Elliott 1993).

The creation of teacher-training institutions constituted a crucial step in the process of professionalization. In the 20th century an increase in the number of university programs represented an essential part of the social and scientific affirmation of teachers. It is not a matter of reducing the intellectual scope of teacher training or of advocating a return to schools as a site of excellence in teacher preparation. The question is elsewhere: it involves installing new procedures and techniques of collaboration between the universities and the schools in a way that promotes training that reflects the actual challenges facing the teaching profession (Adams and Tulasiewicz 1995).

Although raising the level of initial training has been one of the historical demands of teachers, recently the principal debate has centered on in-service education. For several years we have seen that teacher training needs reconsideration and restructuring that will integrate different levels of conceptualization, "organizational context, nature of the professional role, professional competence, professional knowledge, nature of professional apprenticeship, curriculum and pedagogy" (Elliott 1991, 310).

Nevertheless, it is important to recognize that neither the universities nor the schools alone are capable of responding to these needs, a fact that points to the importance of a new basis for cooperation. To institute organizational mechanisms that create connections between the universities and the schools requires putting into place new professional functions that value space for practice and for reflection on practice. A reflective conception of teaching is consonant with this *third way*, which is based on praxis as space for forming a critical consciousness and qualified actions. The reconfiguration of a new *teaching profession* passes through three stages traditionally absent in teacher training: the teacher as an individual, the school as an organization, and the profession as a collective (Nóvoa 1994). The new realities of initial training, and especially of in-service education, cannot ignore these three challenges.

Bodies of Knowledge and Techniques

These reflections touch on the relationship between teachers and knowledge. Are teachers the carriers (and producers) of their own knowledge, or are they merely the transmitters (and reproducers) of a knowledge generated by others? Is the reference knowledge of teachers essentially "scientific" or "technical"? These questions have been the subject of numerous debates in which different visions of the teaching profession and contradictory professional development projects come face to face. The historical analysis of curricula and teacher training reveals an oscillation between three poles: *methodological*, special attention to techniques and instruments of action; *disciplinary*, mastery of a domain of knowledge; and *scientific* (pedagogical), the educational sciences as references framed by other social and human sciences, particularly psychology. These poles tend to reproduce dichotomies (fundamental knowledge/applied knowledge, science/technique, knowledge/methods) that are no longer pertinent to the relationship between teachers and knowledge.

The effort to escape such binary thinking has been pronounced since the 1980s, when the contours of new knowledge about the teaching profession were outlined. Educational literature has advanced a great deal in the demarcation of professional knowledge, beginning with a look at the specifics of concrete actions of teachers (Paquay, Altet, Charlier, and Perrenoud 1996). This underscores the reflective dimension of teachers' actions and, while paying particular attention to the lives of teachers, the need to invest in praxis as the point of knowledge production. According to Pierre Dominicé (1990), theory furnishes us with indicators and with a framework for reading, but what the teacher remembers as reference knowledge is that which is linked to identity and experience. The triple movement suggested by Donald Schön (1990)—knowledge in action, reflection in action, and reflection on action—suggests a conception of the teacher as a reflective practitioner. Currently, teachers' knowledge and techniques can be defined only in relation to their capacities for reflective self-development and the theoretical elaboration coming from references to practice.

The Renewal of Teachers' Professional Associations

The teachers' association movement has played a primary role in the professionalization of teachers. Adoption of the union model is consistent with the consolidation of the role of teachers as functionaries: "To the extent to which teachers are salaried workers like others, their unions are unions like any other, classical defenses by professionals against employers and clients, instruments for negotiating working conditions, salaries, qualifications for employment, rules regulating vacations, status, career paths, continuing education, retirement, social solidarity, etc." (Perrenoud 1991, 31). We cannot forget, as Martin Lawn writes in speaking of England that "teachers were the first major group of white collars to organize into professional associations" (1996, 28) and that "the union became the major link between individuals and groups and acted as an effective way of exerting pressure publicly and mobilizing support" (1996, 107).

The teachers' union movement has its own contours that are related to the specifics of this professional group. Today, however, redefinition of the status of teachers brings with it significant changes in the logic of association. For several years we have seen, on the one hand, a reflection on styles of union action and organization, and on the other hand, the development of new forms of teacher associations. The regrouping of teachers tends to be organized through different modalities; for example:

- disciplinary groups (associations of history or mathematics teachers), which have stimulating dynamics but at the same time risk diminishing a sense of belonging to the teaching force as a whole;
- pedagogical movements, manifested in the sharing of teaching tasks, and/or spaces for cooperation and collaboration;
- structures for exercising professional power in the framework of the affirmation of collegiality, a counterpoint to strategies for reinforcing state control (Smyth 1991).

This last modality is particularly important because it articulates with autonomy, with reorganization of educational institutions, and with the consolidation of collaborative networks within the teaching force. In a study of teacher culture and the structure of schools, we can see the interdependence of three elements: initiative in education, the self-governance of schools, and the collegiality of teachers. André Robert even talks about a "unionism of proximity, characterized by its capacity to multiply the initiatives for local interventions, at the level of the institutions themselves" (1995, 165) as one of the most promising evolutions. Martin Lawn goes so far as to affirm that "in a seller's market power should move to the teachers; this has happened at significant periods in the past" (1996, 138).

Set of Norms and Values

The values that have served as the basis for the historical affirmation of the teaching profession need rethinking in the light of contemporary debates in education. It goes without saying that a certain number of these values remain essential to the professional definition of teachers, but others have become obsolete. This is the case, for example, with the scholarly ideals that founded the teaching profession in the 19th century. The normative framework of the state, furthermore, does not take the same form today; teachers tend to escape from administrative restraints that are too strict. The attachment of teachers to the construction of national citizenship, furthermore, tends to be redefined in a more intimate sense (local and community ties), as well as in a wider sense (transnational affiliations). Teachers need to develop new values that lead to positive reminiscences of the past but do not encourage an indiscriminate "return to the past."

The need to go past the restrictions imposed by a state framework makes it necessary to define other modalities (recruitment, evaluation). In this context, debate on the production of a professional culture for teachers becomes central. This is work that is accomplished both inside and outside the professional group, making necessary a series of interactions, negotiations, and compromises. The new professionality of teachers needs organization according to clearly explicit ethical and deontological rules, notably on relationships with different educational partners and with providers of professional services. In addition to certain traditional dimensions, there are three aspects that deserve mention: pedagogical responsibility, institutional compromise, and collective engagement.

Professional ethics have to integrate a pedagogical component, namely, the refusal of theories and methods that are discriminatory or that contribute to the consecration of social inequalities. Lise Demailly is correct when she emphasizes that this aspect cannot be dissociated from the definition of teachers: "It can seem strange that professional competence implies ethical (philosophical) positions—and perhaps this is true in the case of relational careers—but how else can I name (I will give one example of the ethical dimension of the profession among others) a principle such as belief in the educability of the learner?" (1987, 66). We are confronted here with a definition of ethics very close to the terrain of pedagogy and to professional practices. This is not about a normative system dictated from the outside, but instead the profession's collective production of ways of doing and saying.

This brings us to a second point, that is to say, an ethic that is defined in terms of institutional compromise at the level of educational organization. The capacity of teachers to produce a professional culture leads to the possibility that the teaching profession enjoys autonomous power of self-regulation. Autonomy, however, needs *territoriality*, an institutional space where the organized teaching force can legitimately exercise its power. The definition of politics in a local space, as well as the emergence of schools as organizations, configures new territoriality concerning identity and professional intervention between the too global level of the *macro*-system and the too restrained level of the *micro*-classroom. Reflection on the school and its educational projects is not identical in the different European countries—the most obvious division is that which separates countries with a strong tradition of centralization or decentralization—but we see similar evolution concerning responsibility for teachers, which is also constructed on educational organizations (and not only on the basis of relations, or of references to national citizenship).

It is within this institutional framework that the idea of a collective engagement (collegiality) can take place. This is not simply a matter of consolidating networks of solidarity and esprit de corps, but also of creating spaces for collaboration and regulation of the profession. The new professional culture should be based on strict criteria for a teaching career (recruitment, progression, evaluation, etc.) and on an explicit process for setting rules, responsibilities, and criteria for competence. If teachers do not occupy this space for regulating the profession, other groups (the state, the universities, local authorities) will create apparatuses for controlling their work. However, if a wider participation of social actors is desirable, it is crucial to distinguish those aspects, which must be regulated by the profession itself.

The Social Image and Economic Status of Teachers Today

Analysis of social image and economic status is essential for understanding challenges currently facing the teaching profession. Important changes in the condition of teachers are taking place even though certain traditional divisions are maintained: functionary/contractual labor, primary teachers/secondary teachers, and so on. These divisions reinforce the idea that there is enormous difference from one country to another, that to speak globally about the situation of teachers is difficult (OCDE 1994). It is equally undeniable, however, that problems encountered by teachers within European space are similar. In the thematic dossier about teachers presented in the *Key Data on Education in the European Union* appears the following: "In conclusion, the different lights in which the same subject—the teaching profession—has been shown have revealed again the diversity of the situations in the Member States of the European Union. This approach has also made it possible to see that many Member States are asking the same questions and trying to solve the same problems" (European Commission 1996, 129).

It is important to understand that the modifications produced in recent years, at least in certain countries, tend to bring together various situations. In the countries of Southern Europe, we see the emergence of laws for placing wage

controls on teachers, which, without casting doubt on their status as functionaries, introduce distinctions and specifics between teachers and other categories
of workers. In the European nations as a whole, there is a tendency to reinforce
ties with local communities, often translated into a greater social participation
in the wage control of teachers. Perspectives on school autonomy bring more
meaningful power for controlling the recruitment and the career paths of teachers. These few examples show the existence of problems and discursive practices
that are identical in all of the countries within the European Union.

Another question concerns the traditional debate between unity and differentiation within the teaching force. The union movement, strongly marked by
this division, has leaned toward equality of wages for all teachers. *A contrario*,
certain associations have worked toward deepening distinctions to assure maintenance of prerogatives and privileges. Such a difference still remains marked,
especially between primary teachers (a single teacher in charge of the class;
relationships with children, an essential element in his or her professional identity), and secondary school teachers (one teacher for each academic discipline;
disciplinary knowledge, an essential element of his or her professional identity).
Nevertheless, these divisions are disappearing—a process visible in the leveling
of salaries, "whereas in 1965 a considerable difference was found fairly generally between primary and secondary teachers' remuneration, in 1993 this difference was much less (Belgium, Spain and Austria) or tending to disappear
(Greece, France, Italy, Finland, Sweden and Scotland)" (European Commission
1996, 120). This phenomenon not only relates to questions of salaries, but also
touches on recruitment policies, teacher training, career progression, or participation in the management of educational institutions.

A central point in the sociological analysis of the teaching profession is the
evolution of levels of remuneration. This situation is quite different from one
country to another. Nevertheless, it is possible to delineate a general tendency
toward slow growth in purchasing power, even though the relative position of
teachers with respect to the overall standard of living has slowly decreased over
the last thirty years.[2] The relative economic stability of teachers hides important
differences between countries. For example, German teachers earn almost twice
what Greek teachers earn (OECD 1996). Another relevant aspect is the fact that
there has been a reduction in the spread between maximum and minimum teachers' wages in recent decades. This means that teaching becomes more attractive in the beginning of the career, but is detrimental to a challenging and
financially remunerative professional progression. This option makes it possible
to solve certain problems of recruitment, but contributes to de-skilling and de-
professionalization.

This point has a direct impact on the social image of teachers. This is a
difficult issue to debate. On the one hand, there is without doubt a devaluation
of the social image of teachers; they have lost the prestige of having knowledge
inaccessible to the majority of the population. Paradoxically, teaching as a popular occupation has contributed to a loss of social status among teachers, a group

who sometimes live in the nostalgic dream of a society in which their actions were more highly valued. On the other hand, several studies have demonstrated that the professional image of teachers remains relatively high. Peter Cunningham, for example, has analyzed the English press between 1950 and 1990, concluding that "despite attacks from the political right and their development in the media, public support for teachers and a benign perception of their role was once again ascendant by 1990" (1992, 55). These contradictory sentiments accentuate the ambiguity and malaise of teachers who are incapable of replacing traditional images with images that affirm a new vision of the profession. The social representation of the profession remains attached to a past time period and is not capable of taking the challenges currently facing teachers into account. The identity process is always elaborated in interplay of powers and counter-powers between images carrying different projections for the teaching profession.

The key to the renewal of the profession lies, to a large degree, in the possibility of a status defined by wider autonomy and by identification with excellence and rigor. Questions about training and associative space are essential, but consolidation of ties with local communities and decision making within the framework of educational institutions have become central elements in redefining teachers' professional identity. It is for this reason that debates surrounding educational projects take on increasing importance: liberating teachers from administrative control and stimulating more cooperation at the level of schools. This debate involves, on the one hand, cooperation in professional activities (groups for planning, reflection, and evaluation of pedagogical work), and on the other hand, the search for an active presence in management of educational institutions (Nóvoa 1993).

The five dimensions evoked in the last paragraphs—status, unity/differentiation, salaries, social image, and autonomy/career—make it possible to identify an evolution taking place in Europe, a process that is reconfiguring European education, although in diverse forms. However, the emergence of a new identity brings, above all, the possibility of a *social redemption of the profession*. In fact, the ambivalence that cuts across the relations of European societies with the teaching profession is no longer tolerable. On one side, discourses are outbidding each other to define the role and the mission of teachers, on whom reposes a considerable part of the hopes for Europe's future (OCDE 1990). On the other side, we tend to regard teachers with a certain distrust, to devalue their professional activity, and to blame them for current difficulties in educational systems. The rhetorical inflation thus grows to a social distrust toward teachers, a situation that reinforces divisions and malaise.

The raison d'être of the teaching profession is shaken when we speak now of a post-nation-state Europe, or a post-national identity. In the European context, the process of globalization is added to a project of economic and political integration that has an important impact on the arena of education (Husén, Tuijnman, and Halls 1992; Ryba 1995). Given the multiplication of levels of power between the local and the global, an inevitable question concerns the maintenance of the nation-state as a pertinent space for decision making in educational matters. These tendencies are clearly increased in the context of the European Union, which constitutes the most elaborate legal form for defining a *post-national citizenship* (Soysal 1994). The principle of a *European citizenship*, already consecrated institutionally by the Maastricht Treaty, brings into numerous public spaces a solidarity "which breaks apart forever the idea of the primary alliance on which the idea of national territory is based" (Badie 1995, 222).

This is a conflictual reality in which local identities, regional loyalties, national sentiments, and European ideologies are expressed. This is an extremely complex debate with radical consequences for education that threaten fundamental elements of national systems of education. The changes resulting from contemporary policies of technologization, privatization, and rationalization of teaching are currently defining themselves in a time frame marked by strong contradictions within the teaching force. A look at the evolution taking place in the European Union shows clearly that in this region of the world, perhaps more than elsewhere, teachers are being subjected to a redefinition of their role and of their identity (Nóvoa 1996; Sultana 1994; Vaniscotte 1996). A number of documents even talk about the "new" European teacher to emphasize the moment of transformation we are facing.

NOTES

1. Translated by Theodora Lightfoot. This text has been prepared in the context of a research project dealing with "the Images, the Cultures, and the Politics of Education in the European Context," financed by JNICT (the PCSH/C/CED/908/95 Project).

2. These conclusions are drawn from the releasing of two documents that furnish important facts in this respect: *Key Data on Education in the European Union*, published by the European Commission in 1996; and *Education at a Glance*, published by the OECD in 1996.

REFERENCES

Adams, A., and W. Tulasiewicz. 1995. *The Crisis in Teacher Education: A European Concern?* London: The Falmer Press.

Albisetti, J. 1993. "The Feminization of Teaching in the Nineteenth Century: A Comparative Perspective." *History of Education* 22 (3): 253–263.

Araújo, H. 1993. *The Construction of Primary Teaching as Women's Work in Portugal (1870–1933)*. Ph.D. diss., University of London.

Archer, M. 1979. *Social Origins of Educational Systems*. London: Sage.

Badie, B. 1995. *La fin des territoires*. Paris: Fayard.

Berger, I. 1979. *Les instituteurs d'une génération à l'autre*. Paris: Presses Universitaires de France.

Bernard, F., L. Bouet, M. Dommanget, and G. Serret. 1966. *Le syndicalisme dans l'enseignement*. Grenoble: Institut d'Études Politiques.

Boubou, M. 1925. *La situation matérielle et morale de l'instituteur dans le monde*. Paris: Internationale des Travailleurs de l'Enseignement.

Bourdieu, P. 1993. "Esprits d'état—Genèse et structure du champ bureaucratique." *Actes de la Recherche en Sciences Sociales* 96–97: 49–62.

Chapoulié, J.-M. 1987. *Les professeurs de l'enseignement secondaire—Un métier de classe moyenne*. Paris: Editions de Maison des Sciences de l'Homme.

Charlot, B., and J. Beillerot, eds. 1995. *La construction des politiques d'éducation et de formation*. Paris: Presses Universitaires de France.

Chartier, R., and D. Julia. 1989. "L'école: traditions et modernisation." In *Transactions of the Seventh International Congress on the Enlightenment*. Oxford: The Voltaire Foundation.

Cornu, L., ed. 1992. *Le métier d'instruire*. Paris: Centre National de Documentation Pédagogique.

Cunningham, P. 1992. "Teachers' Professional Image and the Press 1950–1990." *History of Education* 21 (1): 37–56.

Demailly, L. 1987. "La qualification ou la compétence professionnelle des enseignants." *Sociologie du Travail* 29 (1): 56–69.

Dominicé, P. 1990. *L'histoire de vie comme processus de formation*. Paris: Editions L'Harmattan.

Elliott, J. 1991. "A Model of Professionalism and Its Implications for Teacher Education." *British Educational Research Journal* 17 (4): 309–318.

Elliott, J., ed. 1993. *Reconstructing Teacher Education: Teacher Development*. London: The Falmer Press.

European Commission. 1996. *Key Data on Education in the European Union*. Luxembourg: Office for Official Publications of the European Communities.

Florin, C. 1991. "Social Closure as a Professional Strategy: Male and Female Teachers from Co-operation to Conflict in Sweden, 1860–1906." *History of Education* 20 (1): 17–26.

Gardner, P. 1995. "Teacher Training and Changing Professional Identity in Early Twentieth Century England." *Journal of Education for Teaching* 21 (2): 191–217.

Gellner, E. 1983. *Nations and Nationalism*. Ithaca, NY: Cornell University Press.

Giddens, A. 1990. *The Consequences of Modernity*. Stanford: Stanford University Press.

Goodson, I., and A. Hargreaves, eds. 1996. *Teachers' Professional Lives*. London: The Falmer Press.

Grace, G. 1991. "The State and the Teachers: Problems in Teacher Supply, Retention and Morale." In *Teacher Supply and Teacher Quality: Issues for the 1990s*. Edited by M. Lawn and G. Grace. Clevedon, England: Multilingual Matters Ltd., 3–16.

Green, A. 1990. *Education and State Formation: The Rise of Education Systems in England, France, and the USA*. New York: St. Martin's Press.

Hamilton, D. 1989. *Towards a Theory of Schooling*. London: The Falmer Press.

Helsby, G. 1995. "Teachers' Construction of Professionalism in England in the 1990s." *Journal of Education for Teaching* 21 (3): 317–332.

Husén, T., A. Tuijnman, and W. Halls. 1992. *Schooling in Modern European Society*. Oxford: Pergamon Press.

Judge, H., M. Lemosse, L. Paine, and M. Sedlak. 1994. *The University and the Teachers—France, the United States, England*. Oxfordshire: Triangle Books, Vol. 4 of Oxford Studies in *Comparative Education* 1–2.

Julia, D. 1981. "La naissance du corps professoral." *Actes de la Recherche en Sciences Sociales* 39: 71–86.

Julia, D., ed. 1994. *Aux sources de la compétence professionnelle*. Gent: Paedagogica Historica (special issue 30-1994-1).

Landman, M., and J. Ozga. 1995. "Teacher Education Policy in England." In *The Political Dimension in Teacher Education: Comparative Perspectives on Policy Formation, Socialization and Society*. Edited by M. Ginsburg and B. Lindsay. London: The Falmer Press, 23–39.

Larson, M. 1988. "À propos des professionnels et des experts ou comme il est peu utile d'essayer de tout dire." *Sociologie et Sociétés* 20 (2): 23–40.

Lawn, M., ed. 1985. *The Politics of Teacher Unionism: International Perspectives*. London: Croom Helm.

Lawn, M. 1987. *Servants of the State: The Contested Control of Teaching, 1900–1930*. London: The Falmer Press.

———. 1996. *Modern Times? Work, Professionalism, and Citizenship in Teaching*. London: The Falmer Press.

Lawn, M., and G. Grace, eds. 1987. *Teachers: The Culture and Politics of Work*. London: The Falmer Press.

Lawn, M., and J. Ozga. 1981. "The Educational Worker? A Re-assessment of Teachers." In *Schools, Teachers & Teaching*. Edited by L. Barton and S. Walker. London: The Falmer Press, 45–64.

Maurice, M. 1972. "Propos sur la sociologie des professions." *Sociologie du Travail* 2/72: 213–225.

Neave, G. 1992. *The Teaching Nation: Prospects for Teachers in the European Community*. Oxford: Pergamon Press.

Nique, C. 1991. *L'impossible gouvernement des esprits (Histoire politique des écoles normales primaires)*. Paris: Nathan.

Nóvoa, A. 1987. *Le Temps des Professeurs*. 2 vols. Lisboa: INIC.

———. 1993. "The Portuguese State and Teacher Educational Reform." In *Changing Patterns of Power; Social Regulation and Teacher Education Reform in Eight Countries*. Edited by T. Popkewitz. Albany: State University of New York Press, 53–86.

———. 1994. "Les enseignants: à la recherche de leur profession." *European Journal of Teacher Education* 17 (1/2): 35–43.

———. 1996. "L'Europe et l'éducation: Analyse socio-historique des politiques éducatives européennes." In *Challenges to European Education*. Edited by T. Winther-Jensen. Frankfurt am Main: Peter Lang, 29–79.

OCDE. 1990. *L'enseignant aujourd'hui: Fonctions, Statut, Politiques*. Paris: Organisation de Coopération et de Développement Economique.

———. 1994. *La qualité des enseignants: synthèse des études par pays*. Paris: Organisation de Coopération et de Développement Economique.

OECD. 1996. *Education at a Glance—OECD Indicators*. Paris: Organization for Economic Co-operation and Development.

Owen, P. 1988. "Who Would Be Free, Herself Must Strike the Blow: The National Union of Women Teachers, Equal Pay, and Women within the Teaching Profession." *History of Education* 17 (1): 83–99.

Ozga, J. 1989. *Schoolwork—Approaches to the Labour Process of Teaching*. Milton Keynes: Open University Press.

Ozga, J., and M. Lawn. 1981. *Teachers, Professionalism and Class: A Study of Organized Teachers*. London: Falmer Press.

Ozouf, J. 1967. *Nous les maîtres d'école (Autobiographies d'instituteurs de la Belle Epoque)*. Paris: Gallimard.

Ozouf, J., and M. Ozouf. 1992. *La République des instituteurs*. Paris: Seuil.

Paquay, L., M. Altet, E. Charlier, and P. Perrenoud, eds. 1996. *Former des enseignants professionnels*. Bruxelles: De Boeck Université.

Pereyra, M., J. García Mínguez, A. J. Gómez, and M. Beas. 1996. *Globalización y descentralización de los sistemas educativos*. Barcelona: Ediciones Pomares-Corredor.

Perrenoud, P. 1991. "La double face du syndicalisme enseignant." *Educateur* 3: 31–33.

———. 1996. *Enseigner: agir dans l'urgence, décider dans l'incertitude*. Paris: ESF Editeur.

Popkewitz, T., ed. 1993. *Changing Patterns of Power—Social Regulation and Teacher Education Reform*. Albany: State University of New York Press.

Robert, A. 1995. *Le syndicalisme des enseignants*. Paris: La Documentation Française.

Ryba, R. 1995. "Unity in Diversity: The Enigma of the European Dimension in Education." *Oxford Review of Education* 21 (1): 25–36.

Schön, D. 1990. *Educating the Reflective Practitioner*. San Francisco: Jossey-Bass.

Schriewer, J., and E. Keiner. 1992. "Communication Patterns and Intellectual Traditions in Educational Sciences: France and Germany." *Comparative Education Review* 36 (1): 25–51.

Simola, H., and T. Popkewitz, eds. 1996. *Professionalization and Education*. (Research Report 169). Helsinki: Department of Teacher Education—University of Helsinki.

Smyth, J. 1991. "International Perspectives on Teacher Collegiality: A Labour Process Discussion Based on the Concept of Teachers' Work." *British Journal of Sociology of Education* 12 (3): 323–346.

Soysal, Y. 1994. *Limits of Citizenship—Migrants and Postnational Membership in Europe*. Chicago: The University of Chicago.

Soysal, Y., and D. Strang. 1989. "Construction of the First Mass Education Systems in Nineteenth-Century Europe." *Sociology of Education* 62 (4): 277–288.

Sultana, R. 1994. "Conceptualising Teachers' Work in a Uniting Europe." *Compare* 24 (2): 171–182.

Terral, H. 1997. *Profession: Professeur*. Paris: Presses Universitaires de France.

Vaniscotte, F. 1996. *Les écoles de l'Europe—Systèmes éducatifs et dimension européenne*. Paris: Institut National de Recherche Pédagogique.

Viñao Frago, A. 1994. "Les origines du corps professoral en Espagne." In *Aux sources de la competence professionnelle*. Edited by D. Julia. Gent: *Paedagogica Historica* (special issue 30-1994-1), 119–174.

Wideen, M., and P. Grimmett, eds. 1995. *Changing Times in Teacher Education—Restructuring or Reconceptualization?* London: The Falmer Press.

4

Educational Studies in Europe

Jürgen Schriewer

GENERAL PROCESSES AND NATIONAL VARIANTS IN THE FORMATION OF ACADEMIC DISCIPLINES

Modern scholarship, in contrast to older forms of knowledge production, quite rightly lays claim to universal rationality and trans-national validity. In spite of these claims, recent history and sociology of the sciences have brought to light a high degree of contingency in the theoretical, institutional, and social forms within which, and through which, academic disciplines or fields of scholarly study are constituted. This holds true all the more as history and sociology of the sciences have included in their analyses an explicitly comparative perspective. Suffice it to mention, for example, the studies by Wolf Lepenies (1985 [1991]) and Peter Wagner (1990) on the emergence and unevenly successful disciplinary consolidation of social sciences in Western Europe; the analyses by Fritz Ringer (1992) of the interrelationships between educational concepts, epistemological models, and political positions that characterized the French and German intellectual milieu at the turn of the century; the analyses by Bernhard Plé (1996) on the rise of positivism in France, England, and Italy in the last half of the 19th century; and numerous other studies (Bruch 1985; Ranieri 1985; Larson and Deutsch 1988; Schriewer and Keiner 1992; Schriewer and Keiner

This chapter appeared under the title "Etudes pluridisciplinaires et réflexions philosophico-herméneutiques: La structuration du discours pédagogique en France et en Allemagne" (Multi-disciplinary Studies and Philosophical-Hermeneutic Reflexions: The Structure of Pedagogical Discourse in France and in Germany) in vol. 3 of *Paedagogoica Historica*, Supplementary Series (Gent, Belgium: 1998), pp. 57–84.

1993; Depaepe 1993; Drewek, Lüth et al. 1998). It is important to note that even the so-called "hard" sciences have not escaped from being put into a socio-historical perspective. Salient examples include Jonathan Harwood (1992) on the Denkstile or differing cognitive styles used by German and North American geneticists, Dominique Pestre's work on the impact that national styles of theorizing have had on the physics of solid bodies, and analyses of the reception of the theory of relativity in what Fritz Ringer has called different "academic cultures" (Glick 1987).

What these studies actually demonstrate is that general trends linked to the emergence of modern society—the crystallization of a functionally specific social subsystem for science, as well as processes of the scientization and professionalization of academic institutions—intersect in diverse national settings with varying patterns of "university-state relations," distinct intellectual traditions, and diverse cultural meanings. In other words, the "political-institutional positions from which aspiring social scientists started out in the second half of the nineteenth century" differed significantly, not only between the United States and Europe, but also within Europe between the "relative statelessness" of British society and the "state-centered" societies of continental Europe. These positions differed also, however, within the latter group, as is conspicuously illustrated by France, with its long history of consolidated state institutions, and Germany, plus Central Europe more generally, where late nation-state building assigned a key role to the university in forging a cultural identity closely associated with elite education and research (Wagner and Wittrock 1991, Quotations, pp. 342 f.).

The analyses that follow illustrate this contrast between the overarching differentiation, scientization, and professionalization characteristic of the modern university, on the one hand, and divergent discipline formation processes followed by the same field of study in different national settings, on the other. They will do so by focusing on the divergent French and German patterns of modern educational studies. German Pädagogik and French sciences de l'éducation—like educational studies in Britain or its equivalents in other European nations—in no way represent anything corresponding to a logic intrinsic to the phenomenon of pedagogy. The institutionalization of one or another variant of the educational sciences is rather as much the product of the combined effects of university-state relations, of socio-institutional conditions, and of different intellectual traditions, as their development across time is the result of epistemological choices and intellectual exclusions that favor certain theoretical options while excluding others.

Our attempt to describe, in terms of intellectual, political, and institutional history, the emergence of these two national configurations of the educational sciences draws on the concept of *discourse coalitions* developed in the recent historical-comparative sociology of the social sciences (Wittrock, Wagner, and Wollman 1991). Corresponding studies have brought to light the importance, in the academic institutionalization of particular fields of study, of the sometimes intense interactions between actors from different fields of social activity, from science as well as from politics. What is meant, then, by the concept of *discourse coalitions* are alliances established between certain representatives (or groups of representatives) of the social sciences, on the one hand, and certain political actors (or groups of political actors), on the other. These alliances result from the fact that the interpretations (or reinterpretations) of social and political reality advanced by the social sciences show cognitive affinity with the need to interpret (or reinterpret) traditional models of action felt by political actors. In fact, certain representatives of the social sciences may conceive of interpretations of society that are capable of supporting, by their reasoning, the projects of certain political actors and, consequently, of reinforcing the position of the latter in the political struggle. Conversely, the direct support given to certain social science discourses by politicians, as well as the more indirect support these discourses obtain because of the accrued social legitimacy attendant on political support, work together to procure them a reinforced position in the field of science (Wagner 1990, 55).

In the following, the concept of *discourse coalitions* will designate the two-fold character of the phenomena under study: on the one hand, the fact that actors of different origins cooperate and in so doing, surmount the borders between their respective fields of action (or social subsystems); on the other hand, the impact that these interactions have on the discourse of the social science disciplines being studied and on their transformation. With reference to this concept, I would like to explain the following thesis: It was essentially in the period between the two world wars that the French and German configurations in the educational sciences received their decisive form—in Germany, under the impact of a powerful coalition between the universities and leading representatives of the Prussian administration, which was effective during the years of transition between the empire and the Weimar Republic; in France, conversely, following the stepwise decomposition, over the course of the same years, of a once equally powerful discourse coalition which, constituted in the early years of the Third Republic, had displayed a similar impact (see also Schriewer 1998).

THE EMERGENCE OF PHILOSOPHICO-HERMENEUTIC PÄDAGOGIK IN GERMANY

In the German case, one key date—1917—particularly captures the attention of the historian (Tenorth 1989; Drewek 1996; and Drewek 1998). In May of that year, the Prussian Ministry of Education convened a conference, the deliberations of which led to apparently inconsequential conclusions (Pädagogische Konferenz 1917). On the one hand, participants in the conference agreed to recognize the importance of creating chairs in education, a university subject that was no longer to be annexed to other disciplines in Prussian universities. On the other hand, educational theory was eliminated as a required subject from examinations for the state certificate for secondary school (Gymnasium) teachers. Consequently, the decrees adopted in the same year, which reorganized the overall pattern of Gymnasium teacher training, while aligning this pattern with that of jurists and higher-level civil servants, removed its educational components from the universities. These components were reshaped into an essentially practical training period, which was to take place after university graduation under the tutelage of the schools' administration.

The meaning of these apparently contradictory decisions, which have caused serious interpretation problems for historians, cannot be deciphered if one limits oneself to a strictly utilitarian view of educational studies as the professional training of teachers, however logical this goal. What was involved, instead, in a political and social context in which ministerial officials and farsighted politicians were already beginning to prepare for a postwar period, the difficulties of which loomed in their thought, was to provide spaces for reflection or, more exactly, for legitimization of the existing educational system. The philosopher Ernst Troeltsch, spokesman for the faculties of philosophy and rapporteur of the conference, set the tone by specifying the expectations that were to guide the introduction of the new discipline in the Prussian faculties:

What I categorically refuse to do, is to construct this discipline on the basis of psychology; I would construct it instead on the basis of the history of the educational system, of institutional analyses as well as of the philosophy of civilization. On the basis of psychology, it would be impossible to understand either the given educational system, since it has crystallized as a historical and political fact, or—as you, gentlemen, must admit—the objectives of education (*Bildungsziele*) and the ideals of civilization (*Kulturideale*). In cases where people nevertheless proceed in this manner, and where modern psychology is joined with biology and sociology in order to accomplish this task, we can see the development of conceptions of public instruction and its objectives which you would have difficulty applauding, gentlemen. What these conceptions are attempting to do is to put public instruction at the service of a type of progress which is supposed to be justified by sociology and social psychology, and which aspires to bring about educational equality for everyone as well as an essentially utilitarian promotion of the popular masses. Those are the true intentions of a psychology which, in our days, strives for the direction of education, but which, in reality, is nothing but a disguised metaphysics and a doctrine of utilitarian progress. (Troeltsch 1917, 24)

The contrasting positions thus evoked by Troeltsch reveal both the ideological opponents he was trying to block—the left-wing parties, the primary-school teachers and their unions, the supporters of experimental methods in psychology and educational studies—and the alliance being hatched between the Prussian administration, leading representatives of secondary-school teachers, and the faculties of philosophy, led by the chairs of philosophy.

What was at stake, first, for the Ministry of Education was preservation of the existing educational system over social upheavals, which loomed ahead in 1917 and would in the next year bring down the established political order. This concern was all the more pressing because the German educational system at that time, patterned on the structures of a hierarchical and fragmented society, was very socially selective. Its different tracks, whose definition and coordination with degrees leading to differentiated careers did not come to an end until 1900, had taken shape in accordance with the reproduction needs of the social strata of the prewar society (Müller, Ringer, and Simon 1987). This system, however, was increasingly exposed to radical questioning: to political debate by the harbingers of the comprehensive school, affiliated with the primary-school teachers' unions, and strongly supported by Social Democrats; and to scientific scrutiny, as a result of research conducted by specialists in experimental psychology. The former put forward principles of justice and social promotion. The latter denounced the character, largely unjustified from the point of view of the psychology of intelligence, of a premature distribution of children into hierarchically structured tracks leading to very unequal degrees and to differentiated opportunities in life. In this situation, educational theory conceived in terms of Troeltsch—that is, giving preference to historical interpretation of educational realities, and to the broad perspectives of reflection nourished by the philosophy of civilization—became in the eyes of the ministry an antidote to the attempt of "modernist" psychologists to link positivistic research with political involvement, and experimental method with social and educational reform.

For the teachers' associations, furthermore, the debate over the educational system and its overall organization was tightly linked to preoccupations with teacher training. As they were to do later in France, the proponents of comprehensive schooling in Germany called for a training program that would be both unified, that is, common for all groups of teachers, and more academic, that is, given by the universities. Such claims, of course, went hand in hand for the primary-school teachers and their unions with aspirations for increased social recognition, for alignment of their status with that of secondary-school teachers, and for higher salaries. Thus, the primary-school teachers' unions and the supporters of comprehensive schooling agreed in demanding that the unified training of all teachers be organized by the faculties of philosophy. The latter, however, would inevitably see their academic teaching style and their intellectual and moral cohesion jeopardized if they had to enroll great numbers of students from more modest social backgrounds, students whose intellectual training and life experiences differed considerably from that of their traditional clientele. These faculties were naturally disposed, therefore, to reject the idea of organizing a profession-related training program, all the more so as the chairs of philosophy, on their part, insisted on constructing the new field of education as an essentially theoretical discipline. Considerations of social advancement, moreover, were not unfamiliar to Gymnasium teachers. For decades, they had demanded the alignment of their titles and status with that of higher civil service officials who graduated from the law faculties. Throughout the 1917 restructuring of the program for secondary-school teachers, thus, the Prussian Ministry of Education not only succeeded in disarming attitudes of discontent and frustration widespread among members of this group; it succeeded also in gaining

Gymnasium teachers as allies in its defense against the social and intellectual ambitions of primary-school teachers and against the threat to the established educational system coming from these teachers' unions as well as from the newly emerging group of academics specializing in experimental psychology.

The chairs of philosophy, finally, while displaying an intellectual program for the new discipline that was responsive to the ministry's attempts at legitimization, were by the same token defending their own corporate interests. In order to oppose attempts, much in vogue at the turn of the century, to construct the field of education on the model of experimental science, they made use of the methodological paradigm worked out by Wilhelm Dilthey—the development of human and social studies, the *Geisteswissenschaften*, based on philosophico-hermeneutic learning. This model, which had been developed with brilliant success by Wilhelm Wundt at the University of Leipzig, was subsequently adapted for education, notably by Ernst Meumann. Experimental psychology, while still affiliated with departments of philosophy, came to epitomize scientific and methodological modernity for the social and human sciences more generally, and therefore succeeded in attracting a considerable number of young researchers. Since at this time experimental psychology could barely be distinguished from experimental pedagogy, the extraordinary increase in academic staff specializing in psychology also appeared in educational studies programs. In fact, themes dealing with questions of teaching and pedagogy provided psychological researchers with a welcome field of application that allowed them also to combine experimental research with social and educational reform, thus following the example of Meumann himself within the very influential Association for School Reform (Bund für Schulreform). According to statistical data recently compiled by Drewek (1996 and 1998), more than half of the almost 2,000 courses and seminars in educational studies given in German universities between 1911 and 1919 had a psycho-experimental approach. At the same time, courses using philosophical and historical approaches were only about one-third of the total (with the remaining 10 to 15% coming from the faculties of theology). The average age of academic staff teaching philosophy, furthermore, was considerably higher than that of psychologists. Given the numerical preponderance of the latter group, as well as the serious crisis in recruitment for positions in philosophy that therefore loomed ahead, first-class philosophers such as Rudolf Eucken, Edmund Husserl, Paul Natorp, Heinrich Rickert, and Wilhelm Windelband were led, as early as 1913, to denounce publicly the threatening takeover of chairs in philosophy by psychologists, and to demand a clear and clean separation between the two fields. It is thus mostly out of concern for the preservation of their own discipline that the chairs of philosophy, more than any other group, put together every possible means to discard the option, very real at this time, of building the new field of education on the model of experimental psychology.

The significance of the discourse coalition being formed around an intellectual program opposed to experimental psychology, namely the Diltheyan paradigm, was therefore triple. This coalition equally signified: (1) counteracting the questioning, advanced with reference to experimental psychology, of the existing educational system and its functioning; (2) cutting off the aspirations for university training by primary-school teachers, that is, a clientele whose enrollment in the faculties of philosophy could profoundly modify the mission and everyday teaching practices of these faculties; and (3) safeguarding the social reproduction of philosophy as a distinctive discipline within these faculties.

Through the combined activities of the alliance of the Ministers of Education (not only of Prussia, but of other German *Länder* as well), the representatives of secondary-school teachers, and the faculties of philosophy, led by the chairs of philosophy in particular, the paradigm of philosophico-hermeneutic reflection was successfully implanted, then, by those nominated to the first autonomous chairs of education: Eduard Spranger at the University of Berlin, Herman Nohl at the University of Göttingen, Theodor Litt at the University of Leipzig, and Wilhelm Flitner, first at the University of Kiel, then at the University of Hamburg. Once firmly established, this group, which was soon reinforced by Max Frischeisen-Köhler at the University of Halle and Richard Hönigswald at the University of Breslau, also succeeded, incrementally but enduringly, in ousting their theoretical rivals—experimental pedagogy, sociological and psychoanalytic strands of educational studies, and finally the claims of the churches. In fact, although intellectually close to liberal, secularized Protestantism, comparable in this respect to the type of thought developed by Ferdinand Buisson in France, the philosophico-hermeneutic paradigm of educational studies nevertheless cultivated a genuine orthodoxy of its own. It did not tolerate either theoretical or disciplinary dissension, either, to use the terms coined to designate the field's theoretical adversaries—*empiricism* or *psychologism* and *sociologism*. The dominant discourse centered instead on the reiterated interpretation of its own history and the history of its presumed predecessors such as Schleiermacher; on the explanation of its own idiosyncratic concepts (*einheimische Begriffe*); and on the constantly renewed justification, through intricate epistemological reflections, of its theoretical fundamentals (*paedagogischer Grundgedankengang*). It ended up then in a self-centered and strictly disciplinary theoretical orientation, whose historico-reflective style of theorizing and overload with epistemological justifications was to be characteristic of the dominant discourse in German educational sciences up to a recent past. This discourse can be identified in greater detail in the data produced by comparative content analyses of the contemporary knowledge production of German and French educational sciences, which will be outlined below.

THE TWOFOLD INSTITUTIONALIZATION OF SCIENCES DE L'ÉDUCATION IN FRANCE

In France, the science de l'éducation, which came to light at the beginning of the Third Republic, while sharing some traits with the German Pädagogik institutionalized in the early years of the Weimar Republic, followed a largely opposite path. As in Germany, its institutionalization was essentially the outcome of a wide discourse coalition. In this coalition, the Ministry of Public Instruction, the parliamentary majority of the République Triumphante,[1] as well as the academic elites, worked for a far-reaching "intellectual and moral reform" of the country[2]—a reform, in other words, that would encompass both the universities and primary and vocational education; both the renewal of science and the moral education of people; both the achievement of processes of system-differentiation and—using a term coined by recent social history (Müller, Ringer and Simon 1987)—*systematization* of the educational system and the preservation of the cohesion of the social and political body through a secular morality. Among the component groups of this coalition, the intellectual program supported as much by the leading academics as by the high officials of the Ministry of Public Instruction, that is, spiritualism nourished by Kantian philosophy, was considered compatible with the principles of secularism, which directed social and educational reform at the level of public politics. It was on the basis of this ideological complementarity, and with the combined financial support of the three levels of education—primary, secondary, and higher—that the ministry granted the new field of study to the Sorbonne Faculty of Letters, which had not solicited it. From the standpoint of the ministry, as well as of the faculty, the new discipline was considered "a lecture course in speculative pedagogy"—*un enseignement de pédagogie spéculative*—meant to take on a character that was not immediately practical and professional, but deliberately "philosophical" and "theoretical."[3] Inevitably, these definitions bring to mind those that Ernst Troeltsch was to advance more than thirty years later. The correspondences with German pedagogy are even more pertinent if one takes into consideration the functions of legitimization and justification of the reorganized French educational system that were assigned to this—as some people would prefer to call it—*philosophical pedagogy* or *pedagogical philosophy* (Marion 1883). In terms that anticipate almost word for word the preoccupations expressed by Troeltsch, namely to guarantee a deeper understanding of the "objectives of education" and the "ideals of civilization," Emile Durkheim, at the turn of the century, assigned the following role to pedagogy:

not to transmit impersonal recipes, which are mechanically applicable to all circumstances of school life; but to imprint on us a general direction; to aid minds in finding their way in the confusing mêlée of ideas; to facilitate a better understanding of what is and, in particular, what tends to be the very essence of the nation. Above all, its tasks would definitely involve laying bare the major aspects of the ideal to which we aspire. (Durkheim 1901, 134–136)

From the 1910s onward, however, a successive disintegration of the previously effective alliance began to take place. This disintegration, completed in the period between the two world wars, took place at several levels: at the political level, through a recomposition of the parliamentary majorities; at the intellectual level, as a consequence of the "French Enlightenment crisis" (Descombes, cited in Lindenberg 1990, 11); at the ideological level, through the "long descent into hell of the 'republican spirit' after 1918" (Lindenberg 1990, 17); and finally, at the university level itself, as a consequence of the relative weakening of the university system and of its impact on public debate. The "republican synthesis," which during the decades of the République Triumphante had tied together spiritualism, patriotism, and secular republicanism, fell apart, thus allowing its components to deviate into nihilistic scepticism, into pacifist internationalism, and into utopian plans conceived as radical and authoritarian alternatives to the faded bourgeois republic (Dubief 1976; Lindenberg 1990; Sirinelli 1994). This disagregation entailed the delegitimation of the politico-ideological ideals that had been at the center of the important reforms accomplished by the Third Republic and had led to the institutionalization of science de l'éducation as an academic discipline. Indeed, as early as 1912 high officials in the Ministry of Public Instruction denounced the secular "theologism" and "mysticism" they purported to diagnose in the works Emile Durkheim and Jean Delvolvé, respectively, had undertaken with a view toward founding moral education on the basis of a reformulated secular morality.[4] Toward the end of the 1930s, a former minister of education was even able to permit himself to comment ironically, in an almost official encyclopedia launched by the ministry, on the end of an "excessively long parody of the sacerdotal State" (Monzie 1939).

Following the disintegration of a discourse coalition with such powerful origins, the French institutions of higher education, and the academic disciplines within these institutions, ridded themselves to a degree of the politico-ideological considerations implied by the former alliance. As in Germany, where philosophers and experimental psychologists were to become involved in a struggle for influence motivated as much by divergent intellectual orientations as by worries about their social reproduction within the university, the egotistical corporate interests of the disciplines within the faculties of letters made themselves felt with greater and greater force. However, in contrast to German pedagogy, whose philosophico-hermeneutic approach was in accord with intellectual orientations that were particularly strong in the faculties of philosophy, that is, historicism and the Diltheyan paradigm of human and social studies, French "philosophical pedagogy" was much more fragile, fragile in fact from two viewpoints.

First, the methodological eclecticism practiced by the first generation of French philosopher-educationalists—Henri Marion at Paris, Alexandre Martin at Nancy, Georges Dumesnil at Toulouse, Raymond Thamin at Lyons, Jean Delvolvé at Montpellier, and Georges Lefèvre at Lille—soon encountered reservations in a university setting that had just lived through a remarkable period of institutional and intellectual renewal under the aegis of scientific ideals derived from positivism and orthodox philosophy of science. In contrast to the German faculties of philosophy, the French university setting did not offer, to the fundamental problematique of education as an academic field that systematically blends different components of knowledge and cognitive orientation, an intellectual climate favorable to solutions of reflective integration. Instead, the "exoteric discourse," which Ferdinand Buisson (1896, 501)—a key figure in France with a role comparable to that of Eduard Spranger in Germany—proposed to designate the missions of legitimization and justification assigned to pedagogy, immediately collided with Durkheimian claims that the social sciences should "take on the esoteric character which befits all science" (1982 [1895], 163). Furthermore, if Durkheim nevertheless managed to bridge these apparent contradictions by advocating a differentiation of theory styles—namely between "science de l'éducation" and "pédagogie," between, in other words, "scientific theory" and "practical theorizing," that is, between a kind of historical-comparative sociology of education and "reflection applied as methodically as possible to educational matters in view of regulating their development" (1973 [1911])—in the thinking of his successors differentiation would rapidly turn into hierarchization, with the second of the two poles being devalued.

Later, this differentiation and hierarchization was multiplied by strong tendencies toward fragmentation. In effect, in contrast to the accomplishment by German philosophico-hermeneutic pedagogy of defining itself with reference to a problematique peculiar to it and of constituting itself on idiosyncratic concepts, the problematique that had determined the institutionalization of 19th-century French science de l'éducation—that is, moral education based on a secular morality—was part of the intellectual preoccupation, not only of education, but also of sociology, social economics, social philosophy, and ethics. Far, then, from being able to consolidate itself as a clearly delimited field of university-based reflection, education in France found itself torn between different disciplinary approaches, which were, in addition, intellectual rivals.

Therefore, it is in the wake of the combined effects (1) of the disintegration of a discourse coalition forged under the République Triumphante; (2) of the corporate interests that were increasingly asserted by the individual disciplines united in the faculties of letters; and (3) of the tendencies toward hierarchization and disciplinary fragmentation that followed from this, that this intellectually fragile field institutionalized in French universities since 1883–1884 collapsed during the 1920s and 1930s. As the acts and deliberations of the Paris faculty of letters make it possible to reconstruct, in all of its details, the intellectual functions originally attributed to science de l'éducation were taken on by disciplines as distinct as moral philosophy, sociology, psychology—most notably child psychology illustrated by Henri Wallon—and, eventually, a few complementary courses in pedagogy that were largely devalued.[5]

After this collapse of French science de l'éducation as a distinct discipline, educational studies continued to be taught only in substitute forms. These were, on the one hand, several courses integrated into the program of the University Institutes of Psychology, which were established during the inter-war period with a special status outside the faculties; on the other hand, some clearly delimited courses served as component parts of the program for the licenses—the French equivalent of the master's degree—in philosophy, psychology, and sociology. It is in the form of such substitutes that the field of education in France survived a long eclipse, to be reborn only in the late 1960s. Inevitably, the generation of academics then in charge of bringing new life to the reinstitutionalized field and of assuring it a definite place in French universities had received their intellectual training, their paradigmatic frameworks, and their particular research approaches in the context of a whole range of other social and human sciences, most notably psychology and sociology. In consequence, the second institutionalization in French universities of a discipline particularly devoted to the study of educational phenomena took on a deliberately pluri-disciplinary orientation much more aligned with research in the social sciences than with philosophical reflection or historical erudition. It is this orientation that not only resulted in the use of a plural term to designate the field as *les sciences de l'éducation* instead of the late-19th-century singular, but also impinged on the field's contemporary knowledge production.

DISCIPLINE FORMATION PATTERNS REFLECTED IN THE THEORETICAL CONSTITUTION OF THE FIELD

The two national variants of educational science whose emergence (in particular socio-historical settings) and structural elaboration (through the influence of diverse discourse coalitions) have been at the center of the analysis so far, have until recently defined the shape the field has taken on either side of the Rhine. German Pädagogik constituted during the Weimar Republic still preserves, in spite of considerable quantitative and qualitative changes, characteristic traits of its idiosyncratic hermeneutico-reflective style of theorizing. French sciences de l'éducation, in contrast, though not excluding profession-related practical reflection and hermeneutic reasoning, nevertheless show a characteristic preference for social scientific analysis and interdisciplinary study. If this interpretation is correct, the theoretical constitution of the field on one side or the other of the Rhine should mirror the disciplinary configuration of the two national variants of educational science. What follows is a description of some of the major research results from cross-national analyses of scholarly knowledge generated by French and German educationalists. Quite particularly, I shall refer to analyses that attempt to grasp the cognitive relations that are incorporated, in the form of citations, in the French and German educational discourse (for more comprehensive data and analyses, see Schriewer and Keiner 1993).

The rationale underlying this approach follows from analytical models worked out in recent sociology of science (Stichweh 1990 and, more particularly, Stichweh 1994, 52–83). These models are not meant to relativize the concept of *discourse coalition* introduced above to emphasize the socio-historical contingencies that favored or neutralized the consolidation of one or another type of educational discourse. They are, rather, complementary in that they focus on the intrinsically communicative character of science in general and of academic disciplines or fields of study in particular, with publications serving as the mode of communication specific to science. It is indeed publications that represent the basic communicative acts through which the self-regulating flow of a particular discipline's communication process is generated, continued, and reproduced. This is linked to the fact that by incorporating arguments developed in other publications into its own line of reasoning, that is to say, by making statements of its own and at the same time, referring to other authors' statements, each publication not only interacts with preceding ones, but in so doing invites re-actions and further publications. Thus, because it combines statement and ref-erence, proposition and quotation, any scientific publication displays an array of references that may then be analyzed for the cognitive affiliations, the theo-retical affinities, and the disciplinary preferences—or, in certain instances, also for the intellectual negations—to which these references give expression. On this basis, a citation analysis make it possible to grasp the cognitive affiliations woven between educationalists and the authors they prefer to cite, and in so doing, vest with intellectual authority. Furthermore, the reviewing and ranking of the most frequently cited authors make it possible to identify the theoretical stances and methodological options these authors represent, as well as their relative importance in the two national communities of educationalists. As a result, an analysis of the theoretical and epistemological filiations embedded in educational communication reveals the predominant theoretical profiles of the field on either side of the Rhine. In this way, a citation analysis, conducted both quantitatively and qualitatively, serves to reconstruct the largely divergent in-tellectual worlds within which, as if it were the most natural thing in the world, German and French educationalists have become accustomed to thinking, work-ing, and communicating among themselves.

The results of the citation analysis are listed in Tables 4.1 and 4.2. The quan-titative data these tables contain are based for Germany on textual analysis of thirty-two volumes of the *Zeitschrift für Pädagogik* (*German Educational Review*), a journal that until recently has been the most academic and most representative of German education journals. Since French education reviews unfortunately do not have name indexes, a series of alternative documents, con-sidered as functionally equivalent, have been chosen as relevant source material. These are a series of autobiographical portraits published from 1985 onward under the title of "Itinéraires de recherche" and "Itinéraires de lecture" in the journal *Perspectives documentaires en Sciences de l'éducation*. In a concise form, they make possible investigation of French educationalists' intellectual development and theoretical orientation. In what follows, the accumulated data in Tables 4.1 and 4.2 are interpreted in terms of four different analytical per-spectives, with a fifth one being taken up in the concluding section.

Concentration Versus Dispersion of Communicative Space

For Germany, Table 4.1 shows the ranking of those thirty-four reference au-thors who in their 2,104 citations make up the leading group out of thousands

Table 4.1
Ranking of the Authors Most Frequently Cited in the *Zeitschrift für Pädagogik,*
(German Educational Review)

		1955-1967					1955-1967	
		N	%				N	%
1	Spranger	157	26.6	1	Habermas		437	28.9
2	Flitner, Wilhelm	124	21.0	2	Klafki		173	11.4
3	Litt	56	9.5	3	Blankertz		159	10.5
4	Derbolav	39	6.6	4	Piaget		140	9.3
5	Schleiermacher	38	6.4	5	Flitner, Wilhelm		64	4.2
6	Pestalozzi	37	6.3	6	Kant		62	4.1
7	Dilthey	30	5.1	7	Humboldt		53	3.5
8	Nohl	29	4.9	8	Hentig		48	3.2
9	Weniger	26	4.4	9	Hegel		42	2.8
10	Humboldt	20	3.4	10	Mollenhauer		40	2.6
11	Meister	13	2.2	11	Ulich		33	2.2
12	Goethe	11	1.9	12	Brezinka		29	1.9
13	Rousseau	11	1.9	13	Albert		28	1.9
				14	Roth		25	1.7
	Total	591	100.0	15	Bloom		22	1.5
				16	Robinsohn		20	1.3
				17	Bollnow		19	1.3
				18	Schorr		19	1.3
				19	Pestalozzi		18	1.2
				20	Flechsig		17	1.1
				21	Flitner, Andreas		17	1.1
				22	Herrmann		17	1.1
				23	Scheuerl		16	1.1
				24	Lukesch		15	1.0
					Total		1513	100.0

of names quoted in the *Zeitschrift für Pädagogik* over a period of thirty-two years. In addition, the table makes it possible to compare two successive periods—the years between 1955 and 1967, which correspond to the phase of academic reconsolidation of the field after World War II, and the years between 1968 and 1986, a phase of strong expansion and intellectual modernization—thus emphasizing evolution of the field over time. Table 4.2 contains the corresponding ranking for educational sciences in France. It presents the leading group, identified on the basis of 455 citations, of those ninety-nine reference authors who stand out for frequency among a total of 941 authors quoted altogether in the form of 2,534 citations.

In connection with our examination, even these data, though more technical in nature, have an analytical value. Indeed, the ratio of the number of authors who are cited to that of corresponding citations gives a citations quotient that can be used as an indicator of the degree of concentration or dispersion respectively of the referential space peculiar to each of the two national variants of educational studies. For the thirty-four leading authors cited in the *Zeitschrift*

Table 4.2
Ranking of the Authors Most Frequently Cited in the French Educationists'
Autobiographical Outlines (*Itinéraires de recherche & de lecture*)

	N		N		N
Piaget, Jean	22	Debesse, Maurice	4	D'hainaut, Louis	3
Bourdieu, Pierre	13	Descartes, Rene	4	Fourastie, Jean	3
Durkheim, Emile	11	Dewey, John	4	François, Frederic	3
Wallon, Henri	11	Ferry, Gilles	4	Gide, Andre	3
Bachelard, Gaston	10	Foucault, Michel	4	Hegel, Georg W. Fr.	3
Freud, Sigmund	10	Girard, Denis	4	Huberman, A. Michael	3
Crozier, Michel	9	Hameline, Daniel	4	Husen, Torsten	3
Legrand, Louis	9	Hassenforder, Jean	4	Isambert-Jamati, V.	3
Rogers, Carl	8	Havelock, Ronald G.	4	Kuhn, Thomas S.	3
Freinet, Celestin	7	Kant, Immanuel	4	Langouet, Gabriel	3
Morin, Edgar	7	Lefebvre, Henri	4	Lapassade, Georges	3
Peretti, Andre De	7	Levi-Strauss, Claude	4	Leon, Antoine	3
Schwartz, Bertrand	7	Lewin, Kurt	4	Lerbet, Georges	3
Ardoino, Jacques	6	Marcuse, Herbert	4	Lobrot, Michel	3
Chomsky, Noam	6	Moreno, Jakob Levy	4	Martinet, Andre	3
Establet, Roger	6	Passeron, Jean Claude	4	Merleau-Ponty, M.	3
Mialaret, Gaston	6	Pieron, Henri	4	Miles, Matthew B.	3
Nietzsche, Friedrich	6	Popper, Karl	4	Milner, Jean-Claude	3
Rousseau, J.-Jacques	6	Quignard, Jacques	4	Monod, Gustave	3
Avanzini, Guy	5	Reuchlin, Maurice	4	Monod, Jacques	3
Baudelot, Christian	5	Valery, Paul	4	Moscovici, Serge	3
Bernstein, Basil	5	Zazzo, Rene	4	Pages, Max	3
Binet, Alfred	5	Atlan, Henri	3	Papert, Seymour	3
Bloom, Benjamin	5	Baudouin, Charles	3	Perrenoud, Philippe	3
Bruner, Jerome S.	5	Becker, Howard S.	3	Prigogine, Ilya	3
Claparede, Edouard	5	Benveniste, Emile	3	Romilly, Jacqueline	3
Friedberg, Erhard	5	Berge, Andre	3	Rosnay, Joel De	3
Illich, Yvan	5	Berger, Guy	3	Sartre, Jean-Paul	3
Marx, Karl	5	Bergson, Henri	3	Spinoza, Baruch	3
Prost, Antoine	5	Bresson, François	3	Touraine, Alain	3
Snyders, Georges	5	Chombard De Lauwe	3	Vasquez, Aida	3
Barthes, Roland	4	Coleman, James S.	3	Weber, Max	3
Boudon, Raymond	4	Culioli, Antoine	3	Wittwer, Jacques	3

für Pädagogik, this quotient is 1:62, which means that each of these thirty-four
eminent scholars or philosophers on average collects sixty-two citations on his
name. For the leading group of French authors cited, in contrast, the corresponding ratio is only 1:5. In other words, the average number of citations gathered
by each of the ninety-nine authors listed in Table 4.2 is less than five. Even if
we keep in mind the different nature of the German and French sources utilized,

the different ratios show that in Germany, disciplinary communication in education, despite a certain dispersion on the periphery, clearly centers around a compact kernel of almost unanimously acknowledged reference authors. As the frequency with which they are cited emphasizes, these authors represent, to a degree unknown on the other side of the Rhine, the quasi-natural center of educational communication. The French authors who are cited, in contrast, circumscribe citation space that is much less distinctly structured, displays average citation frequencies that are much lower, and fans out widely in consequence. The French figures in no way reveal the consolidation, so convincingly demonstrated by the German data, of a core of theoretical positions, but instead a net tendency toward theoretical dispersion. None of the French authors cited comes close to scores reached in German discourse by scholars such as Eduard Spranger, Wilhelm Flitner, Jürgen Habermas, Wolfgang Klafki, or Herwig Blankertz.

As these few names suggest, moreover, the compact kernel of the intellectual reference space of German Pädagogik is defined essentially by theoretical approaches inherent to the field. The citation scores reached by this group of authors represent positions characteristic of the particular style of hermeneutico-reflective theorizing widespread among German educationalists, and which—in the traditional form of "committed reflection" (Flitner) or in its more modern counterpart of "critico-constructive theorizing" (Klafki)—meets with large socio-communicative consensus. In France, by contrast, the most frequently cited authors do in no way represent the field of educational sciences proper. Instead, they are among the most visible and, in terms of theoretical progress, most advanced representatives of the social and human sciences, belonging to psychology, as in the case of Piaget and Wallon, or to sociology, in the case of Durkheim and Bourdieu.

Intra-Disciplinary Cohesion Versus Pluri-Disciplinary Opening

The last observations already indicate another dimension of analysis. With regard to the distinctive configuration of French and German educationalists' intellectual worlds, classification of cited authors by discipline is of as much interest as the quantitative aspects of concentration or dispersion studied before. Indeed, breakdown by discipline of all of the authors included in Tables 4.1 and 4.2 offers evidence of the extraordinary concentration of German educational discourse, at the level both of socio-communicative relations and of intellectual filiations, on the field of educational theory proper, and on its traditional philosophical foundation disciplines. Thus, an extremely high percentage of the German authors cited are affiliated with the educational sciences and with the broader tradition of educational thinking that goes beyond the boundaries of education as an academic discipline institutionalized in universities. This percentage, on the order of 61.4%, is even more impressive if we add the citation score of authors affiliated with historical and philosophical disciplines, namely

28.5%. The two groups taken together add up to about 90% of all citations of the authors who, because of their academic standing and theoretical prestige, delimit the intellectual profile of educational sciences in Germany. Moreover, among the representatives from the historical and philosophical disciplines thus distinguished, we largely find philosophers who, like Kant, Hegel, Dilthey or Habermas, have defined major stages in the development of German thought. The authors cited from social sciences, in contrast, carry much less weight with the intellectual composition of the field in Germany, the only exception being Piaget, who has attained an impressive citation score.

The French figures, on the other hand, show a largely inverse configuration. The share in the total of citations of authors affiliated with the educational sciences (including the tradition of the grand pedagogical classics) as well as with historical and philosophical disciplines amount to only one-third (21.3%) or even less than a quarter (6.6%) respectively of the German scores. These two percentages taken together do not equal even half of the share of those authors cited, who, at a rate of 58.7%, represent a wide range of human and social science disciplines. Among the authors from these disciplines, in sharp contrast with the citation space of German Pädagogik, the names of psychologists dominate: Jean Piaget, Henri Wallon, Alfred Binet, Edouard Claparède, Henri Piéron, Maurice Reuchlin, or René Zazzo—a group that represents the grand tradition of French psychology. Moreover, psychologists such as Wallon and Piéron, and also Mialaret, who later left psychology to dedicate himself to educational sciences, at the same time represent a scientific transformation through the experimental method of pedagogical concepts that originally emerged from the progressive education movement. They thus represent a successful synthesis between the reform tendencies in progressive education and experimental research in education and psychology—a synthesis whose German supporters, since the first decades of the 20th century, have in their majority been pushed out of the field by a Pädagogik consolidated around the philosophico-hermeneutic paradigm (Tenorth 1989). Finally, the ranking of French citations confirms an overall picture that has already emerged from previous analyses (Schriewer and Keiner 1992 and 1993): It is not intellectual traditions peculiar to the field that define the referential space of educational sciences in France, but instead a wide diversity of positions drawn from other disciplines, quite especially the human and social sciences.

Continuation of Intellectual Traditions Versus Production of Novel Knowledge

While throwing into relief the importance, for German educational discourse, of theoretical stances peculiar to the field, the ranking of the authors German educationalists particularly prefer also indicates the weight they attach to the field's grand intellectual traditions in comparison with current research. The ranking displayed in Table 4.1 reveals, in fact, the high scores attained by the grand philosophical and educational classics belonging to the era preceding the constitution of the modern system of university disciplines—Schleiermacher, Humboldt, Pestalozzi, or Rousseau—and by the academic heroes of the Weimar generation—Herman Nohl, Eduard Spranger, Wilhelm Flitner, Erich Weniger, and Theodor Litt, who endeavored to shape the Pädagogik institutionalized after World War I into an autonomous discipline.

The importance thus attached to the history of educational thinking reveals a peculiar program for pedagogical theory building. This program, on the one hand, positions itself in the original tradition of a "critique of historical reason" formulated by Wilhelm Dilthey. On the other hand, by means of a so-called historico-systematic style of reasoning, it is involved in the profession-related and action-oriented reflection that since Durkheim and Dilthey has been qualified as "practical theorizing." For this type of reflection, recourse to history does not primarily involve "perspectivism," that is, detached analysis that strives for historically contextualizing educational ideas and experiences of the past. Instead, recourse to history is performed with a view to reinterpreting past ideas and experiences from the standpoint of present-day preoccupations, making sure of the normative value and the allegedly trans-historical theoretical substance these are supposed to embody. This recourse, in other words, does not primarily mean historical research practiced in the manner of historians, but instead certain forms of "theoretical and normative traditionalization" (Tenorth 1976). Such forms may be directed, for example, toward reinterpreting educational models of the past with respect to needs or issues of the present as "promises which have not yet been realized"; toward constructing a normative consensus in the continuation of the philosophy of the Enlightenment; or toward the historical justification of forms of reflective reasoning purportedly appropriate to the very nature of education, and therefore supplied with particular authority. In this sense, the extensive recourse to intellectual traditions shown by the German citation scores not only underlines the importance that the history of educational and philosophical thinking have long assumed, and continue to assume, for educational theorizing in Germany, but it also attests to the importance that is systematically attached, in the context of hermeneutico-reflective reasoning, to the history of ideas.

It is true that classical authors have decreased in importance in comparison with contemporary educationalists during the more recent period, between 1968 and 1986. But the impressive citation scores attained by authors such as Wolfgang Klafki, Friedrich Bollnow, Herwig Blankertz, Klaus Mollenhauer, Ulrich Herrmann, or Hans Scheuerl—by authors, in other words, who are closely linked to the philosophico-hermeneutic tradition by both biography and theoretical training—illustrate the continuity, uninterrupted to the present day, of this type of reflection in Germany (Peukert and Scheuerl 1991).

The ranking of reference authors most frequently quoted in French educational journals displays exactly the opposite configuration. The classics representing either the grand tradition of the Western philosophy of education such as Rousseau, or the thought of progressive education such as Freinet, or the academic tradition of education as a university subject such as Durkheim, make up only a very modest group. Its modest size contrasts sharply with the massive block of authors who, be they educationalists or scholars from other disciplines, represent the current state of social science research and theory building. The rare references to philosophers such as Marx or Nietzsche to the French figures attest, point, in this context, to individual theoretical positions, and not, as in the German tradition, to a peculiar type of reflective theorizing that is specific to the field.

From Everyday Knowledge to Scientific Knowledge: Continuity Versus Rupture in Epistemological Reasoning

Oppositions similar to these contrasts between the French and German networks of cognitive filiations may be expected in the epistemological positions prevailing among educationalists on either side of the Rhine. In fact, until the end of the 1960s in Germany, Wilhelm Dilthey indisputably occupies first place among the most often cited epistemological authors. In France, this position is taken by Gaston Bachelard. His voice is reinforced by Emile Durkheim with respect to the positivist philosophy of science tradition, and by Karl Popper and Raymond Boudon, as far as the contemporary reformulation of this tradition along the lines of neo-positivism and analytical philosophy is concerned. The contrasts could not be greater. The program attempting to establish the study of man, history, and society on the model of historical and philological disciplines stands in opposition to the claims of scientific rationalism based on the model of the natural sciences. Dilthey's hermeneutic inductivism contrasts with the experimental logic of falsification supported by Bachelard. The philosopher of epistemological continuity is in conflict with the harbinger of "epistemological ruptures." In fact, whereas the former tried to establish his methodology for human and social studies on the assumption that there exists a gradual progression of knowledge, ranging from the concatenations of meaning rooted in everyday experience to systematic concept building, as is characteristic of science, the latter proclaimed the rupture between "common knowledge" and "scientific knowledge." Bachelard stands out, indeed, as the one philosopher who most firmly emphasized the distance between experiences made in the everyday social world and specifically scientific experiences that result from the methodical and reiterated interaction between conceptual construction and experimental evidence.

On the other hand, the rankings displayed by Tables 4.1 and 4.2 do not merely point to contrasting epistemological positions that contribute, in their turn, to shaping the intellectual traditions prevailing on one or the other side of the Rhine. These rankings make it possible also to trace, at least in the German case, an evolution over time. This evolution is not simply progressive; rather, it combines renewal and continuation. Thus, the period following the end of the

1960s marks the sudden entry, into German educationalists' discourse as well, of the orthodox philosophy of science, especially in the form of the hypothetico-deductive method developed by Karl Popper. The percentages attained by cited authors such as Hans Albert and Wolfgang Brezinka account for this entry on the meta-theoretical level, whereas in parallel the scores of authors such as Piaget, Ulich, Roth, Bloom, and Lukesch are manifestations of the growing importance of theories and methods linked with research-based social science approaches. Such evolutions point not only to a certain weakening of the traditions of philosophico-hermeneutic reflection, but also attest to a noticeable rapprochement of educational studies in Germany to the French configuration, that is, to a field of pluri-disciplinary social science research.

Evolutions such as these, nevertheless, remain limited in scope. The scores attained by the authors representing what has come to be termed the *social scientific turn* in German education, both on the level of epistemology and on that of substantive research and theory building, are limited to the mean values of the ranking. With the sole exception of Piaget, these authors remain far from top positions. These positions are taken by Jürgen Habermas and by authors who—like Wolfgang Klafki and Herwig Blankertz—borrowed substantial ideas from Habermasian philosophy and translated them with great success into German educationalists' communication processes. In view of the total number of citations attained, it is indeed Habermas and the overall system of philo-sophical reasoning and justification he represents, that occupy, for the period following 1968, the position previously taken by the philosophy of "intellectual life" developed by Dilthey. Moreover, the Habermasian scores, which consid-erably exceed those of any other author quoted, reveal their significance only if they are examined from the point of view of the correlation between continuity and change in a given field of academic study. These scores have indeed to be explained against the backdrop of the unique combination, epitomized by his works, of innovation (at the level of critical social philosophy) and continuation (in terms of historico-systematic reasoning). The extraordinary citation scores that Habermas manages to bring together do not really reflect, then, clearly delimited theoretical positions; rather, they delineate, as some scholars have quite rightly emphasized, a consensus-based zone of "liberal thought rooted in Enlightenment traditions" (Tenorth 1986, 52). This common ground of liberal thought presents itself to be combined with a good many other theoretical po-sitions deemed compatible: with the emancipatory ideas intrinsic to the phi-losophy of *Bildung* as well as with modern theories of socialization and communication; with the normative aspects involved by a field of reflective theorizing, which deliberately defines itself on the basis of its "social functions," as well as with expectancies toward a reinterpretation, adapted to present-day conditions of existence, of the "discourse of modernity."

Looked at from the point of view of the correlation between continuity and change, the French data also merit a closer examination. One can indeed iden-tify, among the French authors cited, theoretical positions representing to some

extent the same combination of innovation and continuation as that embodied
by Habermasian ideas in the German educational discourse. These are positions
that remain compatible with the French tradition of educational studies patterned
on the social science model, while at the same time pointing to evolutions likely
to redefine, at the height of current scientific thought, the field's theoretical and
epistemological foundations. In this sense, authors such as Edgar Morin, Henri
Atlan, Jacques Monod, Ilya Prigogine, and Joël de Rosnay attest an increasing
reception by French educationalists of research findings and conceptualizations
related to the "self-organization" paradigm. They represent, therefore, theoretical
options making it possible to transcend, from the perspective of an explicitly
trans-disciplinary "science of complexity," the unitary paradigm thus far inspired
by the natural sciences and neo-positivist philosophy of science.

AT THE END OF THE SECOND MILLENNIUM: GROWING CONVERGENCE OR PRESERVATION OF NATIONAL STYLES?

The major conclusion to be drawn from our examination of the theoretical
constitution of educational studies is that even now, French and German educationalists continue constructing theories, carrying through research, and organizing their debates in the context of largely divergent intellectual worlds.
These worlds, which are by and large accepted within each of the two national
communities, constitute structuring frameworks within which the general problems of any educational science are defined, conceptualized, and studied in diverse ways: deploying concepts such as *liberty* and *indeterminableness* of the
individual subject on one side of the Rhine, and concepts such as *hyper-
complexity* and *multidimensionality* of interrelationship-networks on the other.

Against the backdrop of such findings, the question arises: what reciprocal
exchanges or intellectual intersections exist between the French and German
variant of educational studies? In view of the largely divergent patterns followed
thus far, it is not surprising to see that such exchanges and intersections remain
quite limited. If zones of theoretical overlap do exist, they are organized around
a small number of philosophers representing the grand traditions of Western
philosophy, such as Rousseau, Kant, and Hegel, as well as, regarding current
theory building and research, around the works of Piaget. The latter even turns
out to be the one single author who is represented with equally important citation
scores in the intellectual worlds of both national communities.

Long-lasting blockades in the reciprocal reception of the intellectual traditions
of the Other have had a decisive responsibility in this mutual distance between
the French and German educational discourses. Because of the language barrier,
the theoretical and methodological incompatibilities, and the vicissitudes of politics, such as the two world wars, these reception blockades have contributed
not only to maintaining, but to reinforcing that distance. They thus have contributed also to strengthening the natural corollary of that distance, namely the

long-lasting persistence of the epistemological and philosophical frames of reference prevailing in each of the two intellectual worlds. Reception blockades of this order can actually be seen as specific manifestations of the potential for resistance which "the dominant academic groups, philosophical schools, or intellectual traditions generally oppose against those new ideas that they are unable to incorporate into their theoretical corpus, except at the cost of a more or less radical transformation of their own fundamental premises" (Pollak 1986, 671).

The epistemological authors preferentially quoted on one or the other side of the Rhine are perfect examples to illustrate such reception blockades. Thus, in France, the works of Dilthey that set out to provide methodological foundations specifically suited for the emerging disciplines focusing on the study of man, history, and society have, for decades, encountered complete incomprehension or even rejection by French social sciences rooted in positivist and Durkheimian traditions (Mesure 1990; for another deep-seated epistemological incompatibility of this sort, see the analyses by Hirschhorn 1988). Conversely, in the German— and, incidentally, Anglo-American—debates concerning the methodology or the history of science, there would have been no question, until recently, of "seriously adopting Bachelard's thought" (Lepenies 1989, 125).

Last but not least because of the long-term effects of such reception barriers— which obviously have parallels in other disciplines as well (see for philology, Espagne and Werner 1990)—the communication networks of French and German educationalists have been connected with the more general vicissitudes of communication between what Louis Dumont has described as two "national variants of modern ideology." One should keep in mind, therefore, that these variants not only took shape in a period in which communication between France and Germany, paved over with all sorts of difficulties and misunderstandings (Leenhardt and Picht 1990 [1989]), took on a truly "dramatic" aspect— that is, the decades between the end of the 19th century and the 1930s; the "French and German ideologies," going well beyond the domain of educational studies proper, have also represented two particularly conspicuous variants of the discourse of modernity (Dumont 1983, 115 ff.).

NOTES

1. An expression used to describe the decades following the victory of the Republican and left-wing parties in the elections held between 1876 and 1879 for the National Assembly and the Senate.

2. According to the title of the widely read analyses on *La réforme intellectuelle et morale* (Paris: Michel Lévy, 1871) authored by Ernest Renan after the French defeat in the Franco-German war of 1870–71.

3. "Délibérations de la Faculté des Lettres de Paris, 4 août 1883, "French National Archives, AJ16–4747*, pp. 98 ff.

4. "Direction de l'enseignement primaire. Note sur l'Enseignement de la Morale à l'Ecole publique, décembre 1912," Archives Nationales, F17–11630, pièce 121.

5. "Délibérations de la Faculté des Lettres de Paris," successive volumes covering the 1920s and 1930s, French National Archives, AJ16–4752* to 4756*.

REFERENCES

Bruch, R. vom. 1985. "Zur Historisierung der Staatswissenschaften. Von der Kameralistik zur historischen Schule der Nationalökonomie." *Berichte zur Wissenschaftsgeschichte* 8: 131–46.

Buisson, F. 1896. "Leçon d'ouverture du cours de Science de l'éducation, Faite à la Sorbonne le 3 décembre 1896." *Revue Internationale de l'Enseignement* 32: 481–503.

Depaepe, M. 1993. *Zum Wohl des Kindes. Pädologie, Pädagogische Psychologie und experimentelle Pädagogik in Europa und den USA 1890–1940.* Weinheim: Deutscher Studienverlag.

Drewek, P. 1996. "Die Herausbildung der 'geisteswissenschaftlichen' Pädagogik vor 1918 aus sozialgeschichtlicher Perspektive." *Zeitschrift für Pädagogik. Beiheft* 34: 299–316. Weinheim and Basel: Beltz.

———. "Educational Studies as an Academic Discipline in Germany at the Beginning of the 20th Century." In *History of Educational Studies.* Edited by P. Drewek, C. Lüth et al., 175–194.

Drewek, P., C. Lüth et al., eds. 1998. *History of Educational Studies. Geschichte der Erziehungswissenschaft. Histoire des Sciences de l'Education.* Paedagogica Historica, Vol. 3 of Supplementary Series. Gent, Belgium: C.S.H.P.

Dubief, H. 1976. *Le déclin de la Troisième République, 1928–1939.* Paris: Seuil.

Dumont, L. 1983. *Essais sur l'individualisme. Une perspective anthropologique sur l'idéologie moderne.* Paris: Seuil.

———. *Homo aequalis, II. L'idéologie allemande. France—Allemagne et retour.* Paris: Gallimard.

Durkheim, E. 1901. "Rôle des Universités dans l'Education sociale du Pays." In *Congrès International de l'Education sociale.* Paris, 26–30 septembre 1900. Paris: Alcan, 128–138.

———. "Nature et méthode de la pédagogie [1911]." In *Education et sociologie.* Paris: Presses Universitaires de France, 69–90.

———. *The Rules of Sociological Method.* Translated by W. D. Halls. (Originally published in 1895 as *Les règles de la méthode sociologique.*) New York: Free Press.

Espagne, M., and M. Werner, eds. 1990. *Philologiques I. Contribution à l'histoire des disciplines littéraires en France et en Allemagne au XIXe siècle.* Paris: Editions de la Maison des Sciences de l'Homme.

Glick, Th., ed. 1987. *The Comparative Reception of Relativity.* Boston Studies in the Philosophy of Science, 103. Dordrecht, the Netherlands, Boston: Reidel.

Harwood, J. 1992. *Styles of Scientific Thought. A Study of the German Genetics Community, 1900–1933.* Chicago: University of Chicago Press.

Hirschhorn, M. 1988. *Max Weber et la sociologie française.* Préface de Julien Freund. Paris: L'Harmattan.

Larson, G. J., and E. Deutsch, eds. 1988. *Interpreting Across Boundaries. New Essays in Comparative Philosophy.* Princeton, NJ: Princeton University Press.

Leenhardt, J., and R. Picht, eds. 1990. *Au jardin des malentendus. Le commerce franco-*

allemand des idées. Paris: Actes Sud. (German edition published in 1989 under the title of *Esprit/Geist. 100 Schlüsselbegriffe für Deutsche und Franzosen.* München and Zürich: Piper.)

Lepenies, W. 1985. *Die Drei Kulturen. Soziologie zwischen Literatur und Wissenschaft.* München: Hanser. (French translation 1991 as *Les Trois Cultures.* Paris: Editions de la Maison des Sciences de l'Homme.)

———. *Gefährliche Wahlverwandtschaften. Essays zur Wissenschaftsgeschichte.* Stuttgart: Reclam.

Lindenberg, D. 1990. *Les années souterraines (1937–1947).* Paris: Editions de la Découverte.

Marion, H. 1883. "Cours sur la Science de l'éducation. Leçon d'ouverture." *Revue Internationale de l'Enseignement* 6: 1259–1277.

Mesure, S. 1990. *Dilthey et la fondation des sciences historiques.* Paris: Presses Universitaires de France.

Monzie, A. de. 1939. "Une morale d'Etat." In *Encyclopédie Française* tome 15: Education et Instruction. Paris: Larousse, 40.12–13.

Müller, D. K., F. Ringer, and B. Simon, eds. 1987. *The Rise of the Modern Educational System: Structural Change and Social Reproduction 1870–1920.* Cambridge: Cambridge University Press; Paris: Editions de la Maison des Sciences de l'Homme.

Pädagogische Konferenz im Ministerium der geistlichen und Unterrichts-Angelegenheiten am 24. und 25. Mai 1917. Thesen und Verhandlungsbericht. Berlin, ca. 1917.

Peukert, H., and H. Scheuerl, eds. 1991. *Wilhelm Flitner und die Frage nach einer Allgemeinen Erziehungswissenschaft im 20. Jahrhundert.* Weinheim and Basel: Beltz.

Plé, B. 1996. *Die "Welt" aus den Wissenschaften. Der Positivismus in Frankreich, England und Italien von 1848 bis ins zweite Jahrzehnt des 20. Jahrhunderts. Eine wissenssoziologische Studie.* Stuttgart: Klett-Cotta.

Pollak, M. 1986. "Die Rezeption Max Webers in Frankreich. Fallstudie eines Theorietransfers in den Sozialwissenschaften." *Kölner Zeitschrift für Soziologie und Sozialpsychologie* 38: 670–84.

Ranieri, F. 1985. "Stilus curiae." *Rechtshistorisches Journal* 4: 75–88.

Ringer, F. 1992. *Fields of Knowledge. French Academic Culture in Comparative Perspective, 1890–1920.* Cambridge: Cambridge University Press; Paris: Editions de la Maison des Sciences de l'Homme.

Schriewer, J. 1998. "Etudes pluridisciplinaires et réflexions philosophico-herméneutiques: La structuration du discours pédagogique en France et en Allemagne." In *History of Educational Studies.* Edited by P. Drewek, C. Lüth et al., 57–84.

Schriewer, J., and E. Keiner. 1992. "Communication Patterns and Intellectual Traditions in Educational Sciences: France and Germany." *Comparative Education Review* 36: 25–51.

———. 1993. "Kommunikationsnetze und Theoriegestalt: Zur Binnenkonstitution der Erziehungswissenschaft in Frankreich und Deutschland." In *Sozialer Raum und Akademische Kulturen.* Edited by J. Schriewer, E. Keiner, and C. Charle, 277–341.

Schriewer, J., E. Keiner, and C. Charle, eds. 1993. *Sozialer Raum und akademische*

Kulturen/A la recherche de l'espace universitaire européen. Komparatistische Bibliothek/Vol. 3 of Comparative Studies Series. Frankfurt am Main: Peter Lang.

Sirinelli, J.-F. 1994. *Génération intellectuelle.* Paris: Presses Universitaires de France.

Stichweh, R. 1990. "La communication, l'évolution et la différenciation. Trois notions théoriques dans l'histoire des sciences." In *Philologiques I. Contribution.* Edited by M. Espagne and M. Werner, 189–209.

———. 1994. *Wissenschaft, Universität, Professionen. Soziologische Analysen.* Frankfurt: Suhrkamp. In particular chapter 2, pp. 52–83, on "Die Autopoiesis der Wissenschaft."

Tenorth, H.-E. 1976. "Geschichte und Traditionalisierung." *Bildung und Erziehung* 29: 494–508.

———. 1986. "Transformationen der Pädagogik—25 Jahre Erziehungswissenschaft in der 'Zeitschrift für Pädagogik.' " *Zeitschrift für Pädagogik* 20. Beiheft, pp. 21–85.

———. 1989. "Versäumte Chancen. Zur Rezeption und Gestalt der Empirischen Erziehungswissenschaft der Jahrhundertwende." In *Rekonstruktionen Pädagogischer Wissenschaftsgeschichte.* Edited by P. Zedler and E. König. Weinheim: Deutscher Studien Verlag, 317–343.

Troeltsch, E. 1917. "Schlusswort." In *Pädagogische Konferenz im Ministerium der Geistlichen und Unterrichts-Angelegenheiten am 24. und 25. Mai 1917.* Thesen und Verhandlungsbericht. Berlin, ca. 1917.

Wagner, P. 1990. *Sozialwissenschaften und Staat—Frankreich, Italien, Deutschland 1870–1980.* Frankfurt am Main/New York: Campus.

Wagner, P., and B. Wittrock. 1991. "States, Institutions, and Discourses: A Comparative Perspective on the Structuration of the Social Sciences." In *Discourses on Society. The Shaping of the Social Science Disciplines.* Edited by P. Wagner, B. Wittrock, and R. Whitley. (Sociology of the Sciences. A Yearbook. Vol. 15). Dordrecht, the Netherlands, Frankfurt am Main: Kluwer, 331–357.

Wittrock, B., P. Wagner, and H. Wollmann. 1991. "Social Science and the Modern State: Policy Knowledge and Political Institutions in Western Europe and the United States." In *Social Sciences and Modern States. National Experiences and Theoretical Crossroads.* Edited by P. Wagner et al. Cambridge: Cambridge University Press, 28–85.

PART II

SYSTEMIC GROWTH
AND EXPANSION

5

Equality of Opportunity: Expansion of European School Systems Since the Second World War

Bernd Zymek

DYNAMICS OF SOCIAL CHANGE AND EDUCATIONAL EXPANSION IN MODERN EUROPE

The expansion of European school systems since the Second World War is neither a new phenomenon in European history nor the mere result of a specific policy started by European governments after the war to promote equal opportunities. The expansion of European school systems since the Second World War must be seen instead as the continuation and acceleration of the long-term process of expansion, systematization, and structural change of the key institutions of modern educational systems that were established in the 19th century (Ringer 1979; Müller, Ringer, and Simon 1987). This process has been developing, sometimes more, sometimes less dynamically, in European countries. Indeed, the five decades since the Second World War have been an exceptionally long period of dynamic expansion.

This long-term expansion of school systems in Europe has not been an isolated development. In many respects, it has been linked to the process of economic and social change that was constantly transforming European societies throughout the 19th and 20th centuries. A historic review reveals a significant correlation between the increase of enrollment in institutions of secondary and higher education, and a long-term shift in employment from the agricultural to the industrial and to the service sector. These processes are linked to the decrease of traditional small enterprises—farms, handicrafts, shops—and the employment of a steadily increasing percentage of the population in larger and more formalized organizations and firms. The processes are also associated with the demographic trend in all industrializing societies of reducing the number of children per family, with urbanization and bureaucratization, with an increase in civil services, and with the expansion of the European welfare state.

The apparent correspondence of these long-term processes, which is reflected in the various historical statistics, simplifies and harmonizes the history of education and the social history of European countries. The expansion and structural change of educational systems has never been a mere reflection of an increasing demand for qualified labor in a changing economy. Far more important are the contributions of educational systems to master the social consequences of the permanent economic revolution. To obtain economic and social status, a steadily increasing number of families was forced to change from traditional strategies of social reproduction within the small world of the inherited family and the local community to modern strategies of social reproduction, which demand achievement by individuals in modern schools and modern means of employment. The increase in numbers of institutions of secondary and higher education enabled and fostered processes of social and geographic mobility, which an increasing percentage of the population was forced to adopt. It thus ensured the necessary social cohesion of the rapidly transforming European societies and their political legitimacy.

The more or less formalized connection between certificates granted by institutions of secondary and higher education and access to the upper levels of civil service, large firms, and an increasing number of professions limited the number in privileged social strata. At the same time it stimulated the aspirations of those who had been excluded so far. Contrary to a superficial but common prejudice that views educational systems as conservative and dependent on economic and political demands, the history of European educational systems and their institutionalized connection with the hierarchies of employment has proved them to be exceptionally dynamic and surprisingly resistant to political interventions. The demand in ever broader strata of European societies for higher education and the access to the upper levels of employment and the subsequent growth of enrollment in secondary and higher education were troubling to conservative politicians and professionals. These conservatives lamented the "unreasonable" aspirations of girls and of the lower classes, and prophesied the coming of an "academic proletariat" and political uproar. European history of the 19th and 20th centuries reveals that growth of the economy, development of different sectors of the labor market, an increased demand for secondary and higher education, the existence of institutional barriers, and dynamics in educational systems are by no means a prestabilized harmony but are mostly conflicting processes and the background to political and intellectual controversies (Kotschnig 1937; Barbagli 1974; Ringer 1979; Müller and Zymek 1987; Titze 1990).

These conflicts and debates often reveal an ambiguous attitude toward the foundations of modern European societies and culture. At the end of the 19th and beginning of the 20th centuries, the development of national systems of education characterized by universal standards that open up careers for gifted children from all social classes has been a crucial element in programs and debates in which liberal intellectuals and politicians criticized the social segregation and the systems of privilege and economic stagnation in traditional European societies. The focus was on strategies that free the talent, initiative, and productivity of the social classes whose members had been excluded.

European countries developed different strategies to realize this vision, a process of more than 100 years (Ringer 1979; Müller, Ringer, and Simon 1987; Lelièvre 1990; Schneider 1982; Harney and Zymek 1994). In England and the Netherlands, the early wealthy European societies and the forerunners of the European modernization, the initiative in education was seen as a right of families and of local or religious communities, who limited the influence of the central state legislature and its bureaucracies in this field. In Prussia, a developing country in those days, but also in the Scandinavian and the East European countries, the state and its bureaucracies were seen as the agent and warden in developing a national educational system. In many European countries—France, Belgium, Italy, Spain, Austria—the development of public educational systems had to be enforced against the opposition of the traditional educational systems of the Catholic Church and its international orders. Despite these conflicts, the further development and the steady systematization of national educational systems has become characteristic of European political culture. If a new political era is to start or an economic or social crisis to be overcome, the proclamation of programs and initiatives for expansion of the educational system has been a political option for politicians seeking to demonstrate political strength and vision. This has been the case, firstly for Liberals, later for Socialists, and finally, even for Conservatives (Fuller and Rubinson 1992).

MID-20TH-CENTURY EUROPEAN SCHOOLS

To understand the dynamics of the expansion of European school systems after the Second World War, it is necessary to remember the level from which this expansion started. In the late 1940s and even the early 1950s, about 80 to 90% of youth attended only elementary schools. The length of compulsory schooling varied from five to eight years in those days. In most European countries the majority of the population still lived in rural areas and villages where one teacher taught children in one classroom from the age of 6 to the age of 12 or 14. In the cities, which since the end of the 19th century have provided more developed and differentiated systems of compulsory schooling, more than forty pupils often were confined to a single classroom. Until the middle of the 20th century, elementary education of this kind was considered sufficient for the demands of the private, public, and working life of the great majority of the population.

In those days only 5 to 10% of the population attended schools that prepared them for access to institutions of higher education. The standards for graduation and the subjects that defined the general education of the educated man or woman in Europe were still dominated by the particular kinds of secondary schools developed in all European countries throughout the 19th century: the public schools and grammar schools in England, the *lycées* in France, the *Gymnasien* in Germany, the *licei classici* in Italy, and the *gymnasier* in Sweden. In addition to these classic types, modern secondary schools providing little Latin and no Greek but more modern languages, mathematics, and natural sciences had been developed in most European countries by the end of the 19th century. Traditionally, these secondary schools were exclusively for boys. Most European countries, however, had developed secondary schools for girls by the end of the 19th century. These schools steadily expanded, but academic studies and professional careers for woman remained an exception in those days. These secondary schools were for the European urban middle classes, who were able to pay fees and who wanted employment for their children in public service, in the bureaucracies of great firms, or in the traditional learned professions. However, less than half of the pupils who entered secondary schools at the age of 10 or 12 followed the full course until the age of 17 to 19 and graduated to the universities. The majority of the pupils left secondary schools at about 16 for employment, mainly in the service sector, or for further training in commercial or technical schools.

Between the mass of elementary schools and the relatively small but expanding group of secondary schools, there existed in all European countries in the middle of the 20th century a wide range of very different schools, which responded to specific regional, social, religious, and professional demands. The greater part of these schools consisted of traditional institutions; some were the result of school reforms of the first half of the century. They offered schooling beyond the level of traditional elementary education for members of the middle and upper classes who were able to pay fees and wanted to separate their children from those of the lower classes. Many of these schools were private schools of religious denominations and the Catholic orders; a great number were for girls. They offered schooling that reflected the regional, religious, and social milieu of the families. For some of their pupils, however, they provided preparation for the further transition to urban upper secondary schools. The same function was served by the many secondary schools with no upper-level classes, like the many traditional *collèges* in France found mostly in the smaller cities of rural areas. These schools prepared their students for occupations in the local area or for transition to upper secondary schools in the larger cities. Their number decreased, however, either because private owners did not maintain them or because these communal schools developed upper secondary classes.

In addition, some European countries had begun school reform aimed at raising the level of education of a broader stratum of the population and thus respond to the increasing demand for secondary education. Reform was planned, however, for schools without academic aspirations, those with a "modern" or "realistic" curriculum presumed to correspond to the demands of commercial and technical occupations on an intermediate level. Two models were to become strategies for the further development and expansion of traditional European school systems: on the one hand, advanced classes for gifted children in traditional elementary schools (for example, the *cours complimentaire* attached to primary schools in France, the *Modern Schools* in England, the *högre folkskolar* in Sweden, and the *Aufbauklassen an Volksschulen* in some states of Germany); on the other hand, a new, lower secondary school without upper classes, planned as the intermediate and expanding part of a tripartite school system—for example, the *Mittelschule*, later named *Realschule*, in some states of Germany; the *enseignement primaire superieure* (EPS) in France; some types of the Swedish *real skola*, the *Technical High School* in England (Prost 1992; Zymek 1997).

In the middle of the 20th century, European school systems provided a range of vertically segmented schools that corresponded to settings more or less segmented by region, religion, sex, and social group. Transition from one type of school to another was possible but in fact not very frequent. Most of the school programs discussed and reform acts passed throughout the first half of the century promoted a more systematic connection among the various institutions to open up opportunities for articulation from one level of the school system to the next. In some European countries—England, Sweden, France—even during the war, inquiries and discussions had been started, aiming at such a further structural reform of schools (Leschinsky and Mayer 1990).

POLITICAL, ECONOMIC, AND SOCIAL DYNAMICS OF THE POSTWAR PERIOD

It was a specific historical constellation after the Second World War that induced and furthered the dynamic expansion of European school systems. In East European countries and the eastern part of Germany—areas occupied by the Soviet army after the war and subsequently governed by Communist parties and Soviet advisers—radical school reforms were proclaimed by the late 1940s. These programs and subsequent initiatives for school reform pretended to abolish the so-called social class school system and to establish "united school" systems. This policy of school reform sought recognition as a crucial element of a universal strategy to promote opportunities for underprivileged "children of laborers and peasants." In the following years great efforts were made to expand school systems, not only to realize a policy for equal opportunity but also to ensure political loyalty and to provide enough qualified man power for the socialist economy (Shoup 1981; Baske 1987).

Memory of economic stagnation and civil wars in Europe after the First World War and confrontation with communist policy in East European countries led to a specific economic, social, and political strategy for Western Europe. The United States commitment to a European Reconstruction Program provided the necessary capital for a recovery of West European economies (Marshall Plan). It also implemented new forms and institutions of international cooperation such as the Organization for European Economic Cooperation, founded in 1948 and succeeded in 1961 by the Organization for Economic Cooperation and Development (OECD). On the one hand, the United States government and European governments wanted to get rid of the war economy with its planning and restriction. On the other hand, new policies for a liberal economy were inspired by the conviction that the renaissance of devastated European countries was not only a question of how to promote economic productivity and the restoration of international market relations. There was a broad consensus that economic growth was to be accompanied and intensified by the promotion of mass consumption, thus developing and expanding the inner market of European countries and copying, in a certain sense, the New Deal policies of the United States during the prewar years. In those days the Socialist and Social Democratic parties, as well as Liberal and Conservative politicians and economists in all West European countries, rejected a radical market policy and argued that economic growth and the development of democracy demanded a policy that would promote social security and raise the standard of living (Lutz 1989). The further development of the European welfare state system became the political philosophy and strategy of a hidden or open coalition of all in most Western European countries (Flora 1986 and 1987; Esping-Andersen 1990). The political coalitions, which had prepared and accompanied the Education Act of 1944 in England, as well as discussions and initiatives in Sweden at the same time, indicated that further development of the European welfare state was to include, sooner or later, development of educational systems.

This political strategy was justified and supported by the revival of Keynesian economic theory in the 1960s. According to this economic theory, the state is able to influence economic development and is urged to do so. By means of its budget policy, public investments, and legislation for development of the infrastructure, the state influences private investments, the labor market, and economic cycles. Consequently, the expansion of school systems, the abolition of fees for secondary and higher education, the provision of scholarships for gifted children of the lower classes, and the public promotion of scientific research programs were not viewed as a waste of taxes or as social charges that hinder economic productivity but as a public investment in further economic expansion. The analyses and guidelines published by the OECD in those days were inspired by this economic and political philosophy. These beliefs became the framework and the legitimization for expansion and structural change of European school systems in the 1960s and 1970s (Papadopoulos 1994).

Since the 1950s and inevitably into the 1960s, social dynamics and demands have put increasing pressure on political and administrative authorities. At the same time, a political and economic philosophy favorable to the expansion of European educational systems has offered a strategy for response. The worldwide economic crisis of the late 1920s and early 1930s, the inner conflicts, civil wars, and fascist revolutions in the 1930s, the devastations of the Second World War, and the misery of the postwar years characterized a period of stagnation and destruction in the economic and social history of more or less all European countries. This background and the new framework for economic and social recovery revolutionized the social structures of Europe throughout the postwar years. Millions had lost their lives. Millions of those who survived had lost their original homes, their property, and their occupation, and were unwillingly forced into geographic and social mobility. Economic recovery and expansion led to a period of accelerated structural change, particularly within the traditional sectors of agriculture and small-scale ownership. The social and economic effects of the war and of the postwar years were to change traditional attitudes toward the education of a large stratum of the population. In many European countries this became the structural background for the increasing social demand for secondary education in the 1950s. This development was aggravated by the baby boom most European countries experienced during the years of economic recovery after the war. Since the late 1950s, the political and administrative bodies responsible for educational planning in Europe had to face the question of how to answer to the increasing demand for secondary education and how to recruit teachers for increasing numbers of pupils.

OECD policies of the 1950s for economic growth and international cooperation did not include initiatives for educational reform. For the OECD, however, education was a crucial field from the very beginning. The first conference of the newly founded and enlarged international organization, "Economic Growth and Investment in Education," was held in Washington, D.C., in 1961 (OECD 1961). In the international community, arguments for the further development and expansion of educational systems, which were published in the preparatory papers and the "Reports and Conclusions" of this conference, were viewed as the incentive for educational expansion after the Second World War. Actually, growth of enrollment in secondary education had started earlier, a result of structural changes that transformed European societies. But the conference and the subsequent initiatives and papers of the OECD offered new arguments and new legitimization for public planning, investments, and structural reforms in education that were, so far, not part of European political culture. A state policy to provide universal educational institutions accessible to all was not only seen as a policy to guarantee civil rights, individual development, religious education, and social reproduction in a liberal and modern society. Since this conference, educational policy has become a policy for economic growth rather than predominantly a policy for cultural and social progress. The USSR's first successes in space technology, furthermore, seemed to indicate deficiencies in scientific research and preparatory scientific education in secondary schools of Western countries. Further economic growth seemed to demand a state-planned expansion of the educational systems (Hüfner and Naumann 1977, 1986).

INCLUSION, SYSTEMATIZATION, AND EXPANSION

A political slogan of the 1960s was promotion of equal opportunities by school reform. The pragmatic essence of the educational policy of those days, however, was to realize at least the old claim and promise of *secondary edu-*

cation for all. The great majority of the population and of academic experts in all European countries supported this policy in national parliamentary debates, apparently a response to social and economic demands. Public investments necessary for the development and dissemination of schools and for the recruitment of more teachers were made possible by economic growth in those days.

In the 1960s, *secondary education for all* meant: (1) replacing the juxtaposition of traditional elementary schools with secondary schools by a system of primary and secondary schools, (2) providing such schools not only in the cities but also in suburbs and rural areas, (3) fostering the inclusion of girls, and (4) including children of the so-far underprivileged social classes in the new institutions of lower and upper secondary education.

The great Swedish school reform act of 1962, which established the nine-year *grundskola* in Sweden; the law that installed the *scuola media* in Italy in 1962; the reform decree of 1963 in France, which initiated the progressive unification of the new *collèges*; the famous Circular 10/65 in England, which urged the Local Education Authorities to develop comprehensive schools; the "Mammoth Law" of 1968, which reformed the school system in the Netherlands—to mention only a few examples—suggest that the expansion of European school systems in the 1960s and 1970s was the result of a policy directed toward bringing about a comprehensive school system. Such an assessment overestimates the impact of isolated reform acts, underestimates the long duration of school reform processes, and idealizes an international tendency to equate the development of comprehensive schools with arguments for equal opportunity through school reform. There were, however, a lot of pragmatic reasons for the comprehensive system to become the major type of secondary school in most European countries in those days.

The 1970 Paris Conference on Policies for Educational Growth, organized by the OECD as a sequel to the 1961 Washington conference, fostered the idea of educational growth as a process initiated, planned, and enforced by politicians as managers. The conclusions of that conference declared that the "targets" for 1961 had been "in general terms accomplished, and significantly exceeded in the case of higher education," as if the goals of education were growth of productivity and the profits of an enterprise. This document went on to say: "The structure of this growth of education in the last decade was such that in many Member Countries a high proportion of the age-group in primary and secondary education were now enrolled" (OECD 1971, 136).

This statement of 1970, however, and the figures of secondary school enrollment in the OECD countries that were published shortly afterward (OECD 1974) reveal that the growth of enrollment in institutions of secondary and higher education in the 1960s could not have been initiated by school reform acts passed only a few years before. There are good reasons to interpret the school reform policy of the 1960s not as an incentive to expansion, but as a reaction to the dynamically increasing demand for secondary and higher education and the problems of the still existing and expanding traditional schools. There was no "freewheeling quantitative growth" in the 1960s and 1970s, as the OECD report for the Intergovernmental Conference of 1988 noted in those days in commenting on historic processes and its own philosophy (OECD 1989a, 26). The reform acts of the 1960s and 1970s were accompanied by endless political conflicts in all European countries over how to transform traditional institutions of elementary and secondary education into a modern system that could cope with increasing social demand for secondary and higher education.

The expansion of European school systems, an inevitable consequence of social dynamics during the postwar decades, which had great public support in those days, could not be put into practice as the equivalent of the further expansion and dissemination of traditional institutions of European education. It was neither realistic nor economical to set up the segregated institutions of traditional school systems everywhere in a country. The new historic step of expanding European school systems demanded comprehensive school structures flexible enough to adapt to diverse regional und urban environments. Consequently, various models of comprehensive or united secondary school systems were first established in rural areas and the new suburbs. Apart from all ideological arguments, the advantage of the comprehensive school system had proved itself in the East European countries some years before. The strategy of labeling all schools as part of a comprehensive or united system offered the opportunity to politicians to proclaim a radical school reform, to hide the still existing differences between the different regions and schools, and to develop schools pragmatically (Zymek 1997).

The controversial debates and political conflicts between defenders of the traditional institutions of secondary education and the advocates of the comprehensive system have attracted most of the public interest since the 1960s. Actually, implementation of comprehensive structures for pupils from 10 to 16 has been just one aspect of a universal strategy whereby political and administrative authorities seek to systematize a wide range of diverse educational institutions within sequentially structured levels. A number of traditional schools with specific tasks for specific groups was either abolished or integrated as a stream within the new structures.

The education of girls in schools separate from those for boys had been characteristic of traditional schools for the European upper and middle classes in the 19th and in the first half of the 20th century. The abolition of secondary schools just for girls and the introduction of coeducation of girls and boys in united school systems were an element in postwar school reforms in East European countries from the very beginning. In the 1960s and 1970s, more and more single-sex secondary schools for girls and boys in Western European countries were also transformed into mixed-sex schools. This aspect of school reform, which has been discussed ever since as a strategy to promote equal opportunities for girls (see chapter 8 by M. Sutherland) was supported for pragmatic reasons, too. In those days it was neither economical nor realistic to respond to the increasing demand for secondary education for girls, which has been heard since the 1950s, by further development and dissemination of traditional girls' schools.

The separation of schools for general education on the one hand and the institutions for technical or commercial education and vocational training on the other hand was another characteristic of school systems developed in European countries throughout the 19th century. In the 1960s the integration of general education and vocational training became a crucial aim of school reform strategies, first in the East European countries and later, in the Western European countries as well. A process of continuous experimentation was started, which aimed to put this project into practice. In fact, more and more European countries have set out to integrate elements of technical education into the curriculum of general education schools and to classify the traditional institutions for technical, commercial, and vocational training as a formal equivalent branch of the upper secondary school level (European Commission 1995; Lasonen 1996).

These reforms were crucial aspects of the strategy found in all European countries throughout the postwar decades: to develop and to define the framework of a more systematized national school system legally. This long-term project was realized in different ways in Europe. In the East European countries with Communist governments, the proclamation of reform acts involving the whole educational system was to demonstrate the new political and ideological unity of the Communist Party and the so-called working class, which was identified with the mass of the population. The school reform acts expressed the pretense of being able and willing to plan and achieve societal progress through centralized political leadership and centralized bureaucracies. In the Western European countries such ambitions conflicted with liberal traditions and democratic constitutions. Nevertheless, some European countries have a tradition of a strong, centralized state—for example, France and the former German states that became *Länder* in the Federal Republic of Germany. This includes a tradition of defining more and more details of a universal educational system, such as institutions, curriculum, examinations, certificates, teachers, and funding. In other European countries, such as Norway, Sweden, and Italy, the development of a centralized school system became an important mechanism for forging a cohesive nation out of a dispersed population, and thus founding a national tradition.

In the 1960s and 1970s the tendency in modern Europe to develop universal structures in an educational system was pushed to a new level of systematization and bureaucratization. School reform acts had so far regulated only aspects of the field: compulsory schooling, funds for the communities to provide elementary schools, secondary schools for boys and later for girls, standards for examinations, and teacher training. Many of the school reforms passed in the 1960s and 1970s now made educational systems uniform. Even in European countries with a tradition of decentralized and community-centered schools such as the Netherlands, England, and Denmark, the framework of general regulations for the competencies of local or religious communities, the funding of public and private schools, the articulation between different institutions, and the training, status, and payment of teachers were defined in school reform acts.

The initiatives for reform acts defining the elements of a national school system, the attempts to integrate the formerly dispersed institutions within a new legislative framework, and the activities and institutions for international cooperation and comparison favored the development of rather general structures in transforming school systems. The terminology of primary and lower/upper secondary schools was about to replace the traditional names that characterized institutions and structures of the different national school systems, not only in reports and statistics of international organizations such as UNESCO and the OECD, but also in official documents of the national parliaments and bureaucracies. It often happened that traditional names for a specific group of schools became the name of a level in the restructured school systems. In France, for example, the new lower secondary level of the transformed school system was named *collège*, the new upper secondary level was now labeled *lycée*. The European school systems officially were transformed from vertically segregated schools of very different function and value to schools providing a wide range of opportunities for transition from one level to the institutions or specific branches of the next.

This new terminology of primary, lower secondary, and upper secondary schools became the measuring instrument according to which the expansion of European educational systems was recorded and compared. With respect to those general indicators, there has been an impressive growth: most European countries have prolonged compulsory schooling to the age of 16 (OECD 1989b). However, more and more young people are extending their schooling, young women as well as young men. By the end of the 1980s, the enrollment of young people in full-time education at the age of 18 had risen to 79.7% (girls 77.6%) in Germany; 76.2% (69.1%) in Switzerland; 71.4% (69.2%) in the Netherlands; 72.6% (74.8%) in Norway; 70.4% (73.2%) in France; 67.9% (67.9%) in Denmark; 52.5% (54.8%) in Sweden; 52% (52.9%) in Ireland; and 50.5% (43.2%) in Spain (OECD 1993, 94).

EXPANSION, DIFFERENTIATION, COMPETITION

There are still many conservative commentators who lament the expansion of European school systems as the result of misguided policy and the surrender of traditional standards of quality and competition. On the other hand, a review by those who had promoted a policy of equal opportunity through school reform shows the results of the expansion to be rather disappointing, for it shows "persisting inequalities" (Coombs 1985, 211; Shavit and Blossfeld 1993; see also Müller and Haun 1994). Critics on both sides, however, miscalculate the effects of policies for equal opportunities and the expansion of the European school systems in the last three decades because they neglect to note the social effects of structural transformations that took place within the expanding school systems.

The introduction of comprehensive structures on the level of lower secondary schools in most European countries has by no means meant implementation of undifferentiated forms of schooling for all children in the age groups in question. From the very beginning, the implementation and the development of comprehensive schools have led to a never-ending process of experimentation, evaluation, reform, and re-reform of orientation, of streaming and setting, of tracking, and of curriculum. This has been true not only for the comprehensive schools in Western European countries (Leschinsky and Mayer 1990; Dahmen et al. 1984) but also for the development of the "united school" systems in the East European countries under Communist governments (Anweiler and Kuebart 1984; Anweiler 1986). Recent studies on differentiation and selectivity of East European school systems reveal that the communist school systems guaranteed the social reproduction of new elites in these countries very well (Shavit and Blossfeld 1993). The establishment of comprehensive schools proved to be not the only and not even the crucial factor to stimulate a dynamic increase of aspirations for upper secondary and higher education. The same process happened in countries that had retained traditional differentiation at the lower secondary level. In the Federal Republic of Germany, for example, the policy of maintaining the tripartite system resulted in an unplanned expansion of the former elite model of secondary school, the Gymnasium, which today enrolls the majority of the pupils on this level (Köhler 1992).

Diagrams published by national ministries of education show that national school systems in Europe are primarily characterized by universal structures. These diagrams, however, disguise a crucial separating line in most European countries: the differences between the state sector and the private sector of national school systems. In 1985, 72% of enrollment in secondary schools in the Netherlands, 68% in Ireland, 65% in Belgium, 35% in Spain, 22% in France, 14% in Denmark, 8% in the United Kingdom, Portugal, and Luxembourg, 7% in West Germany, 6% in Italy, and 4% in Greece came under institutions operated by private associations (UNESCO 1989; see also Eurydice 1996). Religious denominations and orders are very often the proprietors of European private schools. Most private schools obtain funds from the state and therefore have to adapt to the curriculum of national schools. These schools offer, however, a religious, cultural, and social homogeneity of pupils, teachers, family background, and school life that makes them attractive in comparison with the cultural and social lack of homogeneity of state schools and the problems they entail. Thus, the role of the private schools in strategies for social and cultural reproduction is far more important than the figures of the statistics indicate. Recent studies in France, for example, reveal that more than 40% of pupils attend private schools for at least some time during the course of their school career. More and more French families are switching their children from state schools to private schools and back, as if they were "zapping" TV programs (Langouet and Leger 1994). The development of the private schools, which has been fostered by legislation, funding, and integration of the school systems in a number of European countries throughout the last decades, has counterbalanced the expansion of comprehensive schools. It has enabled the upper and middle classes to accept integration of the traditional secondary schools into the new universal and comprehensive secondary school structures. The process of transformation from communist to more open societies in the East European countries, which is still continuing today, is likely to bring about an important private school sector in these countries, too (Walford 1989; Himmel 1996).

On the level of the upper secondary schools, even more differentiated structures than on the lower secondary level have developed (European Commission 1995; Lasonen 1996; Klemm and Rolff 1988; Anweiler and Hearnden 1983). This has fundamentally changed the ways and methods of competition and social selection within European schools. The traditional school systems in most European countries provided schools with a compulsory curriculum for all students. The crucial point in the selection process was whether a pupil dared to aspire to the more demanding schools, not the question of whether an individual had access to a particular type of school or the way admission was organized. The inclusion of girls in secondary schools, the transformation of the traditional sex segregation in secondary schools to coeducational systems, the integration of technical and commercial streams and vocational training in general education, and the widened opportunities for individual profiles transformed traditional methods of competition between the sexes and social classes. Nevertheless, the cultural and social background of the family has become even more important in helping students develop strategies to succeed within the specific structures of national educational systems and in influencing them to avoid the choice of subjects and streams that might lead to an impasse (see chapter 7 by Marie Duru-Bellat and Agnès van Zanten).

The new comprehensive structures and the new forms of differentiation and flexibility have even changed the prestige of different subjects in the schools. Traditionally, Latin, literature, philosophy, and foreign languages were the most prestigious subjects of European secondary schools and were used to distinguish among the abilities of the elite of the students. The direct competition between girls and boys in secondary schools produced new hierarchies and profiles of subjects: girls now occupy the first ranks in the most prestigious subjects of yesterday; mathematics and natural sciences have become the profiling subjects of the best male students. Within the institutions and branches of general education on the upper secondary level and even on the level of higher education, girls have become a majority; the boys tend more and more toward the applied sciences, toward technical and commercial schools, toward vocational training programs and engineering colleges. This tendency, first recognized in East European countries such as Poland and Czechoslovakia in the 1970s, is nowadays to be seen in Western European countries, too.

There are, however, highly competitive systems of transition from the institutions of secondary education to higher education in most European countries. To succeed in these times of transition—for example, in the *classes préparatoires* and the *concours* for the *grandes écoles* in France, or in the English university and college admission system, and in the matriculation from secondary to higher education in the former East European countries—it is not enough to be a gifted student with a record of good achievement. Those systems demand a particular family background and culture, which will foster the necessary academic aspirations, lead to the right choices, prepare in the right way, use the right words, and behave in the right manner. This background, in other words, will provide intimate knowledge of the official and hidden structures of the educational system and the labor market.

These structural transformations and continuities have preserved the basically exclusive character of higher education and the social hierarchies in European societies, despite the increase of enrollment and the opening up of secondary education that has happened in Europe throughout the last decades.

THE EXPANSION OF EUROPEAN SCHOOL SYSTEMS AND THE EMPLOYMENT CRISIS

The new relationship between school systems and employment, which developed in the late 1970s, has also had an impact on competition between the sexes and between social classes in European schools. In politics and in the social sciences, four approaches attempt to explain the fact that an increasing number of dropouts in all European countries cannot find employment:

1. Politicians are constantly propagating the idea that the unemployment of school dropouts is a short-term problem, an accompaniment to economic cycles, which will be overcome with the next boom or with the next step of structural change and modernization of the economy.

2. Historians, economists, and sociologists have, however, shown that the expansion of school systems has brought about an increasing number of more highly qualified dropouts but has not been accompanied by a similar increase in adequate jobs. The policy of equal opportunity would necessarily end in great disappointment for the group who have graduated from the expanded institutions of secondary and higher education since the 1980s ("la generation abusé," Bourdieu 1979).

3. In opposition to those who criticize the politics of equal opportunity and the expansion of school systems, sociologists and economists have pointed out that the increasing number of higher-qualified secondary school leavers and university graduates has already changed the structure of employment and the hierarchies within firms. All statistics prove that achievement in secondary schools and universities is not useless. Graduates have better opportunities to find employment and are rarely unemployed. The graduates, however, thrust aside the less qualified. The early school leavers and people without vocational training are the losers in the global process (Blossfeld 1983).

4. The most radical and disillusioning vision is formulated by those who forecast the end of a specific period of the history of modern industrialized Europe, which has been characterized so far by the pretense of providing employment for all who desire it. In the future only a minority of 50% or even 20% will be able to attain occupations in the traditional sense, the majority being forced to switch between jobs and unemployment (Dahrendorf 1994; Rifkin 1995).

Thus, expansion of European educational systems in the last decades and recent structural changes in the world economy that result increasingly in a lack of employment have brought about a new constellation in the educational and social history of Europe. Increasing difficulties in finding employment force more and more young people to extend schooling and even to attend one of the diverse institutions of postsecondary education, hoping to improve in this way their opportunities on the narrowing labor market. This phenomenon induces a constantly fed-back expansion of educational systems. Under these circumstances school systems are going to change their character. In the future, secondary schools and tertiary institutions will not just be a place where pupils acquire learning that leads to employment and social status. The majority of the schools, even the vocational training schools, will probably become more and more a refuge for those who cannot find employment or for the unemployed who want to get at least the status of a student hoping for a new engagement.

The expansion of European school systems throughout the last decades alleviated the pressure on politicians to reduce inequalities and to promote more opportunities for employment (Shavit and Blossfeld 1993, 22). However, there is much evidence that the policy of expansion and systematization of the national school systems, which had been a political option for reform since the 19th century, cannot be continued. The new perspective of educational policy, which is proclaimed by more and more national and international bodies since the 1980s, is the decentralization and reparticularization of universal structures of education and employment, which had been developed in Europe since the 19th century. The policy of deregulation and decentralization is urgent not only for the postcommunist East European countries in their strategies of transformation to liberal societies; the same policy is said to be inevitable for Western European countries, too.

There is much evidence that the educational and social history of all European countries has come to a turning point (Harney and Zymek 1994). Nobody seeks a continuation of the strategy for expansion of educational systems through the development of universal structures; politicians and most experts, however, would like to see decentralized systems of schooling adjusted to the demands of the regional economy (see chapter 6 by François Orivel). Consequently, the slogans of educational policy have changed since the 1980s. It is no longer "equal opportunities for all children" but more choice, more variety, more flexibility, more adjustment of schools to the demands of a changing economy and the principles of the market (OECD 1989a, 1). Public discussions and research programs no longer focus on the question of how to raise the general level of achievement and the output of national school systems, but instead on the question of how to identify the "good schools" (OECD 1989c, 3). The annual publication of a ranking of secondary schools, which has taken place in England and France for several years, introduces new forms of competition and new hierarchies within secondary schools. At the same time, they reveal that the expansion of secondary school systems throughout the last decades has not weakened the impact of the traditional elite schools (Lawton 1989; Le Monde de l'Education 1997).

Today, a series of contradictions characterize the role and the future development of European school systems. Education and educational certificates have become more important than ever in finding employment; at the same time, the opportunities of those who graduate are more uncertain than ever. Within the official framework of national school systems, the gap between those schools that seem to provide occupational opportunities and those that apparently do not is widening, with the result of a development of new hierarchies within European school systems that sometimes reaffirm traditional positions. There is a "growing overlap" between the institutions of education and those of the economy, new measures of "school-to-work-transition," new "competition from new types of education and training institutions, including private enterprises." People without formal education and vocational training risk being marginalized; however, with regard to the labor market, "education is less synonymous than ever with schooling" (OECD 1989a, 18).

REFERENCES

Allmendinger, J. 1989. "Educational Systems and Labor Market Outcomes." *European Sociological Review* 54: 231–250.

Anweiler, O., ed. 1986. *Staatliche Steuerung und Eigendynamik im Bildungs—und Erziehungswesen Osteuropäischer Staaten und der DDR*. Berlin: Berlin-Verlag.

———. 1996. *Bildungssysteme in Europa. Entwicklung und Struktur des Bildungssystems in zehn Ländern: Deutschland, England, Frankreich, Italien, Niederlande, Polen, Rußland, Schweden, Spanien, Türkei*. Weinheim und Basel: Beltz.

Anweiler, O., and A. G. Hearnden, eds. 1983. *From Secondary to Higher Education*. Köln: Böhlau.

Anweiler, O., and F. Kuebart, eds. 1984. *Bildungssysteme in Osteuropa—Reform oder Krise*. Berlin: Berlin-Verlag.

Bach, U. 1977. *Bildungspolitik in Jugoslawien 1945–1974*. Darstellung und Dokumentation. Wiesbaden: Harrassowitz.

Baske, S. 1987. *Bildungspolitik in der Volksrepublik Polen 1944–1986*. 2 vol. Berlin: Harrassowitz.

Baske, S., M. Benes, and R. Riedel. 1991. *Der Übergang von der Marxistisch-leninistischen zu einer freiheitlich-demokratischen Bildungspolitik in Polen, in der Tschechoslowakei und in Ungarn*. Berlin: Dunker und Humblot.

Barbagli, M. 1974. *Disoccupazione intellettuale e sistema scolastico in Italia*. Bologna: Il mulino.

Bereday, G.Z.F. 1968. "School Systems and the Enrollment Crisis: A Comparative Overview." *Comparative Education Review* 12: 126–138.

Blossfeld, H.-P. 1983. "Höherqualifizierung und Verdrängung—Konsequenzen der Bildungsexpansion in den siebziger Jahren." In *Beschäftigungssystem im gesellschaftlichen Wandel.* Edited by M. Haller and W. Müller. Frankfurt am Main/New York: Campus, 185–240.

Bourdieu, P. 1979. *La distinction. Critique sociale du jugement.* Paris: Minuit.

Coombs, P. H. 1985. *The World Crisis in Education. The View from the Eighties.* New York/Oxford: University Press.

Dahmen, K., D. Breitenbach, W. Mitter, and H.-H. Wilhelmi, eds. 1984. *Gesamtschulen in Europa.* Ergebnisse eines Kolloquiums/Comprehensive Schools in Europe. Conclusion of a European Colloquy. Köln/Wien: Böhlau.

Dahrendorf, R. 1983. *Wenn der Arbeitsgesellschaft die Arbeit ausgeht.* In *Krise der Arbeitgesellschaft? Verhandlungen des 21. Deutschen Soziologentages in Bamberg 1982.* Edited by J. Matthes. Frankfurt am Main/New York: Campus.

Esping-Andersen, G. 1990. *The Three Worlds of Welfare Capitalism.* Cambridge: Cambridge University Press.

European Commission. 1995. *Structures of the Education and Initial Training Systems in the European Union.* Brussels/Luxembourg: European Commission.

Eurydice (editor for the European Commission). 1996. *Formen und Status des privaten und nicht-staatlichen Bildungswesens in den Mitgliedsstaaten der Europäischen Gemeinschaft.* Brussels: European Commission.

Flora, P., ed. 1986. *Growth to Limits. The Western European Welfare States Since World War II.* Vol. 1: Sweden, Norway, Finland, Denmark. Vol. 2: Germany, United Kingdom, Ireland, Italy. Berlin/New York: de Gruyter.

Flora, P., et al. 1987. *State, Economy, and Society in Western Europe 1815–1975.* A Data Handbook in two Volumes. Vol. 1: The Growth of Mass Democracies and Welfare States. Vol. 2: The Growth of Industrial Societies and Capitalist Economies. Frankfurt am Main/London/Chicago: Campus.

Fuller, B., and R. Rubinson, eds. 1992. *The Political Construction of Education. The State, School Expansion, and Economic Change.* New York: Praeger.

Harney, K., and B. Zymek. 1994. "Allgemeinbildung und Berufsbildung. Zwei konkurrierende Konzepte der Systembildung in der deutschen Bildungsgeschichte und ihre aktuelle Krise." *Zeitschrift für Pädagogik* 40: 403–422.

Himmel, B. 1996. "Private Schulen in der Tschechischen Republik zwischen Euphorie und Ernüchterung." *Bildung und Erziehung* 49: 57–70.

Hüfner, K., and J. Naumann. 1977. *Konjunkturen der Bildungspolitik in der Bundesrepublik Deutschland.* Vol. 1: Der Aufschwung (1960–1967). Stuttgart: Klett.

———. 1986. *Hochkonjunktur und Flaute: Bildungspolitik in der Bundesrepublik Deutschland 1967–1980.* Stuttgart: Klett.

Husén, T., and T. N. Postlethwaite, eds. 1994. *The International Encyclopedia of Education.* 2d ed. Oxford/New York/Tokyo: Elsevier Science.

Klemm, K., and H.-G. Rolff. 1988. *Der heimliche Umbau der Sekundarschule.* In *Jahrbuch der Schulentwicklung. Daten, Beispiele, Perspektiven.* Band 5. Edited by H. G. Rolff et al. Weinheim/München: Juventa, 75–102.

Köhler, H. 1992. *Bildungsbeteiligung und Sozialstruktur in der Bundesrepublik. Zu Stablilität und Wandel der Ungleichheit von Bildungschancen.* Berlin: Max-Planck-Institut für Bildungsforschung.

Kotschnig, W. M. 1937. *Unemployment in the Learned Professions. An International Study of Occupational and Educational Planning*. London: Humphrey Milford.

Langouet, G., and A. Leger. 1994. *École publique on école prive. Les zappeurs d'école*. Paris: Fabert.

Lasonen, J., ed. 1996. *Reforming Upper Secondary Education in Europe. Surveys of Strategies for Post-16 Education to Improve the Parity of Esteem for Initial Vocational Education in Eight European Educational Systems*. Jyväskyla: University Press.

Lawton, D., ed. 1989. *The Education Reform Act: Choice and Control*. London: Hodder & Stroughton.

Lelièvre, C. 1990. *Histoire des Institutions Scolaire (1789–1989)*. Paris: Nathan.

Leschinsky, A., and K.-U. Mayer, eds. 1990. *The Comprehensive School Experiment Revisited: Evidences from Western Europe*. Frankfurt am Main/Bern/New York/ Paris: Lang.

Lutz, B. 1989. *Der kurze Traum immerwährender Prosperität. Eine Neuinterpretation der industriell-kapitalistischen Entwicklung im Europa des 20. Jahrhunderts*. Frankfurt am Main/New York: Campus.

Mitter, W. 1983. "Schulreform in Osteuropa." In vol. 8 of *Enzyklopädie Erziehungswissenschaft*. Stuttgart: Klett-Cotta, 356–372.

Le Monde de l'Éducation, de la Culture et de la Formation. 1997. *Les résultats des lycées aux baccalauréats généraux, technologiques et professionnels en 1996*. Hors-Série–March. Paris: Le Monde.

Müller, D. K., and B. Zymek. 1987. *Sozialgeschichte und Statistik des Schulsystems in den Staaten des deutschen Reiches, 1800–1945*. Datenhandbuch zur deutschen Bildungsgeschichte, vol. 2, 1. Göttingen: Vandenhoeck & Ruprecht.

Müller, D. K., F. Ringer, and B. Simon, eds. 1987. *The Rise of the Modern Educational System. Structural Change and Social Reproduction, 1870–1920*. Cambridge: Press Syndicate of the University of Cambridge.

Müller, W., and D. Haun. 1994. "Bildungsungleichheit im sozialen Wandel." *Kölner Zeitschrift für Soziologie und Sozialpsychologie* 46: 1–42.

OECD. 1961. *Economic Growth and Investment in Education*. Paris: OECD.

———. 1971. *Educational Policies for the 1970's. General Report for the Conference on Policies for Educational Growth, Paris, 3rd–5th June, 1970*. Paris: OECD.

———. 1975. *Educational Statistics Yearbook, Vol. I, 1974, International Tables, Vol II, 1975. Country Tables*. Paris: OECD.

———. 1981. *Educational Statistics in OECD Countries, Statistiques de L'Enseignement dans les Pays de L'OCDE*. Paris: OECD.

———. 1989a. *Education and the Economy in a Changing Society*. Paris: OECD.

———. 1989b. *Education in OECD Countries. 1986–1987: A Compendium of Statistical Information*. Paris: OECD.

———. 1989c. *Schools and Quality*. Paris: OECD.

———. 1991a. *Education in OECD Countries. 1987–1988: A Compendium of Statistical Information*. Paris: OECD.

———. 1993. *Education in OECD Countries. 1988/1989, 1989/1990: A Compendium of Statistical Information*. Paris: OECD.

———. 1996. *The European Reconstruction, 1948–1961. Bibliography on the Marshall Plan and the Organization for European Economic Cooperation (OEEC)*. Paris: OECD.

Palomba, D. 1988. *Scuola e Societa in Italia nel Secondo Dopoguerra. Analsi di una progressiva convergenza*. Roma: Ateneo.

Papadopoulos, G. S. 1994. *Education 1960–1990. The OECD Perspective*. Paris: OECD.

Prost, A. 1992. *Education, société et politiques. Une histoire de l'enseignement en France de 1945 á nos jours*. Paris: Seuil.

Rifkin, J. 1995. *The End of Work*. New York: Putnam.

Ringer, F. 1979. *Education and Society in Modern Europe*. Bloomington/London: Indiana University Press.

Robinsohn, S. B. et al. *Schulreform im gesellschaftlichen Prozeß. Ein interkultureller Vergleich. Vol. 1. 1970. Bundesrepublik Deutschland, Deutsche Demokratische Republik, Sowjetunion. Stuttgart, Vol. 2 1975. England and Wales, Frankreich, Österreich, Schweden*. Stuttgart: Klett.

Scheipl, J., and H. Seel. 1988. *Die Entwicklung des österreichischen Schulsystems in der Zweiten Republik, 1945–1987*. Graz: Leykam.

Schneider, R. 1982. "Die Bildungsentwicklung in den Europäischen Staaten 1870–1975." *Zeitschrift für Soziologie* 2: 207–226.

Shavit, Y., and H.-P. Blossfeld, eds. 1993. *Persistent Inequality. Changing Educational Attainment in Thirteen Countries*. Boulder: Westview.

Shoup, P. S. 1981. *The East European and Soviet Data Handbook. Political, Social and Development Indicators, 1945–1975*. New York: Columbia University Press.

Stoer, S., and R. Dale. 1987. "Education, State, and Society in Portugal, 1926–1981." *Comparative Education Review* 31: 400–418.

Titze, H. 1990. *Der Akademikerzyklus. Historische Untersuchungen über die Wiederkehr von Überfüllung und Mangel in akademischen Karrieren*. Göttingen: Vandenhoeck & Ruprecht.

UNESCO. 1989. *Division of Statistics on Education. Development of Private Enrollment. First and Second Level Education, 1975–85*. Paris: UNESCO.

Walford, G. 1990. *Privatization and Privilege in Education*. London: Routledge.

Walford, G., ed. 1989. *Private Schools in Ten Countries: Policy and Practice*. London: Routledge.

Wickham, A. 1980. "National Educational Systems and the International Context: The Case of Ireland." *Comparative Education Review* 24: 323–337.

Wulff, K. R. 1992. *Education in Poland, Past, Present and Future*. London: University Press of America.

Zymek, B. 1997. "Die Schulentwicklung in der DDR im Kontext einer Sozialgeschichte des Deutschen Schulsystems. Historisch-vergleichende Analyse lokaler Schulangebotsstrukturen in Mecklenburg und Westfalen, 1900–1990." In *Bildungsgeschichte einer Diktatur. Bildung und Erziehung in SBZ und DDR im historischgesellschaftlichen Kontext*. Edited by S. Häder and H.-E. Tenorth. Weinheim: Deutscher Studien-Verlag, 25–53.

6

The Economics of Education: Incentives, Control of Costs, Allocation of Resources

François Orivel

This chapter reflects the analysis of economists who have focused on European education systems. North American scholars have for a long time dominated economic analysis of education. The founders of the human capital theory in the late 1950s and early 1960s were all American scholars (Schultz 1963; Denison 1962; Becker 1964; Bowman 1966; Mincer 1958 and 1962, among others), and the revival of this theory during the second half of the 1980s was also the product of American scholars, in particular Romer (1986), Lucas (1988), and Barro (1994). Economists have two ways of looking at the economic returns of education: a macroeconomic approach, which is focused on the relationship between education and human capital production and the growth of the economy, or a microeconomic approach, which is interested in the individual returns of education—namely, the influence of education on employability, on income over the lifecycle, and more generally on all rewards that can be attributed to a better education.

When one compares American with European economists of education, one can notice two differences: the European approach is more critical of the human capital theory. This theory better fits an American context in which there is a real market for postcompulsory education. American households often pay for university education but accept this cost because they anticipate higher income for university graduates, a situation that implies that the job market operates in accordance with the laws of supply and demand. The second difference is the lack in Europe of universities such as Chicago, Stanford, Syracuse, or the University of Wisconsin at Madison that are clearly identified as centers of excellence in the field of the economics of education. In Europe the economics of education is found in scattered places where individual university professors show some interest in the field, but the field lacks the continuity and critical size that give strength to the American school.

The United Kingdom is the closest to the American context in the economics of education. In the United Kingdom it is possible to note between 50 and 100 names in this field. This is, furthermore, the only European country that has a specialized journal in this field (*Education Economics*, Lancaster University). Two countries come second as challengers, the Netherlands and France. Both have at least one permanent academic team of a critical size, about twenty personnel or more, and several isolated individuals in other universities. In France, there exists a "who's who" of economists of education (Savoie 1993), which has identified 53 names, among whom about 20 could be considered active producers in this area of research. Germany and Spain constitute a third group of countries where one can identify 20 to 25 scholars who are not associated with a particular institution. These countries are typical of the European scene, where scattered individuals may work temporarily on the subject and then move to a new area of interest. Other European countries have a much lower involvement in the field and remain marginal actors. One should also mention the presence in Europe of two international organizations that maintain a certain level of activity in the field, both of them based in Paris: namely the United Nations Educational, Scientific and Cultural Organization (UNESCO), with its affiliate, the International Institute for Educational Planning (IIEP), and the Organization for Economic Cooperation and Development (OECD). In the former Soviet Union, however, the field is almost unknown, and no significant production of innovative research has emerged from this part of the world during the past decades.

One can estimate, therefore, that there are in Europe about 200 scholars working in the area of the economics of education, a relatively modest number. In a review of the literature worldwide, Orivel (1994) has numbered about one thousand authors who have published in this area during the 1980s. More than half are North American, one-fifth are European, and the remainder are from the rest of the world.

The relatively low involvement of Europe in this field is related to the fact that Europe has not developed a strong research sector in the field of education. Research and development (R&D) expenditures on education in Europe represent only 0.27% of total education expenditure (Orivel 1995), which is about one-tenth of R&D budgets in other sectors of the economy. In addition, a significant proportion of studies on education are undertaken within institutions not academic by nature, but closely linked with education administrations. The clear advantage of this approach for education ministries is closer control of the orientation and public dissemination of such work. Education is often a sensitive social issue, and European education administrations frequently do not trust the academic community to carry out studies whose results can sometimes be embarrassing.

Table 6.1
Average Public Expenditure for Education as a Percentage of GDP

Average (unweighted)	1950	1960	1975	1992
European Union (15 countries)	2.46	3.93	5.55	5.52
Other (5 countries)	2.92	5.14	6.92	5.30
Overall	2.58	4.24	5.89	5.46

The current review of the European scene in the area of the economic analysis of education will cover successively the issues of cost and finance, the issue of the internal effectiveness of educational systems, and finally, the question of the economic returns of education.

RECENT TRENDS IN THE COST AND FINANCE OF EDUCATION IN EUROPE

Public Expenditure for Education

Public expenditures for education have increased substantially since the Second World War in virtually all countries of the world, both developed and less developed, but at a different pace and at different levels. The most commonly used indicator for assessing the public effort for education is the share of the Gross Domestic Product (GDP) allocated for this purpose. A twofold increase took place between 1950 and 1975, as shown in Table 6.1, in which the unweighted average for the fifteen countries of the European Union and five major other economic powers (the United States, Canada, Japan, Australia, and the Russian Federation) approximately doubled, from 2.58% of the GDP in 1950 to 5.89% in 1975. Since the GDP of this group of countries increased quite rapidly during this period, the total volume of public resources allocated to education has known an unprecedented growth.

The year 1975 represents a turning point in this evolution. It signals the end of the expansion of the share of national wealth dedicated to public education and the beginning of a period during which the behavior of developed countries in this respect can be described as "convergence." Countries that used to spend significantly more than the average have shown a tendency toward reduction, whereas those that used to spend significantly less have expanded their education expenditure.

On average, European Union countries have followed a slightly different policy than that of their economic partners. During the period of rapid expansion (1950–1975), they lagged behind the others (about .5% in 1950, more than 1% in 1960, and close to 1.5% in 1975). These differences are not minor, since they represent between one-sixth and one-fourth less than their partners. Since the 1975 turning point, however, convergence has worked quite well. The five major economic powers reduced their effort by more than 1.5% between 1975 and 1992, whereas the European Union countries have maintained theirs more or less at the 1975 level (on average). In 1992, their effort was close to that of their partners, and even slightly superior (5.52% versus 5.30%).

In terms of individual countries, Japan appears to have atypical behavior. It is the only one among the twenty listed in Table 6.2 that has spent no more, and even slightly less in 1992 than in 1950. But it was the biggest spender at the beginning of the period, a period of economic growth significantly above the average. It is interesting to observe that the relations established by macroeconomic studies between human capital development and economic growth apply perfectly to the Japanese case during that era, and that early investments in education created a comparative advantage in the subsequent rate of economic growth of concerned countries.

Within the European Union, there exists a traditional contrast between the Nordic countries (in particular Scandinavia and the Netherlands), and the Mediterranean ones (Spain, Portugal, Greece). The first group used to allocate significantly more public resources to education than the second. But here again, the convergence pattern has worked successfully. The Southern group filled most of its gap between 1975 and 1992, a period during which the majority of other countries have stabilized or reduced their effort.

According to economic theory (see in particular Baumol 1967), the distribution of resources among sectors in a national economy changes over time with respect to two driving factors: the evolution of productivity across sectors and the evolution of the demand of economic agents. If one assumes that the structure of the demand is stable, then the share of sectors where productivity improvement is weak tends to increase, whereas the share of sectors where productivity is improving rapidly tends to decline. For instance, the historic decline of the relative size of agriculture is explained by this type of evolution, and the growing size of sectors such as health or education are similarly linked to the same phenomenon. Productivity increase in agriculture is high, but in health or education, it is supposed to be slow or null because the technology is essentially based on human labor with little capital/labor substitution in comparison with many other economic sectors.

During the period 1950–1975, the increase of the share of public expenditure allocated to education was owing to both a lower productivity improvement of education services with respect to other economic sectors, and to a growing demand for education services from society and from individuals. But how do we explain the evolution of the sector between 1975 and 1992? Stabilization could be the combined result of a declining demand compensated by an equivalent productivity gap with the rest of the economy.

Actually, there are four possible explanations for this stabilization; the evolution of the school-age population, the evolution of the participation rates at

Table 6.2
**Percent of GDP Allocated to Public Education Expenditure (European Union Plus
Five Selected Countries)**

	1950	1960	1975	1992
Austria	n.a.	3.7	5.7	5.8
Belgium	2.1	5.7	6.2	5.1
Denmark	3.1	3.9	7.8	7.4
Finland	3.1	6.6	6.3	7.2
France	1.5	3.2	5.2	5.8
Germany	3.0	3.7	5.1	3.7
Greece	1.3	1.7	2.0	3.1
Ireland	2.7	4.0	6.2	6.2
Italy	2.9	4.6	4.1	5.4
Luxembourg	2.0	1.7	4.8	4.1 (1989)
Netherlands	3.5	5.9	8.2	5.9
Portugal	1.4	2.2	4.1	5.0
Spain	1.2	1.5	1.8	4.6
Sweden	3.5	5.3	9.0 (1980)	8.3
United Kingdom	3.2	5.3	6.7	5.2
Australia	1.8	3.6	7.4	5.5
Canada	3.2	5.8	7.6	7.6
Japan	4.8	5.1	5.5	4.7
Former Soviet Union	1.7	5.9	7.6	3.4
USA	3.1	5.3	6.5	5.3

Sources: UNESCO, *Statistical Yearbook*, 1963, 1967, 1975, 1987, 1995; World Bank, "Russian
    Education in the Transition," 1995.

higher International Standard Classification of Education (ISCED) levels, the evolution of private financing of education services, and the evolution of the productivity of education services. For instance, Germany and Japan, which are considered to have developed reasonably good education services, tend to spend less than average (respectively, 4.7% and 4.1% of their GDP). Both have comparatively high participation rates (above average), and declining school-age populations (more than average). Both also have high, that is, above average, non-public sources of financing for education and training (firms in Germany; firms and, above all, families in Japan). Unfortunately, we cannot tell from available data whether the role of private financing has increased or not during the period, because private-financing data collection has been introduced recently (see OECD, *Education at a Glance* 1992, 1993, 1995). Very likely, the relative situation of Japan and Germany is the result of two dominant factors: the decline of the school-age population and the mobilization of non-public sources of financing.

France is an example of a country that has continued to increase public expenditure for education, even after 1975. This is clearly the outcome of higher participation rates at all levels, from preschool to higher education, in a context of moderate decline of the school-age population. The sharp decline of public resources for education in the United Kingdom (from 6.7% in 1975 to 5.2%), and in the Netherlands (from 8.2 to 5.9%), have different causes, among which the most significant is the commitment of governments to reduce public expenditures in education, thanks to less generous welfare policies for students (the Netherlands), or less generous grants to universities (the United Kingdom). These changes can be interpreted as a combination of finance transfers between taxpayers and households, on one hand, and an attempt to improve the productivity or the cost-effectiveness of resource utilization in education services, on the other. Between 1989 and 1995, per-student public expenditure in the United Kingdom sharply declined, from about £6,600 to £4,600, or minus 30%. (These figures are given in constant pounds, at their 1993/1994 value, and quoted from THES 1996.) It is unclear if this decline is absorbed by deterioration in the quality of service, by higher productivity, or different cost sharing between public and private sources. Unfortunately, no hard fact reveals the respective share of these three possibilities.

In the former Soviet Union, as in other East European countries, the golden age of public commitment to education was the 1960s and 1970s. But since the beginning of the "transition" period, the fiscal difficulties faced by the governments of this part of the world have led to a strong decline of public resources available for education and training systems. The GDP not only declined strongly between 1991 and 1995, but in some cases, the share of the education sector within the GDP significantly shrank. Table 6.3 provides information on the magnitude of education expenditure decline in selected former Soviet Union countries during the transition. In Ukraine and Belarus, the decline has followed more or less the pace of the GDP decline, about half in Ukraine and one-fifth

Table 6.3
Public Resources Allocated to Education in Selected FSU Countries

Country	Russian Federat.		Ukraine		Belarus			Georgia	
Year	1990	1994	1990	1994	1992	1994		1990	1994
GDP Index	100	50	100	49	100	75		100	19
Share of Education (%)	8.2	4.4	4.3	4.6	5.1	5.4		7.4	0.9
Educ. Expenditure Index	100	27	100	52	100	79		100	2.5

Sources: World Bank, "Russian Education in the Transition," 1995; UNESCO, *Statistical Yearbook*, 1993; Ministries of Education (Ukraine, Belarus, Georgia).

Table 6.4
Staff Employed in the Education Sector

Countries	Staff*
Russian Federation	9.7
Ukraine	7.5
Belarus	8.4
Georgia	8.9
OECD average	5.2

*As a percent of the total labor force.

Sources: World Bank, "Russian Education in the Transition," 1995; UNESCO, *Statistical Yearbook*, 1993; Ministries of Education (Ukraine, Belarus, Georgia).

in Belarus. But in the Russian Federation and in Georgia, the share of education within the GDP has also significantly diminished, by half in Russia and by 88% in Georgia. As a consequence, real resources for education in Russia represented only slightly more than one-fourth (27%) their previous level before the transition, whereas in Georgia, their 1994 value was only 2.5% of what it used to be. Here, the evolution is determined by the capacity of the new regimes to collect fiscal resources in a period of deep economic changes, and by the direction of the GDP, which is everywhere in decline but with different levels of severity.

The consequences of the decline are harsh. As in other education systems, the most important share of expenditure is allocated to the salaries of teachers and non-teaching staff. But in the former Soviet Union, the management of education during the Communist period led to massive endowments of staff assigned to schools. Table 6.4 indicates, for some countries of the region, the proportion of active population employed in the education sector in the early 1990s. This proportion is about 9%, almost twice as much as the OECD countries average. During the Soviet period, salaries of staff employed in education used to be slightly lower than in industry. With the decline of real resources allocated to education, the salaries of education personnel have declined further, much below salaries in the other sectors of the economy. In Ukraine, for instance, real teacher salaries fell below twenty U.S. dollars per month in 1994. In Georgia, they dropped to the abysmally low level of five U.S. dollars in 1995.

Such a situation illustrates the low productivity of education in the former Soviet Union. When a country has 30% of its active population employed in agriculture, labor productivity in the agricultural sector is significantly lower than in a country where 4% of the active population work in agriculture and this small proportion is large enough to feed the entire population. If the number of educational services provided to the population is similar in two countries, they should have, *ceteris paribus*, a close enough index of population working in the education sector. It is clear that the quantity and the quality of educational services supplied in the former Soviet Union and in OECD countries are different, but these differences are likely narrower than the differences in the volumes of staff employed. Therefore, it is not unfounded to assume that education productivity is lower in the former Soviet Union.

This conclusion suggests policy orientations for the future. The excessively low teacher salaries in the former Soviet Union will generate mobility of labor away from the teaching sector. The governments will have to manage a reduction in the size of staff employed in education and accompany this reduction with significant increases in teacher compensation. In addition, the hierarchy of salaries according to qualification will have to be modified. The current system is characterized by a relatively small differentiation between the less qualified teachers and the most prominent university professors. To enhance teacher motivation, the scale of salaries should be enlarged according to qualification and merit.

Private Financing of Education and Training

During the period of rapid expansion of public expenditure for education (1950–1975), the debate concerning the role of private financing was quite different from today. The priority of politicians and education lobbyists was to achieve more democratization in the access to higher levels of education for a growing number of children, regardless of the financial capacity and the social background of their families. It was considered inequitable to be excluded from non-compulsory education, especially at the university level, because of a lack of resources.

Unfortunately, as said earlier, historical data on the share of private sources of financing within total education resources are not available. Reliable data have not been properly collected, and the OECD's recent efforts to fill in this information gap are far from complete. In a recent edition of *Education at a Glance* (1995), only twelve out of twenty-five OECD members have provided data on private sources of finance for the year 1992. They indicate that for all the education systems, 80% of financing originated from public sources and 20% from private. Very few countries among the twelve are able to indicate a long-run trend for an increased share in private sources. One may assume that during the golden years, private sources were in decline because of the higher participation of children from underprivileged social backgrounds, but the situation since 1975 is unclear. Some evidence from the United Kingdom and from the Netherlands shows a tendency for lower public expenditure per student at the higher education level. Table 6.5 indicates also that for the United States, fees in the overall cost of higher education tend to increase.

Table 6.5
Evolution of the Share of Tuition and Fees in the Finance of Higher Education in the United States

Year	1977	1992
Private universities	40.3	45.1
Public universities	16.4	22.2
Private 4-year colleges	61.7	68.9
Public 4-year colleges	16.4	22.4
Public 2-year colleges	16.8	22.1

Source: U.S. Department of Education, Office of Educational Research and Improvement, "The Condition of Education," 1995.

As in the United Kingdom and the Netherlands, private participation in the financing of higher education is increasing in the United States, whatever the category of institution under consideration. France, however, has collected data for the past twenty years that show a slightly different picture. In 1975, household contribution to education represented 10.7% of total French education expenditure from preschool to universities. In 1992, this contribution was marginally lower, at 9.2% (Ministère de l'Education Nationale 1993). This slight decline is compensated for by a small increase of the contribution by business, from 4.9% to 6.2%; therefore, in the long run, all private sources combined are stable at about 15% of the total expenditure. This is below the OECD average (20%), and there seems to be a strong resistance from French education lobbies to any increase in the private financing of educational services.

Europe has developed a tradition of public support of education that is more deeply entrenched than in the rest of the world. Perhaps closer exposure to the "socialist" model worked out in the former Soviet Union influenced education policies in Western Europe during the cold war and has spread to all levels of education, including higher education. The break-up of the former Soviet Union has de facto destroyed public monopoly of higher education in this part of the world. Hundreds of private educational institutions are emerging in countries formerly part of the USSR and in Russia itself, meaning that the socialist model is disappearing. But in Western Europe, public debate over whether or not it is desirable for families to finance higher education remains quite tense. A large majority of economists involved in this debate are in favor of higher family participation (see for instance Williams 1992); but the political cost of such a reform seems to be difficult to overcome, and the opposition of students in some countries appears to be very strong. It is particularly strong in France, where a first attempt to introduce modest fees of about $200 for university entrance generated massive social unrest from the student community in 1986 and the resignation of the minister involved, Mr. Devaquet. In 1994, a report commissioned by the Ministry of Education, but not endorsed officially, also recommended the setting up of higher fees. It provoked intense student mobilization before its publication, and consequently was not even published. The issue of higher education fees in the French context has clearly reached a dead end.

Other European countries are close to the French situation, although with less passionate public debate: Denmark, Norway, Sweden, and Austria remain attached to free higher education. Greece has an even tougher approach, since the setting up of fee-paying higher education institutions is not allowed. But as shown by Lambropoulos and Psacharopoulos (1992), this approach is not exempt from hypocrisy. Significant proportions of Greek students, as many as 30%, enroll in foreign universities, where they pay the regular fees. These migrations are dictated by the scarcity of places in public Greek universities and the absence of commitment from the Greek authorities to increase the number of places at the higher education level.

In all other European countries, the question of partially transferring the burden of educational financing from the taxpayer to the user is open and discussed. The word *partially* is important because this transfer of financing is often presented by opponents as a full transfer from public sources to families (see Vinokur 1995). Actually, the question that is raised should be envisaged at the margin: in a context where 80% of financing is borne by public sources and 20% by households, should future policy be oriented toward lower family participation (10% versus 90% from public sources), or should the national policy set up an objective of 30% from families and a reduction in public financing to 70%? The majority of countries where such a debate is going on are interested in the second alternative.

This historical reversal does not necessarily imply that the new financing approach will be more inequitable. One has to remember that current systems in which students have access to free higher education lead to regressive redistribution of income in a society because participation of children from better-off families is significantly higher than participation of children from low-income households. As a consequence, the net beneficiaries of free higher education tend to be high-income families (see for instance Bowman, Millot, and Schiefelbein 1986). It is perfectly possible to imagine a higher financial contribution of families to higher education and a better targeted public subsidy for students from deprived families.

A group of European countries has already decided to set up fees, at a level between 5 and 20% of the total student cost. Among these countries are Belgium, Spain, Italy, the Netherlands, and Switzerland. The most significant change concerns policies aimed at covering the subsistence costs of students. Here, the most common trend is the substitution of student loans for student grants, or for a combination of both. The rationale for this substitution is based on the human capital theory, which assumes that education is an investment for the individual and that this investment will generate higher income during the lifecycle. As a consequence, higher income will make it possible to repay loans contracted during the period of study.

Here again, France seems slightly different, because the last innovation in the financing of subsistence has been a lodging allowance for which students are eligible regardless of their family income. This innovation represents a yearly public expenditure of the same magnitude as scholarships allocated on social criteria. In terms of equity, this innovation has reinforced, not reduced, the regressive pattern of financing in French higher education. One can add that this policy is likely implemented at the expense of teaching cost and is not independent of the fact that French universities are usually considered to be of relatively low quality. According to the OECD (1995), per-student expenditure in French universities is 30% below the level that could be expected from the GDP per capita in France.

COST-EFFECTIVENESS OF RESOURCE UTILIZATION

In spite of an extensive literature on measurement of education outcomes, there is still a long way to go in assessing the relative performance of school systems in resource utilization. For an economist there are two types of education effectiveness, internal and external. Internal effectiveness looks at the production function of education services (input/output function), with outputs standing for learners' acquisitions. External effectiveness looks at the utilization of previous outputs (the different acquisitions of learners after the education process), on the performance of individuals in the job market (processes of employment/unemployment, labor productivity and income, professional careers), or on non-market activities such as individual behavior as a family member, spouse, or parent, as citizen or consumer. It is possible that education reduces the propensity to criminal behavior, or increases concern for environmental protection, or stimulates the adoption of behavior that enhances health or the health of one's children. This second approach to education effectiveness will be addressed in the next section.

Reliable international comparisons on the internal effectiveness of education systems are still scarce, but the concern for improving the evaluation capacity for these different dimensions is on the rise in many European and non-European countries such as the United States and Canada. The OECD has worked at producing new education indicators, but one could also mention those of the European Union (Eurostat) and several individual countries. If international organizations are undertaking this kind of exercise, it is clearly because they anticipate a growing demand from their member countries.

Evaluation of School Performances

Two networks of countries, the International Association for the Evaluation of Educational Achievement (IAEEA) and the International Assessment of Educational Progress (IAEP), have conducted internationally comparable evaluations of school performance. Every three to five years, a network of countries voluntarily participates in a common survey on pupil performances, most of the time at the age of 9 or 13–14. Each round is directed toward one or two topics selected among the most important aspects of school curricula, such as reading capacity, writing, mathematics, or sciences. The number of participating countries varies, but one regularly finds: Northern American countries, the United States and Canada; a significant minority of European countries, including some Eastern European countries; and some East Asian countries, such as Japan and South Korea. There are very few or none from sub-Saharan Africa, from Northern Africa and the Middle-East Crescent, or from Latin America. One can assume that participation is biased in favor of countries in which pupils perform relatively well. This bias may explain why there is a relatively weak relation between per-pupil expenditure (or inputs) and pupil performances (or outputs) in these surveys.

East-Asian countries, whatever their classification as developed or developing countries, perform relatively well, given their level of expenditure, whereas North American countries tend to have lower performance for the money they spend. These counterintuitive observations are less common for European countries, in spite of the fact that one observes also a relative independence between available resources per pupil and pupil performance. But as said above, there would likely be a stronger input-output relation if low-income countries were included.

Several studies carried out by the Institute for Research on the Economics of Education (Irédu), at the University of Burgundy, have shown that to explain the variance of school performances of French pupils, the role of traditional inputs such as class size, teacher qualification, teacher experience, pedagogical material, and per-pupil expenditure has strongly declined in the French context (see Mingat 1991, or Jarousse and Leroy-Audouin 1996). To summarize the major conclusions of this research: One can explain 70% of the variance of pupil performances; 50% are because of pupil characteristics and 20% because of school context (and 30% still unexplained). But of these 20% linked with the school variables, only 5% are still related to the traditional inputs (those mentioned above), and 15% to a residual "teacher" factor, which is not really identified. Some researchers call it the motivation or the charisma of the teacher; some prefer to invoke different pedagogical practices. All think that more research is needed to track this factor.

One can at least draw a more general conclusion from this research: rich countries have reached a level of resource allocation to schools that is more than sufficient, on average, from the point of view of pupil performance. If these countries want to set up policies that will reduce the gap between low achievers and high achievers, or that will improve the average performance of pupils in respect to other countries, the most promising avenues are not to be found in higher budget appropriations. They are more likely related to class or school management, teacher motivation, and personal characteristics other than their training, pedagogical practices, curriculum organization, time spent studying, and pupil motivation. In other words, there are more prospects for improving education outcomes through developing factors that are not related to unit costs than through providing additional costly inputs.

Decentralization and Autonomy in School Management

Recently, both in Western Europe and in Eastern Europe, the issue of decentralization to improve school management has been intensively discussed. The rationale behind such a policy lies in the belief that decisions made at the top, far from the real actors, tend to be poorly adapted to local conditions, and are therefore less pertinent. In some instances, this debate has been oversimplified through associating centralized systems with the idea of bad management and decentralized systems with good management. Plenty of counterexamples could have been analyzed fruitfully. For instance, whereas several continental European countries have pushed for more decentralization in education management, the United Kingdom has tried to introduce more central authority in specific domains such as curriculum development or certification procedures. The same concern is found in the United States, especially in regard to standardized curricula versus an excessively diversified curricula under the authority of more than 15,000 school districts, not all of which have the relevant competencies for carrying out this difficult task.

The most interesting attempt to measure the degree of centralization of an educational system has been undertaken under the OECD/INES project, which has isolated thirty-five different decisions undertaken in routine management (OECD 1993). These thirty-five decisions cover four areas: (1) planning and structures, (2) personnel management, (3) the organization of instruction, and (4) resources. These include four decision-making levels: the school, the first intermediate level (the municipality, the school district), the second intermediate level (the region, the province, the state), and the central level. This analysis takes into account when a decision is made jointly by several of these levels.

The concept of decentralization means transfer of decision-making power from a higher level to a lower level. For instance, decentralization is in process when secondary schools that previously were built and maintained by the central government are now under the control of regional authorities. Sometimes, there is confusion concerning the "local" level of administration. Decentralization exists if a decision that used to be taken at the central or at the state level is transferred to a local level or to municipal authorities or to school district authorities; but the concept of "autonomy" pertains if the lower (local) level is the school itself (and not the municipality).

Table 6.6 summarizes the major results of this project. The first lesson that emerges does not support the assumption that countries shown in this table can be clustered so as to assign each of them to a centralized or a decentralized

Table 6.6
Decisions Taken by Level of Governance as a Percentage of All Decisions

Unit: percent

Level of governance	School	Interm.1*	Interm. 2**	Central	Total
Austria	44	8	26	23	100
Belgium	26	50	24	0	100
Denmark	39	48	0	14	100
Finland	38	50	0	13	100
France	35	0	35	30	100
Germany	32	44	17	7	100
Ireland	74	8	0	18	100
New Zealand	73	0	0	27	100
Norway	31	45	0	24	100
Portugal	42	0	3	55	100
Spain	28	26	14	32	100
Sweden	47	47	0	6	100
Switzerland	9	44	46	0	100
United States	26	71	3	0	100

*Intermediate level 1, namely school district or municipalities.
**Intermediate level 2, namely region, province, or state in federal countries.
Source: OECD, *Education at a Glance*, 1993.

group. There are fourteen countries and fourteen different patterns. Only Denmark and Finland, which are relatively close, can be considered decentralized countries, with only 13 to 14% of decisions made at the central level. The most centralized country is Portugal, which makes 55% of decisions at the central level, but which is also one of the most "autonomous," with 42% of the decisions made at the school level. With the exception of Sweden, almost all countries known as rather decentralized, such as the United States, Switzerland, Belgium, Norway, and Germany, belong at the same time to the group that leaves the lowest share of autonomy to their schools, as if school autonomy and administrative decentralization were contradictory.

Surprisingly, "centralized" France leaves more autonomy to its schools (35% of decisions), than the "decentralized" United States (26% of decisions) or Switzerland (only 9% of decisions made at the school level). French politicians believe that their country's education system moved from highly centralized to decentralized in the early 1980s after the adoption of new laws on the role of the second intermediate level. Such decentralization concerns only one of the thirty-five decisions mentioned previously, however—namely, capital expenditure at the junior and upper secondary levels. This change represents only a 4% shift of national education expenditure from the central to the regional level. Of course, this analysis is dependent on the assumption that all decisions have the same impact on school management and that a different picture would emerge if different weightings of decisions were adopted. Nevertheless, one remains skeptical about the virtues of decentralization as in itself a way to enhance school effectiveness, especially if this is done at the expense of school autonomy. The question is less an opposition between centralization and decentralization than it is a determination of areas likely to obtain better results because the decision is made at a central level, at an intermediate level, or at the school level.

Decentralization policies are not limited to Western Europe. Since the breakup of the Soviet system, a large number of countries that have become independent, Russia included, have introduced a more decentralized approach to their educational systems. Decentralization here is linked first to the fact that the new countries are not any longer managed from Moscow but are individually responsible for education policy. This is in itself a powerful driving force for an extensive diversification of approaches to education in this part of the world. But there is a second aspect to this increased decentralization that is internal to each country: more responsibility is given to local authorities, namely, the regions and the school districts or municipalities.

In some cases, the delegation of authority from the center to the periphery is very great, as in Georgia or Russia, among others, because the fiscal debacle faced at the central level has created a situation in which devolution of appropriate budgets to the local level has simply stopped. Giving more responsibility for managing schools to local authorities has become the only means to help schools survive. One can therefore interpret, at least partly, the adoption of more decentralization in educational management to be the result of major financial constraints at the central level and as a way to ease fiscal pressure by transferring school management responsibility to a lower level. This evolution is clearly illustrated by data provided in Table 6.7, which show that the share of centrally managed school resources in Russia is declining from 30% to about 5%. This evolution is accompanied by a similar withdrawal of support by firms that, during the transition period, also face huge financial difficulties and no longer have incentive to support the cost of vocational training or kindergarten.

Parents and Community Involvement

Zanten (1996) argues that educational systems are progressively opening the doors to new actors who tend to have more influence on the day-to-day management of schools. Parent associations tend to be consulted more often; families

Table 6.7
Russian Educational Recurrent Expenditures by Type of Governing Authority

Unit: Percent

	1992	Present trend
Federal	30	5
Region/oblast	6	30
District/raion	48	65
Enterprises	16	0
Total	100	100

Source: World Bank, 1995.

have more choices about schools in which they can register their children; local authorities are gaining more influence in important decisions in their schools. Local actors are no longer silent on school management and are more often invited to give their views on the schools' future. Internationally comparable evidence on this issue is not easy to collect, but here again it can be useful to examine the results of another OECD survey of a sample of parents in twelve countries (OECD 1995) on certain aspects of school missions and school management. Ten of the twelve countries belong to the European Union. The two others are Switzerland and the United States.

A first series of questions focused on parents' opinions regarding practices considered essential or very important. This series produced relatively disappointing results because a large majority of respondents answered "yes" to most items. Yes, schools should give more advice and guidance to pupils concerning careers (80.2%). Yes, schools should help pupils facing learning difficulties (89.1%). Yes, schools should maintain discipline in classrooms (77.1%). Yes, schools should keep parents well informed concerning the problems of the school and keep them involved in its management (82.3%). But for two questions, the proportion of "yes" answers is significantly lower: the issue of giving regular homework, lowest approval (57.5%), and the desirability of strong leadership from the headmaster (61.4%).

These two exceptions are worth analyzing. A large proportion of the literature on school effectiveness has shown how important it is to have committed and motivated headmasters. Concerning homework, Fuller and Clarke (1994) have demonstrated that this is one of the three most frequent positive determinants of pupils' achievement, together with time spent studying and the availability of a library in the school. Parents' answers may be interpreted two ways: either they are not well informed about factors that have a positive impact on pupil

Table 6.8
Percentage of Parents Who Thought It Was Very Important for Decisions to be Made by Schools Themselves

Question	1	2	3	4	5	6	Aver.
Austria	31	36	28	33	31	18	29.6
Belgium (Flemish)	22	41	27	36	39	26	31.9
Denmark	20	32	16	34	31	12	24.0
Finland	18	35	26	40	34	22	28.6
France	34	56	51	50	59	43	48.7
Netherlands	15	35	22	31	47	24	28.9
Portugal	44	55	50	56	51	37	48.8
Spain	13	19	17	19	20	13	16.9
Sweden	23	38	24	51	44	17	32.8
Switzerland	18	32	21	22	26	14	22.0
United Kingdom	39	50	44	57	50	32	45.3
United States	53	60	57	64	67	57	59.8
Country average	27.7	40.6	31.8	41.0	41.6	26.2	

Question 1: Subjects to be taught.
Question 2: How subjects should be taught.
Question 3: Amount of time spent to teach each subject.
Question 4: How the school budget is spent.
Question 5: Teacher selection and promotion.
Question 6: Teachers' salaries and working conditions.

Source: OECD, *Education at a Glance*, 1995.

performances, or they do not like, among these factors, those that require some attention from them, such as homework. If the latter interpretation is correct, it means that parents are not ready to take a more active part in their children's education, that they consider this attention the school's mission, not their mission.

The second series of questions to parents focuses on their opinion about the importance of making certain decisions at the school level (the issue of the autonomy of the school). For this second series, the proportion of "yes" is much lower on average, 26.2% to 40.6% respectively (see Table 6.8) in all countries combined. This restraint is a clear indication of a certain suspicion by parents about the capacity of school authorities to make pertinent decisions. In certain countries, the proportion of parents in favor of school autonomy is lower than the proportion of decisions made at the school level, as shown by the previous OECD survey. Of course, the two surveys have not been designed for such comparisons, but this potential conflict is worth noting. There is no evidence that parents wish more autonomy for their schools.

This series of questions, unlike the first, tends to show discriminations among countries. The twelve participants could be clustered into three groups: those in which parents largely favor school autonomy (the United States, then Portugal, France, and the United Kingdom); those in which parents moderately favor school autonomy (about one-third of parents in countries such as Austria, Belgium, Finland, the Netherlands, and Sweden); and finally, countries in which parents are little inclined to consider school autonomy in a positive way (less than one-fourth of parents in Denmark, about one-fifth in Switzerland, only one-sixth in Spain). These results are astonishing. In Switzerland the proportion of decisions made at the school level is among the lowest, yet Swiss parents do not ask for more autonomy. The United States, on the other hand, belongs to the group of countries in which few decisions are made at the school level, and there, parents are massively in favor of more autonomy. Are these diverging attitudes owing to cultural differences? to different degrees of satisfaction with school effectiveness? to the nature of the public debate, which would suggest that the merits of local responsibility are more ideological than empirical? The question remains open to further work.

The issue that receives the highest approval from parents who want to improve schools is the question of teacher selection and promotion (41.6% on average). Two countries are particularly willing to introduce more school involvement on this issue—the United States (67% approval) and France (57% approval). In the case of the latter, this opinion strongly contradicts current practices in which schools have virtually nothing to say about the recruitment and promotion of their teachers. As in many other European countries, French teachers are strongly unionized, and the Ministry of Education, which is the direct employer of all teachers, co-manages staff issues with the unions. This means that salaries are determined by diplomas and seniority, not by observed merit, that firing unsuccessful teachers is virtually impossible, and that their nomination in a given school is determined by a complex procedure in which the schools are not consulted.

The consequence of this management system is that inefficient teachers can stay as teachers. The proportion of bad teachers is difficult to evaluate. It likely is relatively low but not insignificant. It is quite common that in a given grade in which a pupil is exposed to about eight teachers, each of them specialized in a given subject, one of the eight has a bad reputation. If the system were open to change, it is possible that 10 to 15% of teachers could be easily replaced by better ones. This issue is well known by parents, who face this situation regularly with their children. It is well known by headmasters and education administrators, who are unable to remove teachers but who try, as much as possible, not to concentrate the less-good teachers in the same school or in the same grade, thus giving all pupils opportunity for alternative exposure to good and less-good teachers. This approach is fair enough, but it may also explain why so many parents have experienced the less-good teachers and why so many believe that schools should be entitled to implement more satisfactory solutions.

The recruitment, promotion, wage scales, and firing procedures of teachers in most European countries are closely controlled by powerful unions, which are able to impose their rules on education managers. These unions are opposed to merit pay and more generally do not sustain personnel management procedures aimed at maximizing labor productivity. This approach has been made possible because of the low level of competition in educational systems. Such a mode of management may suffer in the future with the introduction of new information technologies in educational services. The role of teachers may have to change, and the current organization of schools will have to adjust to unavoidable innovations. Few European educational systems are prepared to face this challenge.

ECONOMIC RETURNS TO EDUCATION

The major problem concerning the economic return of education faced by most European countries is linked with the issue of rising unemployment, an issue that touches a growing proportion of the younger generation, including recent graduates. During the 1980s, a large number of European countries increased participation rates significantly for postcompulsory levels of education, especially at the university level. This expansion has not produced a compensatory reaction from job markets; hence there are lower career prospects for new graduates in comparison with former generations. Countries such as Germany, the United Kingdom, France, Italy, and Spain, where traditions used to be rather Malthusian, have produced a twofold increase in university student enrollments in less than a decade. This expansion of access to higher education has been quite remarkable.

That does not mean that the gap between Western Europe, on the one hand, and North America and Japan, on the other, has been fully filled in, but it has been significantly reduced almost everywhere, except in Switzerland and Greece. The proportion of new entrants to tertiary education at the theoretical starting age is currently about 40% in the European Union, whereas it is above 50% in North America and Japan (OECD 1993, 1995). In Switzerland this proportion is only 24%, and Swiss public authorities do not seem committed to filling in the gap in the near future. Their attitude is reinforced by two considerations: a financial consideration, because Swiss education is among the most expensive in the world (50% more than the OECD average) and current public deficits in Switzerland hamper a larger effort for this purpose; and a job market consideration, which does not show a shortage of higher education graduates in Switzerland.

It is difficult to say whether the expansion of European higher educational systems is driven by a growing demand from families who anticipate increasing difficulties for their children in finding jobs and who view a diploma as a useful

Table 6.9
Unemployment Rates by Level of Educational Attainment 25 to 64 Years of Age (1992)

	<Upper secondary	Upper secondary	Higher (Non-University)	Higher (University)	Total
Austria	5.6	3.2	-	1.3	3.6
Belgium	13.0	4.7	2.3	2.2	7.8
Denmark	15.6	9.2	5.8	4.8	10.6
Finland	14.9	12.1	5.7	3.4	11.4
France	12.1	7.4	4.6	4.4	8.8
Germany	8.9	6.4	4.5	3.7	6.2
Ireland	19.8	9.3	5.8	3.3	13.5
Italy	7.3	8.2	-	6.0	7.4
Netherlands	8.0	4.7	-	3.9	5.6
Portugal	5.3	4.5	1.9	1.8	4.9
Spain	16.0	14.1	12.5	9.9	14.7
Sweden	4.6	4.3	2.3	2.0	3.8
United Kingdom	12.3	8.3	3.3	3.6	8.4
Switzerland	3.5	2.2	2.3	3.0	2.5
United States	13.5	7.2	4.6	2.9	6.6
OECD average	10.5	7.2	4.9	3.8	7.6

tool in avoiding unemployment; or whether expansion is the outcome of a national policy aimed at higher rates of participation in both the upper secondary and the tertiary level. A double objective may be to follow the examples of Japan and North America and to reduce the number of unemployed through the "parking" effect of school enrollments. In the case of France, for instance, the government publicly adopted a voluntary expansion after a comparison with Japan in the early 1980s showed that France lagged far behind Japan in enrollment in non-compulsory levels of education.

Education and Employment

The first way to assess the economic return of education for individuals is based on the relationship between the level of education and the rate of employment. Table 6.9 provides comparable data for the population from 25 to 64 years of age. It shows that there exists a kind of general law associating a decline of the unemployment rate with a rise in the level of education. The average rate of unemployment for the population in the OECD is 7.6%, but it is three times higher for the least-educated group and 10.5% higher for those with no more than junior high school than it is for university graduates, for whom it is 3.8%. The United States is very close to the OECD average, but in Europe one can observe some specific behaviors in certain countries. The law applies quite strongly to Belgium, the United Kingdom, or Ireland (4 to 6 times more unemployed in the least-educated groups). On the other hand, the differences are almost insignificant in Italy (1.2 times more) or in Spain (1.6 times). Portugal appears to have relatively low rates of unemployment at all levels, and Spain to have high levels of unemployment whatever the educational attainment. Switzerland, which used to have a low level of unemployment, is the only case where this rate is higher for the university graduates than for the least educated. That may explain why Swiss authorities show little enthusiasm for enlarging access to higher education, but at 3%, the unemployment rate remains below the OECD average and cannot be considered an issue.

These data refer to the entire active population (from 25 to 64 years of age). It would be more relevant to focus only on youth. Unfortunately, data for new graduates are less comparable than for the previous group, because in some countries, data gathering is done one year after graduation, and in some others, five years after. When one observes unemployment among school leavers, one sees that some countries face an increasingly difficult situation. One year after leaving school, French young people face 57% unemployment within the least-educated group, with 12% for university graduates; in Ireland, Spain, and the United States, one out of three in the least-educated group faces unemployment. In Spain among university graduates, one out of four faces unemployment, and about one out of ten elsewhere. The worst situation is faced by Italian university graduates, who, in 1992, were unemployed at the rate of 39% one year after their graduation (OECD 1995). As a consequence, one may conclude that deterioration of job prospects for young people in general, including university graduates, is a widespread European phenomenon. This phenomenon does not discourage expansion of higher education, because there are relatively better employment prospects in relationship to the least-educated groups for those who have enrolled in higher education. The queuing is longer for everyone, but a diploma allows one to bypass less-educated competitors.

Education and Individual Income

Education not only reduces the likelihood of unemployment, it also gives higher income during the lifecycle. This proposition is illustrated in Table 6.10 by the income index of different groups of active adults, selected according to their level of education. The missing column refers to the index 100 attributed to the income of people who have completed upper secondary education. It

Table 6.10
Ratio of Mean Annual Earnings by Educational Attainment to Mean Annual Earnings at Upper Secondary Level (Population 25 to 64 Years of Age, 1992)

	Men			Women		
	<Upper Sec.	Higher Non-Univ.	Higher Univ.	<Up. Sec.	Higher Non-Un.	Higher Univ.
Austria	85	-	146	81	-	134
Belgium	86	115	149	78	137	164
Denmark	86	110	146	86	111	135
Finland	93	132	192	94	132	176
France	87	127	174	81	131	142
Germany	88	116	170	84	114	175
Italy	84	-	134	86	-	116
Netherlands	84	-	132	73	-	147
Portugal	65	124	179	67	117	188
Spain	78	-	138	71	-	149
Sweden	88	118	160	92	119	156
United King.	80	121	171	70	156	206

Note: For both men and women with secondary school education there is a missing column in this table for which the value of the index is 100.

Source: OECD 1995.

shows that men who finished their school career before the upper secondary level earn between 65% (in Portugal) and 93% (in Finland) of what people with upper secondary education earn. A non-university degree increases the income of its holders by 10% in Denmark (which is low), but by 32% in Finland. And finally, those who obtain a university degree see their income grow from 32% in the Netherlands to 92% in Finland. The returns from education are slightly higher for women, especially in the United Kingdom, where university graduates make more than twice what upper secondary school graduates are able to make. At the other extreme, Italian women earn relatively little with their university degree (only 16% more), a result that is consistent with the high rate of un-employment at this level of education (see previous paragraph).

The growing economic importance of efficient educational systems is clearly understood in Europe by policymakers and by individuals or their families. From a qualitative, as well as a quantitative point of view, European countries are trying to cope with the requirements of what is seen as a "knowledge" society, a society in which economic survival is directly dependent on the performance of educational systems, both at the initial stage and during the entire life of individuals. Reforming European education is not an easy task. There are many obstacles. Some progress has taken place, but there is still a long way to go.

REFERENCES

Barro, R. J., and X. Sala-i-Martin. 1995. *Economic Growth.* New York: McGraw Hill, 539.

Baumol, W. J. 1967. "Macroeconomics of Unbalanced Growth: The Anatomy of Urban Crisis." *American Economic Review* 57 (June): 415–426.

Becker, G. S. 1964. *Human Capital. A Theoretical and Empirical Analysis, with Special Reference to Education.* Princeton: Princeton University Press, 187.

Bowman, M. J. 1966. "The New Economics of Education." *International Journal of Educational Science* 1 (1): 29–46.

Bowman, M. J., B. Millot, and E. Schiefelbein. 1986. "An Adult Life Cycle Perspective on Public Subsidies to Higher Education in Three Countries." *Economics of Education Review* 5 (2): 135–146.

Denison, E. F. 1962. "The Sources of Economic Growth in the US and the Alternatives Before US." New York: Committee for Economic Development, Supplementary Paper No. 13: 67–80.

Eicher, J. C. 1995. "Le financement de l'enseignement supérieur en Europe." Paper presented at the Irédu/DEP Seminar. Dijon, France: Université de Bourgogne, 17.

Fuller, B., and P. Clarke. 1994. "Raising School Effects While Ignoring Culture? Local Conditions and the Influence of Classroom Tools, Rules, and Pedagogy." *Review of Educational Research* 64 (1): 119–158.

Jarousse, J. P., and C. Leroy-Audouin. 1996. "Les nouveaux outils d'évaluation: quel intérêt pour l'analyse des effets-classe?" Paper presented at the Irédu/DEP Seminar. Dijon, France: Université de Bourgogne, 25.

Lambropoulos, H., and G. Psacharapoulos. 1992. "Educational Expansion and Earnings Differentials in Greece." *Comparative Education Review* 36 (1): 52–70.

Lucas, R. E. 1988. "On the Mechanics of Economic Development." *Journal of Monetary Economics*, no. 22: 3–42.

Mincer, J. 1958. "Investment in Human Capital and Income Distribution." *Journal of Political Economy* (August): 201–213.

———. 1962. "On the Job Training: Costs, Returns, and Some Implications." *Journal of Political Economy*, Supplement (October): 50–80.

Mingat, A. 1991. "Expliquer la variation des acquisitions au cours préparatoire: les rôles de l'enfant, la famille, et l'école." *Revue Française de Pédagogie*, no. 95. Paris: INRP: 47–64.

Ministère de l'Education Nationale. 1993. "L'état de l'Ecole," no. 3, Direction de l'Evaluation et de la Prospective. Paris, 77.

OECD, 1992, 1993, 1995. *Education at a Glance.* Paris, 148, 259, and 373.

Orivel, F. 1994. "Stand der Forschung im Bereich der Bildungsökonomie: Allgemeine
    Übersicht und französische Situation." *Zeitschrift für Pädagogik* 32. Weinheim
    und Basel: Beltz Verlag, 135–148.
Orivel, F. 1995. "Three Editions of OECD Education Indicators: Progress to Date and
    Future Directions." Paper presented at the General Assembly of the INES/OECD
    Project. Lahti, Finland, 16 ff.
Romer, P. 1986. "Increasing Returns and Long Run Growth." *Journal of Political Econ-
    omy* 94: 1002–1037.
————. 1990. "Endogenous Technical Change." *Journal of Political Economy* 98: 71–
    102.
Savoie, P. 1993. "Un nouveau champ pour l'histoire: économie et finances de l'éducation,
    Annuaire des chercheurs. Paris: INRP, 69.
Schultz, T. W. 1963. *The Economic Value of Education*. New York: Columbia University
    Press, 92.
THES (Times Higher Education Supplement). 23 February 1996.
U.S. Department of Education. 1995. *The Condition of Education 1995*. Washington,
    DC: National Center for Education Statistics, Office of Educational Research and
    Improvement, 518.
Vimont, C. 1995. *Le diplôme et l'emploi*. Paris: Economica, 173.
Vinokur, A. 1995. "Réflexions sur l'économie du diplôme." *Formation/Emploi*, no. 52
    (October-December): 151–184.
Williams, G. 1992. "Changing Patterns of Finance in Higher Education." Buckingham:
    The Open University Press, 173.
World Bank, 1995. "Russian Education in the Transition." Washington, DC: ECA Coun-
    try Department, 73, plus annexes.
Zanten (van), A. 1996. "École: la nouvelle donne." *Sciences Humaines*. Hors Série, Les
    Métamorphoses du Pouvoir, No. 11.

7

The Impact of Family Socialization Processes and Educational Strategies on the Adaptation and Academic Success of Students

Marie Duru-Bellat and Agnès van Zanten

The level of education attained by European students has steadily increased. In Germany, more than 70% of youngsters between 10 and 13 years of age now stay at school compared with about 30% in the mid-1960s. In Ireland, full-time enrollment of 16-year-olds rose from 39% in 1965 to 98% in the 1990s. Even so, inequalities reflecting geographical or socio-economic background continue to be important. In France, among pupils enrolled in 1980 in a *collège*, a unified lower secondary school, 23.5% of the offspring of factory workers obtained the *baccalauréat*, the leaving examination for higher secondary schools, whereas 76% of the offspring of professionals and top executives and almost 80% of the children of teachers did so.

This chapter deals with the impact of family socialization processes and strategies on these educational inequalities. The first section uses several indicators to describe social inequalities in European schools. The second section shows the more or less explicit strategies used by families with unequal resources and different expectations to prepare children to participate in school activities and to meet school requirements. We will not discuss the specific impact of the students' sex and ethnicity, which are dealt with in other chapters.

SOCIO-ECONOMIC DIFFERENCES IN EDUCATIONAL ACHIEVEMENT

The Impact of Family Background

In every European country, school careers reflect the family background of pupils. Social differences appear very early. In the Netherlands (OCDE 1991), as in France (Le Guen 1991), important differences that reflect the father's occupation are observed at the primary level in language as well as in arithmetic. Dutch research, however, also emphasizes a contrast among 9-year-olds between the strong effect of home background on reading achievement and the lack of its significance on arithmetic achievement (Jung 1993). In Britain (Sammons 1995), the father's occupation is strongly linked to language and arithmetic at the beginning of primary school, but this pattern changes as children progress through junior school (age 10), when mathematics is less dependent on background factors. Nevertheless, children benefit from continuous parental involvement in reading and in the provision of reading resources. Differences in attainment in these areas are still visible in secondary school. However, in Britain (Sammons 1995) as in France (Duru-Bellat, Jarousse, and Mingat 1993a), the gap in absolute achievement widens over time if students follow the same curriculum.

The influence of the mother's occupation is more complicated. The role of mothers is a real issue because the number of women in the workplace in Europe has steadily increased in the last decades. In 1992 at least 70% of women between 25 and 49 years of age were working in Denmark, the United Kingdom, France, and Portugal. Even in countries with lower female participation (Luxembourg, Spain, Ireland), more than 50% work outside the home. Women with a high level of education are more likely to work, whatever the number of their children. In France, at the primary level (allowing for other factors of family background), having a working mother is positively linked with achievement, especially if the job requires further education (Mingat 1991); but at the secondary level this positive effect is no longer significant (Vallet and Caillé 1995). European trends seem relatively far from American results, which show that having a working mother does not, on the whole, have a detrimental effect on children's development or school career. Having a working mother remains slightly harmful, however, to middle- and upper-class boys, but is slightly positive for working-class boys and girls (Bogenschneider and Steinberg 1994). This discrepancy may reflect the quality of European day-care centers. In Sweden, the longer young children attend those centers, the better they adjust to and perform in school (Andersson 1989). In France, children attending nursery schools (*école maternelle*) from age 2, do better in primary school (Jarousse, Mingat, and Richard 1992). The same trend is observed in Britain (Wadsworth 1986). But even if preschool attendance has a beneficial effect on children's verbal scores, the mother's education remains by far the most powerful agent, eclipsing any effect of preschool.

Actually, parental occupation is strongly associated with cultural resources that are directly related to academic achievement. The education of the father or mother is strongly linked with achievement at the primary and secondary level (Paterson 1991b), especially for the most brilliant students (Undheim and Nordvik 1992). To be more precise, the mother's education is strongly linked with the child's performance in the mother tongue (Graaf 1988). French data, taking into account the level of education of both parents, show that when parental educational levels differ, it is the mother's level that is more strongly connected with the child's achievement. This certainly reflects the commitment of mothers to the education of children, for on average, women in France allot five times more of their day to tasks related to children than do their husbands (Héran 1994). Cultural resources remain important, therefore, even when the educational opportunities of children with working or unemployed parents are analyzed (Wesselingh 1996).

Research is less plentiful on the impact of family structure on academic achievement. A French study (Vallet and Caillé 1995) shows that the smaller the family size (controlling for parents' occupation and education), the better the schooling career. Disadvantage is especially strong for families having more than three children. Large families, however, are becoming rare in many European countries: more than 60% of children in France, the United Kingdom, Belgium, and Denmark, come from families of one or two children, but only 20% in Ireland and Portugal come from small families.

As far as the composition of the family is concerned, especially the one-parent family, there is a big gap between rather alarming discussions (Rülcker 1989; Husén, Tujiman, and Halls 1992) and the facts.[1] A strong majority of children live with two parents. About 25% come from one-parent homes in Denmark, the country where divorce rates are highest, and between 15 and 20% in most European countries, although fewer in Mediterranean countries such as Greece, Italy, and Portugal. Although less educated parents are overrepresented in one-parent households, there is little research on the effect of this family structure on child development or achievement that also takes into account the education level and occupation of parents. Research indicates that conflicts between parents have a more detrimental effect than a separation (Ni Bhrolchain, Chappell, and Diamond 1994).[2] However, there is a slight trend among youngsters to leave school earlier when they belong to a one-parent or a recomposed family. There may exist more specific effects, too. In Sweden (Mac Nab and Murray 1985), the mathematics and "world knowledge" scores of junior high school students from one-parent families (with the mother most often the parent at home) are weaker than those of students from two-parent families, but this difference is statistically significant only for children of two well-educated parents. The authors contend that the removal from the home of one of the adult family members does represent a loss to the intellectual environment within the home. But on the whole, the negative effects of a single-parent home remain inconstant and very weak when compared with such traditional factors as parental education (Wesselingh 1996).

Let us emphasize that even if research strives to identify and to separate the effects of different background factors (parents' education proving the most important), these factors often act in combination. In England, for example, seven factors could be used to predict increased risk of low educational achievement at age 11 (Sammons 1995): eligibility for subsidized school meals, large family size, a one-parent family, parental unemployment or semi- or unskilled manual parental occupation, uncontrolled behavior, incomplete fluency in English, and ethnic family background. Only 11% of pupils not affected by any factor would be in the lowest verbal reasoning band, compared with nearly 92% of those affected by at least one of these seven factors.

The Specific Impact of Curriculum Choices

Inequalities in academic attainment do not entirely explain social differences in school careers. Pupils must make numerous choices when going through an educational system. It is not sufficient just to succeed in school; it is also important to be aware of the "best" choices to make, and here parents have an important part to play.

The aspirations of European parents have risen in recent years, so strong is the belief that a degree is the best protection against unemployment. Today, 80% of French parents wish their child to stay at school until the age of 20 (or more). This figure varies between 65 and 94% reflecting parental education (Caillé 1992). In spite of their generally low level of education, parents from ethnic groups may develop even higher aspirations for their children, willing them to acquire the credentials that will allow social integration and mobility (for France, see Vallet and Caillé 1995; for Britain, Sammons 1995). These high aspirations, however, pertain only to parents who do not plan to return one day to their country of origin (Zéroulou 1988).

What is going on when educators responsible for streaming decisions encounter these aspirations? In the Netherlands (OCDE 1991), where pupils are streamed at the end of primary school, the teachers suggest tracks that tend to reflect the pupils' socio-economic level. Such placements lead to wider social differences than would placement based only on a gap in achievement. Among the offspring of top professionals, 10% are told to follow a vocational route, compared with 46% of the offspring of factory workers. A third of the former are invited to follow the academic route leading to higher education, compared with 8% of the latter. Moreover, the poorest or less educated parents follow teachers' advice more often, whereas well-educated parents "resist" when their child is directed to a less prestigious route. The result is a wider social gap than would result from just the teachers' suggestions.

The weight of social inequalities generated through tracking also exists in Germany, where the first and definitive choice between the *Hauptschule* (which gives access to an apprenticeship in craft industry), the *Realschule* (which provides vocational and general studies), and the *Gymnasium* (secondary school that leads to the *Abitür* and then to the tertiary level) is made at age 10. When research is controlled for the academic achievement of students, the choice of *Gymnasium* proves to be linked to the cultural resources of the family, whereas the choice between alternative routes reflects a family's financial resources (Graaf 1988). There results a segregation in the three secondary schools where socialization takes place (Bargel 1994; Trommer 1990). Similar trends exist in countries that have postponed the first selection point. In Spain and in France, as in Sweden, youngsters and families are more likely to choose the academic over vocational routes, the latter more and more becoming "ghetto" tracks for the most underprivileged.

Choice of subjects follows the same pattern. Academic subjects (scientific studies, modern languages), for example, tend to be regarded as middle class and vocational subjects as working class, an opposition linked to the fact that science and modern languages are taught in higher-status schools (and in streams within schools) and are associated with progress into higher education. These subjects are thus perceived to have greater "buying power" in professional life (for Scotland, see Croxford 1994). On the whole, social inequalities in choices are very important because only half of the social class differences in secondary school curriculum choice can be explained in terms of measured ability.

A similar situation pertains in France (Duru-Bellat, Jarousse, and Mingat 1993a). At all levels of academic attainment (but especially for below-average pupils), pupils from low-socioeconomic status (SES) families realize a self-selection, seeking less prestigious routes than their counterparts from high-SES families, as if the former were more afraid than the latter of the risks of failure. Sex differences in access to the different routes of the curriculum, with fewer girls enrolled in science courses, can be explained in the same way: by the choices and aspirations of individual pupils having learned their "place" through the experience of schooling (for France, see Duru-Bellat et al. 1993b; for Norway, Skog 1991).

In every European country, there remain social inequalities in schools in spite of numerous reforms since World War II. Most countries have seen improvement in the situation of low-status pupils, the offspring of farmers, and unskilled workers. Everywhere, also, geographical inequalities and sex differences have seriously diminished. But no country can claim unequivocal democratization. More often, researchers talk of moving inequalities to more advanced levels of the system, or about a growing hierarchy in alternative tracks (B. Zymek, chapter 5).

If social inequalities do remain within schools, that is because they relate to broader inequalities in the larger society. Some sociologists or economists view schools as mainly a screening device, as a way to get a good position in the queue for jobs. As a consequence, families will implement strategies to maximize their youngsters' increasing access to degrees, even though the degrees are becoming devalued. They will, for example, assess what are the best "bargains" in the education market. For other sociologists (especially the French Bourdieu), the stability of social inequalities in schools reflects a cultural mismatch between what is needed to succeed in school and the "cultural capital" pupils enjoy in their family.

From one point of view, the persistence of social inequalities reflecting educational choices leads to an investigation of the strategies families use to choose subjects and schools. From another, the persistence of inequalities in achievement leads to an investigation of family socialization and cultural transmission to children. The review of what we know about parental educational practices, which will be presented in the next section, will show that both paths are worth investigating.

PARENTAL PRACTICES AND SCHOOL ACHIEVEMENT

Families are the most important educational agent and the primary source of support for children in their school careers. As far as the first role is concerned, psychologists are unanimous in emphasizing the importance of family interaction on a child's development. For example, in Belgium, Pourtois (1984) concludes from empirical research on 7-year-olds that 70% of the variance of intellectual development can be explained by family background (level of education, social characteristics, and parental practices), and 75% is attributable to intellectual development.

Parental Socialization in Early Childhood

Europe, like the United States, has increased emphasis on "process" studies that seek to identify features of family environment through which socio-economic and cultural background have an impact on mental development and school achievement. A traditional area of research concerns normative aspects of parental attitudes and practices, the question being, What kind of man or woman do parents want to build?

Since the 1960s, scholars have contrasted parents from the middle and upper classes, who emphasize enhanced self-control, autonomy, and projection into the future, with working class parents, who emphasize respectability, obedience, and solidarity within the family group.[3] In France, a recent study shows that the best-educated parents bring dynamism, a sense of effort, and a moral conscience to their children, whereas the less educated give priority to resourcefulness and respectability (Duru-Bellat and Jarousse 1996). These findings, in line with those previously mentioned, show that one group gives strong weight to qualities that make a self-conscious achiever, and the other, strong weight to accommodation to circumstances.

There is, however, an increasingly dominant model, as illustrated by a recent study from Geneva (Kellershals and Montandon 1991). The child that parents strive to build is autonomous and accountable, self-regulated, and well adjusted to his or her environment. Less importance is given to sensitivity or to the willingness to defend ideals, solidarity, or creativity. But even if self-regulation and expressiveness are more often promoted by well-educated parents and accommodation by the less educated, the model of the efficient and well-adjusted child seems to be shared by every family.

Recently, research has focussed on the cognitive (versus normative or affective) component of the relationships between parents and children. This research has also placed emphasis on parental beliefs about the development of children, with the idea that to understand child development, it is worthwhile to investigate what parents think about this subject. The more educated mothers are, the more often they reject the idea that children's progress relies primarily on innate intelligence and that education is limited to control of impulses (Castro, Monteiro, and Rebelo 1995). Researchers have also focused on parental interpretation of the cause of events affecting their children, on parental locus of control. This locus of control is internal when parents do not attribute good or bad events to chance or to external uncontrollable factors but are influenced by their child's or their own attitudes and behaviors. Parents sharply differ in this respect (Perrez and Chervet 1989). The best-educated are more "internal," and this has consequences for the child's development. A mother's internal locus of control produces stronger motivation to succeed (Fontaine 1994) and strengthened self-confidence (Perrez and Chervet 1989).

Actually, parental values and cognitive beliefs produce an atmosphere that impinges on their children's life. In Europe, as in the United States, a parental style characterized by strong control and by hierarchical relationships within the family is antithetical to a style whose main feature is expressive support, sensitivity to needs, open communication, the granting of autonomy, and horizontal relationships. Again, middle- and upper-class families prove nearer to the latter style, and working-class families nearer to the former (for Spain, see Lopez Bachero 1986; for the Netherlands, Meijnen, Guldemond, and Boomsma 1989; for minority working-class families in Germany, see Flitner-Merle 1992). Contrary to observations in North America, research in some European countries such as Portugal (Fontaine 1994) shows that a certain amount of authoritarianism may not be detrimental to the motivation of young adolescents in families where parental authority is considered unquestioningly as the basis of education and is a strong social norm.

Research today is looking further and further for "mediating variables" between parenting styles and children's achievement. Dutch research (Jung 1993) shows that the relationship between SES and the achievement of 9-year-old children is mediated by two processes: first, the link between achievement and paying attention in school; second, the link between paying attention and parental styles. Some parental discipline practices give children less opportunity to develop and practice the deployment of attention. Among those "mediating variables" some concern children's emotional life. In Switzerland (Kellershals et al. 1992), the self-esteem of adolescents does vary with parenting style. Youngsters educated within families where self-regulation, autonomy, empathy, and negotiations with parents are valued are more prone to develop a strong feeling of self-worth,[4] in comparison with those living in families where parental control and distance from parents dominate. However, in research that controls for parental style, there is no direct influence of SES on self-esteem. The association between high SES and good self-esteem are entirely related to how the family functions and to parental styles.

Another mediating variable whose cognitive effect proves worth investigation is what psychologists call flexibility of rearing practices. Piagetian intelligence theory poses the hypothesis that in daily life, children need rules to anticipate the consequences of their behavior; however, some unpredicted events are also necessary for them to learn how to adapt to strange situations. The presence of rules coupled with a certain amount of flexibility in rearing practices has proved favorable to children's intellectual development and academic achievement. Such flexible structuring in rearing has proved more frequent in average and high SES, whereas working-class families and families from rural areas tend to create a more rigid context for their children (for France, see Lautrey 1989; for Portugal, see Fontaine 1991).

The Belgian Pourtois (1991) shows that mothers implement very different practices with their 5- to 6-year-old children to help them manage daily problems. Some mothers, frequently the most educated, let children explore until they find a way by themselves, whereas others, frequently the least educated or the more depressed, are less confident of their children's ability to succeed and tend to solve problems for them. The former behavior proves more beneficial than the latter. In sum, child-rearing practices associated with better academic achievement will encourage exploration and the assessment of the consequences of actions, will ask numerous questions and will give positive feedback—all behaviors more widespread among middle and upper class, or well-educated, parents. Consequently, daily child-rearing practices prove to be among the mediating variables that explain the relation between SES and achievement, and the unequal fostering of intellectual abilities, especially in the primary grades.

Let us turn to research on the knowledge or know-how parents instill in their children. Because social inequalities in reading achievement exist from the very beginning of formal schooling, there is interest in the way parents help children develop requisite language skills for reading. Numerous pieces of research, especially in countries such as the Netherlands (Bus, Van Ijzendoorn, and Pellegrini 1995) demonstrate the impact of parent-preschooler reading practices, one of the most important processes mediating the impact of SES on academic achievement.[5] Storytelling or fostering verbal argumentation through reading activities (Wadsworth 1986; Meijnen, Guldemond, and Boomsma 1989) are very beneficial. But there are differences among countries: German parents tend to play a specific role in their child's reading attitudes and competencies and are very active in this area, whereas French parents rely more often on the school, on just supervising homework (Prêteur and Louvet-Schmauss 1995).

Let us emphasize that as far as reading practices are concerned, time allotted and the prevailing climate at home differ among SES groups. In Belgium (Grisay et al. 1990), low SES families appear to consider reading a way to promote their children's success, whereas medium and high SES groups view reading as a pleasure to share. The specific impact of reading practices is confirmed by Dutch data (Graaf 1986) showing a strong association between SES and participation in formal culture such as library visits, theater, or museum visits. Nevertheless, reading and writing habits that support a child's academic progress can and do exist among less-educated parents (Lahire 1995).

Parental Support of Children's School Careers at Home

One of the main consequences of the increase in the number of years spent at school and the importance attributed to schooling as a means of access to desirable professions and as a marker of social identity is that parents now spend considerable time supporting their children's school careers. In Bourdieu's and Passeron's (1970) terms, parents cannot content themselves with the initial transmission of cultural capital. They must supervise and intervene on behalf of their children throughout their entire school career, thus becoming "professional" parents (Beattie 1985). Successful reinforcement of schooling implies creation of a home environment that corresponds to implicit and explicit demands of school, supervision of daily homework and related activities carried out at home, provision of complementary cultural and recreative activities inside and outside the home, and interaction with teachers and school personnel.

School demands on families have increased in most European countries, either in the explicit request for school materials, or in the indirect assumption that parents can organize their time, activities, and visits at the school's convenience (Perrenoud 1987a). Recent research conducted in France (Gissot, Héran, and Manon 1994), Great Britain (David et al. 1993) and Spain (Ortega 1983) shows that improvement in living conditions and development of parental awareness of the function of formal education has led to a relative homogenization of immediate aspects of home support for schooling such as buying textbooks or providing a desk for doing homework at home. Important differences still exist, however, between upper-class families, who can buy computers and sophisticated educational equipment for their children, and lower-class families, who cannot afford such investment. Moreover, differences between social groups increase considerably if more subtle mechanisms for creating a learning environment at home, such as the regulation of meals, of sleeping, of television-watching time, or of the content of conversation, are analyzed in detail.

Concerning parental help with homework, social differences are also significant. Research projects conducted in Switzerland (Montandon 1991), in Germany (Ulich 1985) and in France (Glasman et al. 1991; Héran 1994) all conclude that most parents, especially mothers, regularly help their children with homework to an extent that many home activities are organized around it. Homework may even generate stress and tension between adults and children, but the kind of help provided differs considerably. Less-educated mothers are more likely to encounter serious difficulties in understanding lessons and exercises, and in decoding teachers' implicit expectations, so that early in their children's school career they tend to restrict themselves to controlling the completion of homework. Moreover, because they lack the financial resources and information for using outside services such as private lessons, they have to rely on the irregular help of relatives and neighbors or on public after-school sessions provided by school or community centers.

It is therefore not surprising that in the last thirty years, researchers and practitioners in several European countries such as Belgium, the Netherlands, and France have set up programs designed to compensate for children's initial disadvantages in linguistic and cultural capital and to increase parental competence in dealing with homework and curricular activities through conferences, training exercises, and wide dissemination of written information. These programs still reflect an ideology in which the role of the school is to educate parents, but their promoters now want to move from the assistance model to the development of parental autonomy. Some results seem encouraging, but such programs may still create subtle forms of parental dependency on education professionals (Pourtois et al. 1984; van Den Bossche 1994).

Upper- and middle-class mothers are not only more able to help their children at home with school assignments, but also more able to assume a global pedagogic role. They explain lessons and exercises, devote more time to becoming informed about subjects and teacher expectations, and devise tasks and games to reinforce and anticipate learning beyond the requirements of homework. In addition, these parents are, both for financial and for cultural reasons, more able to find and pay for specific kinds of external support. Indeed, recent French research has shown a spectacular development of private lessons and other educational enrichment in these social milieus in the last decades (Glasman 1994).

Parents at the upper end of the social scale are also more likely to provide indirect support for their children's school careers through the organization of cultural activities: reading, watching specific television programs, playing educational games at home; going to the theater, to concerts or museums, or on "cultural" outings or holidays; or encouraging extracurricular activities outside the home such as painting, music, scientific activities, and sports. The growing importance these parents attribute to such activities has been documented in France (Establet 1987), in Switzerland (Kellershals and Montandon 1991), and in the United Kingdom (Beattie 1985). Although such activities fulfill important socializing functions by introducing ethnic or gender groups to certain socioeconomic norms, they are also a way for some parents to capitalize on social and cultural resources for their children that will help obtain better school results. And in fact, recent studies show a strong correlation between parental intervention in homework and the leisure activities of adolescents. The more parents help, the more likely it is that children will prefer reading to television watching (Chambaz 1996).

Parent-Teacher Interaction

Parent-teacher interaction is another central element of support for the school careers of children in Europe. There has been an increase in the number and varieties of these interactions since the 1960s. At one time, problems between families and schools were primarily attributed to failures of communication. If parents, immigrant as well as working-class fathers and mothers, did not visit schools, the main reason was thought to be because they did not have mastery over the teacher's language. If they did not understand school customs, this was thought to be because they lacked information and opportunity to see, discuss, and become involved (Bastiani 1987). As a consequence, a variety of programs were developed to facilitate interaction in England (Cyster, Clift, and Battle 1979; Wofendale 1989), in Belgium (Pourtois and Desmet 1989), in the Netherlands, and in many other European countries. Nevertheless, the development of individual parent-teacher relations is also the consequence in more recent years of the fact that for an increasing number of parents, developing good relationships with teachers appears to be a way to maximize their children's advantages. Teachers can provide useful information on the child and on the school system, and can exert an important direct influence on the child's success in school.

It is important to note that the intensity, the nature, and the effects of parent-teacher contacts vary according to national contexts, school level, and geographical location. In some European countries the local community and local authorities have traditionally encouraged more dialogue between individual parents and teachers. Examples are Denmark, the Netherlands, and to a lesser extent, the United Kingdom, where the school is legally and symbolically accountable to parents. In other countries such as France and Italy, teachers are state agents who have tried to protect themselves from local interference. Recent statistics on the countries of the European Community show, however, that the mean number of annual parental visits to schools is highest in Italy (4.98) and France (2.91), and lowest in Ireland (1.63), the United Kingdom (1.93), and Luxembourg (1.96) (Macbeth 1984).

Nevertheless, these figures vary within each country, especially if the informal/formal nature of contacts is taken into account. School size and location are important factors in this respect. There seem to be more informal individual contacts in small rural schools, more formal meetings and activities in urban settings (Bell and Sigsworth 1987; Zanten 1990). Swiss studies have explored other factors such as school level. They show that parent-teacher contacts, especially informal ones, decrease from preschool to the higher levels of secondary education because of changes in the objectives and the organization of each level and because of students' increasing role as a "go-between," mediating home and school (Perrenoud 1987b). These studies have also shown that teacher and pupil characteristics do play a role. For instance, the eldest and most experienced teachers report more individual contacts with parents, whereas their younger colleagues organize more formal meetings (Huberman 1989). The most important variable for pupils seems to be the level of achievement: the more learning difficulties the child has, the more teachers ask for formal individual contacts, whereas informal interviews initiated by parents decrease (Montandon 1991).

The most important source of variation across countries remains, however, the social and ethnic background of parents. Middle-class parents seem to demand more individual contact with teachers and to have the best contact with them. This appears to be so not only because of similarities in their social position, but because middle-class parents are more likely to consider such contacts an important part of their "professional activity" as parents (Sharp and Green 1975). Upper-class parents are less dependent on teachers to obtain information or to solve their children's problems because they can appeal more easily to principals, to members of the educational administration, or to people in power who have competencies to help them. Nevertheless, they do not seem to neglect contact with teachers as a way to discuss children's progress or changes in school organization (Pinçon and Pinçon-Charlot 1989). At the opposite end of the social scale, working-class parents and minority and immigrant parents are frequently described by teachers as ill at ease in social interaction. Teachers frequently find that these parents misunderstand or refuse to accept what they have to say about their children. Teachers also tend to criticize the socialization practices of these parents and to decry them as irresponsible, repressive, conservative, ignorant "problem parents" (Anderson-Levitt 1989; Reed-Danahay and Anderson-Levitt 1991; Tomlinson 1993).

Research conducted in Switzerland on parental attitudes toward parent-teacher interaction distinguishes four styles of relationships: Some parents who consider that the school has an important socializing function participate intensively in school activities. Their attitude is one of collaboration. Other parents may believe the school has an important socializing role but prefer not to participate, delegating part of their own socializing role to schools. Other parents see schools only as transmitters of knowledge, but they are nonetheless willing to supervise the work of teachers and become involved in school affairs. Their style is one of contribution. Finally, a last group of parents recognizes only a limited role for schools and does not participate. They just give school personnel a mandate. These four styles appear more or less linked to social position. Parents who delegate to schools are more likely to be members of the lower class, whereas parents who collaborate or contribute are more likely to be upper and middle class (Montandon 1994).

PARENTAL INVOLVEMENT IN EDUCATION

School Choice

An increasingly important dimension of parental involvement in schooling in Europe and in other Western countries in the last fifteen years is the issue of choice. Traditionally, most European countries have allowed the possibility of subsidized choice between public and private schools while ensuring, through national curricula and inspection and training of teachers, some conformity between schools. Nevertheless, the nature and extent of choice vary considerably from one country to another. In Belgium, parental freedom of school choice on a religious or ideological basis is a fundamental characteristic of the system. In the Netherlands, parents are entirely free to choose the educational form or type of school that seems most appropriate for their child. As a result, 28% of pupils go to official schools, 38% to Catholic schools, 26% to Protestant schools, and 8% to other private schools (Macbeth 1993). Even in France, the existence of a centralized, well-developed public sector has not prevented the maintenance of a private sector largely subsidized and partly controlled by the state. This private sector receives around 16% of the school population at a given time, but almost one-third of all pupils switch from the public to the private sector at one or several points of their school careers (Langouët and Léger 1991). Only in countries such as Denmark, Sweden, and Norway has the small independent sector subsidized by the state not played an important role in the dynamics of schooling.

On the subject of school choice, most of the debates and changes that have taken place in recent years concern the public sector. The most radical example is the United Kingdom, where since 1988, various pieces of legislation have introduced choice as part of an overall policy of creating an educational market. This educational market, like all markets, is intended to be driven by self-interest: the self-interest of parents, as consumers, choosing schools to provide maximum advantage to their children; and the self-interest of schools or their senior managers, as producers, making policy decisions based on ensuring the survival of their institutions in the marketplace. The result is meant to be competition, emulation, and rivalry, because survival can be ensured only by attracting consumers away from other schools (Ball, Bowe, and Gewirtz 1995). It is important to note, however, that in most countries that have traditionally or recently encouraged choice, real choice is limited to urban areas where different types of schools are concentrated in a small geographical area. An exception to this trend is the Netherlands, where, because of the public financial aid granted to private groups that decide to set up new schools, small towns and rural areas offer a wide variety of school provision (OCDE 1994).

Contrary to the postulates of market ideology that all parents will try to apply to schools with good academic reputations, thus forcing other schools to improve, research shows that reasons for choosing between schools in European countries are quite diverse. In the past, choices between the public and private sector were frequently related to religious affiliation. Today, choices between both sectors or within the same sector are more likely related to perceptions concerning the quality of schooling, although a religious or a moral dimension is still apparent among those who choose the private sector (Héran 1996). What is meant by "quality" can nevertheless be quite different from one family to the other. Parents certainly try to have their children accepted in schools known for their good results and their attractive educational options, but this kind of strategic choosing can apply only where there is real variation between schools and if parents are able to make informed choices (Ballion 1986). Parents, however, are also attentive to the "ethos" of a school, the mix between social and ethnic composition and the values promoted by principals and teachers through pedagogical options, extracurricular activities, and disciplinary techniques (Ball, Bowe, and Gewirtz 1995). Factors such as distance, transportation, and cost also remain important. A majority of parents are not "active choosers" but send their children to the nearest or more accessible schools.

In addition to this, it is important to note that children's "happiness" remains an important criterion of parental choice (Coldron and Boulton 1991). Although mothers are particularly involved in the complex process of choosing, most adults do not make their choices alone. They go over choices with their children, especially late in secondary schooling (David, West, and Ribbens 1994). The importance given to children's opinions, however, seems to vary according to the liberal or conservative character of European societies. Recent surveys show, for instance, that children are more likely to be consulted about their preferences in Great Britain and in France than in Belgium (OCDE 1994).

Choice is not, however, equally distributed among social and ethnic groups. Although urban working-class parents do make choices, as has been shown by Scottish and French research (Adler, Petch, and Tweedie 1989; Léger and Tripier 1986), the proportion of "active choosers" among them is less important than in middle-class communities. Moreover, the circuits and processes of choice can differ considerably. Middle-class parents usually include a variety of schools as theoretical possibilities to carefully explore through visits and contacts with school personnel even when they are also aware of the reputation of these schools among friends and acquaintances. Working-class parents, on the other hand, are more likely immediately to dismiss some schools as being "out of reach" physically or symbolically or to stick to a positive preference for local schools that are important in maintaining the identity of working-class communities (Ball, Bowe, and Gewirtz 1995). British and French research shows that parents from ethnic minorities are less likely to exercise their right to choose and less likely to make really informed choices. Moreover, if one takes into account the fact that the social and especially the ethnic composition of schools are factors that many parents consider part of the "ethos" or the "quality" of school, there is reason to fear that choice may help some parents influence the educational futures of their children while reinforcing inequalities. This fear may seem unfounded, given the fact that the proportion of "active choosers" remains relatively small in countries where choice is a new and minor element of educational policy. Nevertheless, as noted by a recent OECD report (1994), even a limited amount of choice can have important social consequences for school personnel, parents, and children.

Accountability and Participation in School-Governing Bodies

The parental choice movement is related to the accountability movement in that a market ideology is predominant in both. In fact, the notion of the accountability of public services has taken root and spread against a background of economic recession, reduction of public expenses, and falling pupil numbers, on the one hand, and of significant decrease in trust in public services such as education, on the other hand, even in countries such as Sweden, where satisfaction with the welfare state has been very important (Lindblad 1995). Within the context of accountability policies and studies, parents are seen as a major external audience with whom schools need to create and sustain a dynamic and constructive relationship based on mutual respect and the full exchange of information. For politicians and pressure groups, accountability implies an increase in external influence and control, whereas for teachers it implies securing a renewal of trust through increasing efforts to explain and justify policy, actions, and results (Bastiani 1987; Munn 1991). A recent example of accountability practices is the emergence in England and Wales of government "league tables" and in France of an official document comparing the results of each *lycée*.

Parental pressure for accountability and the resistance to it of teachers and school personnel are reflected in increased conflict between parents, teachers, and school authorities in many European countries. Conflict has even been reported between parents and the ecclesiastic authorities and school personnel of Catholic schools (Arthur 1994). From the parents' side, these conflicts stem from a desire to foster the educational future of their children in a context in which education appears to be a major protection against unemployment and in which educational opportunities appear to have increased. At the same time, these parents feel that they do not possess enough information and power to ensure the best choices for their children. Conflicts also stem from dissatisfaction with the possibility of influencing the functioning of schools in democratic societies in which public participation is continuously presented as a guiding principle. From the teachers' point of view, conflict seems to arise from the difficulty of moving from a bureaucratic mode of functioning, which implies being accountable to local or state education authorities only, to a professional mode, which implies being accountable to customers for fear of losing control of the educational activity and of individual autonomy (Montandon 1994). Conflict may also proceed from the feeling of school authorities and teachers that accountability procedures benefit only those parents whose social position and educational level allow them to understand what goes on in school and give them the confidence to contest school decisions.

The degree to which parental participation in school governance is allowed in each European country impacts the positions of parents and teachers. Denmark and Scotland are atypical in having a voting majority of parents in school governance. Other countries with a long tradition of decentralization such as the

Netherlands and Germany have equal numbers of parents and teachers in most educational decisions. In the Netherlands, parents have been members of parents' councils in the public and the private sector for a long time. Legislation set up in the 1980s specifies that each school must have a participatory council on which a third of the members should be parents (and in secondary schools, students aged 16 or up). Although it has only consultative powers, the council can debate on any topic. In Germany, although it is difficult to give a global view because of important differences between *Länder*, the *Skulkonferenz*, which is the central structure of participatory administration and is composed of parents, students, and teachers, can make decisions on such important matters as the organization of homework and examinations, remedial teaching and guidance, choice of teaching materials, and extracurricular activities. On the other hand, in countries such as Italy, Portugal, and France, formal participation of parents in school affairs is not only a recent phenomenon but remains limited by legislation, the attitude of teachers, and the national positions of parents' associations (Macbeth 1984, 1993).

Parent associations exist in most European countries. Although they fulfill similar functions, their specific objectives, their capacity to influence national and local educational policy, and their modes of intervention nevertheless vary considerably. Macbeth (1984) distinguishes four types of parent associations. The first is composed of those associations that function as a support group for teachers; an example of this type is the National Confederation of Parent-Teacher Associations in the United Kingdom. The second comprises associations that see their task as the cooperation of equals, parents with teachers and school personnel, the case of some Belgian and Dutch associations. Other associations found in many European countries see themselves as a group to defend parental interests. Finally, some associations are closer to the model of an ideological group. This is frequently the case of associations of a particular religious affiliation or of an educational affiliation such as "comprehensive" or "progressive." In practice, however, many European parent associations combine more than one of these types.

Parental participation in governing bodies, either as individuals or as members of parental organizations, presents difficulties. A central difficulty is the tension between the search for more parental rights through public confrontation and negotiation, and the conviction that harmony and cooperation between teachers and parents is necessary for the children's sake (Dutercq 1996; Barthélémy 1995). Another problem is the parents' need to acquire sufficient knowledge about school legislation, policies, and daily functioning so that teachers, principals, and other educational professionals will recognize them as competent partners. In fact, many parents who sit in governing bodies have great difficulty contesting professional judgments (Zanten and Migeot-Alvarado 1992). This is the case even in those countries, such as Scotland or England, where recent legislation has considerably increased lay power in local educational decision making (Munn 1993; Field 1993). A third important problem is that of representing other parents and of communicating with them about school matters. Because in many countries only a limited number of parents participate in the election of representatives, and because these representatives are more likely to come from the upper or middle class and have a higher educational level than average parents, the representatives may encounter difficulties in teacher recognition of their legitimacy and in interaction with parents from lower-class and immigrant backgrounds.

As a group, parents in Europe play an important role in supporting the school career of their children. They devote considerable time and energy to helping their children with school assignments, to providing them with materials and activities that complement school learning, to discussing problems and progress with teachers and school personnel, and to choosing the school track. A significant number of parents want to be involved in school affairs, either as individuals or as members of parent organizations. Variations between countries reflect differences in cultural traditions, differences in the political and administrative organization of educational systems and the training of teachers and school personnel, and in their definition of role. Nevertheless, these variations are less important than those that exist within each country between parents of different socio-economic, ethnic, and geographical backgrounds.

CONCLUSION

Persisting social inequalities in school careers attest to the influence of family background on children's academic success and adaptation. Even if European children attend school earlier and for longer periods (and consequently if schooling is prolonged), even if mothers increasingly are working outside the home, and even if divorces occur more often, this does not imply that families are retreating from their educational function or that schools must play the role of substitute parents. Families' cultural resources have more influence than financial resources, and are in turn mediated by rearing practices particularly influential in early childhood. In addition, in more and more undifferentiated educational systems where subtle choices are increasingly required from parents, cultural resources exert a growing impact because parents do not have equal ability to manage their children's careers. Last but not least, with more youngsters staying longer at school and with fewer opportunities for jobs, competition has become harsher, and this has fostered parental involvement in education.

NOTES

1. In all European countries, divorce rates are rising, even if they remain far lower than in the United States: 1.6 divorces per 1,000 people in Europe (ranging from 2.5 in Denmark to 0.5 in Ireland), compared with 4.8 in the United States. The growth of divorce rates and the fact that women work more often outside the home result in young

children spending less time with their parents and more in collective settings in institutions, particularly preschool ones (cf. Husén, Tuijman, and Halls 1992).

2. Many pieces of research underline the impact of emotional disruptions on academic achievement (Campos Luanco and Calero Garcia 1988).

3. In some European countries, these results have been criticized as displaying ethnocentrism from researchers belonging themselves to middle-class families (Combessie 1969).

4. This result can be put in line with what has been observed by Baumrind (1980) about the "authoritative" style: Children oriented toward achievement, presenting more independent goal-oriented behaviors, had parents showing both a high level of demand and a great sensitivity to their children's needs.

5. "Family literacy" has become a movement in countries such as the Netherlands, with many family literacy programs in libraries, adult literacy centers, and community agencies.

REFERENCES

Adler, M., A. Petch, and J. Tweedie. 1989. *Parental Choice and Educational Policy.* Edinburgh: Edinburgh University Press.

Anderson-Levitt, K. 1989. "Degrees of Distance between Teachers and Parents in Urban France." *Anthropology and Education Quarterly* 20 (2): 97–117.

Andersson, B. E. 1989. "Effects of Public Day Care: A Longitudinal Study." *Child Development* 60: 857–866.

Arthur, J. 1994. "Parental Involvement in Catholic Schools: A Case of Increasing Conflict." *British Journal of Educational Studies* 42 (2): 174–190.

Ball, S., R. Bowe, and S. Gewirtz. 1995. "Circuits of Schooling: A Sociological Exploration of Parental Choice of School in Social Class Contexts." *Sociological Review* 43 (1): 52–78.

Ballion, R. 1986. "Le choix du collège: le comportement 'éclaire' des familles." *Revue Française de Sociologie* 27: 719–734.

Bargel, T. 1994. "Jeunesse et système éducatif en RFA: remarques sur la question des inégalités sociales." In *Jeunesses et sociétés.* Edited by G. Mauger, R. Bendit and C. Von Wolffersdorff. Paris: Colin.

Barthélémy, M. 1995. "Des militants de l'école: les associations de parents d'élèves en France." *Revue française de sociologie* 36 (3): 439–472.

Bastiani, J. 1987. "From Compensation to Participation? A Brief Analysis of Changing Attitudes in the Study and Practice of Home-School Relations." In *Parents and Teachers 1: Perspectives on Home-School Relations.* Edited by J. Bastiani. Windsor: NFER-Nelson, 88–107.

Baumert, J. 1991. "Langfristige Auswirkungen der Bildungsexpansion." *Unterrichtswissenschaft* 19: 333–349.

Baumrind, D. 1980. "New Directions in Socialization Research." *American Psychologist* 35: 639–652.

Beattie, N. 1985. *Professional Parents: Parent Participation in Four Western European Countries.* London: The Falmer Press.

Bell, A., and A. Sigsworth. 1987. *The Small Rural Primary School. A Matter of Quality.* London: The Falmer Press.

Bertram, H. 1994. "Jeunesse d'Allemagne." In *Jeunesses et sociétés*. Edited by G. Mauger, R. Bendit, and C. Von Wolffersdorff. Paris: Colin.

Bogenschneider, K., and L. Steinberg. 1994. "Maternal Employment and Adolescents' Academic Achievement: A Developmental Analysis." *Sociology of Education* 67: 60–77.

Bourdieu, P., and J. C. Passeron. 1970. *La reproduction. Eléments pour une théorie du système d'enseignement*. Paris: Minuit.

Bus, A. G., M. H. Van Ijzendoorn, and A. Pellegrini. 1995. "Joint Book Reading Makes Success in Learning to Read: A Meta-Analysis on Intergenerational Transmission of Literacy." *Review of Educational Research* 65 (1): 1–21.

Caillé, J. P. 1992. "Les parents d'élèves de collège et les études de leur enfant." *Economie et statistique* 32: 15–23.

Campos Luanco, M. L., and M. D. Calero Garcia. 1988. "El retraso escolar y su relacion con el clima escolar percibido." *Bordon* 4: 649–657.

Castro, P., M. B. Monteiro, and M. Rebelo. 1995. "Mother's Beliefs about the Development and Education of Children: Content and Sources of Variability." European Conference on Educational Research, Bath, UK (September 1995).

Chambaz, C. 1996. "Les loisirs des jeunes en dehors du lycée et du collège." *Economie et statistique* 293 (3): 95–106.

Coldron, J., and P. Boulton. 1991. " 'Happiness' as a Criterion of Parents' Choice of School." *Journal of Education Policy* 6 (2): 169–178.

Combessie, J. C. 1969. "Education et valeurs de classe dans la sociologie américaine." *Revue française de sociologie* 10: 12–36.

Croxford, L. 1994. "Equal Opportunities in the Secondary-School Curriculum in Scotland, 1977–1991." *British Educational Research Journal* 20 (4): 371–391.

Cyster, R., P. S. Clift, and S. Battle. 1979. *Parental Involvement in Primary Schools*. London: NFER.

David, M., R. Edwards, M. Hughes, and J. Ribbens. 1993. *Mothers & Education Inside Out? Exploring Family-Education Policy and Experience*. London: Macmillan.

David, M., A. West, and J. Ribbens. 1994. *Mother's Intuition? Choosing Secondary Schools*. London: The Falmer Press.

Duru-Bellat, M. 1996. "Social Inequalities in French Secondary Schools from Figures to Theories." *British Journal of Sociology of Education* 17 (3) 341–350.

Duru-Bellat, M., and A. van Zanten. 1992. *Sociologie de l'école*. Paris: A. Colin.

Duru-Bellat, M., and J. P. Jarousse. 1996. "Le masculin et le féminin dans les modèles éducatifs des parents." *Economie et statistique* 293: 77–93.

Duru-Bellat, M., J. P. Jarousse, M. A. Labopin, and V. Perrier. 1993b. "Les processus d'auto-sélection à l'entrée en 1ère." *L'Orientation Scolaire et Professionnelle* 22 (3): 258–272.

Duru-Bellat, M., J. P. Jarousse, and A. Mingat. 1993a. "Les scolarités de la maternelle au lycée: étapes et processus dans la production des inégalités sociales." *Revue française de sociologie* 34 (1): 43–60.

Duru-Bellat, M., and A. Mingat. 1989. "How Do French Junior Secondary Schools Operate? Academic Achievement, Grading, and Streaming of Students." *European Sociological Review* 5 (1): 47–64.

Dutercq, Y. 1996. "La résistible ascension de la cause des parents d'élèves en France." In *L'Ecole et le changement: défi à la sociologie?* Montréal: Logiques (in press).

Establet, R. 1987. *L'école est-elle rentable?* Paris: PUF.

Field, L. 1993. "School Governing Bodies: The Lay-Professional Relationship." *School Organization* 13 (2): 165–174.

Flitner-Merle, E. 1992. "Scolarité des enfants d'immigrés en RFA." *Revue française de sociologie* 33: 37–52.

Fontaine, A. M. 1991. "Le genre de l'enfant influence-t-il la structuration de la vie familiale?" *Enfance* 45 (1–2): 111–126.

———. 1994. "Achievement Motivation and Child Rearing in Different Social Contexts." *European Journal of Psychology of Education* 9 (3): 225–240.

Gewirtz, S., S. Ball, and R. Bowe. 1995. *Markets, Choice and Equity in Education.* Buckingham: Open University Press.

Gissot, C., F. Héran, and N. Manon. 1994. "Les efforts éducatifs des familles." *INSEE Résultats Consommation Modes de Vie* 62–63.

Glasman, D. 1994. *Cours particuliers et sens de la scolarité.* Paris: C.N.D.P.

Glasman, D., et al. 1991. "Le soutien scolaire hors école." *Revue française de pédagogie* 95: 31–45.

Glenn, C. L. 1989. *Choice of School in Six Nations.* Washington, DC: U.S. Department of Education.

Graaf (de), P. M. 1986. "The Impact of Financial and Cultural Resources on Educational Attainment in the Netherlands." *Sociology of Education* 59 (4): 237–246.

———. 1988. "Parents' Financial and Cultural Resources, Grades, and Transition to Secondary School in the Federal Republic of Germany." *European Sociological Review* 4 (3): 209–221.

Grisay, A., A. Delhaxhe, et al. 1990. "Quelle approche du langage écrit à la maison et à l'école?" *Revue française de pédagogie* 91: 47–57.

Héran, F. 1994. "L'aide au travail scolaire: les mères persévèrent." *INSEE Première* 350.

———. 1996. "École publique, école privée: qui peut choisir?" *Economie et statistique* 293 (3): 17–40.

Huberman, M. 1989. *La vie des enseignants. Evolution et bilan d'une profession.* Lausanne: Delachaux et Niestlé.

Husén, T., A. Tuijman, and W. D. Halls, eds. 1992. *Schooling in Modern European Society.* Oxford: Pergamon Press.

Jarousse, J. P., A. Mingat, and M. Richard. 1992. "La scolarisation à deux ans: effets pédagogiques et sociaux." *Education et formations* 31: 3–9.

Jung (de), P. F. 1993. "The Relationship Between Students' Behaviour at Home and Attention and Achievement in Elementary School." *British Journal of Educational Psychology* 63: 201–213.

Kellershals, J., and C. Montandon. 1991. *Les stratégies éducatives des familles.* Paris: Delachaux et Niestlé.

Kellershals, J., C. Montandon, G. Ritschard, and M. Sardi. 1992. "Le style éducatif des parents et l'estime de soi des adolescents." *Revue française de sociologie* 33 (3): 313–333.

Khöler, H. 1992. "Bildungsbeteilung und Sozialstruktur in der Bundesrepublik." Max-Planck-Institut für Bildungsforschung, Studien und Berichte, 53.

Lahire, B. 1995. *Tableaux de familles.* Paris: Gallimard-Le Seuil.

Langouët, G., and A. Léger. 1991. *Public ou privé? Trajectoires et réussites scolaires.* Paris: Pubilidix/éditions de l'Espace Européen.

Lautrey, J. 1989. "Structuration de l'environnement familial et développement cognitif: quoi de neuf?" *Bulletin de psychologie* 62 (388): 46–56.

Léger, A., and M. Tripier. 1986. *Fuir ou construire l'école populaire?* Paris: Méridiens-Klincksieck.

Le Guen, M. 1991. "Réussite scolaire et disparités socio-démographiques." *Education et formations* 27–28: 9–28.

Lindblad, S. 1995. "Missing the Market: Exploring Current Tendencies in the Restructuration of Education in Sweden." Paper presented at the ECER 95 Conference, Bath, England.

Lopez Bachero, M. 1986. *La familia en Murcia*. Valencia: Nau Llibres.

Mac Nab, C., and A. Murray. 1985. "Family Composition and Mathematics Achievement." *Scandinavian Journal of Educational Research* 29 (2): 89–101.

Macbeth, A. 1984. *L'enfant entre l'école et sa famille*. Bruxelles: Office des publications officielles des Communautés Européennes, Education series 13.

———. 1993. "Preconceptions about Parents in Education: Will Europe Change Us?" In *Parents and Schools: Customers, Managers or Partners?* Edited by P. Munn. London: Routledge, 27–46.

Meijnen, G. W., H. Guldemond, and A. Boomsma. 1989. "Socialization and Development of Academic Abilities." In *Educational Opportunities in the Welfare State*. Edited by B.F.M. Bakker, J. Dronkers, and G.W. Meijnen. Nijmegen: Instituut voor Toegepaste Sociale Wetenschappen, OOMO-Series.

Milne, A., D. Myers, A. Rosenthal, and A. Ginsburg. 1986. "Single Parents, Working Mothers, and the Educational Achievement of School Children." *Sociology of Education* 59 (3): 125–139.

Mingat, A. 1991. "Expliquer la variété des acquisitions au cours préparatoire: les rôles de l'enfant, de la famille et de l'école." *Revue française de pédagogie* 95: 47–63.

Monreal, J., and A. Vinao. 1979. "Aspiraciones y expectativas educativas y desigualdad social: procesos de interiorizacion de la realidad social objectiva." *Cuadernos de Realidades Sociales* 14–15: 123–145.

Montandon, C. 1991. *L'école dans la vie des familles*. Genève: Service de la Recherche Sociologique, cahier 32.

———. 1994. "Les relations parents-enseignants dans l'école primaire: de quelques causes d'incompréhension mutuelle." In *Education et famille*. Edited by P. Durning and J. P. Pourtois. Bruxelles: De Boeck, 206–217.

Müller, W., and W. Karle. 1993. "Social Selection in Educational Systems in Europe." *European Sociological Review* 9: 1–23.

Munn, P. 1991. "School Boards, Accountability and Control." *British Journal of Educational Studies* 39 (2): 173–189.

———. 1993. "Parents as School Board Members: School Managers and Friends?" In *Parents and Schools: Customers, Managers or Partners?* Edited by P. Munn. London: Routledge, 87–100.

Ni Bhrolchain, M., R. Chappell, and I. Diamond. 1994. "Scolarité et autres caractéristiques socio-démographiques des enfants de mariages rompus." *Population* 6: 1588–1612.

OCDE (Organization de coopération et de développment economique). 1991. *Examen des politiques nationales d'éducation: Pays-Bas*. Paris: OCDE.

———. 1994. *Le choix de l'école*. Paris: OCDE.

Ortega, P. 1983. "Medios socio-familiares y motivation y ayuda al estudio." *Anales de pédagogia* 1: 207–228.

————. 1983. "Expectativas socio-culturales de los padres y medio socio-familiar."
    Anales de pedagogia 1: 181–206.
Paterson, L. 1991a. "Trends in Attainment in Scottish Secondary Schools." In *Schools,
    Classrooms and Pupils*. Edited by S. W. Raudenbush and J. D. Willms. San
    Diego: Academic Press.
————. 1991b. "Socio-Economic Status and Educational Attainment: A Multi-
    Dimensional and Multi-Level Study." *Evaluation and Research in Education* 5
    (3): 97–121.
Perrenoud, P. 1987a. "Ce que l'école fait aux familles. Inventaire." In *Entre parents et
    enseignants: un dialogue impossible?* Edited by C. Montandon and P. Perrenoud.
    Berne: P. Lang, 89–168.
————. 1987b. "Le 'go-between': l'enfant messager et message entre sa famille et
    l'école." In *Entre parents et enseignants: un dialogue impossible?* Edited by C.
    Montandon and P. Perrenoud. Berne: P. Lang.
Perrez, M., and C. Chervet. 1989. "Rôle de la famille dans le développement des attri-
    butions causales et des convictions de contrôle." In *Les thématiques en éducation
    familiale*. Edited by J. P. Pourtois. Brussels: De Boeck.
Pincon, M., and M. Pincon-Charlot. 1989. *Dans les beaux quartiers*. Paris: Seuil.
Pourtois, J. P. 1991. "L'éducation parentale." *Revue française de pédagogie* 96: 87–112.
Pourtois, J. P., et al. 1984. *Eduquer les parents*. Brussels: Labor.
Pourtois, J. P., and H. Desmet. 1989. "L'éducation familiale." *Revue française de pé-
    dagogie*. 86: 69–101.
Prêteur, Y., and E. Louvet-Schmauss. 1995. "Une pédagogie fonctionnelle de l'écrit à
    l'école peut-elle réduire l'hétérogénéité de départ liée aux pratiques socio-
    familiales?" *Revue française de pédagogie* 113: 83–92.
Reed-Danahay, D., and K. Anderson-Levitt. 1991. "Backwards Countryside, Troubled
    City: French Teachers' Images of Rural and Working-Class Families." *American
    Ethnologist* 18 (3): 546–564.
Rülcker, T. 1989. "Familienbedingungen heutige Kinder." *Grundschule* 5: 16–18.
Sammons, P. 1995. "Gender, Ethnic, and Socio-economic Differences in Attainment and
    Progress: a Longitudinal Analysis of Student Achievement over 9 Years." *British
    Educational Research Journal* 21 (4): 465–485.
Scheerens, J. 1992. *Effective Schooling: Research, Theory, and Practice*. London, New
    York: Cassell.
Sharp, R., and A. Green. 1975. *Education and Social Control*. London: Routledge and
    Kegan Paul.
Shavit, Y., and H. P. Blossfeld, eds. 1993. *Persistent Inequality. Changing Educational
    Attainment in Thirteen Countries*. Boulder: Westview Press.
Skog, B. 1991. "Girls' Avoidance of 'Hard' Science Subjects: Protest or a Rational
    Choice?" *Scandinavian Journal of Educational Research* 35 (3): 201–211.
Tomlinson, S. 1993. "Ethnic Minorities: Involved Partners or Problem Parents?" In *Par-
    ents and Schools: Customers, Managers, or Partners?* Edited by P. Munn. Lon-
    don: Routledge, 131–147.
Trommer, L. 1990. *Demographische Entwicklung und Bildungsbeteiligung von Auslän-
    dern*. Berlin: Max Planck Institut für Bildungsforschung, 25.
Ulich, K. 1985. "Eltern und Schüler. Die Schule as Problem in der Familienerziehung."
    Zeitschrift für pädagogik 31 (1): 45–75.
Undheim, J. O., and H. Nordvik. 1992. "Socio-economic Factors and Sex Differences in

an Egalitarian Educational System: Academic Achievement in 16-year-old Norwegian Students." *Scandinavian Journal of Educational Research* 36 (2): 87–98.

Vallet, L. A., and J. P. Caillé. 1995. "Les carrières scolaires au collège des élèves étrangers ou issus de l'immigration." *Education et formations* 40: 5–14.

van Den Bossche, J. 1994. "Le musée, instrument d'enrichissement culturel de la famille." In *Education et famille*. Edited by P. Durning and J. P. Pourtois. Bruxelles: De Boeck, 235–245.

Wadsworth, M.E.J. 1986. "Effects of Parenting Style and Preschool Experience on Children's Verbal Attainment: Results of a British Longitudinal Study." *Early Childhood Research Quarterly* 1: 237–248.

Wesselingh, A. 1996. "The Dutch Sociology of Education." *British Journal of Sociology of Education* 17 (2): 213–226.

Wofendale, S., ed. 1989. *Parental Involvement: Developing Networks between School, Home, and Community*. London: Cassell.

Zanten (van), A. 1988. "Les familles face à l'école: rapports institutionnels et relations sociales." In *Education familiale. Un panorama des recherches internationales*. Edited by P. Durning. Paris: MIRE/Matrice, 185–207.

———. 1990. *L'école et l'espace local*. Lyon: Presses Universitaires de Lyon.

Zanten (van), A., and J. Migeot-Alvarado. 1992. "La participation des familles au fonctionnement des établissements d'enseignement secondaire, rapport à la Direction des lycées et collèges du Ministère de l'Education nationale." Paris: Equipe de sociologie de l'éducation, 115.

Zéroulou, Z. 1988. "La réussite scolaire des enfants d'immigrés." *Revue Française de sociologie* 29: 447–470.

8

Gender Issues in European Education Today

Margaret B. Sutherland

When we talk of education in Europe, it is useful to consider what our concept of Europe is. Obviously there are various international and political organizations whose European status is precisely defined, but it does not follow that when the term *European* is used, the many components of Europe are recognized and considered. For those living in Western Europe, a group of such countries as France, Spain, Portugal, Germany, Austria, Belgium, and the Netherlands, comes readily to mind. Switzerland's long-recognized policy of political neutrality gives its European membership a special quality: and on another political level the United Kingdom's hesitations about membership in the European Union sometimes cast doubt on how European it is. But there are also the smaller European states and the islands; there are the Eastern Mediterranean countries. And, a possibly distinct entity until recent times, a number of European countries who formerly belonged to the Soviet bloc are now pursuing varied forms of autonomy as Central European states, such as Poland and Hungary, or Eastern European states such as Russia and the Ukraine, or the small Baltic states of Latvia, Estonia, and Lithuania. Yet another separate entity is formed by the Nordic countries whose links with each other seem closer than those with other parts of Europe. The concept of Europe must thus recognize diversity, a rich variety of countries, some large, some very small, working out in their distinctive ways a balance between their history and the demands of the modern world while—some with greater immediacy than others—they accept and are influenced by increasing interaction with the rest of Europe.

A rich variety of social and political aspects is therefore involved in questions of gender issues in Europe, and the tendency to think in terms of only one or other of the distinctive groupings—Western Europe, Eastern Europe, Mediterranean Europe, Scandinavia—is to be avoided. Diversity seems probable as a result of the various political systems that determined the lives of men and women in Europe during the 20th century. Although we can find in the 19th century evidence of parallel struggles by women's groups for the improvement of women's electoral, educational, and social rights in many European countries, radical political regimes and the two world wars have produced other struggles and distracted attention from the situation of women. We may recall in particular the Nazi dictatorship and the spread of the Soviet empire, but also the Franco regime in Spain (1939–1975), the Salazar regime in Portugal (1926–1968), and the civil war, despotic government, and the Colonels' regime ending in Greece in 1974. Thus it is not simply a difference between Western and Soviet countries that might dichotomize women's situation in Europe: women's progress in the various other countries also, as Kaplan (1992) has shown, has been strongly affected by distinctive government structures and policies. Although in some countries that have enjoyed relatively peaceful and liberal government, progress toward the betterment of women's situation has been considerable, we still find, as the following survey shows, a considerable number of common factors that impede the realization of equality between the sexes.

The common factors to be considered now are (1) religious doctrines, (2) equality in higher education, (3) the relative achievements of girls and boys, (4) women's dual role, and (5) some effects of the hidden curriculum. We shall then note the possible effects of governmental and international policies as well as the contributions of individual organizations.

COMMON FACTORS

The Influence of Religions

Throughout Europe (and other continents) the teaching of various religions has encouraged gender-differentiated provision of education. Religious doctrines in the past and in the present have advocated for males and females different role models, behaviors, and interests. In many educational systems at present there is evidence of a considerable conflict between an official policy of nondiscrimination, promoting equality of opportunity for males and females, and the continuing efforts of religious teaching to ensure gender differentiation in school, in society, and in the home.

Let us review the influence of the religions that have been taught in Europe during many centuries: The Christian churches have consistently made clear what qualities and skills are to be developed by a good woman. She should be a good wife and mother, a role commended for centuries to girls and women throughout Europe (and, through missionary efforts, in other parts of the world). The qualities and skills best suiting women to this role strongly affected the aims of female education until recent times: intellectual development and individual autonomy were seen as of secondary importance. Admittedly, some differences have existed, according to the kind of Christianity dominating the country or state. Nicholas Hans (1949) noted that although the Orthodox Church did little to encourage popular schooling, both Catholic and Protestant authorities made provision for at least elementary education. Yet, having comprehensively examined the Catholic and the Puritan traditions in education, he suggested that in Catholic countries the provision of secondary education for girls was inferior to that made in Protestant countries and was associated, in the Catholic systems, with opposition to coeducation.

Religious influences on the provision of education do vary as the teachings of the churches evolve in different periods of history and in different countries. Coeducation, for example, has for some time now become accepted in Catholic schools (De Grandpré 1970). But even within an international church, interpretations of doctrine can vary from one country to another. The Dutch or French interpretations of Catholic doctrines can be compared with that found in the Republic of Ireland, where more traditional attitudes, such as that regarding the permissibility of divorce, have been slower to change. Fine-Davis (1988) found evidence of some change in opinions in Dublin, since in 1975, 70% of those questioned agreed that "being a wife and mother are the most fulfilling roles any woman could want," whereas in 1986 only 39%—still a substantial proportion—agreed with this statement.

An important change in religious doctrines affecting the education of women has been the gradual acceptance, in some churches, of women as ministers of religion, able to accede to all positions of importance and power in the church. It is a change now achieved in some Protestant churches; but as recent controversies show, it is still a matter of dispute in the Church of England and there are obviously deeply rooted beliefs about the incapacity of women to officiate in religious ceremonies and to teach and give guidance in religion. The authority of the Roman Catholic Church is still firmly opposed to the admission of women to the priesthood. Thus in some areas of Europe where Christian religious doctrines are recognized, the education of women and their life work will be restricted not only by the refusal to prepare them for the priesthood and authority in the church, but also by the underlying belief that women are not equal to men, or that at best, they must accept different, less influential, roles in the church and consequently in society.

The survival of traditional attitudes toward women and their role in life is also to be noted in a more ancient religious faith, Judaism. Here, too, the rule has been that girls should be educated to fulfill the respected role of wife and mother, and that many important religious observances are for men only. The acceptance of women rabbis by some Jewish communities since the 1970s has given some women greater access to religious studies, and has been accompanied by a relaxation of rules excluding women from some public religious observances. Yet here also, a division remains in Jewish communities in different countries between those who accept such changes in gender roles and those who prefer to adhere to traditional differentiations.

Clearly the era of the Soviet Union would have been expected to reduce, if not to eliminate, the effects of religious doctrines in Soviet countries. Yet Muslim teaching remained (unofficially) influential in some of the eastern states of the Union. And generally, religion has survived in a variety of ways. In Russia, since the change of regime, there has indeed been a revival of interest, notably among young people formerly deprived of religious education: it is now in some instances a school subject. In Poland during the Soviet era, support for the church was a kind of political statement, an affirmation of national identity. People who did not hold religious beliefs nevertheless chose to attend church services. But already in the mid-1980s there were attempts by church authorities to return women to the traditional role of wife and mother: a document of the Subcommittee of the Episcopate placed "motherhood in front of other tasks of women" (Siemienska 1994). And in the new political climate, the Catholic Church has greater freedom to try to influence the behavior of men and women, encouraging women to return to the motherhood ideal (Dabic 1994). For some women who were actively engaged in political struggles for freedom for the country, the exhortation, backed by religious authority, to return to the domestic hearth is a sad disillusionment. But in the Czech Republic also there has been a revival of political parties aiming at returning women to the care of the house and children (Klimesova 1994).

In Poland and elsewhere, religious teaching is of course one of the factors in recent controversies about abortion. Whereas earlier Soviet regimes made abortion widely available—admittedly it was often an alternative to contraception and effective family planning (Laas 1990)—a reaction against it, with religious support for this opposition, has now become vocal. Such considerations affect female education in many ways, especially in forming concepts of the right way of life for women and their status as autonomous individuals.

On the practical level, religious authorities in many countries seek to influence the amount and kind of sex education provided in the school curriculum for both boys and girls. As the change of regime in Soviet bloc countries has allowed the setting up of denominational schools, the possibilities of religious authorities introducing their interpretations into the curriculum of such countries have notably increased.

At the same time we must recognize that in many Western European countries, adherence to Christian churches has been in decline, and only small proportions of the population can be regarded as practicing believers. Possibly, therefore, today's attitudes toward differentiated roles now rest more on traditions or prejudices than on religion. Yet these traditions often stemmed from religious beliefs. It is indeed difficult to disentangle religion and tradition in many societies: certainly, when changes in social roles are proposed, even non-churchgoers often fall back on vaguely religious arguments.

At the same time, in some European countries where Christian church attendance is in decline, other religions are increasing in strength, often through the effects of immigration. Europe indeed has long been influenced by religious traditions other than the Christian and the Jewish. In the East are Islamic communities whose teaching accords in some ways with the models proposed historically by Christianity and Judaism—the good woman confining herself to caring for her husband, her children, and the home. Although the growth of Islamic fundamentalism has been more notable in the African Maghreb states, some indications of a return to earlier interpretations of women's place in society have been evident in Turkey (Acar 1994), and the Islamic interpretations of women's place in society remains important in many other parts of Eastern Europe. The Bosnian struggles have again provided tragic instances of the violence exercised against women in the name of religion.

Since Europe today is not simply a collection of indigenous peoples but a community to which immigrants have been admitted, more or less willingly, the educational systems of many European countries now face the task of providing for a population of children and young people whose home religion is not the Christian or the Jewish faith. Educators have tried (Mitter and Swift 1985), and are trying, to reconcile respect for the cultural background of immigrants with respect for the traditions and customs of the host nations. Conflicts of role models for girls and young women thus arise when school policies emphasize gender equality and the home background proposes a differentiated role. This conflict has been clearly shown in France, in the affair of the head scarves, when the simple act of wearing head coverings in school—an act that seemed to some young females to be a religious gesture they wanted to make (though others apparently were directed by their family in this)—seemed incompatible with the secular principles of the French educational system, whose aims are to create feelings of common citizenship and to ensure equal rights for women (*Le Monde de l'Education* 1995). Such controversy is not unique to France: it has arisen in minor instances in the United Kingdom and in Canada.

The influence of Islamic requirements that education prepare girls for women's ascribed role has also led in England to demands for separate schools for Muslim girls, to be provided on a par with other religious schools like those of the Church of England, the Roman Catholic Church, and the Jewish community. On the one side it is argued that this is merely a call for equal rights, giving Islamic schools parity with other denominational schools that receive public financing. On the other side it is argued that the teaching in these schools might be prejudicial to the freedom of girls to develop their own point of view and to enjoy the lifestyle typical of society in Britain. They might also encourage racial segregation. However, it is not only girls' moral education that is thought to be endangered by the ordinary schools of the country. Demands for Islamic schools are said to arise partly from fears that the corrupt moral values of Western societies are being transmitted to both sexes.

This problem naturally affects not only Muslim girls but also Hindu and Sikh young people, and unfortunately, the environment of mixed schools can produce not only religious but also racial tensions for both boys and girls. Yet it is especially girls whose families have come from other countries who may face in the ordinary European comprehensive school not only hostility because of their ethnic origin and their religion but also sexual harassment. Simultaneously, they have to cope with adjusting to the norms of behavior set by the school authorities and their classmates while still adhering, possibly watched critically by brothers in the same school, to the standards of behavior determined by the religious outlook of their home. It is a situation that is not sufficiently often recognized as requiring attention by school authorities. Nevertheless, there is evidence that some young women in such a situation are able to evolve defenses against various types of hostility, as well as the ability to see both sides in an objective way, which parents would do well to emulate (MacIntosh 1990). And some, in their school days at least, compare the restrictions imposed by their religion (such as not going out alone on social occasions, leaving the choice of their marriage partner to their parents) with the freedom given by other religions or an absence of religion and still opt for their home religion and its beliefs.

As we recognize these common influences of major religions in prescribing differentiated roles and activities for males and females, we recall that education is not simply a matter of learning facts and developing skills. It creates attitudes and self-concepts possibly even more effectively than it transmits knowledge. We must therefore have in mind the profound effects that religious doctrines and teachings, however conveyed, are going to have on the self-concepts of individuals in either gender group. And these effects may be all the stronger because in many countries, women are found to be more religious than men (Argyle and Beit-Hallahami 1997; Greeley 1992; Jogan 1993). Overall, despite many differences of history and politics, European countries have in common at least the traditions of religion-inspired preparation for gender-differentiated roles in society.

Equality in Higher Education

European countries have also in common the advantage that access to education at all levels is equally open to females and males. That this has not been so in the past is evident in illiteracy figures for the most elderly generations in many countries, for there the percentage of women who are illiterate is greater than that of males, though the gaps—and the percentages—are much larger in some countries than in others. Nevertheless, for a goodly time now, both sexes have had equal access to all levels of education.

At the same time, some inequalities remain. Many of these are in postgraduate studies. Although access is theoretically open to both sexes, women generally are in a minority when it comes to postgraduate and doctoral studies. In teaching in higher education, women also remain a minority, though the size of this minority varies from one country to another. At full professional level, some of the best situations appear to be in Turkey, with 20% female professors, and Poland, with 17%. Overall it can scarcely be claimed that equality in higher education has been achieved (Lie and Malik 1994.)

Two other aspects of women's position in higher education may be noted. If there is a pecking order among institutions, some having reputedly high status whereas others—such as institutes for teacher education—are regarded as of lower rank, the proportion of women is higher in the institutions having lower prestige. Hrubos (1994) illustrates this with reference to universities and colleges in Hungary.

The second example of gender bias lies in the choice of subject. Although women tend to cluster in "women's subjects" in all European countries, some variations in subject choice and subsequent occupations are to be found, especially as a result of Soviet policies for providing industry with a highly qualified workforce. Comparisons of subject choices are admittedly complicated because it is unwise to assume that different professions have the same social standing in different countries. Medicine, for instance, acquired rather lower rank in the Soviet bloc, so women's considerable representation there could not be considered equivalent to the situation of women in medicine in Western Europe (Wimberley 1994). But in former Soviet countries, greater percentages of women have studied subjects that are often considered to be men's subjects: in Bulgaria, for instance, in the 1980s "every third engineer was a woman" (Rangelova and Vladimirova 1994). There are, of course, some similar trends toward breaking gender barriers in subject choices in Western Europe also, such as the high proportion of women studying chemical engineering in Portugal. But even where more women have become proficient in "men's subjects," women's traditional preferences for languages, the humanities, and the social studies remain evident in statistics from both Western and Eastern Europe. And these preferences are evident also in the proportion of women teaching these subjects in higher education (Lie and Malik 1994).

Considering departures from gender-segregated occupations, it is discouraging to discover that changes in the economies and policies of Eastern European countries may cause employment problems precisely for women with high qualifications in "masculine" subjects: in Bulgaria again (Sretenova 1994), as industrial production has lessened, women with higher engineering qualifications are likely to lose in competing with men for the reduced number of posts available. The experiences of two world wars earlier showed women in all countries that women are accepted in male occupations in times of crisis but expected to withdraw from these when men are in competition for employment.

For whatever reason, a common bias in subject choice seems to survive even when a relatively small space has been given to options in the upper secondary school curriculum. Some Western educators have complained that girls can decide at too early a level in secondary schooling that some subjects, mainly scientific, are not for them (Masson 1994), but this explanation cannot hold with regard to girls who followed the firmly prescribed curricula of Soviet schools.

Gender bias seems to have remained strong as soon as a choice of vocational schools was offered. Similarly, young people in Western European countries, notably Sweden, often proceed from a broad junior secondary curriculum including both "masculine" and "feminine" subjects to a more specialized, gender-biased upper secondary diet. At the same time, we must note the vigorous efforts made in many Western countries recently to encourage greater participation by girls in science, engineering, and technology (Clair 1994; Frank 1996).

Some movement of women in higher education toward "men's subjects" may also be noted in law, accounting, finance, business studies, and administration. Regretably, the new subject of computer studies has anomalous status. It has been found that in higher education in some European countries, women are well represented, whereas in others they have regressed to small minorities (*Social Europe* 1989). At the school level some reluctance of girls to pursue computer studies has been noted, though Terlon (1994) reported good responses to new software.

Of course we cannot assume that there should be complete equality in the proportion of each gender group opting for any subject; there may possibly be natural biases. But as experience in some European countries has shown that many more women than at present could be successful and happy in traditionally male studies—and many men, no doubt, could find success in "women's subjects"—some reduction in gender bias in choice of subject can be accepted as a future European ideal.

Girls' and Boys' Achievement

Although equality of access to education has been achieved for both sexes, equality of outcome is not, as we have seen, ensured. Another common inequality in many European countries is that the achievement of girls in secondary general education surpasses that of their male fellow-students. An OECD publication drew attention to this in 1986: similar findings were reported from Soviet countries. This situation has evoked a rather remarkably prompt reaction in some countries (e.g., the United Kingdom) where formerly the lesser achievement of girls was accepted complacently. Alarmed educators and parents have called for research and remedial action so that boys may be enabled to keep up with girls in academic work. (The trend in fact is not confined to Europe: Australia has been experiencing a similar upheaval.) One reason hypothetically advanced for the difference has been that boys are discouraged by the attitudes of girls who are ready to work hard and conscientiously while boys are still at the stage of taking school tasks lightheartedly. Yet the greater academic success of girls chimes oddly with the affirmations of various feminist writers that girls receive a smaller share of teachers' attention than boys do. It is at the same time commonly agreed throughout Europe that girls are more docile pupils—and so less often need to be spoken to reprovingly. But girls' superior achievement also conflicts with a feminist belief publicized in Western countries during the 1970s and 1980s (on the basis of research in perhaps too few schools and countries) that girls play down or conceal their scholastic ability because they do not want to be considered unfeminine and fear that school success will prevent them from attracting the opposite sex. It is an odd counterbalance that we now have the suggestion that boys in some Western European systems, seeing the achievement of girls, play down *their* academic ability because they think it is "sissy" to do well at school.

A further complication in interpreting secondary school success was indicated in Hungary, where indeed, it was found, girls were likely to outnumber boys in the upper levels of the general secondary school, thus acquiring the qualifications necessary to try to enter higher education. But there, it was also noted, boys who left the general secondary system earlier very often went into vocational education, which would provide them with qualifications that led, in the state of the country's economy at the time, to secure and well-paid employment, whereas girls might not after all achieve entry to higher education, and posts as teachers could be less financially rewarding than those in the technical sector (Hrubos 1994).

Thus, in Europe generally, access to secondary and higher education is not a problem, but there is common concern about bias in subject choice and its vocational consequences. There is also continuing concern that women are underrepresented in top academic posts, in the administration of higher education, and so in decision making in research and educational policy (ENWS 1994).

Women's Dual Role

Two reasons are commonly asserted for these common inequalities in higher education and employment. One is the continuing imposition on women of the dual role of worker outside the home and worker inside the home. The other lies in economic factors, the dramatic changes in the economies of the former Soviet countries, and the economic recession that has affected many Western countries.

Yet differences might be expected to result from the efforts made in Soviet countries to ensure the maximum contribution by women to the labor market. Some differences indeed were evident—but did they change women's dual role? A comprehensive system of child care for preschool children was certainly accepted as essential, though urban and rural environments presented different problems. Places were generally available in day care centers and in kindergartens (even if natality policies enabled some mothers to take two or three years at home with their young children). Communal life in preschool establishments was also seen to have advantages in forming good future citizens. At the same time, some parents expressed (and continue to express) doubts about the desirability of having children under the age of 3 looked after outside their home for a large part of the day. Yet for women students in higher education, baby-care facilities (as in the East German "baby étages" of student hostels) were certainly an important factor in being able to continue in higher education and "weekly" kindergartens did make it easier for some women to combine work with caring for a child.

Maternity leave in the Soviet countries was reasonably generous, at least in theory. Indeed some heads of schools in East Germany could be horrified but powerless when teachers newly appointed to their school arrived to announce that they would be on maternity leave within the very near future.

In Western Europe, on the other hand, provision at the preschool level has often been restricted, but does vary greatly—France, Belgium, and Denmark offer nursery school places to a very high percentage of children in the relevant age groups, whereas provision in other countries is scant and often expensive (OECD 1995). The effect in the latter countries has been to limit women's employment outside the home while their children are young and to introduce often disadvantageous breaks in career or in study, or, when women feel obliged to take on outside work, to produce a stress situation for the family.

But in Soviet bloc countries the availability of child care has changed. Factories that formerly provided facilities for workers' children may have closed down, and in the new capitalist society, employers no longer see it as an obligation to make such provision freely available. Thus women who are going out to work have to make very great efforts to find child care; some, with luck, can call on members of their own family, but this is increasingly less possible.

The day-to-day problems of domestic work in fact have always meant a heavier load for women in countries where household gadgets have not been readily available and where food supplies have been less regular and lavish than in more favored countries. Thus in the Soviet bloc countries, many more hours of a woman's week have had to be devoted to shopping, to finding ways of getting repairs done, to budgeting for the family.

Such circumstances have inevitably affected the situation of women seeking to achieve postgraduate qualifications and make a career in the academic world. Many—in Western Europe also—have abandoned the attempt because they could not do justice to family demands, or they have postponed the completion of their studies till later.

Thus in the former Soviet countries, women's "advantage" of generous maternity leave may serve in the new economic conditions to handicap them (Mironova 1994). Women's chances of employment are easily reduced by the prospect of obligatory maternity leave, the more so, perhaps, because under privatization the great majority of employers are men. In Western countries similarly, maternity leave can be a handicap when women are seeking employment or promotion and employers foresee inconvenient absences looming ahead, even if equal opportunity policies prevent asking about plans for children. There is also the enduring belief—common to all European countries, though now reducing in frequency in Western countries, especially in Scandinavia (Siemienska 1993)—that if jobs are scarce, those available should go to men, the traditional breadwinners for the family, rather than to women.

Other common factors affect women's opportunities to use their skills and knowledge. Women in many Western countries are more likely than men to be part-time workers, and in all parts of Europe many women see the availability of part-time employment as beneficial, partly because this enables them to cope with family responsibilities more easily. But part-time working has considerable disadvantages, since it is likely to affect adversely such things as holiday entitlement, sick pay, and promotion. Employers, too, may be more likely to provide in-service vocational training for full-time male workers.

Doing paid work at home has been hailed by some Westerners recently as a useful solution (for men and women) to the problem of combining earning with family care. It can be an excellent solution for those with high computer or specialist skills, but the situation of women home workers, as a recent European survey has pointed out is very often that astonishingly low rates of pay are received for large amounts of repetitive work (*Social Europe* 1995). It is, although flexible, very often a most insecure form of employment, and by its very nature it is less likely than other types of work to lead to the formation of effective trade unions to protect workers' rights.

Such employment prospects and complications must give girls and young women going through the process of education in European countries many discouraging messages—for instance, that women's chances of employment are limited, and that reconciling family and outside work is difficult (and not always socially approved), so women should not be too ambitious about a career. Solutions to the problem of maternity leave remain elusive.

It is not surprising that in considering its Medium-Term Social Action Plan for 1995–1997, the European Commission noted "the possibility of negotiating an agreement on the reconciliation of professional and family life. The aim of such a proposal will be to promote equal opportunities and encourage the introduction of new, flexible models better suited to the changing needs of European society" (*Social Europe* 1995).

The Hidden Curriculum

Given these common factors in the education and employment of women in Europe, it is worthwhile to consider the effects, not simply of the overt curriculum of the educational systems but also the hidden curriculum, which is highly influential in forming attitudes about sex differences and social roles. Awareness of the hidden curriculum has been most evident in some Western countries where the development of women's studies has highlighted it in the last twenty years, but UNESCO also published in the 1980s a series of analyses of schoolbooks in different countries that revealed how the transmission of gender stereotypes can be affected by such materials.

It is, of course, not only in schools that a hidden curriculum is in operation. Very obviously, children learn in the home and the neighborhood what behaviors are expected of the two sexes—and much of this teaching is unspoken. It is amply documented in Europe and in other continents that girls are more likely to be given the responsibility of looking after younger siblings and that girls are normally expected to learn domestic skills from their mother and to carry out increasingly more complex domestic tasks. Boys, on the whole, escape lightly, being given only the "masculine" tasks, which may involve greater physical effort (though this is by no means always the case) but which occur fairly infrequently. A Swedish study found, as many others have done, that men and women's share of household tasks is unequal (women spending thirty-seven hours a week on them, men about seventeen), that it is perceived as unequal by children, and that boys and girls engage in a different set of tasks, girls spending more hours per week in this way than boys (some 40% of boys spent no time in the week on such work, but only some 23% of girls) (Andersson, Hedman, and Sundstrom 1986).

Yet men and women's share of domestic tasks is affected also by the economic situation. An unexpected result of recent changes in Poland has been that from 1988 to 1992, there was a slight increase in adult sharing of household tasks—not necessarily because of attitude change but because of practical factors such as non-availability of public facilities, high costs for various services, and, unfortunately, the increasing amount of male unemployment (Siemienska 1994). Nevertheless there is some evidence that in some other countries, men are indeed taking an increasing share in domestic work and the care of children because attitudes have changed (Kiernan 1992). But such changes are slow (Séguret 1993) even in the most advanced societies and seem non-existent in others (Kanopiene 1994).

Responsibility for cultivating equality thus reverts to the school curriculum, but explicit teaching about sex roles is inadequately developed—possibly such teaching may be included indirectly in social studies in different countries. But even where the need for explicit teaching has been recognized, as in Sweden, change in gender bias seems slow to come. Moreover, in countries with large numbers of immigrants, there is, as noted earlier, the likelihood of conflict between the school's advocacy of equality in performing household tasks and the traditional beliefs of the home cultures.

The staffing of schools is in itself part of the hidden curriculum. In many Western European schools, positions of authority are more often held by men than by women. For example, in Great Britain it was recently noted that although in primary schools 90% of teachers are women, less than half the head teachers are women; in secondary schools, women make up three-fifths of the total staff, but only one-fifth of the head teachers are women (EOC 1993). Such a hierarchy must foster stereotypes.

But there may be conflicts of principles when attempts are made to change the hidden curriculum. Coeducation, for instance, was expected to increase equal opportunities for all, but in some systems it had the effect of reducing the probability of women becoming heads of schools or colleges (Sutherland 1985). In France, when single-sex secondary schools were the norm, women had a clear career prospect of headship, which was reduced with the advent of coeducation. Similarly in Finland, where teaching is increasingly a woman's profession, men have a disproportionate number of headships. It can at the same time be argued that it is essential to the well-being of the profession, and of the pupils, to maintain a balance between men and women teachers, and that if men see a good chance of becoming heads, they may more readily be induced to enter the profession (*Context* 1996).

The potentially adverse effect on boys of the feminization of the teaching profession has been keenly debated in many countries. In Europe, the balance in secondary schools generally remains fairly even: the average percentage of secondary school women teachers in 1992 was 59 (a slight increase from the 55% of 1980); the average for primary school teaching was 77% (again a slight increase from the 73% of 1980); and of course women are approximately 99% of the profession at the preschool level (UNESCO 1994). But anxiety is expressed because (apart from the general observation that a profession that is largely followed by women attracts lower pay than others, and possibly enjoys less social prestige) boys in school might suffer from a lack of male role models. This point has been especially emphasized by those who note the breaking up of the traditional family in many European countries and the increasing frequency of divorce: they argue consequently that many boys no longer have a father at home who can serve as a role model.

The possible effects of a mainly female teaching profession relate also to a point mentioned earlier, the apparently lower success of boys in secondary education—and even, in some countries, in primary education. It has been suggested that are female teachers emphasize qualities of neatness and orderliness, which are more acceptable to girls than to boys. Hence, it is said, there is a danger that boys develop a feeling of alienation in school or that in the primary classes they live in a female-dominated world that seeks to develop qualities not natural to them. Yet it has seldom been possible to distinguish typically male and typically female styles in teaching; research tends to show that there are indeed different teaching styles, but that none is found only among men or only among women: each style may be found in both groups. And although it may often be the case that divorce deprives children of a father's influence or a mother's influence, women quite often find a new partner who brings a male influence into the household, just as fathers left tending daughters may find a second mother for them.

Also important is the meaning to be attached to a "masculine" role model and a "feminine" role model. Obviously there can be differences in behavior when the individual is in a same-sex group or a mixed group, differences when physical reactions are being discussed, or—relatively superficially—differences when choosing clothing or beauty care; in such cases, someone of the same sex may give more appropriate guidance. But there is the danger that in using the term *role model* we may reintroduce the traditional stereotypes that affirmed an absolute dichotomy between forms of behavior and attitudes that are masculine, and those that are feminine.

Certainly a highly influential part of the hidden curriculum is found in the general atmosphere of the school and the attitudes of individual teachers. Undoubtedly, in all European countries, there are some teachers—not only in the older age groups—who still hold traditional views about inevitable differences in gender roles and attributes. What is needed, obviously, is reasonable discussion of this topic in courses of teacher education. Some efforts are now being made to introduce this in some Western countries, but such topics are too often given little time and less prestige in the program of studies. Demands for comprehensive knowledge of many subjects and narrow concentration on teaching methods tend still to characterize too many European systems of teacher education.

Other aspects of the hidden curriculum affect participation in politics. Here, in all countries, men achieve greater prominence and authority. How far this can be attributed to the overt curriculum of schools or to the hidden curriculum of everyday life is doubtful, though some studies (e.g., Torney, Oppenheim, and Farnen 1975; Stradling 1977) have indicated that already at school, European boys and girls differ in their knowledge of, and interest in, political matters. Naturally, in Soviet educational systems, all pupils were theoretically expected to show equal interest and enthusiasm—and on a practical level, devotion to the dominant political party could improve chances of progress through the educational system and of promotion within it. But certainly in all European countries, the lesson likely to be learned from the hidden curriculum of society outside the school is that men more than women take an active role, and the leading positions, in politics, in political organizations and government—and this despite the outstanding success of some women as prime ministers of their countries. Quite commonly, where women take part in politics, they serve on local councils and communities, with smaller numbers proceeding to regional activities, and still fewer to central government.

A curious effect of the change of regime in the former Soviet Union has been that whereas formerly, quota systems guaranteed women a place—though still a minority place—in councils or parliament, the return to free elections has much reduced the representation of women. This has been noted in Slovenia, Russia, the Czech Republic, Hungary, and Romania (Jogan 1993; Klimenkova 1993; Siklova 1993; Timar 1993; Zernova 1993; Ionescu 1994), even if, at the same time, there has been an upsurge of activity by women in new political parties in these countries (Einhorn 1993).

In the European Parliament, meanwhile, some increase in women members was noted for nine of the fifteen countries between 1989 and 1994, Denmark being outstanding with 43.5%. In national parliaments of the European Union, Denmark again tops the list, with women making up 33% of its members, and the Netherlands follows with 30%. But in nine of the fifteen countries, the percentage of women in parliament was less than twenty, and in four, less than ten (Hoskins 1996).

It is also pointed out in many cases that women do not vote for women in political elections. Women seem less electable candidates. Yet it is difficult to know what action can be taken. In the United Kingdom in 1996, when the Labor Party attempted to redress the balance by imposing some women-only lists of candidates, two men (prospective candidates) invoked equal opportunities legislation to have this affirmative action declared illegal. When in 1995 the European Court found in favor of a man in Bremen who had complained of sex discrimination because preference was given to women candidates for a job (Hoskins 1996), many makers of political policies became worried and uncertain as to how permissible affirmative action may be.

In all European countries, therefore, political education seems to merit greater attention in the overt curriculum, to encourage both sexes to take an intelligent and active interest in politics. This is not an easy prescription to follow when examples of indoctrination have been conspicuous in the past and when charges of renewed indoctrination may readily be made.

GOVERNMENT POLICIES AND EQUAL OPPORTUNITY

Given the common factors producing inequalities in the education of the two sexes in European countries and in their career chances of using skills and knowledge they have acquired, we come to the question of constructive intervention by governments. Have governments shown awareness of the need for action?

In the Soviet countries, it was customarily assumed that because equality was stated in the formal constitution of the country, no real problem could exist. There was normally a women's committee or women's organization created under the aegis of the ruling political party, with responsibility for attending to matters affecting women, yet these organizations were expected to promote cooperation with, and understanding of, central political decisions rather than introduce innovations. Since the Soviet system has been replaced, various women's groups and political parties, sometimes related to former organizations, have come into being (Einhorn 1993) but nationwide provision seems lacking.

In Western European countries governments have created committees, institutes, councils, or ministries specifically concerned with matters relating to women. France indeed from 1965 onward produced a remarkable sequence of committees, delegations, and ministerial secretariates, leading in 1985 to a Ministry for the Rights of Women (Cacouault and Zaidman 1994). Such official bodies are normally concerned with all matters relating to women—their health, welfare, and employment, as well as their education—but education normally plays an important part in their activities. Yet these governmentally established bodies tend to act mainly as distributors of information, as makers of recommendations, and as agencies for the raising of consciousness rather than as distinctive reformers (Baudoux and Sutherland 1994).

An alternative kind of organization was created in the United Kingdom by the 1975 Sex Discrimination Act: this is the Equal Opportunities Commission, which is concerned with all aspects of life in society but which does—in addition to publications, research promotion, and conference organization—give support in courts or tribunals to individuals who claim to have suffered sex discrimination. Such support may lead to cases being referred to the European Court of Justice, whose rulings may produce changes of policy or legislation in member states. The EOC, it should be noted, has the duty of assisting men and boys as well as women and girls and has in fact supported many male complainants against discrimination: indeed, in 1996, the number of cases brought to the EOC by men surpassed the number brought by women, a situation that some journalists interpreted as showing that men are now the disadvantaged group.

INTERVENTIONS BY INTERNATIONAL ORGANIZATIONS

For many years now, the European Community/European Union has taken as one of its objectives the amelioration of women's situation, especially in the field of vocational training. Since the European Community originally intended to ensure harmonization in the coal and steel industries, it has naturally been mainly concerned with vocational education and employment, though it has increasingly extended its interests into the social field. Its directive of 9 February 1976 affirmed the "principle of equal treatment for men and women as regards access to employment, including promotion and to vocational training and as regards working conditions" (*Social Europe* 1991). Many other directives and recommendations have related to securing equal opportunities and reducing unemployment among women. The special concern with vocational education was instanced in a recommendation of 24 November 1987 that "the Member States should adopt a policy designed to encourage the participation of young and adult women in training schemes, especially those relevant to occupations of the future, and should develop specific measures, particularly as regards training, for occupations where women are under-represented" (*Social Europe* 1991).

Much obviously depends on the willingness of governments to attend to and implement the various directives and recommendations of this and other European organizations and to devise relevant projects for which aid may be obtained. The Social Fund of the European Union, which has to be associated with national projects, has financed various schemes intended to encourage the entry of women into formerly male-dominated occupations. It has also given grants to schemes for enabling people to set up their own firms and to develop business enterprises of their own. But the tendency has been for women to benefit from Social Fund grants for training schemes rather than from grants for the development of entrepreneurship.

New Opportunities for Women (NOW), established in 1990, is in fact geared toward assisting women to create their own business opportunities, in accordance with market developments. Schemes to upgrade women's existing qualifications and facilitate returns to the labor market after some years of absence have also been supported. Allied in some of its activities to NOW, another organization called IRIS has, from 1988, created a network of projects for the development of women's vocational skills.

In many instances, the progress of women to employment in which they can use their knowledge and skills is inhibited because of their ignorance of the legal situation. Here the Information Office of the European Union has provided a database of legal provisions, circulated information, and organized conferences to enlighten women in different parts of Europe about legal conditions.

Beyond initiatives specifically aimed at promoting vocational educational opportunities for females, a remarkable variety of international projects has been created in the attempt to promote better understanding, communication, and coherence among the peoples of Europe. The list of acronyms and the specific type of provision each scheme makes would take too long to include here (but see Palomba and Bertin 1993). In considering these far-reaching provisions in the European Union, we can note the gain in confidence as well as in ability likely to be achieved by young women embarking on, for example, an ERASMUS exchange, which takes them to study in universities in another country. And increasingly, programs such as the COMENIUS project foster similar exchanges at the school level (*Context* 1996).

The Council of Europe, which has always had a wider membership than the European Union (forty-one member states by 1999, and with a number of agreements with countries in Central and Eastern Europe likely to lead to closer cooperation and eventual membership), has set up a steering committee to deal with questions relating to equality between men and women (Olafsdottir 1994). Each year, the committee's program includes seminars, meetings of specialists, and workshops. In general the council has acknowledged four main concerns: women's rights, human rights (including elimination of violence), tolerance and cultural diversity, and guidance for new member states.

Less specifically European, but also of importance, have been OECD activities, notably research and publications on female education and employment. Similarly, the overarching concerns of UNESCO and the United Nations have contributed to awareness of the need to improve the situation of women.

There is, therefore, no lack of international expressions of goodwill and of plans that clearly benefit a certain number of women. But again the major factor remains the willingness of national governments to implement the recommendations made by international authorities and to accept seriously—and act upon—the principles affirmed in the wider world.

THE ROLE OF NON-GOVERNMENTAL ORGANIZATIONS

Although development of activities through governmental agencies, the European Union, and the Council of Europe is to be welcomed, it is clear that much also depends on the initiative of local authorities, of smaller groups, or of individuals in promoting programs leading to better education for equality: governments have to be urged to implement international recommendations and convinced that these moves have popular support. Hence the importance of the many non-governmental and voluntary organizations that are now devoting themselves to spreading information and awareness of the need for action.

One development contributing to the advancement of women has been the European Network of Women's Studies (ENWS, also known as the European Network of Scientific and Technical Cooperation on Women's Studies), which came into existence in 1989 under the auspices of the Council of Europe, the Dutch Ministry of Education generously undertaking to fund this development for five years. The ENWS has not simply contributed to the development of women's studies in different countries of Europe, but has organized a number of international conferences bringing together women from all parts of Europe and enabling them to discover similarities and differences in their experiences of education and employment. Courses have been organized to teach management skills useful in business ventures. Overall, the ENWS has produced a number of good conference reports and monographs as well as a newsletter maintaining contact among women in different parts of Europe. It has thus contributed to raising awareness of the problems of gender in education and of proposals for effective reform.

In sometimes similar ways, a number of international women's organizations are active in many if not all the countries of Europe, exchanging information and arranging international meetings and visits for their members. Here may be noted the International Federation of University Women—which extends, of course, beyond Europe—and the University Women of Europe, centered in Geneva. Organizations such as the Soroptimists and the Business and Professional Women's Clubs have a similar role in reinforcing women's awareness of the advantages and defects of their own education and situation, and in facilitating communication between different countries and comparisons of progress.

THE FUTURE

In this review, it has been indicated that although each country of Europe has its own personality and its own history and traditions in education, there are strong similarities in the provision of formal and informal education for both sexes, and similarities in the employment situation, social roles, and status offered to women. It is indeed astonishing that experiences of so many different political regimes should still have left intact so much that is common in women's careers and way of life.

Obviously, common problems remain. There is need for fuller development of women's postgraduate studies, for reduction of gender bias in choosing subjects of study, for ensuring equal opportunities in employment, and in political decision making. There is a need to solve the problems of women's dual role, as they work in the home and outside it, and a need to find a system of maternity leave (and paternity leave) acceptable to all concerned. There is a need to reconsider the definition of individual roles in society.

Much encouragement is certainly given by the strengthening cooperation between women in different countries of Europe and by the development of international projects that facilitate study and vocational training. An effective realization of many proposals resulting from the United Nations Congress of Beijing in 1995 could of course benefit women throughout the world.

At the same time, there are signs of a backlash in many places, a lingering on, or a renaissance, of the belief that women should revert to the traditional role of housewife. Revival of religious beliefs may in some instances serve to confirm that view. Such attitudes may well be reinforced by increasing economic difficulties in various countries, especially by growing unemployment. Men suffering unemployment may further be tormented by uncertainty as to their role when the tradition of being the breadwinner is broken. The definition of partnership in child care is not easy to establish. There is moreover a reaction, not only among men, against some demands for better opportunities for women— indeed, the claim is made in some countries that women already have all they can reasonably desire and that it is time to reassert the rights of men.

It remains to be seen which trend will prevail. It may be that the international declarations of principles and the example of successful women in different parts of Europe will serve to help all women, and especially those still handicapped by poverty or by adverse social conditions. At the same time, the forces of reaction are strong. Yet even some increase of participation by women in economic, political, and social life may lead to the provision of an education that will give better chances of equality and of individual development to both sexes.

REFERENCES

Acar, F. 1994. "Higher Education in Turkey: A Gold Bracelet for Women." In *The Gender Gap in Higher Education*, World Yearbook of Education 1994. Edited by S. S. Lie, L. Malik, and D. Harris. London/Philadelphia: Kogan Page.

Andersson, I., B. Hedman, and P. Sundstrom. 1986. *Kvinno-och mansvär(l)den*, Statistics Sweden, Stockholm.

Argyle, M. and B. Beit-Hallahmi. 1997. *Religious Behavior, Belief and Experience*. London/New York/Boston: Routledge and Kegan Paul.

Baudoux, C., and M. B. Sutherland, eds. 1994. *Femmes et education: Politiques nationales et variations internationales*. Canada: Université Laval.

Borcelle, G. 1985. *Jobs for Women*. Paris: UNESCO.

Cacouault, M., and C. Zaidman. 1994. In *Femmes et education: Politiques nationales et variations internationales*. Edited by C. Baudoux and M. B. Sutherland. Canada: Université Laval, 139–175.

Clair, R., ed. 1994. *The Scientific Education of Girls*. London and Paris: Jessica Kingsley Publishers/UNESCO Publishing.

Context: European Education Magazine. 1996. Special Issue, no. 13: COMENIUS. (The Netherlands).

Dabic, M. 1994. "Women and Academic Careers in Poland." In ENWS Wolfheze Conference Report, 85–89.

De Grandpré, M. 1970. "La Coéducation dans les Ecoles Officielles et les Ecoles Catholiques de 45 Pays." Montréal, Canada: Université de Montréal.

Einhorn, B. 1993. "An Allergy to Feminism: Women's Movements before and after 1989." Conference Report, *From Dictatorship to Democracy*, University of Barcelona.

ENWS (European Network of Scientific and Technical Cooperation on Women's Studies). 1994. Conference on Equality and Partnership towards Higher Education, Employment/Entrepreneurship and Environmental Management in Central and Eastern European Countries; Future Strategic Goals and Objectives. Wolfheze, the Netherlands. Report published by the Netherlands Ministry of Education, Culture, and Science, Zoetermeer.

ENWS *Newsletter*. "Woman, Man and Family: The Division of Labour within the Family in Southern European Countries." October 1993, no. 9.

EOC (Equal Opportunities Commission). 1993. *Men and Women in Britain*. London: HMSO.

European Community Action Programme. 1988. *Info*; IRIS, a European Network of Training Schemes for Women. Brussels: European Commission.

Fine-Davis, M. 1988. "Changing Gender Role Attitudes in Ireland, 1975–1986." In First Report of the Second Joint Committee on Women's Rights. Dublin: Stationery Office.

Frank, E. 1996. *Schulversuch Physik*. Fachabteilung Mathematik, Physik, Informatik. Ostfildern, Germany: Otto-Hahn-Gymnasium.

Greeley, A. 1992. "Religion in Britain, Ireland, and the USA." In *British Social Attitudes*. Edited by R. Jowell, L. Brook, G. Prior, and B. Taylor. Aldershot, England: Gower Publishing, 51–70.

Hans, N. 1949. *Comparative Education*. London: Routledge and Kegan, 252.

Hoskins, C. 1996. *Integrating Gender*. London and New York: Verso.

Hrubos, H. 1994. "Women in Higher Education and Research in Hungary." In ENWS Wolfheze Conference Report, 67–73.

Ionescu, S. 1994. "Some Considerations on the Present Condition of Women in Romania." In ENWS Wolfheze Conference Report, 147–151.

Izhevska, T. 1994. "Women and Employment in the Period of Transition: The Case of Ukraine. In ENWS Wolfheze Conference Report, 171–174.

Jogan, M. 1993. "Democratisation and Re-domestication of Women in the Contemporary Development of Slovenia." Conference Report, *From Dictatorship to Democracy*, University of Barcelona.

Kanopiene, V. 1994. "Women on the Labour Market: The Case of Lithuania." In ENWS Wolfheze Conference Report, 129–135.

Kaplan, G. 1992. *Contemporary European Feminism*. London: UCL Press.

Kiernan, K. 1992. "Men and Women at Work and at Home." *British Social Attitudes*. Edited by R. Jowell. Aldershot, England: Dartmouth Publishing.

Klimenkova, T. A. 1993. "Problems and Strategies of the New Russian Women's Movement." Conference Report, *From Dictatorship to Democracy*. University of Barcelona.

Klimesova, H. 1994. "Women—Employment—Family." In ENWS Wolfheze Conference Report, 117–119.

Koncz, K. 1994. "Women and Employment in Hungary." In ENWS Wolfheze Conference Report, 122–127.

Laas, A. 1990. "The Future for Estonian Women: 'Real Women Are Mothers.' " ENWS Monograph, Zoetermeer, the Netherlands.

Larive, J. 1994. "Policy of the European Union Towards Women in Central and Eastern Europe." In ENWS Wolfheze Conference Report, 43–46.

Lie, S. S., and L. Malik. 1994. "Trends in the Gender Gap in Higher Education." In *The Gender Gap in Higher Education*, World Yearbook of Education 1994. Edited by S. S. Lie, L. Malik, and D. Harris, London: Kogan Page, 205–213.

MacIntosh, M. 1990. " 'Caught Between the Two': Gender and Race in a Scottish School." In *Girls in their Prime*. Edited by F.M.S. Paterson and J. Fewell. Edinburgh: Scottish Academic Press, 71–88.

Masson, M. R. 1994. "Sex Differences in the Study of Science in Scotland and England." In *The Scientific Education of Girls*. Edited by R. Clair. London and Paris: Jessica Kingsley Publishers/UNESCO Publishing.

Mironova, N. 1994. Thesis of the report "On the Problem of Women's Employment in Russia of Today." ENWS Wolfheze Conference Report, 159–164.

Mitter, W., and J. Swift, eds. 1985. *Education and the Diversity of Cultures*. Report of the 11th Conference of the Comparative Education Society in Europe, Bildung und Erziehung, Beiheft 2/1, 2/1. Böhlau, Köln, Wien.

Le Monde de l'Education. 1995. Foulards: Stopper les Exclusions: Edito 222 (January): 3; "Courrier des Lecteurs" 223 (February): 15–16.

OECD (Organization for Economic Cooperation and Development). 1986. *Girls and Women in Education*. Paris: OECD, 10–29.

———. 1995. *Education at a Glance*. OECD Indicators. Paris: OECD.

Olafsdottir, O. 1994. "Intergovernmental Cooperation in the Field of Equality Between Women and Men in the Council of Europe: Framework and Priorities." In ENWS Wolfheze Conference Report, 13–17.

Palomba, D., and N. Bertin. 1993. *Insegnare in Europa*. Milano: FrancoAngeli, 174–181.

Rangelova, R. and K. Vladimirova. 1994. "Employment and Entrepreneurship of Women with Higher Education in Bulgaria." In ENWS Wolfheze Conference Report, 109–115.

Scott, J. 1990. "Women and the Family." In *British Social Attitudes*. Edited by R. Jowell, S. Witherspoon, and L. Brook. Aldershot, England: Gower.

Séguret, M-C. 1993. "La division du travail au sein de la famille." In ENWS *Newsletter*, no. 9, 2–4.

Siemienska, R. 1993. "Gender as a Factor Differentiating Social Position: Transition to a Market Economy in Poland." Conference Report, *From Dictatorship to Democracy*. University of Barcelona.

————. 1994. "Women on the Labour Market in Poland and Their Gendered Perception."
    In ENWS Wolfheze Conference Report, 137–145.
Siklova, J. 1993. "Basic Information about Women in the Czech Republic." Conference
    Report, *From Dictatorship to Democracy*. University of Barcelona.
Social Europe. 1989. "IRIS—The New Community Network of Demonstration Projects
    on Vocational Training for Women." In Commission of the European Commu-
    nities, Directorate-General for Employment, Social Affairs, and Education 2/89,
    49–51.
————. 1991. "Equal Opportunities for Women and Men." In Commission of the Eur-
    opean Communities, Directorate-General for Employment, Industrial Relations,
    and Social Affairs. Luxembourg, 3/91.
————. 1993. "Occupational Segregation of Women and Men in the European Com-
    munity." In Commission of the European Communities, Directorate-General for
    Employment, Industrial Relations, and Social Affairs. Brussels, 70–73.
————. 1995. Medium-term Social Action Programme 1995–97. In European Commis-
    sion Directorate-General for Employment, Industrial Relations, and Social Affairs,
    Brussels, 1/95, 212.
Social Europe Magazine. 1996. "1996–2000: A Fourth Community Action Programme."
    March, no. 3: 3–4.
Sretenova, N. 1994. "The Nation's Show-Case. Bulgarian Academic Women Between
    the Scylla of Totalitarianism and the Charybdis of Change." In *The Gender Gaps
    in Higher Education*. Edited by S. S. Lie et al. London: Kogan Page, 55–65.
Stradling, R. 1997. *The Political Awareness of the School-Leaver*. London: The Hansard
    Society.
Sutherland, M. B. 1985. "Whatever Happened About Coeducation?" *British Journal of
    Educational Studies* 33 (2): 155–163.
Terlon, C. 1994. "Girls and the New Information Technologies." In *The Scientific Edu-
    cation of Girls*. Edited by R. Clair. London and Paris: Jessica Kingsley Pub-
    lishers/UNESCO Publishing, 118–123.
Timar, J. 1993. "The Changing Rights and Conditions of Women in Hungary." Confer-
    ence Report *From Dictatorship to Democracy*. University of Barcelona.
Torney, J., A. N. Oppenheim, and R. F. Farnen. 1975. *Civic Education in 10 Countries*.
    Stockholm: Almqvist & Wiksell.
UNESCO. 1994. *Education for All: Status and Trends/1994*: Basic Education, Popula-
    tion, and Development. Paris: UNESCO.
Wimberley, J. 1994. "Higher Education in Europe." In ENSW Wolfheze Conference
    Report, 19–25.
Zernova, E. 1993. "Situacion Actual en Rusia: Problemas Femeninas." Conference Re-
    port, *From Dictatorship to Democracy*. University of Barcelona.

PART III

EUROPEAN EDUCATION IN AN ERA OF GLOBAL CHANGE

9

The Heritage of Socialism and *Perestroika*: Transformation Processes in Central and Eastern European Education

Jürgen Wichmann and Val D. Rust

PERESTROIKA AND THE TRANSITION TO POST-COMMUNISM

In this essay we give an overview of the transformation taking place in Central and Eastern European education. We include a period of time from *Perestroika* until the end of the 1990s, with a main focus on Russian education. Of course, Russia doesn't represent Central and Eastern Europe, but it seems to be the most significant and dramatic case.

Perestroika symbolized reform-oriented shifts in general social developments in the Soviet Union and its socialist satellites from the middle 1980s. *Perestroika* meant transformation or reconstruction of the existing system with a clear tendency toward openness and democracy. Officials of socialist educational systems were rarely oriented toward change at the time of *perestroika*, though they reluctantly attempted to maintain some semblance of legitimacy by co-opting changes taking place. According to Kerr (1994), "the most interesting indicator of change on the Soviet educational scene in the post-1985 era was the rise of diversity outside the official governmental structure." Divergent tendencies emerged that challenged existing socialist structures as divisive, irreparable, inefficient, and brittle. Those in the educational establishment were so intent on stabilizing the system that change initiatives were usually overwhelmed and paralyzed. In this context, *perestroika* took on a certain ambivalence in that it represented both a success and a failure.

On the one hand, it was a failure when measured by the intentions of those who initiated the movement. The collapse of the whole empire came to represent

an "existential vacuum" for the people, who experienced the "loss of the meaning of life, the collapse of the paradigm of human existence" (Nowikow 1994,
54). Children and youth were especially affected as demoralization, crime, drugs,
homelessness, loss of values, and resignation manifested themselves in societies
unprepared to help children and youth deal with such problems (Jones 1994;
Rybinsky 1994). The crisis brought with it, after 1991, chaos, anarchy, massive
poverty, hunger, and moral decay, accompanied by ethnic conflict and political
turbulence, which threatens to derail the changes taking place. Even in the present time, the children's situation is quite dramatic (Document 1998).

On the other hand, *perestroika* was successful in that it demonstrated the
incapacity of the exhausted socialist system and forced a rapid social and structural transformation. In addition, *perestroika* manifested an incipient dynamic
on the part of many people to become engaged and participate in political,
economic, and cultural activities. Of course, this did not occur with most people.
In fact, those in the marginal republics of the former Soviet Union have often
described the *perestroika* period as something that resembled a breeze passing
through a tree. Only the top of the tree was moved by the breeze, while the rest
of the tree remained as solid and stationary as ever. However, as social eruptions,
problems, and grievances came into open discussion, many people who had been
held speechless for decades gained the courage to speak out.

The post-*perestroika* period documents a social receptivity, as well as the
political will, toward a market economy, political pluralism, and democratic
conditions. The transition from monism to pluralism in the thinking of people
has been so pervasive, that the old regimes of thought have been swept away.
The notion of a single political party, for example, has been replaced by a full
spectrum of political streams and parties.

Of course, many critics claim that changes taking place are not democratic,
that the transformation of the economy is detrimental, and that society in general
is characterized as "gruesome, exploitative, and criminal" (Solschenizyn 1994,
131). Even more radical is the claim that societies have reverted to a "primitive
atavism." Societies appear to some to move along "an unknown path toward
nowhere" and the countless reform initiatives find little resonance by incom-
petent administrations (Sokolov 1994). Even by the end of the 1990s, the complex social reforms, including the reform of the educational system, were not
yet finished.

The characteristic phenomena and tendencies of the broad social system provide the context for analogous and necessary changes taking place in education.
In Russia, for example, the extreme material problems and conflicting ideals
(Gershunsky 1994b, 15–26) were so monumental that every attempt to bring
about fundamental educational change, in the sense of humanistic and democratic ideals, must be counted as a significant accomplishment. The system had
been run for decades by a pedagogical intelligentsia that was focused mainly on
its own social status and material security (Beyrau 1993). This has been com-
pounded by the collapse of material conditions of educators. The monthly in-

come of a Russian teacher in 1992 was only 53% of the average wage in the industrial sector, shifting from 83% in January 1994 to 51% in December 1994. Teachers and workers in the health sector are the worst-paid professional income groups (Karakovsky 1993; Jakovlev 1995). In Ukraine, in September 1994, the monthly wage of the teacher was equivalent to ten dollars (Orivel 1994, 13). In Estonia, the May 1992 income of a teacher in classes one to nine ranged from 2,850 to 4,125 rubles, which was then equivalent to 23–34 U.S. dollars (Rajangu 1993, 188 and 194). Fortunately, the conditions in Central Europe have usually been better. In Romania, for example, the before-taxes income of an average teacher in January 1995 was 122 U.S. dollars, which was 2 dollars above the average income in the country.

Theoreticians and practitioners were alarmed at the extreme decline in education, science, and culture, as well as the threatening "shade of a moral and spiritual vacuum in Russia" (Gershunsky 1994b, 15) and they began to define future programmatic and economic requirements. It clearly requires a great infusion of money. As early as 12 July 1991, President Boris Yeltsin declared that 10% of the state budget would be devoted to education. Such an allocation would have restored the educational commitment to a condition that existed in the 1950s. But only 3% of the budget was actually dedicated to education, and the budget has not increased since Yeltsin's declaration. Education remains a "marginal aspect" of social development in Russia (Mel'nikov and Smolin 1998).

The situation is also precarious in other postsocialist societies. In the former Czechoslovakia, the percentage of the state Gross Domestic Product (GDP) devoted to education rose from 7.1% in 1975 to 8.6% in 1988 but fell again to approximately 5% in 1993/94 (Svecov 1994). In Romania, the percentage of the national budget for education was 3.9% in 1994. In Poland, the school law of 1991 could ensure little more than a "minimum curriculum," and parents were obliged to carry 20% of their children's school costs (Mieszalski and Siemak-Tylikowska 1993). In Hungary, the total expenditure on education in real terms did not decrease between 1990 and 1994, in spite of a 20% decrease in the GDP (Lannert 1997, 52).

Even the period of compulsory schooling has been reduced in many lands (for example, in Russia from eleven to nine years, in the former Czechoslovakia, in 1990, from ten to nine years). One of the purposes of this reduction has been to rid the systems of incentives to engage in corrupt practices, where students are obliged to pay for their grades and school-leaving certificates.

The failure of *perestroika* does not fully explain the sources of the failure of the educational reform endeavors. Sources of failure certainly existed in the regressive phase of the Soviet educational system taking place prior to the beginning of *perestroika*. One indicator of this failure might be that the Soviet educational system, when judged against international UNESCO-coefficients of educational attainment, was given an impressive second place in the rankings in the 1960s but had fallen to forty-second place in 1985 (Razumovskij 1990a,

163). Within two years after he initiated *perestroika*, Mikhail Gorbachev declared that education was in a desolate condition and attained a poor efficiency (Holmes, Read, and Voskresenskaya 1995, 27).

The core of our consideration shall be to clarify a number of parallel and divergent conceptualizations and developments taking place in the former socialistic countries of Europe. Our aim is to unravel a general profile of what we feel has been a set of unique revolutionary processes in education.

IMPLEMENTATION OF EDUCATIONAL LAWS IN THE NEWLY INDEPENDENT STATES

The establishment of national educational laws occurred early after various states established their own independent legal base. After the general school laws were passed, further legal provisions were usually necessary concerning preschools, general schools, vocational education, and institutions of higher learning.

Certain countries, such as Poland and Hungary, had a better foundation for their school laws, because their school laws were based on the laws that had been passed prior to the collapse of the Soviet Union. However, almost all of the laws were established in a rapid process that did not allow for any type of consensus building to take place.

The school laws in the region reflect a high degree of consensus in terms of general aims and purposes. Schooling is dedicated to the aims of humanization and democratization, to human values and rights. However, it remains clear that the transformation of these states into genuine entities based on the rule of law is a problematic and complicated process (Tkatschenko 1994).

The new school laws were little more than embryonic expressions and represent "a kind of spiritual anarchy" (Sting and Wulf 1994, 14). In some cases, the laws were so vague or open-ended that they did not guide developments (Birzea 1995). The moment a law came into force, it was often irrelevant to actual needs. In Russia, for example, the 1992 School Law did not correspond with the constitution with regard to financing the upper secondary schools, and it was necessary, in June 1994, to add a supplement. This School Law was modified again in 1996/97 and remains controversial even now.

In Latvia, there was great inconsistency and incompatibility between the School Law of June 1991 and the subsequent laws and directives, so that a completely new school law is being recommended (Berzina 1993, 221). Added to this was the fact that in June 1993, a new parliament was elected that challenged many of the legal provisions. In Estonia, the formulation of the School Law was preceded by a set of documents and theses, an educational platform for Estonia formulated by teachers and other professionals in November 1987. The new general School Law, passed on 23 March 1992, replaced the old School Law of 1981 (Rajangu 1993, 173–174). The new Polish School Law, passed on 7 September 1991, was the product of formal discussions and controversies that had raged since 1989 (Pachocinski 1994). In Bulgaria, a new Law for General Education, passed on 10 January 1991, took effect in April 1992, and was modified again in 1997. Difficulties in the law were especially evident with regard to secondary education (Taulova 1994). In August 1995, Romania was the last of these former socialist countries to craft a school law, even though a provisional set of decisions had been formulated in May 1990, and an initial draft prepared by the Ministry of Education in 1992. This draft had inspired a wide discussion, resulting in more than 10,000 replies and recommendations (Birzea 1995).

The establishment of new school laws for the new states of Germany came with less drama than in the rest of the region, because in 1991 the various state parliaments established temporary rulings and, in a further step, provisional school laws based on the laws of the old states of Germany. Critics claimed the new laws were largely a consequence of the imposition of almost all the agreements the old states had entered into for the previous forty years as a condition of unification (Vogel 1991; Rust and Rust 1995).

In Hungary, a revised school law was in many respects based on the Education Act of 1985 and the 1978 National Standard Curriculum. The 1990 School Law was also subsequently revised many times. Its basic framework was the elimination of the state monopoly of education. In conjunction with the Local Government Act of 1990, state schools were declared to be the property of the municipalities, which were given the responsibility to finance schools. The 1992 Public Employment Act stipulated that the financial and social status of teachers be improved. However, the financial resources have simply not been available (Nagy 1994). The Education Act of 1993 specified the responsibilities and functions of the new system (responsibility of the municipalities, the extension of the full-time general education from 14 to 16 years of age, etc.) (Lannert 1997, 21).

In the former Czechoslovakia, three primary educational laws were passed in 1990: higher education, general education, and educational management. The Higher Education Law provided the most immediate significant changes, whereas the other two remained rather dormant. Since the Czech Republic and the Slovak Republic became realities on 1 January 1993, more radical changes were sought.

FROM THE SOVIET SCHOOL TO NATIONAL SCHOOL SYSTEMS

The creation of national educational systems in the newly established states is largely based on intense nation-state impulses and the current unique moment of European educational history (Neumann 1991, 57; Anweiler 1992, 254; Brunner 1995; Golczewski and Pickhan 1998). Closely connected with these impulses are attempts to engage in fundamental reforms that are oriented toward individual, cultural, spiritual, and historical traditions, although extensive borrowing from Western educational systems has also occurred. A dialectic process of renationalization and internationalization of educational systems has taken place in the post-*perestroika* period. Russian education considers itself a part of global educational space (*mirovoe obrazovatel'noe prostranstvo*) and views Western models through the prism of national traditions and internal needs (Batyukova 1996; Johnson 1996). At the same time, Russian education reinforces its own tradition (education of the 19th century and of the early Soviet period), emphasizing students' patriotic and national education. Furthermore, Russian education contributes to a re-creation or revitalization of a partial Slavic world (Makarceva 1998; Schriewer et al. 1998; Wichmann 1999).

The establishment of national educational systems in the republics of the former Soviet Union has been within the context of a desire to create a genuine national state. Significantly, these initiatives were already evident in some republics prior to *perestroika*. The 1984 educational reform initiative witnessed, for example, attempts on the part of the Baltic republics and Azerbaijan to allow the individual republics to define the content of history, geography, and literature courses, although these attempts were rejected.

Although in August 1990, Gorbachev exclaimed that the very existence of the Soviet Union was at stake, he agreed to a number of administrative compromises that would allow greater and greater autonomy on the part of individual republics (Grotzky 1991). Gorbachev had never intended for *perestroika* to lead to the breakup of the Soviet Union, but his declaration of openness provided an opportunity for national and ethnic groups to push for a greater independence and allowed the emergence of separatist, nationalistic, and fundamentalist movements and the collapse of the Soviet Union (Simon 1995, 96).

The collapse resulted in a geopolitical collage of units moving to establish some form of state existence, political autonomy, and economic means of survival. Although nationalism and separatism had previously been proclaimed as instruments to break away from the rule of Soviet imperialism, those same factors have presented unresolvable barriers to the establishment of multiethnic societies providing basic human rights to all people (Holmes, Read, and Voskresenskaya 1995, 252). This situation created a genuine paradox. A whole group of nations emerged based on a certain type of national isolation, but each appealed for international recognition and some form of political, cultural, and economic integration. These entities were particularly keen on establishing closer ties with the European Union.

It must be understood that the elimination of the socialist value system has not resulted in the development of a clear set of new values and norms. Unfortunately, many supporters of "pluralism" would simply like to exchange the dogma of communism for some other dogma. In Poland, for example, some are alarmed that the Catholic Church is asserting itself as yet another dominating and all-pervasive value system. In addition, many of the values being declared, including freedom and democracy, are not a part of most national traditions, and so the incipient democracies have too often consisted of unbridled individualism (Sobolev 1994, 52).

Many people maintain that the primary task of the school should be the transmission of a new set of values and ideals, a paradoxical task in that these values and ideals are not yet manifested in the larger social and economic world. Education is then seen as a value and a prerequisite of freedom and individualism. The professional literature of Russia continually makes such an argument in the context of national and classical traditions (Bim-Bad 1993; Egorov 1995; Nikandrov 1998).

The movements toward pluralism have had grave consequences for certain nation-states. Yugoslavia long maintained a radical pluralistic policy. Unfortunately, such a policy contributed to the dissolution of the country rather than helping it resolve its ethnic divisions (Soljan 1991, 189–191). The Russians now face severe problems related to ethnic pluralism. From the time of Lenin, many borders were disregarded, and under Stalin, whole populations were forced to change their place of residence. Russians especially were mixed with peoples throughout the Soviet Union so that their children ceased to identify with Russia as a homeland. At the same time, each republic found itself with a powerful Russian presence.[1]

In addition, the Russian Republic consists of a multitude of different minority groups, many of which live in areas designated as autonomous regions, whereas others have special economic, cultural, or demographic privileges. In independent Russia, educational policies and practices took on spontaneous differences in the various regions. In the Leningrad region, where 64% of all schools are in the countryside and twenty different nationalities exist, the structural, economic, and cultural-ethnic uniquenesses were so great that a self-initiated educational program known as *regional'naia obrazovatel'naia systema—ROS* was developed. It is clear that structural developments in formal and nonformal education in Russia must maintain regionally defined components (Koshkina and Rastchetina 1994). In the autonomous region of Buriat, having approximately 250,000 Buriats, a general council was called together in February 1991 to consolidate and revive the Buriat nation. A national school was defined as an instrument to achieve this goal. With the sanction of the Russian Ministry of Education, the Buriat national school would "create an educational system for children and adults, based on the principle of inclusion of adults in the native ethnocultural tradition and having the purpose of rearing the new generation as carriers and creative conveyors of this tradition having the foundation of a complete responsibility of the mother language" (Elaev 1995, 46). The core of the educational content would consist of national components: mother language, national literature and history, national art, and cultural expression. The newly created Buriat program consists of traditional intellectual subjects of study, Central Asian ethnography, and Buddhist and Shamanist religions.

We contend that school and education must have some capacity to establish the necessary social bonds of different cultures and ethnic groups in any country, while breaking down ethnocentrism and hostility toward foreigners within the boundaries of a state, so that a genuine sense of national identity can exist. Some countries are attempting to achieve this promise. Since independence in Ukraine, for example, those peoples who are not Ukrainians, primarily Poles, Moldavians, Russians, and Jews, have been promised extensive autonomy to cultivate their own national and ethnic traditions. The Ukrainian Educational Law of 23 May 1991 mandates that minority groups can maintain their own schools. In 24.6% of the 21,079 primary schools and 39.2% of the secondary schools, the language of instruction is not Ukrainian (Golik 1993, 231). In Kiev, a Jewish university has even been established. A similar endeavor can be found in Belorussia, through an educational policy that extends even to economic guarantees. The schools have dedicated themselves to the rewinning of national identity and cultural autonomy through the acceptance and integration of other cultural minorities. In this regard, Russians are accorded the rights of other minorities (Tomiak 1993, 407). In both states an enormous level of tolerance, especially toward the Russians, is evident.

In both Ukraine and Belorussia, however, a problem has arisen regarding the restoration of cultural and national identity. The Russification process that was part of Soviet policy has resulted in the fact that a large portion of the population of both countries does not speak Ukraine or Belorussian. A long process has been initiated to rebuild national autonomy and cultural identity by relearning the previously marginalized mother languages.

Since the early 1990s, Lithuanians have been diligent in establishing schools where the mother language of minority groups is the language of instruction (9.4% of the population is Russian, 7% is Polish, 1.7% is Belorussian, 1.8% is Ukrainian). There existed 1,987 Lithuanian language schools, 87 Russian language schools, and 53 Polish language schools (Bulajeva 1993, 226). The basis for such a development may be found in the National Minorities Law of 1989, modified in 1991, which ensured equal political, economic, and social rights to all groups and recognized their desire to cultivate national identity. Especially with regard to education, Lithuanian educators have declared a commitment that schools may be dedicated to the preservation of cultural continuity but also to create the necessary foundations to build understanding, tolerance, and openness between minorities (Jackunas and Lakis 1994, 125).

Even with the above formal provisions for schooling in the mother language, caution must be expressed. We recall that similar provisions were found in the Soviet Union in the 1920s and 1930s. The school laws in the mid-1960s also stressed the importance of mother-language instruction. Efforts to achieve genuine equity must be continuously renewed and acted on.

PRIMARY AND SECONDARY SCHOOLING

The disestablishment of the unified school system and the centralized educational administrative structure are the most visible aspects of transformations that have taken place in the former socialist states. Marxist theory is anchored on the idea of a socially homogenized (classless) society that is guided by a centrally run state. The unified school system was seen as a necessary instrument to attain homogeneity, in that every individual should be accorded equal opportunity for education, from preschool through higher education. Unity required a set of porous institutions, but also a continuous consideration for the "work principle" as well as the scientific principle in terms of educational content.

With regard to current educational reforms, the principle of unity has been replaced by differentiation and pluralism. The new trends are to make unity the exception and multiplicity the dominating theme of reform (Panov 1994). On the basis of new and modified educational laws, it is clear that commitments are strong in all Central and Eastern European countries for primary and secondary schooling, for an extension and diversification of secondary schooling, as well as a stronger inner differentiation of specific educational institutions. In addition, individualized instruction claims a stronger place in schooling programs (Shirokova 1992).

In the Soviet Union during the period of *perestroika*, discussion was already under way concerning the creation of differentiated schooling in terms of content, length of schooling, and quality (Razumovskij 1990b). The unified middle school structure took on various forms as individual schools began to experiment with alternatives. A specific national reform proposal first emerged through a special temporary research committee, known as VNIK (*vremenny nautchny issledovatel'ny kollektiv*), or the Provisional Research Group on the Basic School, founded in June 1988 and headed by Edward Dneprov. Those reforms that took place came mainly from spontaneous and local initiatives by teachers working in individual schools. A typical example of such initiatives was the work of the so-called innovator pedagogues, who became visible in the years 1986–1988 (Amonaschvili, Lysenkova, Volkov et al. 1987; Suddaby 1989). Their main concern was to establish alternative schools that deviated from the typical unified school. By 1992 more than 500 "alternative schools" existed, and each school usually attempted to identify itself by a special profile, especially related to a field of study. Of the 7,000 students engaged in these schools in 1992, 40% were oriented toward the humanities, 30% toward mathematics and physics, 20% toward general natural science, and 5% toward religion (Jones 1994, 5). This unchecked diversification led to some new problems, such as the incompatibility of programs, contents, and certificates. Even in the second half of the 1990s, there were some controversial discussions concerning the *pro* and *contra* of educational standards that ensure the compatibility of schools and the contents of learning (Ginecinsky 1999; "Obazovatel'ny standart" 1997; Ministry of Education 1996).

It was only after 1992 in Russia that a multiplicity of state schools began to emerge. One of the important distinctions we must draw among these schools is their structure and organizational character in urban areas as opposed to the countryside. In the cities, the full spectrum of school types can be found. Many are private and take a variety of forms. At the secondary level one finds *Gymnasien* (grades 5–11/12), *lycéen* (grades 8–11/12), experimental schools focusing on modified instructional approaches, free-time programs, social and psychological services, and many special schools focusing on specific fields of study. Of these institutions it is significant that 31 of the 300 *Gymnasien* and 11 of the 200 *lycéen* are found in Moscow (Bandau 1995, 236). There is a strong Russian tradition of the *Gymnasium* in the context of the general cultural and national heritage of the Russian people (Kondratjeva 1994, 80).

A further element in the change process taking place in the Russian school system is what Russians call "author schools," or schools that take on the name of their founders and directors. Such schools are rarely oriented toward nationally imposed initiatives but instead toward local and individual undertakings, and they focus on the uniqueness of children and the diversity of personalities (Sinjagin 1994, 66).

Along with attempts to restructure the unified school tradition, progressive education and what Europeans call New Education are being revived. Russians attempt to link themselves with the "international activity school movement" that focuses on various levels of school organization. Instruction content is global in nature and attempts to provide an integrated field of study or interdisciplinary research collective centered around six major blocks of study (Krasnojarsker Forschungskollektiv 1994). In principle this movement seeks to restore notions akin to the so-called complex- or project-method that was so popular in the 1920s, using the ideas of John Dewey.

The establishment of so-called teaching- and learning-complexes (*uchebnovospitatel'ny kompleks*) has constituted a further aspect of the general lower-secondary school landscape in Russia. In fact, this was under discussion as early as 1985, particularly in the countryside, where its defenders argued that the creation of such complexes constituted an optimal foundation for social, intellectual, moral, and ethical development (Maljarova 1990). It was argued that symmetry was necessary between school and society and that the growing complexity of social processes and requirements, particularly with regard to regional peculiarities and the ambivalent role of the media in an information society, demanded that the school no longer assume that it could be the only transmitter of knowledge.

In the private sphere a number of different types of school sponsors, financial arrangments, and curriculum content possibilities exist. Typical examples are the Classical *Gymnasium* Nr. 610 and the Ioffe Physical Technical High School in Saint Petersburg (Westbrook 1994). Private tuition schools might charge as much as $400 a month (Bandau 1995, 242 f).

The partial return to traditional educational institutions, particularly *Gymnasien* and *lycéen*, represents a general phenomenon and signals the return of these countries to a Western oriented, neo-conservative paradigm, and a joining with global capitalistic trends (Kozma 1992, 98). However, part of this thrust must be seen as an attempt to break away from the socialist ideology and to restore some contact with what reformers perceive to be their own national educational and pedagogical traditions (Razumovskij 1990a).

Russia is not the only country where dramatic changes are taking place. Estonian children begin school at the age of 6 or 7, when they attend a four-year common school. They then attend either a nine-year general secondary school that has two levels, a five-year and a further four-year level, or they may attend a continuation school for eight or nine years, which is also divided into two levels (Rajangu 1993, 60 f).

In the Czech and Slovak Republics, the basic school is four years in duration, followed by grades 5 to 8 or 9 in different types of schools. At the secondary level are three school types: *Gymnasium*, secondary specialized schools, and secondary vocational schools. In the Slovak Republic, there are both primary and secondary schools where Hungarian is the language of instruction (Svecov 1994; Rummerov 1993, 254).

In Poland, which has a long tradition of middle schools, the primary school now covers the group from 7 to 15 years. If parents wish, their child may enroll as early as 6 years (Pachocinski 1994, 124). Secondary education, however, is much more differentiated than in other countries and provides extensive options to students. It consists of postprimary schools (basic vocational schools and incomplete middle schools), general secondary schools (*lycéen* and general *lycéen*), secondary technical schools, vocational *lycéen*, basic vocational and secondary vocational schools, and special trade schools.

In Hungary, after a long discussion concerning the length and profile of primary schooling, compulsory education was extended two years (in so-called special classes) to 16 years of age. The traditional eight-year general primary school was tentatively retained in the 1990 School Law. After 1995, the length of primary education for all was reduced to four years. Students can transfer at an early age to an appropriate secondary school: a *Gymnasium*, a general secondary school, a vocational secondary school, or a short vocational school (Lannert 1997, 26). This represents partially a restoration of the educational tradition that existed at the time of World War II (Nagy 1994, 58), especially of the educational policies introduced by J. Eötvös and the Hungarian General Education Law of 1868 (Németh and Pukánsky 1994, 39–40).

In Romania, in contrast to political, economic, and finance reforms begun mainly in 1990 and expected to take from ten to fifteen years, experts maintain that changes in the general cultural sphere, including education, will require at least twenty-five years (Birzea 1995, 2). Structural changes, however, are expected to be made rather quickly. The compulsory school consists of eight years (four years primary and four additional years at the *Gymnasium*). Approximately 25% of the pupils conclude their schooling after eight years. Secondary education consists of four years beyond compulsory schooling (age group: 14–18), and it takes place in a variety of institutional settings: four-year academic *lycéen* (24% of secondary students), four-year technical *lycéen* (44% of secondary students), or two- and three-year vocational schools (32% of secondary students). The academic *lycéen* are intended to restore the tradition of schooling that existed in Romania prior to World War II.

Of course, after a process of fundamental structural reforms in all these countries, there have been some additional modifications throughout the whole decade. As of the end of the 1990s, this process was, in the main, finished.

VOCATIONAL TRAINING

Within the socialist context, vocational education played an important role. Training, in the form of apprenticeships, usually took place within the context of communal farms, industries, and businesses. With the collapse of socialism and the wholesale privatization process, almost all of these training places were abolished, and during the 1990s very few training places existed, although new incentive schemes are emerging to attract employers to participate in apprenticeship programs. In addition, the entire vocational training process is being reconceptualized in various countries.

In Russia a wide variety of vocational processes are at work. As Russia became independent, vocational training remained the most resistant to change. Those running vocational programs have finally begun to recognize that changes must be undertaken as the whole economy undergoes a radical transformation (Sowtis 1991, 30), requiring new institutions, training programs, and value orientations (Vul'fov 1993; Beljaeva 1993). The market economy in Russia was (and is?) in its embryonic stage and does not provide a clear picture of the types of vocational skills necessary to address its special needs and developing character. A well-functioning market system is far more complex than anyone imagined. The market is mythologized as a "wonder process" that promises to provide social and individual benefits (Zimmer 1994, 83), but no functioning market system exists in the current phase of development.

The task facing those attempting to develop a vocational education program is how they can provide a bridge between general education and the demands of a weak market system, based on dubious legal provisions. Just as we have stressed the need for regional differences in terms of general education, vocational education must also satisfy individual needs as well as vastly different economic and technical developments in various parts of Russia. Training programs must deal with the conflicting "demands of various markets, the quality of production, the professionalism of workers, the socio-cultural status, and the level of vocational training for personnel, who must be able to compete" (Beljaeva 1993, 68). Priority is now being placed on harmonizing, at the regional level, the developments of general education, the economic structures that are emerging, and the needs and interests of the workforce. In addition to already existing "typical" vocational schools, colleges, *lycéen*, and special vocational schools, there is a tendency in various regions to create so-called general/professional complexes (*uchebno-professional'ny kompleks*), in which a general, preprofessional, and vocational education is possible. For example, the complex *Ishora-obrazovanie* in Saint Petersburg was developed through a cooperative effort between the Russian Academy of Education, the local Educational Office, the Ishora-Industries, and the Technical Lycée Nr. 6.

In close connection with structural innovations, one finds the development of various types of training approaches within the framework of democratization and humanization of the vocational/technical education system. These are related not just to training, but also to the selection of foremen and advisers, the constitutionality of laws affecting trainees and trainers, and the methodological approaches to training.

In Estonia, vocational education has become a part of the general schooling system. It begins with the so-called vocational middle schools, where both vocational and general knowledge are taught. Young people who complete the nine-year general secondary school are able to obtain a vocational and a secondary school-leaving certificate at the same time (Rajangu 1993, 62–63, 73).

In Poland since 1990, the tendency has been to expand and diversify the vocational programs of study. Programs are intended to become more porous, in that students are no longer bound to specific vocations but have the flexibility to shift vocational tracks. Such a scheme requires a stronger individualization of programs. The general framework is that vocational students will not seek narrow training in a specific craft but will have a broadly based vocational profile to offer to prospective employers. To achieve this aim, the Polish are developing a new institution, known as the technical *lycée*, which parallels more conventional vocational schools (Hörner and Wompel 1994, 26; Steier-Jordan 1995, 37 f).

In Hungary, some attention was being given to vocational training issues prior to 1989, but subsequent developments led Hungarians to adopt the so-called dual model of vocational training found in Germany. In this system, the vocational student attends vocational school one or two days a week and is placed directly in the work environment for the remainder of the week. Hungary's main difficulty is that of its own problems regarding economic structures, performance effectiveness, and so on. The dual system in Germany has a whole set of vocational institutions, such as a Labor Ministry, Central Institute of Vocational Education, and Information Centers for Vocational Education, which the Hungarians must develop if they wish to adopt rather than adapt their dual system (Farkas 1993).

In the Eastern part of Germany, vocational education has been reformed by the implementation of the dual system of West Germany. The problem is that there are not enough industrial firms to ensure the practical component of this dualism. Some new-founded firms do not admit young people, arguing that the integration of an "azubi" (trainee) is too expensive.

INSTITUTIONS OF HIGHER LEARNING

One of the most important conditions for the necessary renewal of former socialist societies and the establishment of an effective economy is a professional intelligentsia. This necessitates the reform of the entire system of higher learning. Academics throughout Central and Eastern Europe claim that a significant aspect of the transformation of institutions of higher learning, along with the decentralization, restructuring, democratization, and humanization processes, is the establishment of pluralism as the driving force of the research and teaching institutions of higher learning. All institutions must become open to foreign endeavors and become connected with appropriate international "scientific communities." In practice, however, these expressed desires in all countries have been variously accentuated. Above all else, the lack of financial resources and mounting social problems have prevented the full development of appropriate networks and the building of appropriate institutions.

Almost no reforms in higher education were undertaken in the Soviet Union during the period of *perestroika* (Avis 1990; Balzer 1994), except some critical elements modifying but not rejecting the Marxist-Leninist basic paradigm, as in the field of the history of education in the second half of the 1980s (Wichmann 1996). This means that the problems higher education was facing were never resolved and they continued to accumulate. The current situation in higher education, especially in Russia, must be seen in the context of the terrible economic and social crises, and changes are being made with an awareness that "survival is the greatest present need." In 1994 a questionnaire was sent to the rectors of higher schools in Russia, with the following results: only 8% claimed to be in a "normal" situation, 81% judged their institutions to be in a state of deterioration, and 11% claimed it had reached a crisis stage (Matrosov 1995, 3).

The network of state universities and other higher education institutions has changed since independence, at least in qualitative terms, although a number of private institutions have come into existence, most of which are of questionable quality. Certain changes in the public sector have been in name only. For example, the Humanities University in Moscow is little more than a continuation of the old Historical Archives Institute, and the Technical University, also in Moscow, is a new name for the old Bauman Moscow Higher Technical School. In Saint Petersburg, a regional Higher Education Committee changed the name of forty-two higher education institutions (VUZy) to universities. Of course, it was more than only a juggling with names. The most active changes in name came from former pedagogical institutions, which were attempting to enhance their status and financial support by becoming pedagogical universities. In addition to declaring themselves universities, they also began to require higher tuition fees, offer new and often questionable programs of study, and hire poorly prepared academic personnel (Kitaev 1994b).

A further tendency of structural-institutional reform could be called hybridization. The purpose of such hybridization has been to create what Russians describe as additive or integrative educational complexes. For example, in the end-phase of the *perestroika* period, a number of so-called research-educational complexes were organized (*nautchno-obrazovatel'ny kompleks*—NOK), such as the teacher-training institute in Magadan. This process continued after independence. The institution in Magadan has faculty members from the university, from the Northern Humanistic Lyceum, from the teacher-training institute, from a psychological center, the Research Institute for Biological Problems of the North, various *Gymnasien*, a mathematics/natural science *lycée*, a biological/ ecological *lycée*, an art/aesthetics school, and a school complex with a kindergarten, middle school, and *Gymnasium* (Gadshieva 1993, 39). The basic notion behind such an undertaking was to provide a smooth transition from one type of education to another, such as general to technical education, or from basic to specific to regional educational components.

A further problem manifests itself in the creation of a modified system of higher education-leaving certificates. Since September 1992 a multilevel system has come into existence.

1. Basic higher education

2. Further basic higher education

3. Specialized higher education, with a possible master's degree

4. Graduate study leading to a candidate or doctoral degree

Each university must make its own decision if it will accept this new, more Western form of study (Balzer 1994). Any decision will have fundamental structural, content, and personnel consequences.

Privatization is a further element of the reform in higher education. In Russia, 141 private institutions were licensed in 1994 (Mühle 1995, 80). Currently, however, lack of money seems to be the main problem for all (state) universities with different structural and personal implications (Davydov 1997). But these problems do not concern higher education only in the focused region. Higher education is in a (financial) crisis worldwide (Hüfner 1995, 30).

In Estonia, the six universities that existed at the beginning of the 1950s were able to maintain a semblance of self-determination despite major efforts by political leaders to bring them under ideological control. The greatest changes in the universities are to be found in the kinds of research projects being undertaken, the types of courses being offered, and the new masters and doctoral programs being offered (Rajangu 1993, 63 and 74).

The new states of Germany offer the greatest possibility for change because more resources are available in those states than anywhere else in the region. In these new states, in July 1991, the Science Council of the Federal Republic issued a conceptual framework for the transformation of the institutions of higher learning. From a total of 54 institutions (6 universities, 4 technical universities, 9 teacher-training colleges, 14 colleges of engineering, 3 colleges of medicine, 12 colleges of music and fine arts, 6 specialized institutions), 5 were closed. It was also found that the establishment of a federated system in East Germany meant that Brandenburg did not have a single university. Two general universities and a technical university were consequently established, such as the *Viadrina* in Frankfurt/Oder. At the current time there are 16 universities, 21 specialized universities (*Fachhochschulen*), and 10 colleges of music and fine arts. The number of academic personnel in the former East Germany has fallen from 30,000 to 13,000 (Lange 1993). After a period of generous financial support and against the background of well-functioning institutions, the second half of the 1990s experienced strong financial restrictions step by step. New reforms of the entire German higher education system seem to be necessary.

PRIVATIZATION

An effective means of achieving certain aspects of differentiation in education is through privatization, one of the guiding principles of education policy in an increasing number of countries, including the postsocialist countries (Weiß and Steinert 1996, 1). Privatization and the establishment of confessional, free, or independent schools are a fundamental aspect of all new school laws, although certain restrictions and the activities of private-school lobbies are causes of differing levels of privatization. Once conditions are met to allow private schools to be established, their existence and productivity depend on their capacity to obtain financial resources through tuition, sponsors, and so on. Often it has become clear that the label *non-state schools* is misleading because many private schools have obtained extensive state support and are quasi-state institutions (Darinsky 1997). Over the decade, however, reductions in this generous support mean that some private schools now have to fight for their existence.

In general, private educational institutions are considered a sign of a liberal society and an indicator of political freedom and plurality in which each citizen is given the right to pursue education according to personally defined needs and interests. However, the process of privatizing education in these countries has been marked by ambivalence. The motivation for private schools is not always the ideal of liberalism. For example, private schools are one means for state authorities to reduce their financial obligations to education (Kozma 1992).

In the socialist period, private schools were not tolerated. It takes a certain adjustment of attitude on the part of major segments of the population to entertain the possibility that they have options from which to choose and that the financial obligation for some of these options might fall on their shoulders. One major adjustment in attitude has to do with the notion that privatization signals the return of social class distinctions and a certain elitism in education. It is not surprising to find that 87% of the parents in the Czech Republic believed in 1993 that private schools provide a better education than schools in the public sector, and that 68% also believed that private schools are a privilege of the wealthy (Svecov 1994, 113).

In the new school laws, a distinction is often drawn between "private" and "confessional" schools, even though they are both non-public institutions. After the Czech School Law of 1991–92 was established, a total of 104 private educational institutions was quickly established: 1 kindergarten, 8 basic schools, 20 *Gymnasien*, 48 secondary vocational schools, and 27 apprentice training centers. The major sponsor of these institutions is the church, with 21 schools. In the Slovak Republic in the same period there were 10 private schools (3 *Gymnasien*, 1 secondary vocational school, and 6 apprentice training centers). The number of confessional schools in the Slovak Republic was significantly greater than in the Czech Republic: 28 basic schools, 9 *Gymnasien*, 1 secondary vocational school, and 1 apprentice training center (Svecov 1994, 103). Two years after the School Law had been established in the Czech Republic, more than 500 private and confessional primary and secondary schools existed.

In Poland in 1991, a total of 1,091 general secondary schools, including 65 so-called civic schools, 18 confessional, and 6 private schools existed. Beyond that number there were 155 "non-state primary schools," of which only 17 were truly private schools. By 1993, that number had escalated to 430 non-state schools, including a number of communal schools that were receiving some financial support from the state (Mieszalski and Siemak-Tylikowska 1993, 249). From 1992 to 1996, the number of state primary schools decreased from 17,691 to 13,249, and at the same time the number of confessional schools increased from 12 to 22. The Polish situation is interesting in that communities have initiated a type of privatization process, establishing schools that veer from the state school norms and doing it in the name of "non-state schooling" (Hörner and Wompel 1994). There is also a category of private schools labeled "non-public schools." From 1988 to 1994 approximately 150 such schools in the primary sector and nearly 100 schools in the secondary school sector were established. Currently, approximately 12% of the private-school children attend such schools. Pupils come from wealthy families, so there are "no children of farmers and only a few children of blue-collar families" (Kruszewski 1994, 213).

In Hungary in the fall of 1992, 142 confessional schools had already been established: 88 Catholic, 35 Protestant, 16 Evangelist, 2 Jewish, and one other religious school. Now there are approximately 140 private schools that are not confessional. Most of these private schools (68%) are in the major city of Budapest, whereas most of the confessional schools (85%) are in the countryside (Nagy 1994, 41). Approximately 140 private schools are found in Hungary, although many of these receive state support. In addition there are approximately 200 confessional schools. This means that the private sector represents approximately 4% of all schools. This is remarkable compared with Russia, where about 0.2% of all students go to private schools (Gromyko 1996, 63).

In addition to confessional and more conventional private schools there are alternative and so-called reformed pedagogy schools, including those based on the ideas of Rudolf Steiner, Maria Montessori, and Celestin Freinet.

ADMINISTRATION

One of the tendencies found in almost all postsocialist educational systems is the reduction of central control. The excessive centralization of the former educational system must be counted as one of the most difficult and restrictive factors in the entire system, especially with regard to the ideological deformation of the instructional processes (Botlik 1993). Decentralization has been enhanced both through political and parliamentary initiatives, but also by various social movements.

It would be a mistake to suggest that these differentiation processes began only after the collapse of the Soviet empire. Decentralization efforts have deep roots in certain lands. In Russia, for example, local administrative units known as *Semstvo* have existed for more than 100 years. We can say that when decentralizing the educational system, Russia refers to its own traditions as well as to Western models.

As early as the 1970s, Hungary was toying with so-called alternative school experiments, which attempted to modify the unified school model. Curriculum developments also included attempts to depoliticize history instruction and to introduce optional subjects (Birzea 1994, 58). The former Czechoslovakia maintained for many decades a school system structured around ethnic minorities (von Kopp 1993). In Bulgaria as early as 1956, the centralized school system was modified, a move that represented a shift in the policy of unreflectively copying the Soviet system (Bachmaier 1991, 187). Behind the facade of uniformity there were many forms of differentiation.

At the beginning of the 1990s, the differentiation processes accelerated. In spite of impulses toward decentralization, one of the important discoveries most countries had to make was that a decentralized, functioning educational system did not come automatically with the establishment of new laws and policies or from the demand of people to have "external input" in education. In fact, certain new republics of the former Soviet Union simply carried over the old administrative structure and imposed it on the level of the republic. When viewed from the classroom of an individual school, teachers often have remained subject to a highly authoritarian, uniform system of education (Rust and Rust 1995).

One also finds the other extreme at work. One of the important discoveries made, at least in Russia, was that an "uncontrolled autonomy" was taking place at the local administrative units (Pilipovsky 1991, 57); a type of anarchistic independence was taking hold in each administrative unit. The need was to engage in an educational discourse sufficient to achieve a productive balance between the central state and regional-local-institutional interests (McGinn 1992, 164).

A terrible difficulty is that these systems are attempting to achieve some semblance of professional quality in the middle of a severe political and financial crisis. The effect of the financial shortages is clearly evident in Hungary, for example. The various administrative levels carry some formal responsibility, but the responsibility for enhancing the educational level of the regions, states, and districts has simply fallen on the shoulders of those at the local level (Nagy 1994). In Russia, one of the major accomplishments of the first minister of education, Edward Dneprov, was to decentralize the administrative structure in March 1992. Now the process of decentralization is organized by a more effective administration and is finished in the main (Malakhov 1998). In Poland, also, new administrative arrangements for centralized and decentralized control have emerged. This took place in the context of active political struggles, in which political forces advocated liberal-democratic, populist, and socialist views. It was decided that the administrative structure would center around three basic levels: state (ministry), province (*voivodeships*), and school (Kruszewski 1994, 215).

In the five new states of Germany, great efforts were undertaken to help administrators cope with their new roles and responsibilities. One strategy was to bring experienced administrators from the old states. On the one hand, this proved to be helpful and valuable. On the other hand, they had little understanding of the situation in the new states and were often insensitive to these problems. This has led to resentment and frustration on the part of administrators from both parts of Germany, and it has contributed to a sense of superiority and a "victor mentality" on the part of West Germans and feelings of inferiority and frustration on the part of East Germans.

In other postsocialist countries the educational administrators usually have continued to maintain their posts. Of course, some cleansing of personnel took place, the most extensive in the former German Democratic Republic where a high percentage of administrators were released, leaving the whole bureaucracy in the hands of novices (Rust and Rust 1995). The other lands struggled to cope with the tensions between new, innovative personnel, who wanted to change things, and "old experts," who defended the established ways of managing the educational enterprise (Nagy 1994, 65). In Russia, Edward Dneprov was moved to characterize those from the old establishment in the Pedagogical Academy as "the nest of the Black Hundreds" (Kerr 1994, 55).

REFORM OF THE CURRICULA

The coincidence of structural and curricular innovations is yet another characteristic of educational reform. In every system, curriculum changes occurred prior to the collapse; however, the changes in the 1990s have represented a qualitatively new level. In fact, they have been so fundamental that they are based on different theoretical perspectives. A major change has been textbooks. Previously, the state maintained a monopoly in terms of the publishers of textbooks, and the policy was that single sets of textbooks would be produced throughout the country (Karakovsky 1993). In Hungary, for example, textbooks are now selected by individual schools from a list of appropriate textbooks available in a catalog published by the Ministry of Education. These books are developed and produced by a number of different publishers.

During the period of *perestroika* in the Soviet Union, demands for greater cultural and ethnic autonomy led to a discussion of adjustments in the curriculum plan. The major issue was schools' right to make curricular decisions. Most of the energy for such changes came from the teachers themselves (Kerr 1994, 50).

The Russian first-grade pupil had been expected to spend at least 6 hours on union components, 14 hours on republic components, and two hours on school components each week. A student in the eleventh grade was required to take a 14:10:12 ratio of instructional hours (Razumovskij 1990a, 174). After 1991 the differentiation process was accelerated and modified, so that responsibility for the content of instruction was shifted to the nation/republic, region, and school, and it was decided that consideration must be given to natural, economic, ecological, historical, socio-cultural, demographic, and ethnic shifts that were constantly changing (Butorina 1994). The "Basic Curriculum of the General Secondary School" of 1993–94 clarified and operationalized the appropriate articles of the School Law of July 1992. This curriculum was also outlined on the principle of three parts: the basic curriculum (the core curriculum or the national element); the regional curriculum; and the school curriculum. In contrast to the last curriculum of the Soviet Union, spelled out in 1989–90, the sphere "Literature of the USSR" gave priority to the national literature of the Soviet Union, and the literature of the various republics was very limited. In grades 10 and 11 the subject of mathematics was also reduced by an hour (Zajda 1994, 194). A further emphasis in the Russian curriculum reform was with regard to the quantitative reduction of the content (Karakovsky 1993).

In Ukraine, the major curriculum decisions were driven by the fact that approximately 28% of the people are not Ukrainian. This has necessitated dividing the state curriculum into two parts: the core curriculum (70%) concentrates on mathematics, natural and social sciences, the Ukrainian language, literature, history, and geography, and the optional subjects (30%), which can be determined by the school. The core curriculum is compulsory for all schools. In the ethnic schools the optional subjects focus on the language, literature, folklore, and cultural foundations of the ethnic group (Golik 1993, 232).

In Estonia, two types of curriculum programs of study have been developed since 1990–91, one for ethnic minorities and the other for Russian language schools. Both distinguish themselves mainly by the way they define the main language and secondary languages. In contrast to those countries that focus on scientific disciplines, Estonia has opted to concentrate on learning about the full spectrum of global cultures rather than the academic sciences (Rajangu 1993, 101 and 163).

By 1990, Hungary was already mired in different social, political, and confessional conflicts related to educational policies, though consensus was reached that a new national curriculum must be developed and that at the primary level the curriculum must be devoted to providing the foundations of Hungarian culture (Ladányi 1991). Given this aim, a whole set of issues was addressed. The grading system was revised. A core curriculum was being developed that would have a national base and be compulsory for all students. Above all, however, was the belief that the local environments and the individual schools could adapt this core curriculum to their own special interests and needs (Nagy and Szebenyi 1990, 251).

In Poland, new curricula were being developed as early as 1990–91. The driving principle guiding curriculum development was that encyclopedic knowledge would be reduced and everyday knowledge would be more strongly emphasized. From September 1994, the primary school curriculum was to be built around eight theoretical subjects (Polish, history, social studies, mathematics, physics, chemistry, biology, and geography), a practical subject of sport (including swimming), and foreign languages. The secondary level would be reduced from four to three years, although those preparing for university study would continue to attend for four years. One of the most intense issues facing Polish authorities has been the role of religion in the school program. Religion is now compulsory, but it is possible to substitute an ethics class for religion. It will be a subject in the examination structure of Poland (Pachocinski 1993, 133). One can say that the curriculum reform is essentially finished in all countries. But there is a constant process of curriculum modification, a search for the "optimal" curriculum, because of the emergence of new needs and conditions (Matros 1999).

This estimation can be seen in a general manner: The transformation processes in all postsocialist countries led in this decade to principally new structures, institutions, and forms of administration as well to mainly new contents, goals, and values in education. There are, of course, clear differences between these countries concerning results and problems at the end of the 1990s. In the 1990s there was in Central and East European education a shift in a double sense: from a socialist to a postsocialist system in the first half, as well as a shift from unstable transitional structures to relatively stable structures in working order in the second half. Further reforms in details are, however, still necessary. We think that our analysis proves that in spite of different results and existing problems, educational reforms in Central and Eastern Europe are of concern not just to this region. The entire European educational landscape has been changed so that all national educational systems must confront new challenges.

NOTE

1. There are pockets where Russians are in the clear majority, such as in the eastern area of Latvia, where Russians dominate free elections and continue to hold enormous professional and political power.

REFERENCES

Abbreviation

DIPF Deutsches Institut für Internationale Pädagogische Forschung

Reviews

BuE: Bildung und Erziehung
CE: Comparative Education
NO: Narodnoe Obrazovanie
OvD: Obrazovanie v Dokumantakh
SP: Sovetskaya Pedagogika
TC: Tertium Comparationis
VP: Vergleichende Pädagogik

Amonaschvili, S. A., S. N. Lysenkova, I. P. Volkov et al. 1987. *Pedagogicheskij Poisk* (Pedagogical Search). Moscow: Pedagogika.

Anweiler, O. 1992. "Politischer Umbruch und Pädagogik im Östlichen Europa." *BuE* 43 (3): 237–247.

Avis, G. 1990. "The Soviet Higher Education Reform: Proposals and Reactions." *CE* 26 (1): 5–12.

Bachmaier, P., ed. 1991. *Bildungspolitik in Osteuropa. Systemwandel und Perspektiven.* Wien: Jugend und Volk.

Balzer, H. D. 1994. "Plans to Reform Russian Higher Education." In *Education and Society in the New Russia*. Edited by A. Jones. Armonk, NY/London: M. E. Sharpe, 27–46.

Bandau, S. 1995. "Vielfalt in der Moskauer Schullandschaft." *Osteuropa* (3): 232–246.

Batyukova, Z. I. 1996. "Integracia Rossii v mirovoe obrazovatel' noe prostranstvo" [Russia's integration into the global educational space]. *Pedagogika* 58(3): 98–102.

Beljaeva, A. P. 1993. "The Regional System of Vocational Education" (Russian). *Pedagogika* 56 (4): 68–72.

Berzina, Z. 1993. "Transforming Processes in Latvian Education." In *European Forum on Education. Restructuring Education and Educational Administration after the Breakdown of Socialism*. Edited by H. Avenarius et al. Frankfurt am Main: DIPF, 220–221.

Beyrau, D. 1993. *Intelligenz und Dissens. Die russischen Bildungsschichten in der Sowjetunion 1917 bis 1985*. Göttingen: Vandenhoeck & Ruprecht.

Bim-Bad, B. M. 1993. "Education for Freedom in Russia" (Russian). *Pedagogika* 56 (6): 3–8.

Birzea, C. 1994. *Les politiques éducatives dans les pays en transition*. Strasbourg: Les éditions du Conseil de l'Europe.

———. 1995. "Educational Reform and Educational Research in Central-Eastern Europe: The Case of Romania." Paper presented at the IBE/NIER International Meeting on Educational Reform and Educational Research, Tokyo, 4–14 September 1995.

Botlík, O. 1993. "Recent Developments of the Czech Educational System." In *European Forum on Educational Administration. Restructuring Education and Educational Administration after the Breakdown of Socialism.* Edited by H. Avenarius et al. Frankfurt am Main: DIPF, 222–225.

Brunner, G., ed. 1995. *Osteuropa zwischen Nationalstaat und Integration.* Berlin: Arno Spitz GmbH.

Bulajeva, T. 1993. "The Present Situation of Education in Lithuania." In *European Forum on Educational Administration. Restructuring Education and Educational Administration after the Breakdown of Socialism.* Edited by H. Avenarius et al. Frankfurt am Main: DIPF, 226–227.

Butorina, T. S. 1994. "The Incorporation of National and Regional Components into the School Curriculum as a Means of Promoting Integration into the European Educational System." In *Education in a Period of Social Upheaval. Educational Theories and Concepts in Central East Europe.* Edited by S. Sting and Ch. Wulf. Münster: Waxmann, 119–130.

Darinsky, A. V. 1997. "Non-State General Education in St. Petersburg" (Russian). *Pedagogika* 59 (3): 32–36.

Davydov, Yu. S. 1997. "Higher Education: State, Problems, Solutions" (Russian). *Pedagogika* 59 (2): 61–67.

Document. 1998. "It Is Allowed to Consider a Healthy State When Its Children Are Ill?" (Russian). *Pedagogika* 60 (1): 3–9.

"Educational Standard: For and Against" (Russian). 1997. *NO* (5): 4–33.

Egorov, S. F. 1995. "The Value of General Education" (Russian). *Pedagogika* 58 (3): 90–93.

Elaev, N. K. 1995. "The Present and Future of the Buriat National School" (Russian). *Pedagogika* 58 (2): 45–47.

Farkas, P. 1993. "Die Berufsbildungspolitik in Ungarn nach 1989." In *Halbjahresbericht zur Bildungspolitik und pädagogischen Entwicklung in ausgewählten Ländern Mittel- und Osteuropas.* Bochum: Ruhr-Universität, 1–27.

Gadshieva, N. M. 1993. "The Scientific Educational Complex in Magadan" (Russian). *Pedagogika* 56 (3): 38–41.

Gershunsky, B. S. 1994a. "Offener Brief an den Präsidenten Russlands, Boris N. Jelzin." In *Curricula in der Schule: Russland 1992.* Edited by W. Mitter. Köln: Böhlau, 9–11.

———. 1994b. "Russland: Bildung und die Zukunft." In *Curricula in der Schule: Russland.* Edited by W. Mitter. Köln: Böhlau, 13–38.

Ginecinsky, V. I. 1999. "Obrazovatel'ny standart—problema teoreticheskoy pedagogiki" [The educational standard as a problem of theoretical pedagogy]. *Pedagogika* 61 (8): 12–15.

Golczewski, F., and G. Pickhan. 1998. *Russischer Nationalismus.* Göttingen: Vandenhoeck.

Golik, L. 1993. "Educational Reform in Ukraine." In *European Forum on Educational Administration.* Restructuring Education and Educational Administration after the Breakdown of Socialism. Edited by H. Avenarius et al. Frankfurt am Main: DIPF, 231–233.

Gromyko, Yu. V. 1996. "Bildungswesen im Spannungsfeld von Demokratisierung und Privatisierung: das Beispiel Rußland." *TC* 2 (1): 48–55.

Grotzky, J. 1991. *Konflikt im Vielvölkerstaat.* München/Zürich: Piper.

Holmes, B., G. H. Read, and N. Voskresenskaya. 1995. *Russian Education. Tradition and Transition*. New York: Garland Publishing.

Hörner, W. 1991. "Von der Autonomie der Pädagogik zur Autonomie des Schulsystems. Vergleichende Aspekte einer Begründung von Schulautonomie." *BuE* 44 (4): 373–389.

Hörner W., and R. Wompel. 1994. *Die polnische Schule im Umbruch*. Wiesbaden: Harrassowitz.

Hüfner, K. 1995. *Higher Education Reform Process in Central and Eastern Europe*. Frankfurt am Main: Peter Lang.

Jackunas, Z., and J. Lakis. 1994. "National Minorities and Education in Lithuania." In *Education and the Values Crisis in Central and Eastern Europe*. Edited by V. D. Rust, P. Knost, and J. Wichmann. Frankfurt am Main: Peter Lang, 119–130.

Jakovlev, V. M. 1995. "Who Swallowed the Wages of Teachers?" Letters of the Leadership of the Union of Colleagues in the Educational System and in Science on the President of the Russian Federation (Russian). *Ovd* 2 (4): 67–69.

Johnson, M. 1996. "Western Models and Russian Realities in Postcommunist Education." *TC* 2 (2): 119–132.

Jones, A. 1994. "The Educational Legacy of the Soviet Period." In *Education and Society in the New Russia*. Edited by A. Jones. Armonk, NY/London: M. E. Sharpe, 3–23.

Karakovsky, V. A. 1993. "The School in Russia Today and Tomorrow." *Compare* 23 (3): 277–286.

Kerr, S. T. 1994. "Diversification in Russian Education." In *Education and Society in the New Russia*. Edited by A. Jones. Armonk, NY/London: M. E. Sharpe, 47–74.

Kitaev, I. V. 1994. "Russian Education in Transition: Transformation of Labour Market Attitudes of Youth and Changes in Management of Higher and Lifelong Education." *Oxford Review of Education* 20 (1): 111–130.

Kondratjeva, M. A. 1994. "The *Gymnasium* of the Fatherland: Historical Experiences and Contemporary Problems" (Russian). *Pedagogika* 57 (1): 75–80.

Koshkina, V., and S. Rastchetina. 1994. "The Regional Program: The Way Towards a New Quality" (Russian). *NO* 76 (7): 2–10.

Kozma, T. 1992. "The Neo-Conservative Paradigm: Recent Changes in Eastern Europe." In *Emergent Issues in Education. Comparative Perspectives*. Edited by R. F. Arnove, P. G. Altbach, and G. P. Kelly. Albany, NY: State University of New York, 93–103.

Krasnojarsker Forchungskollektiv. 1994. "Conceptions of a Modern General Educational and Vocational" (Russian). *NO* 76 (2/3): 104–116.

Kruszewski, K. 1994. "Reform in Polish Education." In *International Perspectives on Education and Society*. Vol. 4: Educational Reform in International Perspective. Edited by A. Yogev (series editor) and V. D. Rust (volume editor). Greenwich: JAI Inc., 205–226.

Kruszewski, K., and K. B. Kruszewski. 1994. "Playing Monopoly Polish Style." In *Education and the Values Crisis in Central and Eastern Europe*. Edited by V. D. Rust, P. Knost, and J. Wichmann. Frankfurt am Main: Peter Lang, 89–105.

Ladányi, M. 1991. "Gesellschaftlicher Umbruch und aktuelle bildungspolitische Initiativen in der Ungarischen Republik." *VP* 27 (1): 71–78.

Lange, J. 1993. "Hochschulen und Forschungseinrichtungen in den neuen Bundesländern zwischen gestern und morgen." *BuE* 46 (2): 207–224.

Lannert, J. 1997. *Education in Hungary 1996*. Budapest: National Institute of Public Education.

Makarceva, N. N. 1998. "Spiritual Values in a Russian Popular Culture in Education" (Russian). *Pedagogika* 60 (1): 81–86.

Makarceva, N. N. 1998. "Dukhovnye cennosti russkoy narodnoy pedagogicheskoy kul'tury" [The spiritual and mental values of the Russian popular pedagogical culture]. *Pedagogika* 60 (1): 81–86.

Malakhov, N. D. 1998. "The Development of a Municipal Educational Management" (Russian). *Pedagogika* 60 (7): 20–26.

Maljarova, N. V. 1990. "The Instructional and Educational Complex: Toward the Creation of Interests of the Learner" (Russian). *SP* 54 (2): 60–64.

Matros, D. Sh. 1999. "Experiences in Creation of an Optimal Curriculum" (Russian). *Pedagogika* 61 (1): 24–30.

Matrosov, V. L. 1995. "Difficulties and Hopes of the Higher School in Russia" (Russian). *Pedagogika* 58 (3): 3–6.

McGinn, N. 1992. "Reforming Educational Governance: Centralization and Decentralization." In *Emergent Issues in Education. Comparative Perspectives*. Edited by R. Arnove et al. Albany: State University of New York Press, 163–172.

Mel'nikov, I. I., and O. N. Smolin. 1998. "Educational Reform in Russia: The Parliament Committee's Arguments" (Russian). *Pedagogika* 60 (7): 3–10.

Mieszalski, S., and A. Siemak-Tylikowska. 1993. "The Polish Educational System in Conditions of Political and Economical Transformation—Hopes, Projects, Reality, Prospects." In *European Forum on Educational Administration. Restructuring Education and Educational Administration after the Breakdown of Socialism*. Edited by H. Avenarius et al. Frankfurt am Main: DIPF, 247–251.

Ministry of Education of the Russian Federation. 1996. "Some Experiences of the Process of Standardization in Education in the Vologodsk Oblast" (Russian). *OvD* 6 (21): 10–15.

Mühle, E. 1995. *Die Entwicklung der russischen Hochschule*. Bonn: Dokumente der Hochschulrektorenkonferenz.

Nagy, J., and P. Szebenyi. 1990. "Hungarian Reform: Towards a Curriculum for the 1990s." *The Curriculum Journal* 1 (3): 247–254.

Nagy, M. 1994. "Hungary." In *Education in East Central Europe. Educational Changes after the Fall of Communism*. Edited by S. Karsten and D. Majoor. Münster: Waxmann, 29–75.

Németh, A., and B. Pukánsky. 1994. "Tendencies and Reforms in the Hungarian School System in Historical Perspective." In *Education and the Values Crisis in Central and Eastern Europe*. Edited by V. D. Rust, P. Knost, and J. Wichmann. Frankfurt am Main: Peter Lang, 37–56.

Neumann, P. 1991. "Hauptrichtungen, Gemeinsamkeiten und Unterschiede in Reformbewegungen Osteuropas." *Vergleichende Pädagogik* 27 (1): 57–61.

Nikandrov, N. D. 1998. "Values as the Basis of Goals in Education" (Russian). *Pedagogika* 60 (5): 3–11.

Nowikow, A. 1994. "Die Zukunft ist verschwunden." *Die enterbte Generation. Russische Jugend nach der Perestroika*. Edited by W. Schlott. Leipzig: Reclam, 47–56.

"Obrazovatel'ny standart: za i protiv" [Educational standard: for and against]. 1997. A collection of articles, opinions and criticisms in *Narodnoe obrazovanie*, no. 5: 4–46.

Orivel, F. 1994. *Education in Ukraine: Organization, Public Expenditure, and Unit Cost.* Dijon: IREDU.

Pachocinski, R. 1994. "Poland." In *Education in East Central Europe. Educational Changes after the Fall of Communism.* Edited by S. Karsten and D. Majoor. Münster: Waxmann, 119–155.

Panov, V. 1994. "From Pluralism to Unity" (Russian). *NO* 76 (6): 19–23.

Petrovitchev, V. M. 1994. "Regional Aspects of a Unified Educational Policy" (Russian). *Pedagogika* 58 (5): 30–34.

Pilipovsky, V. Ja. 1991. "Schulreform und pädagogische Wissenschaft in der Sowjetunion." In *Bildungspolitik in Osteuropa. Systemwandel und Perspektiven.* Wien: Jugend und Volk, 52–60.

Rajangu, V. 1993. *Das Bildungswesen in Eastland. Grundlagen, Tendenzen, Probleme.* Köln: Böhlau.

Razumovskij, V. G. 1990a. "Inhalte der mittleren Bildung in der UdSSR: Probleme und Lösungen." *BuE* 44 (2): 159–176.

———. 1990b. "More Differentiation of Schools, Textbooks, Conceptualizations . . ." (Russian). *SP* 53 (2): 88–92.

Rummerov, A. 1993. "The Reconstruction of the Educational System in the Slovac Republic." In *European Forum on Educational Administration. Restructuring Education and Educational Administration after the Breakdown of Socialism.* Edited by H. Avenarius et al. Frankfurt am Main: DIPF, 252–255.

Rust, Val D., and Diane Rust. 1995. *The Unification of German Education.* New York: Garland.

Rust, Val D., P. Knost, and J. Wichmann, eds. 1994. *Education and the Values Crisis in Central and Eastern Europe.* Frankfurt am Main: Peter Lang.

Rybinsky, E. M. 1994. "The Condition of Children in Russia" (Russian). *Pedagogika* 57 (6): 3–12.

Schriewer, J., J. Henze, J. Wichmann, et al. 1998. "Konstruktion von Internationalität. . . ." In *Gesellschaften im Vergleich.* Edited by H. Kaelble and J. Schriewer. Frankfurt am Main: Lang, 151–260.

Shirokova, G. 1992. "A Multifunctioning System of Preschool Education" (Russian). *Doshkol'noe Vospitanie* 67 (2): 25–30.

Simon, G. 1995. "Russland: Imperiale Restauration oder national-staatlicher Neubeginn?" In *Osteuropa zwischen Nationalstaat und Integration.* Edited by G. Brunner. Berlin: Arno Spitz GmbH, 91–104.

Sinjagin, J. 1994. "A Creative, Free, Independent Personality: Conception of an Author-School" (Russian). *NO* 76 (2/3): 65–67.

Sobolev, V. N. 1994. "How Should One Train for Ideals in a Multinational Environment?" (Russian). *Pedagogika* 57 (6): 51–54.

Sokolov, V. S. 1994. "Concerning State Policies Related to Education" (Russian). *Pedagogika* 57 (6): 13–17.

Soljan, N. N. 1991. "Hochschulpolitik in Jugoslawien. Entwicklung, Veränderung, Tendenzen." *BuE* 44 (2): 187–199.

Solschenizyn, A. 1994. *Die russische Frage am Ende des 20. Jahrhunderts* [The Russian question at the end of the 20th century]. München/Zürich: Piper.

Sowtis, D. 1991. "Soviet Industrial Strategy and Reforms in Vocational Education, 1984–1988: Policy Implications and Implementation." *CE* 27 (1): 23–29.

Steier-Jordan, S. 1995. *Die Reform der beruflichen Bildung in Polen seit 1989*. Münster: Waxmann.

Sting, S., and Ch. Wulf. 1994. "Preface." In *Education in a Period of Social Upheaval. Educational Concepts and Theories in Central East Europe*. Münster: Waxmann, 9–22.

Suddaby, A. 1989. "An Evaluation of the Contribution of the Teacher-Innovators to Soviet Educational Reform." *CE* 25 (2): 245–256.

Svecov, J. 1994. "Czechoslovakia." In *Education in East Central Europe. Educational Changes after the Fall of Communism*. Edited by S. Karsten and D. Majoor. Münster: Waxmann, 77–118.

Szymanski, M. S. 1991. "Tendenzen der Veränderungen des Bildungssystems in der Republik Polen." *VP* 27 (1): 66–71.

Taulova, R. 1994. "The New Bulgarian Secondary School." In *Education and the Values Crisis in Central and Eastern Europe*. Edited by V. D. Rust, P. Knost, and J. Wichmann. Frankfurt am Main: Peter Lang, 27–35.

Tkatschenko, E. V. 1994. "Interview with the Minister of Education of the Russian Federation at an International Educational Conference: Towards a Global Culture, Human Rights, and Democracy." *NO* 76 (9–10): 4–6.

Tomiak, J. 1993. "Erziehung, kulturelle Identität und nationale Loyalität in neu entstehenden Staaten. Die Fälle Ukraine und Belarus." *BuE* 46 (4): 393–409.

Vogel, J. P. 1991. "Administration statt Konzeption—Bemerkungen zu neuen Schulgesetzen." *Pädagogik und Schulalltag* 46 (3): 299–304.

von Kopp, B. 1993. "Kontinuitäten und Brüche. Ethnische Schulen in der Tschechoslowakei 1918–1992." *BuE* 46 (4): 411–430.

Vul'fov, B. S. 1993. "Education and Market in the Transition Period" (Russian). *Pedagogika* 56 (2): 3–9.

Weiß, M., and S. Steinert. 1996. "Markt und Privatisierung im Bildungsbereich: Internationale Tendenzen." *TC* 2 (1): 1–17.

Westbrook, M. A. (with L. Lurie and M. Ivanov). 1994. "The Independent Schools of St. Petersburg. Diversification of Schooling in Postcommunist Russia." In *Education and Society in the New Russia*. Edited by A. Jones. Armonk, NY/London: M. E. Sharpe, 103–117.

Wichmann, J. 1996. "Sozialer Wandel und paradigmatische Prekarität: Reformindikationen in der Historischen Pädagogik im Kontext der Perestroika." *Magister* (Moscow) 6 (2): 68–88.

———. 1998. "The Transformation of Educational Systems in Central and Eastern Europe: Some Prospects and Problems." In *Education and the Structuring of the European Space*. Edited by A. Kazamias and M. Spillane. Athens: Seirios Editions, 269–284.

———. 1999. "The Russian Educational Discourse between Global, Regional and National Driving Forces." Paper presented at the 43rd Annual Meeting of the Comparative and International Education Society, Toronto, 14–18 April 1999.

Zajda, J. 1994. "Educational Reforms and the Discourse of Democracy in Soviet and Post-Communist Education." In *International Perspectives on Education and Society*. Vol. 4: *Educational Reform in International Perspective*. Edited by A.

Yogev (series editor) and V. D. Rust (volume editor). Greenwich: JAI Inc., 165–203.

Zimmer, S. 1994. "Der Mythos von der Macht des Marktes." In *Osteuropa im Umbruch. Alte und neue Mythen.* Edited by C. Friedrich and B. Menzel. Frankfurt am Main: Peter Lang, 81–90.

10

Schools, Separatism, and Assimilation: The Education of "Others" in Europe

Elizabeth Sherman Swing

INTRODUCTION

The existence throughout Europe of minority communities, both indigenous and immigrant, challenges a persistent myth: the myth of national cultural homogeneity. Indigenous groups—Scots, Welsh, Flemish, Frisians, Basques, or Germans and Hungarians in Czechoslovakia—have challenged this myth for centuries. So, more recently, have refugees from many parts of the world, immigrants from former colonies, and "guest workers," many from the Mediterranean rim. A third generation of these newcomers still lives in ethnic enclaves, unassimilated "others." Recent easing of naturalization restrictions makes it difficult to chart accurately the population of foreign origin in the countries from which case histories in this chapter are drawn, but approximations are revealing. In Belgium, 9.1% of the population is of foreign citizenship; in Germany 8%; in France 6.2%; in Britain 3.4% (CE 1994). How dominant groups perceive such strangers within the gate (Wirt 1979) remains an unresolved and at times disturbing issue.

The education of the children of these "others" presents a dichotomy. For *individuals* to succeed, they must *integrate*, master mainstream languages, customs, and values that will bring them into ongoing activities and objectives of the dominant group (Schermerhorn 1978 [1970], 4). This is the agenda of most publicly funded schools. The survival of *communities*, on the other hand, depends on preservation of cultural referents: languages, religions, and values—a process that implies separation from the mainstream. A tenuous relationship

Table 10.1
From Separatism to Assimilation: A Taxonomy

SEPARATISM	SEGMENTED PLURALISM	CULTURAL PLURALISM	AMBIGUOUS ASSIMILATION
Flemish Nationalism in Belgium	The clearly defined *Ausländer* in Germany	Bicultural identity in Flanders	*L'étranger* in France
Language revival in Wales		Intercultural exploration in the Francophone schools of Brussels	The hidden agenda of the National Curriculum in England

exists between the perpetuation of disparate cultures and the hidden curriculum of many schools.

This chapter examines seven models of separation and integration in the schools of selected nations in Europe: Belgium, Wales, Germany, France, and England. There is no attempt to examine every program of every non-mainstream group in these locales. The focus instead is on a spectrum: at one end, the separatism of indigenous groups in Belgium and Wales; in the center, the segmented pluralism of "others" in Germany and the multicultural pluralism of pilot projects funded by supranational agencies; at the other end, the ambiguous assimilationism of a national curricula in France and in England (Table 10.1).

None of these modes of accommodation represents the only educational pattern in the society in which it is found. In England, a national curriculum still seeks to provide a common reference point for all students at the same time Muslim groups are petitioning for the funding of separate schools. In Belgium—now a federation of semi-autonomous communities—bilingual, bicultural, and intercultural programs coexist within the federation in both the Flemish and the Francophone communities. In France, *les étrangers* can sometimes look like an *Ausländer* in Germany, for whom schools have experimented with bilingual, bicultural, and intercultural programs. Disparate goals and procedures are part of every society.

TWO INDIGENOUS SEPARATIST MODELS

The Separatism of Flemish Nationalists

In Belgium, a centripetal-centrifugal matrix has existed since the invasion of the Franks in the 5th century A.D.—a Dutch-speaking north, a French-speaking south. In the past, although French was the language of the court and of government, the linguistic prowess of the population in areas where the Dutch and French languages were in contact was the object of interest and praise (Guicciardini [1567] 1943). For centuries, Belgian bilingualism was viewed as a model by other bilingual societies. In 1902, for example, the Welshman T. R.

Dawes journeyed to Belgium to study educational practices that might be emulated in Wales. Dawes was impressed with what he found (Dawes 1902). But what Dawes overlooked, and what began to become increasingly clear to Flemish Nationalists who were gaining power in the early 20th century, was that this was a one-way bilingualism. Upwardly mobile Flemings, who migrated to Brussels and other cities, learned French in schools where French was the language of instruction or in the ubiquitous dual medium Dutch-French schools (Verheyen 1929). Flemings needed French, the language of the power elite. Francophones, on the other hand, saw no need to learn Dutch. For Flemings, moreover, such migration was frequently the first stage in a three-generational language shift to French and to assimilation with the Francophone community (Swing 1980, 1988, 1997).

By the middle years of the 20th century, Flemish Nationalists had rejected bilingualism in education. "Le bilinguisme dans l'enseignement doit être condamné," states the Final Report of the Harmel Center (Centre de recherche, ca. 1950, no. 326, 6), a conclusion that set the stage for stringent language legislation. The Language Law of 1932 had already established *separate* geographical and community educational structures: Dutch-language schools in the north, French-language schools in the south, plus German-language schools in a small area, and *either* Dutch- *or* French-language schools in two *separate* networks in the "bilingual" capital city, Brussels. The Language Law of 1963 set out to plug loopholes in the 1932 legislation: to close transmutation schools in Flanders, where Francophones had managed to retain instruction in French, and to enforce stringent separation of Flemings and Francophones in the schools of Brussels. Even study of the second national language was limited to the *foreign* language classroom, and then only after the fifth year, although in Brussels it could begin after the second year.

Between November 1966, when a special *Arrêté* mandated immediate rigid separation of Flemish and Francophone children in the schools of their respective language regimes in Brussels, and 1971, when partial restoration of parental choice (*liberté du père de famille*) took place, the linguistic segregation of people who had lived for centuries side by side in a bilingual city had de jure status. Confrontation between those who wished to continue what they considered a basic right to select the language of education for their children and those who viewed such choice as illegal became the most explosive political conflict in Belgium (Swing 1980, ch. 8). For parents who chose to go to court, frequently the parents of bilingual offspring of Flemish/Francophone marriages, the stakes were high. Language inspectors entered schools, examined language declarations, observed the linguistic behavior of students, then notified the parents of children found to be illegally enrolled that a school transfer must be effected. One father lost his case because the first years of his son's education had taken place in Dutch in Flanders (Dossier 50/69 Jury). Others resorted to filing two language declarations, one French, one Dutch (Dossier 31/69 Jury). The courts were *very* strict in upholding the letter of the law when dealing with an individual who had matriculated in a territorial language, less strict with children of Francophone Flemings in Brussels.

That the cultural identity of Flemings and Francophones can best be preserved within separate institutions is the premise from which modern Belgium has evolved. That schools are the agent for the formation of this identity is the assumption from which this premise is derived. In modern Belgium it is the separate communities that define the role of the schools. In the not-too-distant past, there was *one* national Ministry of Education; after 1969, there were *two* national Ministries of Education—one for Dutch-language, the other for French-language schools. There is now no *national* Ministry of Education in a federalized Belgium, whose new constitution, completed in February 1994, provides for a federation of separate linguistic communities and regions. Except for laws governing compulsory education, minimal standards for awarding diplomas, and pensions for teachers (Constitution 1994, Art. 127), it is the communities that formulate and carry out school policy, including language policy (Constitution 1994, Art. 127, 129). The old nation-state no longer exists.

Since 1971, when tensions eased in Brussels because of partial restoration of *liberté de père de famille*, a new, somewhat surprising educational pattern has appeared. Traditionally it was Flemish parents who enrolled their children in French-language schools as a way of providing for social and economic advancement, whereas Francophones tended to fear and to avoid Flemish institutions. Since 1971, however, a number of Francophone parents have reversed the traditional pattern by actively seeking a Dutch-language education for their children—a phenomenon partially attributable to a smaller number of students in Flemish schools, partially attributable to "white flight" from schools with large immigrant populations, and partially attributable to recognition of a new balance of power in Belgium in which knowledge of Dutch has pragmatic value. See, for example, the second entry in Table 10.2, which shows that in 1991, 33.1% of children in Dutch-language nursery schools and 19.9% of children in Dutch-language elementary schools in Brussels came from homes in which both parents spoke a language other than Dutch, usually French. Anecdotal evidence exists for what would have been impossible during the era of rigid separatism twenty-five years ago: parent-teacher meetings in Flemish schools that are conducted in French, the only language shared by teachers and many of the parents.

The presence of Francophone children in schools dedicated to the formation of Flemish cultural identity raises questions about the meaning of a cultural center. Does the emergence of such a pattern indicate a shift in cultural priorities within the French-language community? Is a new form of diglossia emerging among Francophones in Brussels, a group that in the past refused to learn Dutch? What does the presence of Francophone children in Flemish schools reveal about a continuing pattern of separatism, even in federal Belgium? What impact does such a centripetal pattern have on cultural identity in both communities? Nev-

Table 10.2
Linguistic and Nationality Background of Children in Brussels Dutch-Language Nursery and Elementary Schools

	Nursery Schools		Elementary Schools	
	Number	Percent	Number	Percent
Native speaker of Dutch	2430	37.2	5020	53.9
Both parents speak a language other than Dutch, usually French	2167	33.1	1850	19.9
One parent speaks Dutch. Child may be raised in a language other than Dutch	1943	29.7	2442	26.2
Belgian nationality	5499	84.1	8414	90.4
Foreign nationality	1041	15.9	898	9.6

Source: Figures provided by Brussels Hoofdstedelijk Gewest Vlaams Gemeenschapscommissie, May 1990.

ertheless, the existence of a federated Belgium with virtually autonomous linguistic and cultural communities is evidence that separatism has triumphed.

Cultural Renewal in Wales

In the debate over the Education Reform Act of 1988, Dafydd Elis Thomas, one of three Welsh Nationalist members of parliament, envisioned a Wales with the same level of cultural autonomy as the "nations" of Scotland and Northern Ireland, which were to be exempt from the "National Curriculum" imposed on Wales (Parliamentary Debates 1988, 82). In the semi-independent Wales he envisioned, Welsh would be one of two national languages, "a modern European language—albeit a minority one" (Parliamentary Debates 1988, 223). There is no doubt that difficulties lie ahead. The Education Reform Act makes instruction of Welsh mandatory within Wales, but only 20% of the 2.9 million people in Wales are Welsh speaking, and there is a serious shortage of teachers of Welsh. Even so, many dedicated Welsh Nationalists are confident that by the year 2006, every child in every school in Wales will be learning Welsh starting at the age of 5 (Roberts 1990).

Welsh revivalists must rely both on legislation to realize their language goals and on the goodwill of the many residents of Wales who are monolingual in English. No strong Welsh Nationalist government is in power, nor are there many people elsewhere who speak Welsh. Within Wales, furthermore, the parents who have fought (and lost) the battle to exempt their children from the study of Welsh are still feeling bruised. Some of them point to the paradox of teaching French through the medium of Welsh or to the difficulties of non-Anglophone Asian children who must study Welsh. At the same time, a curious reality is the number of Anglophone parents, including "ethnic converts" not of Welsh ancestry, who voluntarily enroll their children in Welsh medium schools. That a significant number actively cultivate a "feeling of Welshness," not necessarily a part of their own linguistic identity, marks a particular milestone. As Thomas has pointed out: "We should not consider that the Welsh language belongs only to those who are born into a Welsh-speaking family. It belongs to all Welsh people as part of their national heritage" (Parliamentary Debates 1988, 222).

Meanwhile, structures to accommodate Welsh language study have begun to evolve (Swing 1992). Of particular interest are Welsh medium schools. In Ysgol Gymraeg Melin Gruffydd (Primary), 4-year-old children, a majority of whom come from non-Welsh speaking homes, begin their formal education in Welsh. In addition, there are schools where Welsh is taught as a modern language. The "traditional" sector of Llanishen Fach, for example, does not offer instruction in Welsh until the age of 7 and then for only one hour a week. There are also "bilingual" schools, which use both Welsh and English. The "bilingual" sector of Llanishen Fach Primary School is English medium except for a daily Welsh class approximately one hour in length. Ysgol Maesyryrfn, an "official" bilingual school, on the other hand, teaches history, geography, humanities, music, drama, and art in Welsh; and science and math in English.

The avowed goal is to transmit a standard Welsh free from English inflection. This ideal notwithstanding, regionalisms creep in. In Welsh medium schools in southeastern Wales, the most anglicized section of the country, school inspectors have noted a variety of uncodified Welsh words and inflections (Welsh Office 1987, 1989) and a lack of native speakerlike control. For some sociolinguists, non-standard inflection and syntax represent "linguistic vitality," but for more traditional Welsh Nationalists, standard Welsh remains the goal.

Welsh educators have gone to elaborate measures to separate immersion-class children from casual contact with students who are dominantly Anglophone. They also attempt to curb the use of English and to extend the domain of Welsh in activities outside the classroom. For instance, Ysgol Gymraeg Melin Gruffydd (Primary), the Welsh medium school mentioned previously, shares its building with another school whose medium of instruction is English, but its students are not allowed on the playground with their English-language peers. Nevertheless, the National Curriculum for England and Wales is a source of considerable concern. What happens to "Welshness" when the content of study for tests reflects a middle-class *English* culture that is largely irrelevant to Wales? Is "Oh to be in England" really an appropriate cultural referent in a National Curriculum anthology? A tenuous relationship exists between the perpetuation of minority identity and the cultural agenda of the dominant group.

SEGMENTED PLURALISM: THE CLEARLY DEFINED "OTHER" IN GERMANY

In Germany, the existence of many who are perceived to be "others" poses a particular problem when juxtaposed with the ideology of one nation, one language, one people. Some of the "others" are indigenous: Danes, Frisians, and Serbs, who are protected by special legislation that guarantees mother tongue education for those who desire it. People of German origin, moreover, can claim German citizenship (*jus sanguinis*) even if they do not know the German language and have never lived in Germany, a preferential status widely resented by other immigrants. More germane to this study are those categorized as *Ausländer*, a group who can never be of German origin. Eight percent of the population of Germany, 6.5 million people, are *Ausländer* (CE 1994, 121), a term that conveys a wide range of connotations: foreign, different, strange, unknown, and ultimately unknowable (Schäffter 1991, 1996). The word *immigrant* is not frequently used because Germany is understood *not* to be an immigration country.

There are two categories of *Ausländer*: asylum seekers and guest workers (*Gastarbeiter*). Asylum seekers came to Germany in response to the liberal provisions of Article 16 of the Basic Law, which grants to anyone who enters Germany the right of asylum until status is determined. Political refugees may stay; economic refugees must leave. Stringent regulations now govern which countries can be the entry point for asylum seekers, so that by 1990 the approval rate was down to 5% (compared with 57% in 1971); by 1993 only 3.2% were approved out of 323,000 who applied. The trend in the 1990s is toward fewer approvals. There are nevertheless 309 asylum seekers for every 10,000 German inhabitants (compared with 70 in the United States)—this in a time of chronic unemployment (Hoff 1995; Horrocks and Kolinsky 1996).

From the end of World War II until the early 1960s, *Gastarbeiter* (guest workers), the largest category of *Ausländer*, came from the Eastern Bloc. After the Berlin Wall cut off this supply of labor, guest workers were actively recruited from southern Europe, the Mediterranean, and Turkey. It was originally assumed that they would return to their country of origin, and some did. After recruitment stopped, the percentage from Spain, Portugal, Greece, Italy, and Yugoslavia remaining in Germany decreased by 46%. Even so, in 1995 *Ausländer* made up 11% of the population of Berlin (*Migration* 1995). At the same time, many, particularly among the Turkish population, sent for wives, children, and parents instead of returning home. By the 1990s, nearly 2 million Turkish citizens lived in Germany, 41% of the non-German population, the group with the highest birth rate (OECD 1995, 77).

The children of most *Ausländer* have gone to regular German schools. Others, however, have participated in pilot projects similar to those found throughout Europe. An early educational experiment was a separation policy (Hoff 1995; Luchtenberg 1994)—national schools, classes, or lessons for larger homogeneous groups from the main groups of guest workers: Turks, Yugoslavs, Italians. Next came assimilationist goals with emphasis placed on learning German, even though German schools have no tradition of teaching German as a second language (Luchtenberg 1994). A so-called 'double strategy' has focused on mother tongue language education, plus education in German, but does not apply to refugee children or children with an ethnic German background.

Some German states have imported mother tongue textbooks from the country of origin; some have used textbooks written in Germany, including textbooks developed for evaluation by German institutions (Luchtenberg 1994). But that only the *official* languages of sending countries can be taught produces problems for Turkish children and for North Africans, whose home language is likely to be non-standard. In some schools *Ausländerpädagogik* (education for foreigners) emphasizes intercultural education: establishment of cultural identity, mother tongue literacy, multicultural values, and introduction of major and local religions—a strategy that we will encounter again in this chapter in a discussion of intercultural education in Brussels. A United Europe policy (*Kulturübergreifende Erziehung*) reflecting the advent of the European Union emphasizes replacement of nationalism with a European perspective, although there is some conflict between those who focus only on member states of the European Union and those who want to integrate Eastern European countries. There is also concern over possible racism from groups who want to exclude all non-Europeans, non-Caucasians, non-white, non-Christian people (Hohmann 1989; Uçar 1996).

The goals and outcomes of these programs are complicated by the nationality question (CE 1994). Germany still has one of the lowest naturalization rates in Europe. Only 0.5% a year of resident foreigners become German citizens. In Britain, 2% become citizens; in France, 1.2%; in Sweden, 5.2%. Nationality is a particularly complicated issue for Turks. In the past, most retained Turkish citizenship, but an increasing number have applied for German citizenship— since 1990, more than five thousand Turks a year. Application for naturalization is partly in response to recognition that the only way Turks can participate in elections is to become citizens, partly a response to somewhat more liberal naturalization procedures. The stakes are high. To become citizens of Germany, Turks must give up Turkish citizenship; they cannot inherit property in Turkey; they are liable for German military service; and they must demonstrate capacity to integrate into German society, a somewhat nebulous qualification widely viewed as discriminatory. Leaders in the Turkish community estimate that 85% will eventually become German citizens, and the 15% who don't will most likely go back to Turkey (Pohl 1996).

Turks appear to have rejected assimilation—in response perhaps to recognition that the concept of a Turkish German does not exist, that even with citizenship, Turkish *Ausländer* remain clearly defined "others." According to Mustafa Turgut Cakmakoğlu, president of the Turkish community of Berlin, an organization founded in 1983 but only recently activated, the focus is now on employment, housing, and job training. A complex identity problem is nevertheless illustrated by problems faced by a new association, Turkish Minorities in Germany, which plans to establish a special bilingual grammar school enrolling equal numbers of Turkish-speaking and German-speaking students. The fact that most students of Turkish origin in this school will have German language skills, plus German citizenship, and will be counted as Germans, means that equal representation of Turks and ethnic Germans is an illusory goal. Meanwhile, at the same time German industry seeks workers who know English, not Turkish, many Turks continue to seek self-identifying markers, whether they be head scarves or language.

CULTURAL PLURALISM: THE PILOT PROJECTS OF SUPRANATIONAL AGENCIES IN BELGIUM

Belgium has been host to several generations of migrant workers since World War II, most recruited from southern Europe or North Africa (Commissariat I 1989, 17–21). The first wave, workers in the coal mines of Wallonia, came from Italy. Thereafter, Belgian employers sought workers in Spain, Portugal, Greece, Morocco, and Turkey. Intensive recruitment came to an end during the economic retrenchment of the 1970s, but immigrant communities have continued to grow through the arrival in Belgium of family members and the greater fertility of immigrant groups over that of native Belgians. A statistical dip in the official number of immigrants reflects liberalization of the nationalization laws in 1985, when 63,824 took Belgian nationality. But even with this "dip," by 1994, 9.1% of the population of Belgium were classified as foreigners (CE 1994, 75). In Brussels, 29.6% of the residents are "foreigners." Some of these foreigners are European Union executives, but most are guest workers and the descendants of guest workers in the old coal mining regions of Wallonia, or in Hasselt, Genk, or Antwerp in Flanders (Roosens 1981).

The pilot projects of supranational agencies found in the 1980s and 1990s in Belgium—and in most other Western European countries with significant populations of immigrants, guest workers, and refugees—were at one time a partial response to the European Economic Community Directive of 1977 (77/486/EEC) calling for the education of migrant workers' children in their mother tongue *and* in the language of the receiving country, a directive premised on the assumption that these workers would return to their country of origin. The bilingual-bicultural project in Antwerp discussed in the next section reflects these assumptions. In Belgium and elsewhere in Europe, recent projects provide tacit acknowledgement that reverse migration will *not* take place. Emphasis is more likely to be on mutual exploration of cultures (ECCE 1990) and on "medium-term integration strategies which take account of the cultural pluralization of society" (7) while rejecting "a crude distinction between 'foreigners' and 'natives' " (5). The intercultural project in selected Francophone Brussels schools discussed later in this chapter reflects this set of assumptions.

A Bilingual-Bicultural Curriculum in Antwerp

The Council of Europe pilot project for children of migrant workers at *Rijksmiddenschool Borgerhout* began in 1979 in Antwerp as a parallel undertaking to the European Community pilot project, "Mother Tongue Teaching in Five Secondary Schools in the Limburg Region." At the time the project began in the *Rijksmiddenschool Borgerhout*, a lower secondary school where student ages range from 12 to 17, 84% were of foreign origin. Many came directly from their native country: 77% from Morocco; 6% from other nations such as Chile, Turkey, Spain, Egypt, Portugal, Laos, and mainland China. Many then, as now, were illiterate when they arrived in Belgium. This pilot project had an ambitious goal: to prepare these minority students for the economic realities of their current environment while protecting and reinforcing their ethnic and cultural identity (Baert 1985; Corijn 1982; Haesendonckx 1981; Rapport 1982).

For the first year in the prescribed program the minority students, mostly Moroccans, follow a flexible timetable (1B Variant): eight periods a week of Dutch, two of French (a mandatory second language), two of Arabic as a modern language, five of mathematics, four of environmental studies, two of plastic arts, three of gymnastics and four of technical activities. In addition, two periods each week of religion are required—a choice among Catholicism, Judaism, Protestantism, secular humanism ("morals"), and, since 1978, the Muslim religion—a subject that provides a rubric under which Arabic, a formal language of religion, might be taught in a country in which there are very strict language laws (Corijn et al. 1985). A curious paradox is the fact that the ethnolinguistic center of this project is not a mother tongue, for the mother tongue would have to be one of the several competing Moroccan dialects, and most students learn Arabic as a foreign language.

Thereafter, Moroccan students are assigned to the same courses as their Belgian counterparts. But they also reinforce their cultural identity through contact with Moroccan teachers and teacher aides who know a range of Moroccan dialects, a group recruited by the Dutch-language Cultural Community and the Moroccan government. Some of these recruits teach the Arabic/religion courses. Others are assigned as teacher aides to classrooms in which Moroccan students are enrolled—an arrangement that occasionally gives rise to conflicts with Belgian teachers. Conflicts notwithstanding, the continued presence of Moroccan teachers in this and in other bicultural pilot projects provides strong evidence of the significance of ethnic identity.

This model curriculum is based on a series of assumptions about the function of schools. A program that stresses environmental arts, plastic arts, and technical studies does not expose minority students to Eurocentric humanist values explicit in traditional programs. Nevertheless, the project, despite the stringency of Belgian language laws, provides continual reinforcement of cultural and linguistic identity as Moroccan students learn Arabic in their religion classes. At the same time, prescribing the language of Flemish Belgium for minorities from the beginning, and, after the first year, having the same common core curriculum as Belgian peers in the same classrooms, *does* communicate the reality of a Flemish cultural environment. The assumption is that each minority student will identify with *two* disparate cultures: one based on a Flemish-Belgian worldview, the other on a Moroccan worldview.

It is only the minority students, however, who are expected to achieve this dual frame of reference. Inherent in the design is belief in the existence of both a Flemish worldview grounded on ethnic absolutes and a Moroccan worldview grounded on its own absolutes. At the same time, there exists the practical reality that Moroccan immigrants in Flemish Belgium might have difficulty acquiring a unicultural Flemish identity. The paradoxical assumption is that it is possible to transform a group of minority students who know only the culture of their home into bicultural adults ready to integrate into a Belgian (Flemish) world. The question unasked is whether mutually contradictory cultural referents can coexist within a single person.

An Intercultural Curriculum in Brussels

Unlike the pilot project at the *Rijksmiddenschool Borgerhout* with its bicultural goals directed just at minority students, a project in selected Brussels Francophone schools has intercultural goals that include both Belgians, in this case Francophone, and minorities. This intercultural curriculum, which is similar to intercultural projects found throughout Europe, diverges from the dominantly assimilationist pattern of many other Belgian Francophone schools. Goals of this pilot program begin with social needs: the need for better integration of immigrant students and their families into the Belgian social fabric, better scholastic success for students of immigrant origin, better access to the teaching of the language and culture of origin (*Le Soir* 1990). It is a curriculum that sees richness rather than liability in multicultural diversity (Leunda and Deprez 1988, 215). It is a curriculum, in other words, that views schools as agencies for diffusing cross-national perspectives (Jones and Kimberley 1986, 55), a curriculum based on the assumption that truths from one culture can be of interest and value to members of another culture.

Recognition of non-European languages is therefore part of the agenda. A first-year French language text even makes allusions to Arabic and Turkish literature in its instructional sequence (IAM 1989a). Belgian language laws regulate the language of instruction, which in the Francophone community case must be French, but Arabic, a formal language of worship, may be used in the Muslim religion class without violating Belgian law. In addition, schools may use professionals recruited from the immigrants' countries of origin to teach mother tongues, as long as these are taught as *foreign* languages rather than treated as the language of instruction. That "embassy teachers" are encountering difficulty in defining the culture of immigrant students who have never lived in their parents' country of origin (Leunda and Deprez 1988, 244) is an evolving issue. Success in this project, furthermore, is as likely to be equated with the *French* language competence of ethnic students as with mother tongue competency. As a publicity brochure prepared by one of the participating schools points out, it is essential that a student of immigrant background acquire full knowledge of the structure of French in order to succeed in Belgian (Francophone) society (IAM ca. 1990).

This is a curriculum based on relativist assumptions. The study of secondary school history and geography at the Institut des Arts et Métiers, Ville de Bruxelles has the overt intent of introducing all students, Belgian as well as minority, to a world beyond Belgium and Europe. The first-year history course stresses Roman roots in Africa and the Near East (IAM 1989c). The following year emphasizes "intercultural" evolution: contacts with the Orient, formation of the Arab world, the civilization of the Arabs in Spain, the expulsion of Jews from Spain, the implications for Morocco of the reconquest of Spain (IAM 1989d). The birth of the city of Fès in Morocco—its geography, history, historical monuments, cultural life, its arts and artisans, origins of its bourgeoisie and nobility—parallels a history of the city of Brussels during the Burgundian period (IAM 1989d). Geography lessons emphasize, in addition to Belgium and Europe, the countries of origin of immigrant students—Morocco, Italy, Turkey (IAM 1989b).

Unlike the relativism of the bicultural curriculum model in Antwerp, which is based on the coexistence of absolute but different truths within minority students, an intercultural model is a design based on the concept of multiple worldviews, a diffused, reciprocal relativism in which *both* majority and minority students are expected to adapt to the worldview of each other. Which is the geographic center of these students? Brussels? Fès? How do Muslims adapt to Catholic schools while remaining Muslim? How do Catholic schools remain Catholic while teaching a Muslim population? Students are implicitly invited to construct their own patterns of truth, pragmatically adapting what works best from each culture. Nevertheless, this is a one-sided interculturalism. The Francophone majority is not expected to enroll in Arabic classes, whereas the success of the program is linked to acquisition of French by minority community members. The dominant culture still controls the curriculum—a symbol, perhaps, of the difficulty of achieving balance in any multicultural, pluralist design.

Interculturalism becomes even more complicated within the framework of religion. Francophone schools like Flemish schools must offer two hours of religious instruction a week, selected from among Roman Catholicism, Protestantism, Judaism, "secular humanism," or the Muslim religion. This requirement does not pertain to schools in the Catholic network, however, where instruction in Catholicism is expected to take place as a matter of course—although in certain urban schools with heavy Muslim enrollment, Islam may also be taught if parents request it. Administrators in Catholic schools insist that religion should permeate the teaching of all subjects, not just the formal religion class; but they also point out that a habit of religion, even among Muslim children, is easier to deal with than no religion at all (Bruneel 1990). Nevertheless, Catholic schools have their own problems when a majority of students come from Muslim homes.

There is consensus within the Office of Catholic Education that schools with different cultures invite an "intercultural pedagogy," a concept that means situating children within their own culture, recognizing the diversity of student cultures, and opposing assimilationist strategies (Conseil Général 1990). The problem is not whether these school officials agree on these intercultural goals. The problem is how to realize this agreement, how to provide respect for the religion of Muslim children while providing young Catholics with the education that caused their parents to enroll them in a Catholic school in the first place. The relativist premises of intercultural education and the absolute premises of Catholicism manage to coexist, but with some sense of strain.

ASSIMILATIONIST MODELS

The Enigmatic Stranger in France

Like the United States, France has traditionally received immigrants. Indeed, immigrants constitute a demographic bulge in France, one of the highest in Europe: 8%, but more likely 6.2% now that a number have attained French citizenship (Horowitz and Noiriel 1992)—either way, a reflection of the open admissions policy that existed until recently. One-third of the French population have an immigrant grandparent, but unlike the third generation in the United States who frequently adopt a hyphenated identity with pride, the French are not likely to view themselves as descendants of immigrants. Furthermore, intercultural education was never a serious development in France. Bilingual, bicultural pilot projects are criticized because they are not "good for foreigners" (Silberman 1996). An underlying assumption is that assimilation is a covert goal. Even so, the concentration of ethnics in the suburbs continues to be an issue masked in part by the fact that French nationality on a passport may be recently acquired.

It is not just a matter of incidents involving head scarves or the use of churches as asylums, although incidents involving scarves and churches have taken on symbolic significance. According to Véronique De Rudder (1996), the political right has defined its terms by rejecting individual integration in favor of an Anglo-Saxon style communal integration of ethnics. What remains are terms such as *étranger*, not being French, a situation similar to that implied by the German word *Ausländer*; or "second generation," an ambiguous and fragile category; or *jeunes issue de l'immigration*, an even more fragile category. For an individual to be a non-national foreigner implies that he or she is an "outsider," an "other," a stateless person. Such a definition has practical consequences: French citizens have the right to public employment (as in Belgium), but this employment is closed to immigrants.

Since the arrival of the post–World War II group, several waves of immigrants have appeared in France (*L'immigration en France* 1992). Between 1960 and 1975, migrant workers, mostly from Senegal and other parts of Africa, rotated between France and their country of origin. Recently, others have arrived: students, asylum seekers, families of immigrants reunited. In the mid-1990s, of the 3,607,590 immigrants in France (out of a total population of 57,803,600), 1,652,870 were of African origin (CE 1994), mostly from countries previously under the control of France. Many such "foreigners" disappear from official statistics once they become citizens (Silberman 1996). So do children born in France to Algerians, if their parents were born in Algeria before 1962 (the year of independence). These children are French by birth. Other individuals born in France of immigrants may declare their choice of citizenship at the age of 18 (French by acquisition) but are not entitled to French citizenship just because they are born in France.

As in the United States, schools play a major role in socializing the newcomers (Boyzon-Fradet 1992). No matter what the legal status of the parents, foreign children must enroll in school if they are under the age of 16. Although there are Catholic schools, most "foreigners" enroll in public schools, schools that are secular and where equal opportunity requires uniform treatment. For those who have recently arrived, a few temporary programs provide intensive French language training: a one-year maximum for elementary school, two for secondary school.

There was opportunity, introduced in 1973 sporadically and experimentally, for three hours of weekly instruction in the language and culture of the home, with classes given by teachers from the country of origin, the result of agreements with immigrant countries—but only for children of countries that have an agreement to do so with France: Algeria, Spain, Italy, Morocco, Portugal, Tunisia, Turkey, and Yugoslavia. From 1976 to 1979, a pilot project of the Commission of European Communities replaced these language courses with activities shared with all children, both French and foreign, under both foreign and French teachers. This intercultural concept devolved into folkloric and "cultural activities." There was, in other words, difficulty reconciling this mother tongue instruction with the integration of immigrants into a unified system, a concern over marginalizing students in an era when English or German would be more useful. Meanwhile, debate over teaching the language and culture of immigrant children continues (Boyzon-Fradet 1992).

Many "foreign" children are concentrated in particular schools where it is widely believed that a number of problems exist: deportment, lack of class participation, refusal to accept the authority of the teacher, and aggression with peers (L'immigration en France 1992). Language is the chief divider (Tribalat 1996). Those who are products of a marriage between a French person and a member of a minority group are likely to know some French, but differences in knowledge of French are connected to social practices. Schoolchildren of Algerian background may initially know some French, particularly when one parent was born in France. Moroccans, who have their own vernacular and are likely to be illiterate in Arabic, have more difficulty. Most critical is the situation of Turkish schoolchildren whose parents, particularly the mothers, tend to continue speaking Turkish to their children. Girls of Algerian and Moroccan background also have difficulty, in part because the premises underlying female education in France are contrary to their customs. Youngsters of Spanish background, on the other hand, are likely to do well in French and to take prizes in Spanish.

There appears at first glance to be a big distance between the performance of foreign children and those of French origin. Immigrant children in the problem schools have indeed obtained inferior results in French and math on evaluation examinations (Vallet 1996). By secondary school, however, differences between foreign children and the children of French origin are no longer significant in math and are significant in the French language primarily for newcomers. What is critical is the time spent in French schools, the degree of ambition, and the educational level of the family from which the child comes, particularly the educational level of the mother (Silberman and Fournier 1996; Vallet and Caille 1996). When scores are compared with those of French children from the same socioeconomic backgrounds, "foreign" children are actually doing better than French children from a similar background. They have, however, higher aspirations than do the families of working-class French children. An ambivalent assimilation is in the process of taking place.

A Common Core Curriculum for England

That England has become a multilingual, multicultural society is a fact not mitigated by restrictions on immigration in the Nationalities Act of 1981. In 1983 the Inner London Education Authority reported no fewer than *141* different home languages among its students (ILEA 1983). One child in seven came from a home in which a language other than English was spoken (ILEA 1982), many from a second- or third-generation minority tongue background. In 1989 the Inner London Education Authority reported in the last language census before its demise that it had found *184* different languages among students in its schools. One student in *four* came from a non-English language home (ILEA 1989). In London today, the language of the street is as likely to be Bengali, Greek, Turkish, Spanish, Gujarati, Punjabi, Italian, Urdu, Chinese, French, Arabic, or Portuguese as English. That 70% of the speakers of these mother tongues are not yet fluent in English, a figure that has risen to 87% in the Tower Hamlets section of the East End of London (ILEA ca. 1988), gives testimony to the social dimensions behind these demographics.

The National Curriculum for England and Wales mandated in the Education Reform Act of 1988 has the democratic intent of providing equal access to materials and testing procedures to *every* student in *every* Local Education Authority (Lawton 1989). All students are expected to master the same core subjects: English, mathematics, and science. All must study history, geography, physical education, music, art, a modern language, plus technology—a postindustrial symbol. All, with few exceptions, must also participate in religious education. That acceptance of these goals is far from unanimous is hardly surprising. For many teachers, nationally prescribed programs of study, attainment targets, and assessment instruments represent loss of a cherished tradition of independent planning. In minority communities there is tension between a common core and the maintenance of a linguistic and cultural heritage.

These realities notwithstanding, it could be argued that the Education Reform Act has a hidden agenda: the assimilation of *all* students to a common set of cultural referents and values—the assumption that *all* students, even minority students from India, Pakistan, or Africa should share the same Eurocentric worldview. There is minimal opportunity for study of a non-European language, only marginal attention to the world beyond Britain and other areas of Europe in the history curriculum, reluctant recognition of non-Judeo-Christian religions.

This is a worldview that ignores the unique cultural boundaries of minorities. The same Eurocentric curriculum is prescribed for all (Swing 1995).

The Education Act mandates that all secondary school students study a language other than English until the age of 16. Some schools, particularly those with pilot projects subsidized by the European Union or the Council of Europe, have included languages such as Urdu or Arabic in their curriculum, in addition to one or more European languages (EC 1987). Some have even offered a General Certificate of Secondary Education (GCSE) or Advanced (A) level examination in these languages. Such options, however, are dependent on subsidy by outside agencies, and there is little incentive for tax-supported schools to continue to offer these languages once funding has expired (Kroon 1989, 123). Furthermore, secondary schools must offer at least one European language. Even schools that want to offer minority languages face a dilemma. This dilemma is exacerbated by the demise of what were once primary school bilingual programs. "Section 11" funds, which in the early 1980s subsidized primary school transitional instruction in mother tongues such as Bengali, Punjabi, and Gujarati, may now be used only to "interpret" the new curriculum but not for instruction in a minority language (Gibbon 1990; OFSTED 1992–1993). For linguistic minorities the status of non-European languages is abundantly clear.

The study of history follows a similar pattern. According to the working group that planned it, the history curriculum should include study of individual, group, and family inheritances (DES 1990, 10–11) in a program that will "give pupils a sense of identity," "an understanding of their own cultural roots and shared inheritances" (17). Despite this vision, the curriculum is Brito-centric first, Euro-centric second, with the non-Western world treated as a marginal option. It begins with Roman Britain, then concentrates on Anglo-Saxons; Viking invaders; British medieval realms, 1066–1500; Tudor and Stuart times; the making of the United Kingdom, 1500–1750; expansion, trade, and industry; Britain 1750–1900; Victorian Britain; Britain since 1930; Britain in the 20th century; the era of World War II, 1933–1948. Options that expand on this center focus on Europe or on peripheral areas of the British Isles. Only a handful of non-required units explore the rest of the world: Islamic civilization, China, India, the Americas. The Greek-Roman classical world is part of the core, but no more than a nod is given to other aspects of world history. The homelands of immigrants from non-Western areas of a British colonial past are treated as peripheral.

Requirements in religious education are even more culture specific. The law calls for religious education (ERA 1988, I.6) and collective worship that is "wholly or mainly of a broadly *Christian* character" (I.7). Exceptions to this mandate are possible. The curriculum may take into account "practices of the other principal religions" (I.8). Parents have the right of withdrawal. Teachers need not participate if they do not wish to do so. The daily act of collective worship may even take place in separate groups, and schools with a large minority population may seek exemption through the Standing Advisory Council

Table 10.3
A Taxonomy of Curricula for a Multicultural Population

Curriculum Model	Example	Content	Frame of Reference	Intended Outcome
Separatism	Flemish nationalism	Flemish as the language of instruction in Flanders and in separate Flemish schools in Brussels	Culture is centered in the language and traditions of both nationalist groups	Separate national institutions
	Welsh nationalism	Mandated study of Welsh in Wales		Revival of Welsh Welsh/English bilingualism. Future political autonomy
Segmented Pluralism	A variety of programs for *Ausländer* in Germany	Multicultural elements, plus a common curriculum	Assumption that differences persist whatever the educational program	Dominant group continues to view *Ausländer* as "others"

236

Cultural Pluralism Within Nations	A bicultural pilot project in Flanders	Curriculum of the majority community, plus separate courses in language and religion for minority students	Absolute but different truths within each cultural framework	Coexistence of two sets of cultural referents within individuals in the minority group, their own and those of the dominant group
	An intercultural project at Francophone schools in Brussels	Infusion of ethnic elements into the curriculum of all students	Diffused reciprocal frame of reference. Majority students introduced to a nonEuropean frame of reference. Relativity.	Both groups adapt their cultural referents to one another. Dominant group controls curriculum
Ambiguous Assimilationism	Undifferentiated curricula in France	Same expectations and curriculum for "others" as for native French	Assumption that curriculum of French schools meets the needs of all students	Narrowing of gap in performance of "others" but continued perception of differences
	National curriculum in England	A traditional humanist curriculum even for non-"Western" students.	Assumption that all students should accept the same cultural premises	Continued attempts to assimilate minority students to the worldview of the dominant culture

on Religious Education (SACRE) of their Local Education Authority. But when seeking exemption, the burden of proof is on non-Christians. The starting point is a law calling for transmission of traditions that are "in the main Christian" (I.8), an unambiguous message about the content of a common cultural core.

Mandating a curriculum based on Western humanist traditions *could* be considered a beneficent educational policy guaranteeing minority students the best of an elite education. But imposing a worldview that is not shared by all students and their parents carries its own inner tensions. Not everyone within the large multicultural population now living in England accepts the assumptions on which this curriculum is grounded—witness the criticism of the Christian worship mandate by both the Archbishop of York and leaders of the National Association of Head Teachers, who found that two-thirds of their members were unable to comply with requirements. Like the Americanization school programs of the first half of the 20th century in the United States, the National Curriculum seeks to acculturate *everyone* to the values and worldview of the dominant culture even when not everyone desires such acculturation. From this vantage point, a traditional humanist canon looks more like an instrument for assimilation than a beneficent cultural experience.

A TAXONOMY OF CURRICULA FOR A MULTICULTURAL POPULATION

In this chapter we have focused on a spectrum of curricula for the multicultural populations found in most large cities in Europe (see Table 10.3). At the separatist pole is the program of the Flemish Community, a cultural, territorial, and political entity that includes a network of schools in Flanders and in Brussels. The goals of Flemings include use of their language in schools, transmission of their culture and traditions, and the use of institutions that are separate, whether these institutions be symphony orchestras, radio and television stations, or schools. With the transformation of Belgium from a nation-state to a federation in which linguistic communities have semi-autonomous status, Flemings have already won a significant part of their agenda.

Like the Flemings, Welsh Nationalists tend to view schools as a vehicle for cultural and political autonomy, as well as a vehicle for language reform. They, too, have separatist impulses, but only the future will tell whether mandated Welsh instruction in the schools of Wales will lead to the level of cultural and political autonomy that Flemings have already attained. Both of these separatist groups view schools as tools in a battle for political change. Both, to one degree or another, seek greater autonomy.

In the center of the spectrum are two forms of pluralism: segmented pluralism and cultural pluralism. Segmented pluralism is illustrated in this chapter by the position of Turks in Germany, where, despite a variety of programs for *Ausländer*, perceived differences between "others" and Germans persist and will continue to persist, whatever the educational program. Cultural pluralism, as illustrated by bilingual, bicultural pilot projects, on the one hand, and by inter-cultural projects, usually funded by supranational agencies, on the other, pro-vides a somewhat different frame of reference. Bilingual, bicultural programs are premised on the belief that minority students will internalize two sets of cultural referents, that of the dominant *and* the minority community. Such pro-grams are likely to offer a program in the minority language and religion to minority students but not to students from the dominant culture. In addition such programs attempt to induct minority students into the culture and language of the majority community. Intercultural projects, on the other hand, exist within a diffused, reciprocal frame of reference in which minority students *and* students from the dominant culture are expected to learn from one another. Even so, the dominant group continues to control the curriculum.

In most European countries the curriculum most frequently encountered by minority students is an unmodified assimilationist curriculum. In France, for example, experiments with bicultural curricula have given way to a common core curriculum, to a belief that it is in the best interests of the "others" for them to cope with the same curriculum as their French peers. Paradoxically, many, but not all, of the minority students in France who have had to cope with this ambiguous assimilationism are beginning to do as well in school as French children of similar background. In England, the national curriculum has operated under a similar assumption, an attempt to educate all students to the same cul-tural premises, although leaders of minority communities still attempt to find accommodation for their linguistic and cultural needs. Indeed, Muslims continue to petition for separate schools, thus emphasizing the reality that "others" may refuse to accept a definition of themselves that is not of their own making, even if this defiance means that they face an ambiguous future.

REFERENCES

Baert, Georges. 1985. Interview with E. S. Swing, Ministry of Flemish Education, Brus-sels, Belgium, 24 June.

Boyzon-Fradet, Danielle. 1992. "The French Education System: Springboard or Obstacle to Integration." In *Immigrants in Two Democracies, French and American Ex-perience*. Edited by Donald L. Horowitz and Gérard Noiriel. New York and Lon-don: New York University Press.

Bruneel, Gerda. 1990. Office of Catholic Education. Personal communication. Brussels, Belgium, 28 May.

Cakmakoğlu, Mustafa Turgut Cakmakoğlu. 1996. President, Turkish Community of Ber-lin. Interview with E. S. Swing. Berlin, 21 May.

CE (Council of Europe). 1994. *Recent Demographic Developments in Europe*. Stras-bourg: Council of Europe Press.

Centre de recherche pour la solution nationale des problèmes sociaux, politiques, et juridiques en régions wallonnes et flamandes [Harmel Centre]. No. 326. Photo-copied ca. 1950. typescript, p. 6.

Commissariat Royal à la Politique des Immigrés. November 1989. *L'Integration: une politique de longue haleine.* 3 vols. Bruxelles: Institut Belge d'Information et de Documentation.

———. May 1990. *Pour une cohabitation harmonieuse.* 3 vols. Bruxelles: Institut Belge d'Information et de Documentation.

Conseil Général de l'Enseignement Catholique. May 1990. "Ecole et immigration: Pistes de reflexion et proposition d'action." Typescript. Brussels.

Corijn, Herman. 1982. *Pilootexperiment. Rijksonderwijs, 1979–1982. Pedagogische Opvangvormen voor Migrantenkinderen in het Secondair Oderwijs.* Borgerhout: R.M.S. Borgerhout.

Corijn, Herman, Roland Leemans, Johan Verhult, and Jean Xhoffer. 1985. Interview with E. S. Swing. Borgerhout, Antwerp, Belgium, 27 June.

Dawes, T. R. 1902. *Bilingual Teaching in Belgian Schools.* Cambridge: University Press.

De Rudder, Véronique. 1996. "Quelques problèmes épistémologiques liés au définitions des populations immigrantes et leur descendance." Communication au colloque européen. *Réussite scolaire et universitaire, égalité des chances et discriminations à l'embauche des jeunes issues de l'immigration.* Paris: Université Denis Diderot, Paris VII, 6–7 March.

DES (Department of Education and Science and the Welsh Office). April 1990. *National Curriculum.* History Working Group. Final report.

Dossiers. 1967–1970. *Bestuur Gemeenschappelijke Diensten voor Nationale Opvoedingen Nederlandse Cultuur-Taalinspectie.* (Language cases tried before jury or commission.)

EC. 1987. *European Community Pilot Project: Community Languages in the Secondary Curriculum.* Report 1984–1987. "The Inclusion of Community Languages in the Normal Curricular Arrangements of Local Education Authority Maintained Schools in England and Wales." London: University of London Institute of Education, Centre for Multicultural Education.

ECCE Interkulturell. 1990. The European Communities Comparative Evaluation Project, "Pilot Project Programme of the European Communities, 'The Education of the Children of Migrant Workers.' Results and Recommendations from the Comparative Evaluation." Landau. EWH. Im Froty, D-6840, West Germany.

EEC (European Economic Community). 1977. *Council Directive of 25 July 1977 on the Education of the Children of Migrant Workers.* (77/486/EEC).

ERA. *Education Reform Act of 1988.* Chapter 40. London: Her Majesty's Stationery Office.

Gibbon, Pam. 1990. Interview with E. S. Swing. Ewell, Surrey, England, 24 January.

Guicciardini, Ludovico. [1567] 1943. *Belgique 1567.* Paul Ciselet and Marie Decourt. Brussels: Office de Publicité.

Haesendonckx, Martine. 1981. "Ideas and Educational Research Concerning the Education of Immigrant Children in Belgium Flanders." In *The Education of Migrant Workers' Children.* Council of Europe. Lisse: Swets & Zeitlinger, 136–140.

Hoff, Gerd R. 1995. "Multicultural Education in Germany: Historical Development and Current Status." In *Handbook of Research on Multicultural Education.* Edited by James A. Banks and Cherry A. McGee Banks. New York: Macmillan, 821–838.

Hohmann, Manfred, and Hans H. Reich, eds. 1989. *Ein Europa für Mehrheiten und Minderheiten.* Diskussionen um Interkulturelle Erziehung. New York/Münster: Waxmann.

Horowitz, Donald L., and Gérard Noiriel. 1992. *Immigrants in Two Democracies. French and American Experience*. New York and London: New York University Press.

Horrocks, David, and Eva Kolinsky, eds. 1996. *Turkish Culture in German Society Today*. Providence/Oxford: Berghahn Books.

IAM. 1989a. Institut des Arts et Métiers, Ville de Bruxelles. "Français Textes 1ère. Degré d'observation." Etablissement désigné comme École Pilote pour l'intégration des Cultures sous l'égide de la Communauté Economique Européenne.

———. 1989b. Institut des Arts et Métiers, Ville de Bruxelles. "Géographie 1ère observation. Degré d'observation." Etablissement désigné comme École Pilote pour l'in-tégration des Cultures sous l'égide de la Communauté Economique Européenne.

———. 1989c. Institut des Arts et Métiers, Ville de Bruxelles. "Histoire 1ère Obs. Degré d'observation." Etablissement désigné comme École Pilote pour l'intégration des Cultures sous l'égide de la Communauté Economique Européenne.

———. 1989d. Institut des Arts et Métiers, Ville de Bruxelles. "Histoire 2ème Obs. Degré d'observation." Etablissement désigné comme École Pilote pour l'intégration des Cultures sous l'égide de la Communauté Economique Européenne.

———. ca. 1990. Institut des Arts et Métiers de la Ville de Bruxelles. "L'école du futur . . . ta future école. 3 Implantations." Etablissement désigné comme École Pilote pour l'intégration des Cultures sous l'égide de la Communauté Economique Européenne.

ILEA. 1982. Inner London Education Authority. "The Educational Implications of the 1981 Language Census." 8 (7) ILEA 2249 (h), 6 June.

———. 1983. Inner London Education Authority. "Bilingualism in the ILEA." Briefing Paper no. 1. March.

———. ca. 1988. Inner London Education Authority. *Bilingual Pupils in Tower Hamlets Schools*.

———. 1989. Inner London Education Authority. Research and Statistics Branch. *Language Census*. RS 1261/89.

L'immigration en France. Des resortissants des pays d'Afrique noire 1992. Rapport du troupe de travail interminsteriel. Juin.

Jones, Crispin, and Keith Kimberley. 1986. *Intercultural Education. Concept, Context, Curriculum Practice*. Council of Europe. CDCC's Project No. 7: "The Education and Cultural Development of Migrants." Strasbourg, Council for Cultural Co-operation. School Education Division.

Koninklijk Commissariaat voor het Migrantenbeleid. 1989. *Integratie (Beleid): een werk van lange adem*. November. 3 vols.

Kroon, Sjaak 1989. "Opportunities and Constraints of Community Language Teaching. An Evaluation of the EC Pilot Project Community Languages in Secondary Curriculum." *The European Communities Comparative Evaluation Project*. Landau, Belgium. Photocopy.

Lawton, Denis. 1989. "The National Curriculum." In *The Education Reform Act: Choice and Control*. London: Hodder & Stoughton, 27–43.

Leunda, J., and P. Deprez. 1988. *Rapport d'Evaluation de l'expérience-pilote d'enseignement multiculturel (1984–1987)*. Bruxelles: Commission des Communautés Européennes. Ministère de l'Education Nationale Communauté Française de Belgique.

Luchtenberg, Sigrid. 1994. "Perspectives on Bilingual Education in Germany." *Journal of Intercultural Studies* 15 (2): 73–84.

Migration. Berlin: Zuwanderung gesellschaftliche Probleme, politische Ansätze. 1995. Berlin: Fakultätsinstiut Sozialwissenschaften, Humboldt Universität.

OECD. 1993. *Trends in International Migration. Annual Report*. OECD Paris, 68, 75, 77, 84, 100.

————. 1995. *Education at a Glance OECD Indicators*.

OFSTED. 1992–1993. Office for Standards in Education. *Educational Support for Ethnic Minority Communities. A Survey of Educational Provision Funded under Section 11 of the 1966 Local Government Act*. April 1992–November 1993. Ref. 130/94/NS.

Parliamentary Debates, House of Commons. 8 December 1987–14 January 1988. Official Report of Standing Committee J. Education Reform Bill. London: Her Majesty's Stationery Office.

Pohl, Frau. 1996. Foreigners' Office (*Ausländerbeauftragte*). City of Berlin. Interview with E. S. Swing. Berlin, 22 May.

Rapport. 1982. *Rapport International Colloquium onder de Auspicien van de E. G. Pedagogische Opvangvormem voor Migrantenkinderen in het Basisonderwijs. Moedertaalonderricht aan Migrantenkinderen in het Lager Onderwijs*. Houthalen, Belgie, 26–29 April.

Roberts, Wyn. 1990. Welsh Office. Interview with E. S. Swing. Whitehall, London, 29 January.

Roosens, Eugen. 1981. "The Multicultural Nature of Contemporary Belgian Society: The Immigrant Community." In *Conflict and Coexistence in Belgium: The Dynamics of a Divided Society*. Edited by A. Lijphart. Berkeley: University of California, 61–92.

Schäffter, Ortfried. 1991. "Modi des Fremderlebens. Deutungsmuster im Umgang mit Fremdheit." In *Das Fremde. Erfahrungsmöglichkeiten zwishen Faszination und Bedrohung*. Edited by Ortfried Schäffter. Westdeutscher, 11–42.

————. 1996. Interview with E. S. Swing. Humboldt University, Berlin, 21 May.

Schermerhorn, R. A. [1970] 1978. *Comparative Ethnic Relations: A Framework for Theory and Research*. Chicago: University of Chicago Press.

Silberman, Roxanne. 1996. Interview with E. S. Swing. IRESCO, Institut de Recherche sur les Societé Contemporaine. Paris, 29 mai.

Silberman, Roxanne, and Irène Fournier. 1996. "La position sur le marché du travail des enfants des immigrés." Communication au colloque européen, *Réussite scolaire et universitaire, égalité des chances et discriminations à l'embauche des jeunes issues de l'immigration*. Paris: Université Denis Diderot, Paris VII, 6–7 mars.

Le Soir, 11 November 1990. "Un projet pédagogique multiculturel." Brussels.

Swing, Elizabeth Sherman. 1980. *Bilingualism and Linguistic Segregation in the Schools of Brussels*. Quebec, Canada: International Center for Research on Bilingualism/Centre international de recherche sur le bilinguisme.

————. 1988. "Bilingualism and Linguistic Separatism in Belgian Schools." In *International Handbook of Bilingualism and Bilingual Education*. Edited by Christina Bratt Paulston. Westport, CT: Greenwood Press, 63–83.

————. 1992. "Bilingual/Multilingual Education: Reaction and Reform in Belgium, Wales, and England." *European Education* 23 (winter): 32–44.

————. 1997. "Education and Separatism in Multicultural Belgium: An American Perspective." In *Studies in Comparative, International, and Peace Education. Liber*

Amicorum Henk Van daele. Edited by Karel de Clerck and Frank Simon. Ghent, Belgium: C.S.H.P., 235–252.

———. 1995. "Humanism in Multicultureland: A Comparative Looking Glass." *Educational Foundations* 9, no. 1 (winter): 73–94.

Tribalat, Michèle. 1996. *De l'immigration à l'assimilation. Enquête sur les populations d'origine étrangère en France*. Paris: La Découverte/INED.

Uçar, Ali. 1996. Technical University of Berlin. Interview. Berlin, 23 May.

Vallet, Louis-André. 1996. "Niveau en français et en mathématiques des élèves étrangers ou issue de l'immigration." *Economie et Statistique*, no. 293: 137–153.

Vallet, Louis-André, and Jean-Paul Caille. 1996. "Les élèves étrangers ou issus de l'immigration dans l'école et le collège français." Dossiers d'Éducation et Formations. Paris: Ministère de l'Éducation nationale, de l'Enseignement supérieur et de la Recherche.

Verheyen, J. E. 1929. "Le bilinguisme en Belgique." In *Le bilinguisme et l'éducation. Travaux de la conférence tenue à Luxembourg du 2 au 5 avril 1928*. Genève: Bureau International d' Education, 137–145.

Welsh Office. 1987. *Report by H. M. Inspectors on a Survey of the Teaching and Learning of Welsh in the Primary Schools of the Gwendraeth Valley*. Inspected during autumn term 1987.

———. 1989. *Report by H. M. Inspectors on Ysol Gyfun Ddwyieithog Maesyryrfa Cefneithin, Dyfed*. Inspected during summer term 1989.

Wirt, Frederick M. 1979. "The Stranger Within My Gate: Ethnic Minorities and School Policy in Europe." *Comparative Education Review* 23 (February): 17–40.

11

Developing the European Dimension in Education: The Roles of the European Union and the Council of Europe

Raymond Ryba

INTRODUCTION

The continuing evolution of European integration creates new realities for the peoples of European countries. If these realities are to be fully appreciated and fully integrated into the lives of future citizens of those countries, it is clear that the national educational systems concerned, and particularly the curricula of those systems, need to respond appropriately. Opportunities have to be created for the adaptation of such systems and their curricula to the new needs, opportunities, and responsibilities implied if the results of greater European integration are to be made fully meaningful to the populations involved. What is needed is the development and inclusion of a proper European dimension in the curriculum and the other activities of schools. Only when this is achieved will education in European countries be appropriately adapted to the new situation.

Evidence has made clear over the years that curricular adaptation of any kind does not generally happen very quickly. The case of attempts to develop a European dimension in education in European schools is further confirmation of this state of affairs. Despite the obvious need for its development, the changes that are required are not happening satisfactorily or sufficiently quickly. Nor is the process of natural change in the schools and other educational institutions involved taking place quickly (Ryba 1992). It is evident that some help and guidance from outside authorities and institutions are essential. As will emerge below, it is also evident that the help and guidance given to individual countries over the years has so far generally failed to effect, by itself, a sufficient degree or rate of change, proving inadequate to Europeans' current educational needs

(Ryba 1992). Meanwhile, further developments in the field of European integration continue to add new considerations. It is in this context that attention is given in this chapter to the part being played by pan-European influences and, most particularly, to the involvement of the two most important of these: the European Union and the Council of Europe.

WHY INTRODUCING THE EUROPEAN DIMENSION IS PROBLEMATICAL

It is clear that difficulties still exist in the satisfactory introduction of the European dimension of education into the curricula and extracurricular activities of schools in most, if not all, European countries. Where does that difficulty lie? It should be said at once that it does not lie at the level of explicit intention in virtually any single European country. Some—Germany is an example—have included explicit resolutions on the inclusion of the European dimension within their educational legislation for as much as twenty years (Kultusministeriums Konferenz 1978). Fuller discussion of this example will be offered below. But whether or not earlier efforts had been made by 1988, all the then European Community countries committed themselves in that year to a council resolution to develop the teaching of the European dimension (CEC 1988); and in 1989, all the then members of the Council of Europe did likewise (Council of Europe 1989). So *acceptance* of the need for its development was not a problem at the national level. More will be said about these commitments below.

The key difficulty about developing an adequate European dimension in the educational provision offered in most European countries is that although national governments have all officially recognized the importance of doing so, acting on that recognition remains far from easy. The problem is implementing what has been agreed upon. No doubt reasons for this lie partly in the still evidently different social contexts of individual European countries and partly in difficulties that individual schools have in implementing agreed-upon policy. The importance still attached to the distinctive nature of the historical evolution and traditions in different countries remains particularly strong. Regarding education, this has not only led to the development of distinctive educational systems in different European countries but also accounts for a reluctance to brook any interference from outside (Ryba 1994a). Changes leading to a more European, less nationalistic, development of these educational systems, and in particular, of their existing curricular structures, are therefore especially difficult to introduce. And, with some honorable exceptions in most countries, what is true at the level of national systems is *a fortiori* true at the level of individual schools and other educational institutions.

These realities are by no means new. There is a long history of efforts to Europeanize national education systems in European countries. This goes back at least to the time of Comenius (1592–1670) and extends forward since then through the efforts of a large number of illustrious and well-intentioned individuals (Shennan 1991). Pim de Boer, in a recent analysis, notes a string of famous names associated with these efforts, including thinkers such as Voltaire and Adam Smith, politicians such as Aristide Briand, writers such as Victor Hugo, and others who believed that despite the constant wars between European nations, there was a fundamental unity of European culture that was shared and which, if only developed and made explicit, could lead to greater peace and harmony (Van der Dussen and Wilson 1993, Essay 1). However, despite their efforts, little progress was made in that direction until the post–Second World War period. Indeed, particularly in the 19th-century and the early part of the 20th century, growing tendencies toward extreme nationalism in most European countries, paralleled and supported by the development of nationalist curricula in education, led to the dominance of centrifugal rather than centripetal tendencies in the evolution of European politics and society. Citron offers a masterly analysis of how this affected education in France (Citron 1987). She shows clearly how myths about the continuity and grandeur of the French nation were forged and disseminated by schooling in the 19th century. But similar forces were at work in other European countries. So it was only after the shock to the European nations of the two world wars that any real and consistent progress toward greater European unity first began to be evident. It was also only after the Second World War that developments such as the Council of Europe and then the European Economic Community, from which the European Union has grown, were initiated and continued to grow.

THE COUNCIL OF EUROPE AND THE EUROPEAN UNION

Before considering in more detail the developing roles of the Council of Europe and the European Union in the evolution of the European dimension of education, it might be well to remind ourselves of the differences between these two organizations that are so often confused with each other. Of the two, the Council of Europe, based in Strasbourg, is by a long way the less powerful and less well-funded organization. On the other hand, it was set up as long ago as 1949, considerably earlier than the EEC. Moreover, it has always involved more European countries in its membership than has the European Union and its predecessors. Ten countries set up the council at its outset. In 1999 the number of full members was forty-one and still growing. Also, being a body essentially founded to encourage cultural cooperation, it has always seen the development of cooperation in the field of education as one of its major tasks. Furthermore, its Council for Cultural Cooperation (CDCC), which involves itself particularly in educational matters, has always made a point of offering involvement to non-member countries who nevertheless shared its educational and cultural objectives. By 1996 it had grown to offer a forum for European debate in educational matters involving forty-four European countries. However, although the organization has its own Parliamentary Assembly and holds regular international meetings of ministers of education, and although it engages in various cooperative activities, it has been given no legislative powers. This means that its influence is limited to the successful results of discussion, exhortation, advice, publication, and the application at the national level of common decisions.

The European Union is a quite different and separate organization. Although altogether more powerful than the Council of Europe, it is limited to a much smaller number of countries. Starting from its six founding member states, which set up the European Economic Community in 1957, it still comprises no more than fifteen of the Council of Europe's members (1999). Its central purposes, at least until relatively recently, are essentially economic and political, rather than the educational and cultural ones of the Council of Europe. Moreover, although it has developed its own range of educational activities over the years, it is significant that the Treaty of Rome, the founding treaty of the organization, actually contained no article referring to education (Treaty of Rome 1957).

Unlike the Council of Europe, the European Union does have clear legislative powers, over and above those of its member states. These are determined by its Council of Ministers, a body not to be confused with the Council of Europe. The Council of Ministers is made up of the ministers of the union's individual member states relevant to the particular decisions being taken. When matters of the highest importance and generality are under discussion, the Council of Ministers is made up of the heads of government of the member countries. The financial ministers meet for discussion of matters of finance, transport ministers when transport is under discussion, and so on. Decisions made by this council are administered and executed by the European Commission, which has its headquarters in Brussels. The European Commission is therefore essentially the civil service of the union.

There is also a related elected European Parliament, again not to be confused with the Council of Europe's Parliamentary Assembly. This parliament has powers of its own, though relatively limited ones compared with those of the parliaments of the individual member states. New proposals agreed upon by the member states are certainly discussed by the European Parliament, but their final acceptance remains a matter essentially for the parliaments of the individual states.

In the case of education, the relevant meetings of the Council of Ministers are those of ministers of education, meeting as the council. Since the acceptance by member states, in 1992, of the Maastricht Treaty, these have become more regular and important. This is because the treaty, which formally amends and extends the Treaty of Rome, contains an article directly referring to education. This is article 126, which begins by stating that "the Community shall contribute to the development of quality education by encouraging cooperation between Member States and, if necessary, by supporting and supplementing their action, while fully respecting the responsibility of the Member States for the content of teaching and the organization of educational systems and their cultural and linguistic diversity" (CEC 1992).

Prior to the Maastricht Treaty, the powers of the European Union's Council of Ministers were strictly limited by preserved states' rights in educational matters. However, even after the signing of the Maastricht Treaty, the powers of the council to make educational decisions remain heavily circumscribed by the "subsidiarity" principle. This principle, stated in article 3b of the treaty, makes clear that in areas that do not fall in the exclusive competence of the community, it shall take action "in accordance with the principle of subsidiarity, only if and in so far as the proposed action cannot be sufficiently achieved by the member states and can therefore, by reason of the scale or effects of the proposed action, be better achieved by the Community." Thus national educational systems are protected from supranational decisions other than those agreed upon as not interfering with decisions best made at the appropriate national or regional level.

DEVELOPING THE EUROPEAN DIMENSION AFTER THE SECOND WORLD WAR

If we trace the development of the European dimension in education in European countries from the immediate post–Second World War period, we initially find it relatively neglected. What is more, insofar as it was present, it was in continuing competition with the more nationalistically determined elements of curricula. Generally, national rather than international elements of the curriculum continued to dominate education in most countries. Relatively little attention was as yet paid to more "European" dimensions of the curriculum. To be sure, some European geography and history was taught in most schools. Schooling also included the possibility of learning one or more foreign, generally European, languages. But even these elements were usually taught from a national perspective rather than a European one (Mulcahy 1989). Moreover, in spite of growing efforts to increase the Europeanization of education, efforts that began in the 1950s and that have continued at an increasing pace ever since, progress was very slow and continued to be difficult.

To begin with, greater Europeanization of education in schools and other institutions depended essentially, as in prewar days, on the largely unaided efforts of a minority of dedicated teachers who did their best to Europeanize the curriculum in their own subject areas and in their own schools and colleges. Among these schools, from the 1950s onward, were the European Schools. These were set up in different places to cater to the needs of parents working in various international organizations. However, there were very few of them. So although interesting examples of schools with a resulting European outlook were to be found in a number of Western European countries, wider dissemination of the ideas that gave rise to them remained almost entirely absent.

Already by the 1950s, the Council of Europe had begun to sponsor interesting studies in education aimed at fostering a more European, less nationalistic, attitude. Thus, for example, among its earlier studies was one that investigated the existence of national biases and prejudices in history textbooks with a view to seeking their elimination (Shennan 1991). This and similar work continued into the 1960s and 1970s. At the same time, national agencies for the encouragement of international visits and exchanges within Europe began to be set up. Examples included the Central Bureau for Visits and Exchanges, set up in the United Kingdom in 1948, and the very influential Office Franco-Allemande de la Jeunesse, set up in the early 1960s. Such centers aimed to contribute to European understanding through the exchange of students and teachers between European countries. Again, however, their influence in the early postwar years was not very great. Moreover, many of the exchanges arranged were limited to foreign-language teachers.

Although the European Economic Community had come into being by 1957, it played absolutely no part in the development of a European dimension in education until the 1970s (Neave 1984). We have already seen that the Treaty of Rome had excluded any clauses to take account of education in the work of the community. Throughout these earlier years of the community, education was therefore seen only as a national responsibility of the member states. Indeed, it was not until some fourteen years after the foundation of the community that its ministers of education first actually met together formally. So at the international level, the Council of Europe was left virtually on its own in trying to reduce the always present nationalistic and ethnocentric elements in many European education systems.

By the late 1960s and early 1970s, however, various subject teachers' associations in a number of European countries, particularly those concerned with the teaching of modern languages, history, geography, and economics, began to interest their members in the European dimensions of their respective fields of study. By the 1970s, efforts were being made to link national subject associations with their counterparts in other EEC countries. Thus, for example, European groupings of geographical and economic associations were set up at this time. Also, other associations of a trans-frontier European nature began to come into existence and to play a part in the greater Europeanization of education (Ryba 1995). Early examples of these were the European Association of Teachers (EAT/AEDE) and the Association of Teacher Educators in Europe (ATEE). European groupings of university scholars in the area of education were also set up in this period. Thus the Comparative Education Society in Europe (CESE) came into being in the early 1960s. Originally quite small, these and other similar organizations arranged European conferences and meetings and published European publications. As a result, many of them have now become reasonably powerful influences, in their different ways, on the development of the European dimension of education.

FURTHER DEVELOPMENTS IN THE 1970s AND 1980s

During the 1970s and 1980s, the Council of Europe continued to support the further Europeanization of education in its member countries by means of its educational program of activities. Particularly important were a number of resolutions and recommendations of the council, as well as its program of projects. One important example was its secondary education project on "Preparation for Life" (1978–82). The activities of the various associations and non-government organizations concerned with education in Europe also continued to grow.

In some cases, individual countries within Europe began to develop explicit policies to improve curricular Europeanization. The Federal Republic of Germany, an early example of this trend, has already been mentioned. That country's resolution, in 1978, proposed curricular offerings "designed to fit young people for their tasks as citizens of the European Community" through the communication of knowledge and ideas on a list of relevant topics (Kultusministeriums Konferenz 1978). These included:

- "the special character and diversity of Europe;
- the principal historical forces at work in Europe;
- social and economic structures in Europe;
- the development of European legal and political thought and ideas of freedom;
- the efforts to organize and integrate Europe since 1945;
- the importance of joint action and supra-regional institutions to solve economic, social and political problems;
- the need to achieve a fair balance of interests in Europe;
- the importance of cooperation within the European Community;
- the importance of cooperation between the member states of the European Community and other countries in the world;
- the values and interests which govern decisions in Europe."

It further stressed that "the fundamental values . . . which inspire the school's educational aims must be set in the context of life within the European family of nations and states," thus implying:

- "a readiness to understand and dismantle prejudices and to recognize what is held in common while at the same time appreciating European diversity;
- the development of European legal instruments on the basis of the principles and aims of the European Human Rights Convention and the Social Charter;
- good neighborly cooperation and a willingness to compromise in order to do justice to the different interests in Europe;
- the realization of human rights, the desirability of equality of opportunity, and economic, social and legal security and freedom of movement." (Shennan 1991, p. 147 for English version)

But the key change that occurred, especially after 1976, was the increased involvement of the European Community, as the former EEC had by then come to be known. This change took place in the 1970s, following the accession of

Denmark, Ireland, and the United Kingdom to the community and the publication of the Janne Report (Janne 1973). This important report stressed the need to develop a European education policy at the level of the community.

The change intensified still further in the 1980s, following the accession of Portugal, Spain, and Greece. As we have already noted, the first meeting of the community's ministers of education took place in the early 1970s. This was followed in 1976 by the setting up of the community's first purely educational program of activities, significantly directed particularly at the development of the European "dimension" of education (CEC 1976). Subsequently, the term *European dimension of education* has come to be used almost universally instead of older terms such as *Europeanization*. It has come to be accepted as more representative of what most workers in this particular field have felt needed to be done.

To begin with, the work of the European Community in the European dimension of education field, having no clear basis in the Treaty of Rome, was cautious and limited. In the main, it was restricted to helping various nongovernment organizations (NGOs) already working in the field to develop their activities, and to the development of its own understanding of what needed to be done by the commissioning of specialist papers. However, more regular meetings of ministers and their officials were instituted, and these gradually led to international agreement between the community countries to increase their cooperation in educational matters. The legal basis for these developments, in the absence of appropriate articles in the Treaty of Rome, lay in the unanimous agreement of the ministers concerned with each specific issue.

By the 1980s, intensification of these activities had led to the establishment of a department within the Directorate for Social Affairs (DG5) concerned specifically with educational initiatives and developing new lines of action on behalf of the community. Two major kinds of development occurred that were significantly related to support for the European dimension of education. The first and most financially significant of these was the setting up, from the mid-1980s onward, of a number of important exchange programs. These involved participants from at least two community countries and was open to all of them. The most important of these, and probably the best known, was the Erasmus Program for inter-university exchanges. This afforded partial support to exchanges of various kinds between staff and students at university level, leading, in many cases to university programs in which credit was given for studies undertaken in one or more community countries other than the students' own country. The Erasmus Program has proved to be a successful way of stimulating higher education cooperation across frontiers. It has continued to grow and develop ever since its foundation and to involve more and more universities and other institutions of higher education, as well as more and more university departments within these institutions.

In addition to the Erasmus Program, a number of other significant programs of an exchange nature were also set up. These included the Arion Program, concerned with promoting and supporting study visits by education specialists, the Comett Program, devoted to promoting cooperation between higher education and industry in the training sector for advanced technology, and Youth for Europe, a program aimed at supporting exchanges in non-formal education (CEC 1989).

Eventually, at the very end of the 1980s, two further big programs, known as Lingua and Tempus, were set up. Lingua was aimed at supporting international initiatives that improved linguistic competence in European languages, ranging from that of foreign language teachers in schools and universities, to students and users of these languages in schools, colleges, vocational institutions, and the world of work. Tempus was set up following the collapse of the Iron Curtain to support the Central and Eastern European states by promoting research, development, and exchange activities with those countries.

Most of these exchange activities have continued to grow in importance, though also to change somewhat in character, since the 1980s. But what they have had in common is what might be called a dedication to the indirect development of the European dimension of their participants' education through the programs. The implication has been a belief that practical cooperation across frontiers will develop the European dimension in education. The exchange programs also helped establish activities in all fields of education in addition to becoming directly involved in the schools themselves in the different countries. Direct intervention in the activities of students and of the schools themselves, an area of policy responsibility that at least some of the involved countries felt to be nationally sacrosanct, was studiously avoided as being clearly outside the community's remit. However, work involving teachers, many of whom worked in the schools, was seen as coming within the remit.

The second major kind of development with which the European Community concerned itself was precisely related to the schools as well as other institutions. This led it to be somewhat indirect in nature, that is, by obtaining agreement of member states to common paths of action. It was thus concerned with teaching a European dimension in education within the curricula of educational institutions at all levels, but particularly at the levels of schools and teacher training. In the later 1980s, surveys carried out by the European Commission revealed that much remained to be done to introduce young people to the opportunities and responsibilities associated with membership in the European Community. This led, in May 1988, to the passing of the important Council Resolution, referred to previously on the development of the European dimension in education. This resolution set out agreed-upon tasks to be carried out by member states of the community and also other supporting tasks to be carried out by the commission itself (CEC 1988).

The general objectives set out in the resolution were to strengthen the European dimension in education as follows:

• strengthen in young people a sense of European identity and make clear to them the value of European civilization and of the foundations on which the European peoples intend to base their development today, that is, in particular the safeguarding of the principles of democracy, social justice, and respect for human rights (Copenhagen declaration, April 1978);

- prepare young people to take part in the economic and social development of the community and in making concrete progress toward European Union, as stipulated in the European Single Act;
- make them aware of the advantages the community represents, but also the challenges it involves, in opening up an enlarged economic and social area to them;
- improve their knowledge of the community and its member states in their historical, cultural, economic, and social aspects and bring home to them the significance of the cooperation of the member states of the European Community with other countries of Europe and the world.

Within these general objectives, member states agreed to take various measures to incorporate the European dimension into their education systems and into their school programs and teaching. They also agreed to take steps to ensure that appropriate teaching material was made available, that the European dimension was introduced into teacher training in various ways, that measures would be promoted to boost contacts between students and teachers from various countries, and that related complementary measures, such as the formation of "European clubs" and the organization of appropriate colloquia and seminars, should be stimulated.

At the same time, it was agreed by all the twelve community countries then involved that action by the member states should be backed up by the European Commission in various ways. These included measures to promote exchange of information in the different member states, various measures related to the development and exchange of appropriate European dimension teaching materials, and the development of study visits and other forms of cooperation between teacher trainers in the member states. Additionally, various further measures were proposed to encourage cooperation, such as support to non-government organizations (NGOs) and the fostering of cooperation between educational research institutes working for the introduction of the European dimension in education.

Significantly, the main responsibilities outlined in the 1988 resolution remained with the individual governments, with only supportive activities thought best handled at the community level being left in the hands of the commission. Thus the resolution subscribed in advance to the principle of "subsidiarity" which, as has already been explained, was subsequently to underlie the provisions of the Maastricht Treaty.

Following the passing of the resolution, there was undoubtedly an increase in government activity in the member states aimed at increasing provision for the teaching of the European dimension in education across the curricula of primary and secondary schools. Greater attention was also given to European dimension training within teacher education, both at the pre-service and in-service levels.

At the same time, at the commission level, a special support unit for the European dimension of education was set up in 1989. This monitored the work that was being developed at national levels through regular meetings of a co-ordinating committee. It also helped to organize several annual summer schools related to various aspects of the resolution. In addition it set up a pilot school exchange program (TEX), which supported proposals for joint work by teachers in schools in two or more member countries, and a program of appropriate international curriculum development activities at the teacher education level (RIF). However, compared with the needs of the whole of the European Community area, the dimensions of these programs remained relatively small and circumscribed.

DEVELOPMENTS AFTER 1989

The great political changes that occurred in Central and Eastern Europe in 1989 substantially affected the educational work of both the Council of Europe and the European Community. Careful rethinking was required in both these international institutions in the light of the new situation that had been created.

For the European Community, which was to be renamed the European Union on the signing of the Maastricht Treaty in 1992, the changed political situation simply added new exogenous pressures to those endogenous ones that had been initiated by the signing of the Single European Act (CEC 1986). It will be remembered that this act included various measures directed at encouraging an ever closer union of the member states and their peoples in social as well as economic terms. From 1995, the accession of the three additional countries of Austria, Finland, and Sweden also had to be taken into account. We have already seen how the Tempus Program was created in response to the new external pressures. Later, also responding to these pressures, the Tacis and Phare programs were created to extend the possibility of similar cooperative activities, with the latter offering opportunities for cooperation with the various new states created from the former Soviet Union. But in spite of requests from some Central European states to accede to the European Union, there has so far been no question of this happening for at least some time to come.

In this situation, the main new developments of interest in the evolution of the Union's educational activities have been in the developments subsequent to the signing of the Maastricht Treaty in 1992. This treaty, whose correct name is *Treaty on European Union*, amends and enlarges the original Treaty of Rome, and goes further than any previous EC agreement. In the field of education, it introduces for the first time a specific article, Article 126. This article is concerned, as has already been made clear, with all aspects of education, including schools and colleges as well as with higher education and teacher training. The treaty also contains, in Article 127, an enlarged and more explicit article concerned with the wider field of training (CEC 1992). These two articles, despite careful wording that preserves the "subsidiarity" principle of reserving actions for the individual states except where there is agreement that they can be done better at union level, provide for the first time a treaty basis for educational action in a way that did not previously exist.

This new situation has led to a considerable increase in the union budget attributed to education and training activities and to a reconsideration, expansion, and reorganization of the commission's previous work in these fields. As far as education is concerned, a new Directorate of the Commission has been set up (DG22), and following unionwide discussion of a "Green Paper" (discussion paper) on education, the previous educational activities of the union and some new ones have been reorganized into two main education and training programs. These have been named, respectively, Socrates and Leonardo. Alongside these, Youth for Europe III continues to support educational activities outside formal educational provision.

Broadly speaking, the Socrates Program brings together all the programs in the education field, and the Leonardo one concerns itself with training initiatives. These programs both replace and subsume the previously existing activities of the commission in these fields and add some new ones. Particularly important among the latter, within the Socrates Program, is the new development of the Comenius Program. This gives support to a wider-based teacher and school exchange scheme than previously, involving schools of two or more union countries. This new school-based initiative is a considerable and significant addition to the previous activities of the commission. It is particularly significant because of the way, following the acceptance of Article 126 of the Maastricht Treaty, it extends considerably the commission's support for activities at the school level.

In early 1996, the European Commission published an important "White Paper" on its education policy, "Teaching and Learning: Towards the Learning Society." This paper, which had been completed at the end of 1995, charts the basis for future action by the commission on behalf of the union in the field of education, linking its proposals closely to the field of employment and social affairs (European Commission 1996). It begins by stressing the need for educational policy in the European Union to respond appropriately to three factors of current and future upheaval: the internationalization of trade; the impact of the developing information society; and the march of science and technology. It sees the solution to these current and future pressing problems in two major directions: the reintroduction to schooling and vocational education of "a broad base of knowledge," which it defines as "the ability to grasp the meaning of things, to comprehend and to make judgments"; and "the building up of employability," which it sees as requiring "integration within a network which cooperates, educates, trains and learns."

To further these proposals, the White Paper goes on to propose five main guidelines for action:

1. encouraging the acquisition of new knowledge by proposing, for example, new ways of accrediting technical and vocational skills;

2. bringing school and the business sector closer together through, for example, the development of new forms of apprenticeship;

3. combating exclusion from education and training by the offer of "second chance" routes through schooling, supported, where appropriate, by European funding as well as national funding;

4. developing proficiency in three community languages, as "a factor in European identity" and "a cornerstone of the knowledge-based society";

5. treating material investment and investment in training on an equal basis by "making education and training a priority as regards European competitiveness," supported by appropriate measures, for example, in the field of taxation.

The White Paper seeks to promote "a wide-ranging debate" around its contents as a preliminary step toward submitting concrete proposals for future action. In line with the principle of subsidiarity, however, it makes clear that although its purpose is "to plot out the route" toward the learning society "by identifying the options available to the EU in education and training," its aim is to "support and supplement education and training policies, the responsibility for which rests first and foremost with national, regional and local authorities."

In the case of the Council of Europe, developments have taken a different course, one that has, however, significantly affected and expanded its educational work toward a more European dimension in education. As has already been pointed out, the Council of Europe, untrammeled by the powers accorded to the European Union by its member states, continues, as always, to have a larger membership than that of the union. Following the events of 1989, this membership was rapidly enlarged to include, first, the states of Central and Eastern Europe and then, some of those of the former Soviet Union, now including Russia. Taken together with several other states that have been given membership in the Council for Cultural Cooperation, this meant that by 1996, as has already been pointed out, there was an inclusive forum for educational debate encompassing forty-four European countries. These of course included, but were not limited to, the countries within the European Union.

These developments have opened up a new and quite different arena for educational debate and action. It is one that, unlike that of the European Union, is truly pan-European in its extent. Within this context, the Council of Europe has developed, with renewed vigor, a wide range of educational activities devoted to extending the European dimension of education, conceived in terms of all its member countries and not simply those of the European Union. These developments, amounting to a new and wider mission than in the past, have once again increased the importance of its educational efforts.

In 1989, the council's Parliamentary Assembly passed its own resolution on the development of the European dimension in education, this time applying to all the countries in its wider membership as well as to its union members (Council of Europe 1989). Subsequently, in 1991, the 17th Standing Conference of Ministers of Education of its member countries, held in Vienna, devoted the whole of its time to the subject and passed further supporting resolutions about it (Council of Europe 1991 [a]).

At the same time, the council's own work and development programs have been emphasizing educational projects relating to these objectives, including work on school links and exchanges, on history teaching, and in the area of civics education. Particularly important among these projects over the past few years has been the Council's Secondary Education for Europe Project (Council of Europe. 1991 [b]). Within this project, which is one of the largest ever undertaken by the council, programs concerned with teacher and student exchange and with the development of European dimension pedagogical materials are particularly pertinent to European dimension objectives, as is a continuing series of monographs on successful case studies in developing the European dimension (Ryba 1994b).

Of these programs, the European Dimension Pedagogical Materials Program, coordinated as part of the Secondary Education for Europe Project by the author of this chapter, had carried out the task, by the end of 1996, of creating fourteen major teaching and learning dossiers on a variety of subjects suitable for inclusion across the secondary curriculum of schools throughout Europe (Ryba 1996a). The dossier subjects chosen varied widely from "Environmental Damage in Europe" through titles such as "The Industrial Revolution: Birth of a European Technological Space," "The Rights of Man in Europe," and "Greek Drama and its Influence on European Theatre, Literature and Ideas," to others concerned with "Conflict in Europe," "Identity, Solidarity and the Development of a New Europe," and "A European Economic Database." These teaching and learning resources, produced within a framework laid down by the Council of Europe, are expected to be directly usable by secondary school teachers in different European countries and to function as a model for future dossiers. They are also expected to be useful in pre-service and in-service teacher training courses concerned with the European dimension in education.

ACHIEVEMENTS, PROBLEMS, AND PROSPECTS

It is clear from the foregoing sections of this chapter that after centuries of relative failure to achieve a meaningful Europeanization of educational curricula and activities in European countries, the last fifty years, and particularly the last twenty years, have at least seen a growing success and seriousness in the notion of establishing a greater level of European dimension in educational provision in those countries. It is also clear that this applies not only to the countries belonging to the European Union but also to those belonging to the wider grouping of European countries represented by the membership of the Council of Europe. Progress in these regards has in fact been great enough for some educational writers to begin suggesting that the international bodies involved are in danger of becoming too powerful in the determination of educational policies (Sultana 1996). The appearance of such arguments, though hardly justified as

yet by the reality of the actual situation, at least suggests that meaningful progress at the level of official intentions has indeed been made (Ryba 1996b).

What is far less clear, and also rather more doubtful, is how much progress
has actually been made in implementing these intentions. Moreover, the degree
of effectiveness of what implementation has taken place is also far from clear
(Ryba 1995). Certainly, at the level of higher education, the Erasmus Program,
and to a lesser extent, the Lingua and Tempus programs are now well established, involving every year, as has already been said, a greater number of higher
education institutions and departments within institutions. As a result, the number of higher education students taking a part of their courses in at least one
European country other than their home base has increased dramatically during
the past decade. Certainly, this has had an effect on courses and on teaching in
the institutions involved and has led to higher education cooperation across
European frontiers (CEC 1994). On the other hand, little is really known about
the effects of this development on the attitudes of students involved. Positive
outcomes are assumed rather than established. Much less has so far been done
at the level of the schools. Moreover, even at the higher education level, the
number of students involved is still very much a minority of the total student
population.

At lower levels of education and in relation to non-formal education, the direct
impact of exchange programs has so far remained marginal, to say the least.
This will continue to be the case even with the current expansion implied by
the setting up of the new Comenius Program. Within the funding available, only
a tiny minority of the relevant populations will have any chance of being involved, and it is difficult, for cost reasons, to see this situation changing for a
very long time if at all. Moreover, such evaluations of their effectiveness as
have been carried out tend frequently to emphasize the difficulties encountered
in making these really successful. International student exchanges are difficult
to organize. They tend to be relatively short. They are also inevitably expensive
for the participants, since only a small part of the cost of such activities is borne
by the funds made available by the commission.

So the best chance of introducing a European dimension into education more
widely than at present must be through its introduction into the curricula and
extracurricular activities of schools in European countries. Only in this way is
it likely that all pupils and students will be able to benefit. For this to occur,
there is general agreement that the main efforts needed are those that can introduce the European dimension across the whole curriculum rather than simply
adding a bolt-on course or module. There is also general agreement that what
is required is not simply limited to a greater knowledge of factual content.
Efforts are needed to introduce learning directed at developing relevant skills
and competencies within the context of Europe as a whole; and, in particular,
efforts need to be made to help pupils and students develop values and attitudes
that are explicitly less ethnocentric and more tolerant of other people in the
European context. This applies both with regard to the people of other countries

and to the many minorities that are to be found within and across European countries. It is generally appreciated that greater efforts are still needed to develop the European dimension of an understanding of human rights and responsibilities, as well as a knowledge of the new opportunities to be found within the European frameworks of both the European Union and the Council of Europe countries.

There can be little doubt that the efforts of both the international organizations concerned have contributed greatly over recent years to an improvement in the understanding of the European dimension in these respects. The same may be said for the authorities concerned in the member countries. This has been particularly so within the countries of the European Union, where unionwide and national efforts to develop the European dimension of education have been established for the longest period. On the other hand, such evidence as there is suggests that the improvements that have taken place have so far remained patchy and limited when seen against the context of all the schools and other educational institutions in which it is generally agreed, at the official level, that progress needs to be made. Similar evidence suggests that teacher-training efforts in the area of the European dimension remain far from well developed, either at the pre-service or the in-service levels, and that appropriate teaching materials to help teachers introduce the European dimensions into their classrooms, although increasing in quantity and quality, are still very limited in their availability (Ryba 1992). All this is particularly true of those Council of Europe countries in Central and Eastern Europe, which have only relatively recently rejoined the mainstream of European educational debate. Quite understandably, these countries have been first and foremost concerned with re-establishing their own national identities within the changed political situation. They have therefore not yet had sufficient time or resources to devote to initiatives connected with the European dimension in education.

In the end, the ultimate test of successful implementation of policies to further develop the European dimension of education must be found in the schools, colleges, and other educational institutions and in the hearts and minds of their pupils and students as they move into the adult world. So far, there is very little actual evidence of a sufficiently successful implementation of accepted policies in this area. Much therefore remains to be done at every level of educational influence, from the international, through the national, down to the regional and local. Within this context it seems likely that both the European Union and the Council of Europe will continue to develop their own activities directed at improving the provision and effectiveness of teaching, as well as other initiatives directed at improving the general appreciation of the European dimension in education. How successful they will be remains to be seen.

REFERENCES

CEC. 1976. *Resolution of the Council of Ministers of Education Meeting within the Council.* 9 February. Brussels, European Commission.

————. 1986. *The Single European Act.*

————. 1988. *Resolution of the Council of Ministers Meeting within the Council, on "the European Dimension in Education,"* 24 May. Brussels, European Commission.

————. 1989. *Guide to the European Community Programmes in the Fields of Education, Training and Youth.* Brussels, Commission of the European Communities, Task Force on Human Resources, Education, Training and Youth.

————. 1992. *Treaty on European Union.* Maastricht, 7 February. Chapter 3.

————. 1994. *Cooperation in Education in the European Union, 1976–1994.* Brussels. Education, Training and Youth Studies, No. 5.

Citron, Suzanne. 1987. *Le Mythe National.* Paris: Les Editions Ouvrières.

Council of Europe. 1989. *Recommendation No. 1111 of the Parliamentary Assembly, on "The European Dimension of Education."* Strasbourg.

————. 1991(a). Standing Conference of European Ministers of Education. 17th Meeting, Vienna, October, on *"The European Dimension in Education."* Strasbourg.

————. 1991(b). CDCC Resolution No. 1. Setting up the council's "Secondary Education for Europe Project."

Janne, H. 1973. *Towards a European Education Policy.* Brussels, European Commission.

European Commission. 1996. White Paper on Education and Training: "Teaching and Learning—Towards the Learning Society." Luxembourg, Office for Official Publications of the European Communities.

Kultusministeriums Konferenz. 1978. *Europa im Unterricht*, Resolution of the Ministers of Education of the *Länder* of the Federal Republic of Germany. A revised version was adopted in 1990.

Mulcahy, D. G. 1989. "The European Dimension in Education: The Case of Ireland." In *La Prise en Compte de la Dimension Européenne dans l'Education.* Edited by F. Vaniscotte. Actes de Palerme. Paris: ATEE/ISAS/Hatier, 134–140.

Neave, Guy. 1984. *The E.E.C. and Education.* Stoke on Trent: Trentham Books.

Ryba, Raymond. 1992. "Toward a European Dimension in Education: Intention and Reality in European Community Policy and Practice." *Comparative Education Review* 36 (1): 10–24.

————. 1994(a). "Aspects of Tradition and Change in Modern European Schooling." University of Ghent.

————. 1994(b). "La création des ressources pédagogiques européennes pour l'enseignement de la dimension européenne de l'éducation au secondaire." *Education Comparée* 47: 27–37.

————. 1995. "Unity in Diversity: The Enigma of the European Dimension in Education." *Oxford Review of Education* 21 (1): 25–36.

————. 1996a. "The European Pedagogical Materials Programme: Its Conception, Implementation and Outcomes." In Council of Europe, *Summary Report on the European Dimension.* Strasbourg: Council of Europe, 344–360.

————. 1996b. "The Powers of the European Union in Educational Matters." In *Educational Dilemmas: Debate and Diversity.* Edited by Keith Watson et al. London: Cassell.

Shennan, Margaret. 1991. *Teaching about Europe*. London: Cassell/Council of Europe.

Sultana, Ronald. 1996. "The European Union and Its Educational Agenda: A Wolf in Sheep's Clothing?" In *Educational Dilemmas: Debate and Diversity*. Edited by Keith Watson et al. London: Cassell.

Treaty of Rome. 1957.

Van der Dussen, Jan, and Kevin Wilson, eds. 1993. *The History of the Idea of Europe*. Milton Keynes: Open University.

Index

Accountability movement: and decentralization, 61; different perceptions of politicians and teachers, 157; in England, 37–38; and participation in school governing bodies, 157–59; resistance of teachers, 157; role of market ideology, 157; and school choice, 157–59; source of conflict between parents and teachers, 157; and tolerance for diversity, 25. *See also* Parents

Administrative infrastructure, 5; in England and Wales, 35–38; in France, 29–32; in Germany, 32–35; in the Netherlands, 39–42; in school-oriented systems, 27–28; in state-oriented systems, 26–27, 28. *See also* Stein, Lorenz von

Arnold, Matthew, and formation of modern education systems, 2

Assessment. *See* Evaluation

Assimilationism: assimilationist curriculum in Europe, 239; in Belgium, 221; in England, 220, 234–38; in France, 220, 232–34; and integration, 219–20; rejected by Turks in Germany, 227; in the United States, 17. *See also* England

and Wales, education in; France, education in

Ausländer, 17, 220. *See also* Germany, education in

Australia: achievement of girls, 173; GDP allocated to education, 122

Austria: decisions taken by level of governance, 132; GDP devoted to education, 122; opposition of Catholic Church to public schools, 101; parents' attitude to school decision making, 135; preference for free higher education, 128; ratio of earnings to education, 140; school decision making, 132; unemployment by level of education, 138, 140

Autonomy of educational institutions: and administrative framework of schools in Germany, 35; and anarchistic independence in Russia, 208–9; and control of recruitment of teachers, 66; and decentralization in school management, 131–33; and ethnic identity in education of former Soviet Union, 210; and ethnic identity in federalized Belgium, 220–24; and ethnic identity in Wales, 224–25; and national identity in former Soviet

European Network of Women's Studies
(ENWS), also known as European Network of Scientific and Technical Cooperation on Women's Studies, 183
European Parliament, 247; women members, 179
European Union: average public expenditure for education as percentage of
GDP, 120; compared to Council of Europe, 247–48; contrast between Nordic
and Mediterranean countries, 121; and
cooperation of educational institutions,
42; Council of Ministers, 247–48; developments after Maastricht Treaty,
254–57; and European dimension in
education, 245–59; GDP for education,
119–123; European Commission as
civil service of the European Union,
247; Eurostat, 120; and former Soviet
states, 24, 196; increase in number of
teachers in member countries, 59; Information Office, 182; limitation of influence on education, 27; percentage in
tertiary education, 137; promotion of
women's issues, 181; social fund, 181;
role in the professionalization of teachers, 45; Socrates and Leonardo programs, 255; symbol of European
integration, 16; United Europe policy
in education, 226; women in national
parliaments of members, 179. *See also*
European Community; European Economic Community
Eurydice (Information Network on Education in the European Union), 43n. 2,
110, 115
Evaluation: conclusions from evaluation,
130–31; Eurostat, 129; evaluation of
school performances, 129–31; external
evaluation and self-evaluation in the
Netherlands, 39–41; HMI partially
abolished in England, 37–38; Institute
for Research on the Economics of Education (Irédu), 130; International Assessment of Educational Progress
(IAEP), International Association for
the Evaluation of Educational Achievement (IAEEA), 129; OEDC indicators,

129; OFSTED, 38; role of *Schulaufsicht* in German secondary schools, 34,
35; in school-oriented systems; 27

Families: decrease in family size, 145;
educational inequity and socio-
economic differences, 143–46; influence of family structure, 145; influence
of parental occupation, 143–45; as major source of socialization, 143–60;
single parent families, 145. *See also*
Parents
Finland: coeducation, 178; decisions by
level of governance, 132; decisions
taken by level of governance, 132;
GDP and education, 122; parental decision making, 135; ratio of earnings to
education, 140; unemployment by educational level, 138
Flemish Nationalists, 220–24. *See also*
Belgium, education in; Ethnic groups;
Multiculturalism.
Former Soviet states: abortion, 169; administration, 208–9; alternative education, 15, 199, 208; "author schools,"
200; autonomy and break-up of Soviet
Union, 196; autonomy of local units,
208; Belorussia and cultural identity,
198; budget for education, 193; Buriat
nation, 197; changes in child care provisions, 175; crisis after 1991, 192;
curriculum reform, 199, 209–11; decentralization, 133, 208, 209; decline
in public resources for education, 123,
192–93; demise of intelligentsia, 192;
demoralization, 192; difference in educational services from OECD countries,
126; differentiation and pluralism, 199;
educational complexes, 205; educational exchange with Western Europe,
24; education in former Soviet states,
191–218; educational laws, 194–95;
emergence of national schools, 195–98;
fewer girls enrolled in science courses,
147; GDP allotted to education, 122,
193; gender bias, 173; higher education
leaving certificates, 205; humanization

About the Editors and Contributors

HERMANN AVENARIUS is Professor of Public Law and Administration at the German Institute for International Educational Research in Frankfurt am Main. His publications focus on constitutional law as it relates to education, educational law, and the impact of European Union law on educational law in Germany.

MARIE DURU-BELLAT, a sociologist, is a professor at the University of Burgundy, Dijon, France, where she conducts empirical research within the Institute for Research on the Economics of Education (Irédu). Her research interests include social and gender inequalities in school, tracking, the effects of schools, and the operating of the educational systems.

THEO M. E. LIKET was a "school leader" at a Gymnasium, a senior chief in the Ministry of Education, and senior chief inspector of the Netherlands Educational Inspectorate. Most recently he had been an international educational consultant and president of University Post-Academic School Leader Training, University of Amsterdam.

ANTÓNIO NÓVOA is Professor of Education at the University of Lisbon, Portugal. He has published articles and books on the history of education (history of teachers, "new education," educational historiography) and comparative education (educational policies, educational sciences, comparative methods and theories).

FRANÇOIS ORIVEL is a senior researcher at the Institute for Research on the Economics of Education, University of Burgundy, Dijon, France. He specializes in issues related to finance of education, cost-effectiveness of educational systems, relations between educational investment and economic development, design of efficient educational policies, and the potential of new information technologies in education. He has had extensive comparative education experience in both developed and developing countries, has worked for international organizations active in the field of educational assistance, and has published numerous articles and books in this domain.

VAL D. RUST is Professor of Comparative and International Education at the University of California, Los Angeles. He has served for several years as the head of the Social Sciences and Comparative Education Division and currently serves as the UCLA Director of the Education Abroad Program. Recent books include *The Unification of German Education* (1995), *Education and the Values Crisis in Central and Eastern Europe* (1996), and *Toward Schooling for the Twenty-first Century* (1996).

RAYMOND RYBA, for many years Secretary General of the World Council of Comparative Education Societies, was instrumental in expanding participation in the World Council from its initial European and North American base to its current worldwide membership of comparative education societies. He was formerly Dean of the Faculty of Education, University of Manchester, then a Senior Research Fellow to that faculty. In the past decade much of his work had been as an expert consultant in European education to both the European Commission and the Council of Europe.

JÜRGEN SCHRIEWER is Professor of Comparative Education and head of the Comparative Education Centre of Humboldt University, Berlin. His research interests include comparative history of education, education as an academic field of study in Western Europe, issues of globalization and world-system research, and methodology of cross-cultural research. A former president of the Comparative Education Society in Europe and a founding member of the Research Group on Comparative Studies in History and the Social Science, Humboldt University, his recent publications include *Theories and Methods in Comparative Education* (1992), *Welt-System und Interrelations-Gefüge* (1994), and *Diskurse und Entwicklungspfade* (1999).

MARGARET B. SUTHERLAND, Emeritus Professor of Education, Leeds University, United Kingdom, is a Fellow of the Scottish Council for Research in Education, an honorary member of the Comparative Education Society in Europe, and past president of AFEC (Association Francophone d'Education Comparée). In books and articles, she has published extensively on the subject of the education of girls and women.

ELIZABETH SHERMAN SWING, Professor Emerita of Education, Saint Jo-
seph's University, Philadelphia, is the Historian of the Comparative and International Education Society and Honorary Fellow of that society. Her research
has focused on languages in contact and on the education of minorities and
immigrants. In 1990 she was made *Ridder in de Kroonorde* (Knight in the Order
of the Crown) for research on the Belgian language controversy. She was co-
chair (with the late Raymond Ryba) of the European Commission of the World
Congress of Comparative Education Societies in Prague and in Sydney.

JÜRGEN WICHMANN was a teacher of foreign languages (French and Russian) from 1982 to 1986. Since 1986 he has worked in the Humboldt University
Department of Comparative Education.

AGNÈS VAN ZANTEN, whose publications are in sociology and educational
anthropology, is a senior researcher in sociology at the Centre National de la
Recherche Scientifique in Paris. Her major research interests include the local
context of schools, markets in education, families, and schools.

BERND ZYMEK is Professor at the Department for Educational and Social
Sciences at the Westfälische Wilhelms-Universität Münster (Germany). His
fields of research are history of education and comparative education. He is
author of *Das Ausland als Argument in der pädagogischen Reformdiskussion*
(1975) and co-author of the *Datenhandbuch zur deutschen Bildungsgeschichte*
(1987).

ISBN 0-275-95202-9